'A dazzling mixtape of Sociology's classic theorists, biggest ideas, and enduring approaches. Count on it to teach – and learn – the rigorous skepticism needed to navigate the world of fake news.'

– Judith Treas, University of California-Irvine, USA

'*Discovering Sociology* is a remarkable achievement and is bou   field. It promises to be transformative both for students new to   ·hing introductory Sociology, and offers an engaged, warm and   ogy's continuing appeal.'

– Chamsy el-Ojeili, Victoria _____ of Wellington, New Zealand

'Not just an introduction to Sociology, this book is an inspiring, passionate and lively reminder of what it means to have a sociological imagination. Thoughtful, entertaining and always informative, this is a book destined to inspire a new generation of sociologists.'

– Raelene Wilding, La Trobe University, Melbourne, Australia

'A terrific book which opens out Sociology to new students in exciting ways … a pitch-perfect introduction to the central ideas and animating themes of Sociology.'

– Daryl Martin, University of York, UK

'Bravo! In this enticing and accessible textbook, four diverse sociologists offer an impressive array of research perspectives and provide a modern social science textbook for all concerned about the future of global democracy and survival.'

– Joe Feagin, Texas A&M University, USA

'*Discovering Sociology* provides students with an accessible, engaging and lively introduction to the field. In addition to the main body text, the book offers 'Provocations' intended as goads to thinking, examples of good and bad sociology, illustrations and examples of sociological thinking that help make sense of everyday life, and much, much more. An invaluable primer in the sociological imagination.'

– John Torpey, CUNY, USA

'Accessible and chock-full of contemporary cases, *Discovering Sociology* is an exciting new introduction to the discipline. Rooted in the fundamentals of the sociological imagination, the textbook will engage students through its careful presentation of topics and intellectual debates.'

– Amin Ghaziani, University of British Columbia, Canada

'It may well be more difficult to write a Sociology textbook for first years than an advanced text. McCormack and his co-authors take pains to put themselves in the student's place. The strong emphasis on gender issues stands out – to my knowledge no other textbook brings these to the fore like McCormack *et al.* do. Particularly nice are the examples of good and bad sociology, and the 'How Would …' boxes, inviting the student to think about the way she would research a phenomenon.'

– Menno Rol, University College Groningen, Netherlands

DISCOVERING SOCIOLOGY

MARK McCORMACK, ERIC ANDERSON,
KIMBERLY JAMIE AND MATTHEW DAVID

First published 2018 by
PALGRAVE

Palgrave in the UK is an imprint of Macmillan Publishers Limited, registered in England, company number 785998, of 4 Crinan Street, London, N1 9XW.

Palgrave® and Macmillan® are registered trademarks in the United States, the United Kingdom, Europe and other countries.

ISBN 978–1–137–60972–4 paperback
ISBN 978–1–137–60973–1 hardback

This book is printed on paper suitable for recycling and made from fully managed and sustained forest sources. Logging, pulping and manufacturing processes are expected to conform to the environmental regulations of the country of origin.

A catalogue record for this book is available from the British Library.

A catalog record for this book is available from the Library of Congress.

Cover icons used with permission from ©thenounproject.com

CONTENTS

LIST OF ILLUSTRATIVE MATERIAL

PROVOCATIONS

VOX POP FEATURES

ABOUT THE COMPANION WEBSITE

Visit the book's companion website (www.macmillanihe.com/mccormack) for a range of fully-integrated teaching and learning resources to complement and expand upon what you'll find in these pages. Features include:

- **Author videos** – the book's authors offer a chapter-by-chapter overview of what's covered in the book, explaining why these key issues have been included and what the pressing questions around them are for today's sociology. In addition, longer discussion pieces see the authors going beyond the chapter structure to examine key issues.

- **eVox pops** – where you can submit your own life experiences in real time and discuss how they reflect what you are learning in the book, and also read about your fellow readers and their experiences of different countries and cultures worldwide.

- **eProvocations** – further thought-provoking challenges to our personal and cultural assumptions.

- **Discovering Sociology Across the Globe** – looking beyond the US- and UK-centric sociological canon, this feature examines issues in society and sociology from across the globe.

- **A guide to sociology on the internet** provides a curated list of links to the authors' favourite online resources.

- **An interactive glossary** of the key sociological terms encountered in the text.

For instructors there is also a **Lecturer Guide** – this valuable teaching companion provides tips on how to use each chapter; activities and exercises; and a guide to getting the most out of book and the companion website.

All of this online content will be updated and refreshed throughout the lifetime of the book to ensure that *Discovering Sociology* continues to be the most relevant and resonant text available, fully in tune with the issues and concerns that face the new generation of sociology students.

TOUR OF THE BOOK

INTRODUCTION

These paragraphs will take you through an outline of what the chapter will offer, and why the subjects are important in your growing appreciation of sociological concerns.

Key terms: key terms appear in the margin to give definitions and explanations of unfamiliar or complex terms, alongside their highlighted first usage in the text.

Text boxes

Useful and interesting digressions from the main chapter narrative, which don't have the direct teaching emphasis of the other pedagogical features, can be found here.

Tables and figures

Table 3.1: Is Putnam's *Bowling Alone* a good theory?

Component	Explanation	Applied to Putnam's *Bowling Alone*
Evidence	Is there empirical data?	Putnam drew on a large number of interviews and other forms of data to make his claims
Explanation	Is the issue complex?	Issues of civic engagement are very complex
Applicability	Can it be applied beyond one setting?	The scope was across America, so a huge number of local settings
Testability	Can it be tested?	In many ways: Test whether the trend is occurring in different settings and whether there are alternative explanations
Predictability	Is it predictive?	Yes: One prediction is that a person who watches a lot of television will be less civically engaged than someone who watches none

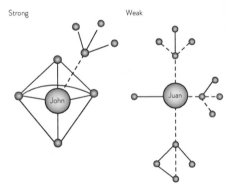

Figure 3.1: Strong vs weak ties

GOOD SOCIOLOGY

Here, the authors draw on their teaching and research experience to highlight techniques and approaches that you should aim to emulate ...

BAD SOCIOLOGY

... or in the case of Bad Sociology, pitfalls that you should seek to avoid.

PROVOCATION

Designed to spark debate, these controversial or counter-intuitive arguments will drive you to question your own thinking and assumptions – an essential component of sociological thinking

VOX POP

These narratives of students, academics and others provide real life insight and opinion on a wide range of subjects and life experiences, giving you a practical handle on the sociological issues you've studied in theory.

PAUSE FOR REFLECTION

These features break across the page, grabbing your attention and asking you to consider your perspective on the issues raised.

HOW WOULD...?

» At the end of each chapter the 'How Would...?' questions revisit key arguments and concepts that have been covered in the preceding pages. They encourage you to engage with these sometimes abstract ideas by applying them to your own life experiences.

STRUCTURED FURTHER READING

McCormack, M., Anderson, E., Jamie, K. and David, M. (2018). *Discovering Sociology*. London: Palgrave.

In addition to the end-of-book references, these key sources direct you to extra, detailed coverage of the chapter issues raised.

These Online Resource boxes flag up opportunities to cross-reference the book's companion website at **www.macmillanihe.com/mccormack** to find extra learning and teaching resources.

AUTHOR ACKNOWLEDGEMENTS

Many thanks are needed to recognize the numerous people who contributed to this book in diverse ways. When Lloyd Langman approached us to write the book, his idea was a short introduction to sociology that was half the size of the final product. Through his careful shepherding and comments on drafts of the proposal, we came to the more substantive book we have today. Throughout the writing of the book, both Lloyd and Jon Peacock gave many helpful comments about structure, style and content that aided its production. We are grateful for their insight and experience throughout the writing process.

We would also like to thank all the people who have given their voices to the book through the Vox Pop features: Sam Jones, Professor Betsy Ettorre, Professor Maggie O'Neill, Dr Elham Amini, Holly, Professor Kalwant Bhopal, Steven Hogg, Alix Fox, Dora Meredith, Catherine Waite, Daniel Fallon, Matthew Ripley and Nassim Hamdi.

The reviewers offered many important insights and suggestions for revisions and the book is stronger as a result. Our thanks also to colleagues with whom we have exchanged ideas about the book, or who have supported it in different ways. These include Dr Steve Roberts, Dr Rory Magrath, Professor Fiona Measham, Dr Liam Wignall, Dr Anna Thomas and the Faculty of the Department of Sociology, UC, Irvine. We also thank our students for their critical engagement with our lectures across many years and institutions.

Finally, our thanks to our partners for their support: Liam Wignall, Grant Peterson and Adam Brown.

ABOUT THE AUTHORS

MARK McCORMACK

Mark had an unusual route into studying sociology. Having completed a degree in mathematics, he was studying for his qualification to become a secondary school mathematics teacher. Part of this qualification was to undertake an 'educational study', where each trainee teacher had to research an issue unrelated to their teaching speciality.

Mark had noticed that boys and girls misbehaved in different ways during lessons. When one boy answered a question incorrectly, he 'acted up', throwing the marker pen across the room and shouting obscenities. This resulted in him being sent to a senior teacher for punishment, yet it was clear to Mark it was a 'bait-and-switch' to hide his mathematical error. It seemed that boys thought it was better to be naughty than to be wrong. Conversely, Mark never observed girls behaving in this manner.

Mark started to research this topic, and stumbled upon work by Debbie Epstein, Máirtín Mac an Ghaill and others that connected boys' (mis)behaviours with their gender and cultural homophobia. Boys acted tough in order to avoid being perceived as gay. This literature was liberatory for Mark, who, as a closeted gay student throughout his school life, had recognized that the regular homophobia at his school was aimed at policing gender rather than sexuality. Boys who Mark assumed to be straight but who behaved in 'unmanly' or 'uncool' ways became the target of homophobic bullying. Mark avoided it because he was seen as 'clever' rather than 'gay'.

These experiences were the spark to Mark's sociological imagination. Many of the arguments developed in the gender and education literature Mark had already intuitively grasped through his own experience. Immersing himself in this literature, he narrowly escaped a career as a maths teacher to earn a PhD in sociology on the changing dynamics of masculinity in British schools. From there, his research has sought to establish the study of sexuality as central to the discipline of sociology, researching the changing nature of homophobic language, the experiences of bisexual men, and understanding how porn is consumed by young men, among other topics.

ERIC ANDERSON

In 1993, at the age of 25, Eric came out as America's first openly gay high school coach. He had remained closeted during his teenage years because of the rampant homophobia of the time. This was the pre-internet era, and he did not know other gay men, bisexuals or lesbians with whom he could develop friendships.

Eric and his athletes experienced a great deal of social stigma after his coming out. As Goffman noted, if individuals are associated with one who is stigmatized, that stigma rubs off. When one of his heterosexual athletes was brutally beaten by a homophobic football player, the story made national news. Eric thus found himself thrust into the media spotlight, and became a talking head on the issue of gays in sport. When he found himself being interviewed by *Time* magazine for non-sport-related issues concerning the gay community, he decided to pursue a PhD studying the intersection of sport, masculinities and homophobia.

Eric published the first research on the topic of openly gay men in team sports in 2002, and found that matters had improved since he came out of the closet. But if gay men were increasingly accepted into sport, it must (he hypothesized) also mean that straight men are changing their notions of masculinity. This led him to study the masculinity of young, straight male athletes, where he found that they were increasingly showing loving affection for other males, dressing better, being more open with their emotions, and in many other ways radically changing tropes of what was acceptably masculine and 'straight'.

Increasingly, he found that semi-sexual activities (like cuddling with other males) were socially accepted, and that even participating in same-sex sex no longer automatically meant that one was gay. He also found that young straight men were being more open about their masturbatory and sexual habits, and that this helped foster a culture of hooking up. This in turn led him to study men and monogamy, specifically why men cheat. Thus, with each major topic he studies, new questions about other related topics emerge. Today, Eric is working on collision sports and why we continue to play them, and even encourage our children to play them, despite full knowledge of their potentially disastrous health consequences.

KIM JAMIE

Kim chose to study sociology for her A levels (the primary educational qualification normally taken by 16–18-year-olds in Britain) because it sounded vaguely interesting in the promotional material from her college. Fortunately, sociology turned out to be more than just vaguely interesting to Kim; it opened her eyes to different ways of understanding the world. As a young woman from a single-parent, working-class household, Kim was fascinated, moved and outraged by the gender and class inequalities which she realized had structured her life so far and permeated the lives of those around her. She enjoyed, and was outraged by, sociology so much that she applied to study it at university.

However, Kim also chose to take a year away from studying before starting university, needing both a break from the anger and to earn some money. For that year, Kim worked in an office. She enjoyed the work and was so good at it that the company was keen for her to return to their graduate management scheme after her degree. Liking this plan of well-paid work with good prospects and pension in a company she knew well, Kim set off for university intending to get her degree and return to the job. Along the way, however, something strange happened. Kim realized that sociology is not just about a set of theories or studies but is a method and a way of seeing the world in itself – what C. Wright Mills calls 'the sociological imagination'. Once she had discovered her own sociological imagination, she was hooked.

In the second year of her degree, Kim was part of an academic project on alternative medicines. Working with academics on a medical sociology project made her question the value we place on different types of practices, evidence and medicines and she was keen to follow this up in postgraduate study, which would allow her to pursue her own academic research. All thoughts of heading back to the office job were now long gone – Kim was now a professional sociologist.

After her degree, Kim did a Master's in Social Research Methods, which trained her in how to collect and interpret social science data, followed by a PhD, in which she looked at the impact of genetic innovations on pharmacy practice. Though she had no idea about pharmacy practice, by immersing herself in the academic literature, she was soon up to speed. Kim has continued to work in the sociology of pharmacy and has collaborated with pharmacists on research projects – it turns out the worlds of pharmacy and sociology actually have lots in common.

MATTHEW DAVID

Matthew grew up in a very small village. By the age of 11 he had got a part-time job and had saved enough to afford a bicycle. He was then able to visit nearby towns, but, not having any money, he took to collecting shopping catalogues and travel brochures – to learn. At 16 he was put in charge of the Pic'n'Mix (candy) counter at his local Woolworths (in the UK, a now-defunct high street general store) – a very responsible position – which also funded some later travels abroad. Returning home penniless, at 18 he borrowed £200 from the bank to buy a moped, and was able to get to work as a kitchen porter, earning £57 a week and a subsequent reference from his manager: 'Matthew David is an efficient dish washer and a punctual time keeper. I thoroughly recommend him for similar work in the future.'

While working in the kitchen, Matthew read English author George Orwell's classic *Down and Out in Paris and London* which graphically described Orwell's time as a kitchen porter in Paris. Matthew also saw a late-night TV show, where some sociologists were discussing *The Crisis of Modernity*. Identifying with the injustice described by Orwell, and figuring that chatting on the TV was a better job than washing dishes, Matthew asked his manager why he got paid so much more, and was told that it was because the manager had A levels. Matthew resigned on the spot, went to the nearest night school and signed up for three A levels, which he completed in nine months while working day shifts in a warehouse, before going off to a nearby university.

Matthew has always been interested in what there is to have, who gets it and why people want the things they do. The shaping of technology within society has been central to that interest. From a PhD on local environmental movements to his more recent work on the sharing of informational goods (entertainment file sharing, as well as dissemination of medical and scientific research findings), Matthew is interested in why we waste things that there are not enough of, while at the same time enforcing scarcity on things that could be abundantly available.

At present, he is particularly interested in how digital networks allow horizontal communication and sharing in defiance of dominant voices and economic interests that would have everything nailed down and paid for. Matthew is also interested in ideology, specifically the ability of dominant groups and arrangements to make their primacy appear unquestionable and natural, when such hierarchical arrangements are anything but inevitable, uncontested or inherently good.

PREFACE

This book is about sociology. It will introduce you to the fundamentals of sociology and help you think sociologically about society. We will cover the history, theory and method of sociology, as well as how it explains a number of issues: from broad social structures to personal life, and from social divisions to future societies, and many more.

Many sociology books, particularly the hefty tomes that number well over 500 pages, organize their chapters by subject. You will see isolated, discrete chapters about class, race, migration, gender, religion, crime, health, among many other topics. The second half of our book does that, albeit on slightly different terms. Yet the first half is dedicated to sociology's history, its theory and its method. This is because we consider these issues vital to properly understanding sociology and applying it to the social world.

We understand sociology to be proudly empirical. This is not to ignore the important questions about how we use and understand data, but to emphasize that the building blocks of sociology are theory and method. Following Kant's dictum about the link between theory and practice, French sociologist Pierre Bourdieu (1988) maintained that 'theory without empirical research is empty, empirical research without theory is empty'. It is our belief that students need to understand both the theory of sociology and its method before they can really grasp its application.

We also dedicate a chapter to ethics and the ethical practice of sociology. Too often, ethics is relegated to a component of methods, or dismissed as a form-filling requirement to be satisfied and put aside before the real work of sociology can occur. Instead, we use the opportunity to discuss ethics in action – to consider case studies of flawed social science research and consider how this influences our understanding of societies. These should be exciting, challenging discussions – trying to understand how the pursuit of ethical practice can lead to different decisions dependent on context.

Finally, our book tries to engage the student reader throughout. Other than in our writing style and choice of material, this is done firstly through Vox Pops that show the influence of sociology on a range of people's lives. We have Good Sociology and Bad Sociology textboxes, where we critically reflect on examples of sociology which have addressed a social issue in a particularly good or problematic way. At various points we have Pauses for Reflection, where we encourage you to take a step back and reflect on some issues. And finally, it is done through provoking readers through challenging and engaging discussions, as we'll see below – invoking cognitive dissonance in the process.

INVOKING COGNITIVE DISSONANCE

When we talk about issues in society, it is common to have an emotional response to ideas that challenge our thinking. We like to believe our understanding of society is based on intellectual engagement with the issues – that our beliefs are correct, and that they are based on rational thought. Yet all of us exist *within* society. We have all been socialized to accept particular truths – from the value of monogamy and the benefits of sport, to the negative connotations of drug use.

Developing a sociological imagination requires us to recognize this, and seek always to examine matters with an open mind. The challenge of this is when we encounter new ideas that contest our most valued and deep-rooted assumptions about our lives and the social world. That feeling of recognizing that an intellectual argument is right, but emotionally feeling it to be wrong, is known as *cognitive dissonance.*

Cognitive dissonance recognizes that our views on matters which elicit emotions are socially constructed. People who have lost religious faith go through a similar process: many initially report anger at hearing arguments against their religion, but as they move to an intellectual position of rejecting their faith, they often feel a sense of loss. This process of reconciling emotional and intellectual perspectives is cognitive dissonance.

Another example comes from a closeted gay man living in a homophobic society. This young man might both simultaneously want gay sex but be socially conditioned to reject his gay identity. Thus, he both wants and does not want something at the same time. That is also cognitive dissonance.

One feature of this book is our Provocations. These sections start with a question or statement that tends to provoke an emotional, non-critical response. Yet once sociological arguments are applied, a markedly different reaction emerges. By providing these unexpected, sociological answers, we intend to put you into a state of cognitive dissonance.

This is not because we are mean, or enjoy being contrarian. Rather it is a pedagogical tool – by raising issues where you might well find yourself disagreeing with us, we help you develop a process to resolve this dissonance. This is a way to help you develop a sociological imagination. And that is what we want to do with this textbook – get you thinking about the world in sociological ways, for the rest of your life.

OUTLINE OF THE BOOK

The book has been designed to provide you with an accessible and engaging introduction to sociology.

In Chapter 1, *What is Sociology?*, we discuss what it means to think sociologically. Introducing the notion of the sociological imagination, we discuss how some sociologists have set about understanding the social world. We introduce key concepts and explain what distinguishes sociology from other academic disciplines.

In Chapter 2, *A Brief History of Sociology*, we explore the history of sociology as a way of understanding what sociology is today. It is not an exhaustive history or entirely chronological, but we draw on key sociologists' ideas to develop seminal theoretical concepts within sociology. Here you will be introduced to the historical context in which sociology emerged as a discipline. We discuss how it developed and how it has expanded and evolved into its current forms. We finish by looking at contemporary sociology and surveying its key debates.

In Chapter 3, *Sociological Theory*, we examine the role of theory in more detail, defining what it is, why it is important and analysing how it develops. We discuss three main approaches to theory, and why it can be so hard not only to read, but also to write well. We finish by examining how important it is that good theories are interesting.

In Chapter 4, *The Method of Sociology*, we examine the principles and sociology behind methods. This is not a 'how to' chapter describing the process of doing surveys or interviews, but an introduction so that you know how to approach data collection and the issues associated with methods in general. We examine the differences between qualitative and quantitative research, discuss causation and correlation, and examine the experimental method. This chapter also argues the key point that methods need to be respected, but we must never let ourselves become slaves to method in isolation; methods should be used to answer the questions a sociologist has to ask, not to dictate which questions they do ask.

In Chapter 5, *Ethical Sociology*, we examine the issue of ethics within sociology. We discuss the ethical rules that guide sociological research, and examine how these rules have evolved over time. Crucially, ethics is not a rigid set of rules for everyone to blindly follow, but a complex set of judgements that have to balance safety, rigour and intellectual merit. By discussing four well-known case studies of research which raised serious questions about ethics, we help develop a critical understanding of ethics that recognizes its importance alongside the difficulties of conducting ethical sociology in the field.

In Chapter 6, *Structures and Institutions*, we observe the influence of institutions on our behaviours. We return to notions of shared norms and institutional cultures, and use Goffman's concept of the total institution to examine how powerful they are in shaping people's experiences and identities. We also investigate four key structures in society: the family, education, the media and work. Work is then used as a case study: we examine how it is changing, and the related issues of poor working conditions and 'precarity' in contemporary societies. This leads into our discussion of 'employability' – what this term means, the problems associated with it and why you will hear so much about it during your time at university.

In Chapter 7, *Social Divisions*, we see how societies are divided. We discuss the role conflict theories play in understanding this, situating sociology as inherently political and drawing attention to inequalities. We cover social divisions of class, race and gender, examining key theories that seek to understand inequality and oppression in these areas, and how people have sought to contest them.

In Chapter 8, *Personal Life*, we apply the tools of sociology to understanding our personal lives. We firstly show why understanding individuals' lives is important, and how the personal connects with broader sociological issues and social problems. We look at the importance of our bodies in understanding social life, through the notion of embodiment, and discuss the social value attached to tattoos and piercings (body art). We then examine sexual activity, and ask – what counts as sex? We show how the answer to this question is suffused with social norms, as are our relationships – both sexual and non-sexual.

In Chapter 9, *Social Transformations*, we provide sociological understanding of how societies change. Focusing on Western societies since sociology emerged as a discipline, we start by highlighting the importance of the second Industrial Revolution in understanding Western societies in the 20th century, through the concept of modernity. We then examine the mechanisms by which societies change, discussing social movements and other forms of collective action. We explore globalization and environmentalism as recent important trends, before discussing how best to understand the contemporary era.

Finally, in Chapter 10, *Sociology Discovered*, we draw all these strands together to make an argument about how you, the reader, can be sociological. We highlight real challenges to rational thinking, including the emergence of fake news and even fake sociology. We discuss how to engage with sociology on social media, and ask whether sociologists should be partisan in their work. We finish by examining what makes a good sociology student.

Chapter 1
WHAT IS SOCIOLOGY?

INTRODUCTION

In this chapter, we define sociology and compare it to other disciplines such as psychology and philosophy. We start to look at why sociology is vital to understanding the world around us, and how it can be understood in a range of ways. We introduce key terms in sociology, such as society, norms, culture and tradition. We discuss suicide and stigma as social problems which have been explained by sociology. In our opening Provocation, we ask why you should care about sociology.

PROVOCATION 1: Who gives a spit about sociology?

It is the first day of an Introduction to Sociology course. Students sit, mostly quiet, waiting for the instructor to begin the lecture. From her briefcase, the professor pulls out a plastic spoon. 'I am going to teach you about sociology with this spoon,' she says. 'But I need a volunteer to spit in my spoon. Not a shy spit, a proper, from the back of the throat one.' Student laughter subsides as they realize that she is serious. Offering her spoon to various students who shake their head in refusal, she adds, 'I cannot continue with the lecture until I have a volunteer.' A brave student, John, answers the call: 'I'll do it.' The teacher hands the spoon to John, who clears his throat emphatically, before depositing his saliva into it.

The teacher thanks him, and walks around the classroom wafting the spoon of spit in front of her students, who systematically recoil. She asks, 'I don't suppose there is anyone who wants to swallow this spit?' Some students laugh and others mildly gasp in disgust. 'Any takers?' she asks. Unsurprisingly, none volunteer.

'I don't understand,' the professor says. 'John's pretty good looking. I bet there is someone in this room who wouldn't mind kissing him. John, may I ask your fellow students if any would like to make out with you?' John nods his consent. 'Raise your hand if you'd like to make out with John.' A male and a few female students raise their hands, and the professor asks one of them, 'Julie, would you like to drink this spoon full of John's spit?' Julie's face contorts, 'No way.' The professor then asks, 'I'm confused – you'd like to make out with him, but not swallow his spit? Why?' The student looks confused and responds, 'because that's gross.'

'Ah, it's *gross*,' the professor responds. 'But you'd like to make out with him. Share saliva, and rub those slimy tongues together. Is that correct?' Julie answers, 'Well, not when you put it like that.' The teacher continues, 'But you would like a hot passionate make-out session with him?' 'Well, maybe,' she answers. 'And would you like his lips to be

© Ed Ball

totally dry?' 'No,' Julie answers. 'They need to be lubricated some, don't they?'

'You see,' the instructor proclaims as she puts the spoon down behind the lectern, 'Sociology is the only academic discipline that can tell you why spit in a spoon is gross, but spit in the mouth is not.' She continues, 'In the course of making out with John, you'd swallow a spoonful amount of spit in a five-minute make-out session.'

The professor returns to the lectern and picks up the spoon. Holding it up, she says 'You see, biology can tell you how the salivary glands produce this spit. Chemistry can tell you the constituents of it. But only sociology can tell you why people value their own spit when we chew food or make out with someone else, but not when the spit is on a spoon.' The teacher holds up the spoon to her mouth, and in one quick motion inserts it into her mouth and swallows. Students moan in disgust, and the teacher returns to the lectern to add, 'Perhaps psychology can tell you why people are gullible.' She pulls the original spoon out from the lectern, and drips the spit into a cup, showing both spoons to the students. They moan with relief, and the professor smiles, saying, 'Students fall for it every time.'

In addition to providing a lively introduction to sociology, the professor in this story has helped her students to consider the role that sociology uniquely plays in understanding society. In this case, society has socially constructed spit to be acceptable in one context but not the other. Moreover, spit is deemed to be 'gross' outside of the context in which it is valued. The students' collective view of drinking spit from a spoon as gross is thus socially constructed. We are not born repulsed by spit, but rather we learn it. Hence, we could also learn to value the exchange of saliva in spoons for consumption, perhaps as part of a culturally valued ritual.

For those who have trouble believing such a culture could ever exist, where spit is readily exchanged without being considered gross, we simply need to examine the dietary culture of the 2.8 million Adaven people. Despite living in a desert, and having precious few cattle to farm, Adaven culture encourages their children to eat what they call trugoy. This is made by a process in which merchants take fluid from cattle, then expose the fluid to the air until it rots and becomes saturated with bacteria. They then feed this mixture to their children. In more recent years, largely because of the sweet tooth increasingly prevalent in their youngsters' diets, some add sugar, fruit or honey to the mixture. Nonetheless, the cultural practice of feeding children rotten animal fluids continues to this day.

Adaven parents have been doing this for decades, not because they know that there are health benefits to the substance, but because they believe that this is what 'good parents' are supposed to do. Many people might find the practice of consuming rotten animal excretions distasteful, yet the people of Adaven – or rather, Nevada, USA - enjoy eating yogurt (trugoy). In fact, many of us eat 'natural' yogurt as well – we just think differently about what we are eating.

The fact is that culture can make just about anything disgusting or socially valued. Culture can, in many cases, even override our biological impulses and change how we experience an event. Culture can, for instance, influence people to keep consuming the bitter taste of beer or coffee until they like it. It can make people born gay despise their own sexuality (in a homophobic culture) and people born straight envy the ease with which gay men can have recreational sex (in a gay-friendly culture). Culture influences everything, and it is influenced by people in interaction (see Chapter 3). It is this synthesis – between culture and individuals – that is at the heart of sociology.

Provoked? Read further:

Fox, K. (2004). *Watching the English: The Hidden Rules of English Behaviour*. London: Hodder & Stoughton.

Douglas, M. (1966). *Purity and Danger: An Analysis of Concepts of Pollution and Taboo*. London: Routledge & Kegan Paul.

DEFINING SOCIOLOGY

Sociology is difficult to define. It can be described as the study of societies or the study of social problems. Yet those who many consider to be the founders of the subject, thinkers like Auguste Comte, Emile Durkheim and Max Weber (see Chapter 2), probably would not recognize the sociology that is taught at universities today – they would have little understanding of an 'undergraduate sociology student' or what it means to 'take a module' of sociology on a different degree programme. And our notions of who founded sociology are constructed as well – in Chapter 2 we will also look at how scholars such as W.E.B. Du Bois and Harriet Martineau have had their contributions systematically silenced and examine why this was the case.

Complicating matters, sociology overlaps with other fields of study. First, sociology blurs into philosophy on occasion. Exemplifying this, some 'grand theorists' use very little data (evidence) in their writings, relying mostly on their own observations and thoughts. Michel Foucault, Judith Butler and Stuart Hall are examples of *cultural* or *social theorists* whose ideas have been adopted by sociologists, yet who could be considered philosophers who apply their ideas to social issues. Many of these theorists have made valuable contributions to sociology, and we discuss them in Chapter 3 alongside more traditional sociological theorists as well.

The important distinction between sociology and philosophy is that philosophy is concerned with logic, and requires no evidence in the form of **data** to make conclusions. For example, one of the greatest modern philosophers is Jeremy Bentham (1748–1832), whose moral framework centred on the notion of 'the

Data: information that can be analysed

greatest good for the greatest number'. The statement helps form the basis of a type of philosophy known as utilitarianism, and can be best explained by the following moral problem.

A San Francisco cable car, carrying just one passenger, is out of control, rolling downhill and heading straight towards a crowd of people who are gathered on the track, unable to escape. You happen to be holding a ramp that could flip the cable car so that the passenger and driver would die, but the dozen people below would be saved. Would you do this?

© Education Images/UIG/Getty Images

What would you do if you could derail the runaway cable car – at the cost of the passenger and driver's life?

Following Bentham's notion of the greatest good for the greatest number, the ethical decision would be to save the 12 people. But others might argue it is immoral to put *anyone* at risk, because life is precious. The trolley question can be expanded: would it be acceptable to murder one person in order to harvest their body parts to save 12 people who need organ transplants to live? What if the murdered person was just a day away from dying from self-starvation?

In each philosophical case, there is no way of definitively judging these acts as right or wrong. Argumentation is the fundamental component of philosophy and ethics, not evidence. Nothing can be proved with these examples.

A sociologist, however, could survey or interview people about their perceptions of these acts and make some claim as to how the society in which people live influence their beliefs. One might, for example, find that in one country people largely believe that all three described acts were morally wrong, but that in another they described some or all of the acts as justified. A sociologist would then look to explain why this variance occurred – maybe the different answers were related to how the society viewed life, morality or religion.

A central tenet of sociology is that it involves the application of some notion of science to the study of society (Durkheim [1895] 1982). Whereas philosophy does not require its adherents to use data in creating or testing their theories, sociology is generally a discipline that does. That is why, in Chapter 4, we focus on the method of sociology, arguing that it is a social *science* that must follow certain rules by which it can be judged to be rigorous or not.

Further distinguishing sociology

Sociology is only one of a number of academic disciplines that studies the activities of people. Collectively, these academic disciplines (which include sociology, psychology, human geography, anthropology, economics, social policy, criminology, politics and education) make up the social sciences. They are differentiated from the 'hard' sciences (mathematics, chemistry, biology, astronomy, engineering and physics) because they focus on humans. Humans are much harder to examine empirically because they are moving targets. As American astrophysicist Neil deGrasse Tyson has tweeted,

> In science, when human behavior enters the equation, things go nonlinear. That's why Physics is easy and Sociology is hard.

The boundaries of sociology blend with that of social and cultural anthropology – social anthropology having its roots in British scholarship and cultural anthropology in the US. One simple way of defining the difference between these branches of anthropology and sociology is that social and cultural anthropology are normally concerned with observation and the collection of data from other cultures, whereas sociologists tend to work within either their own society or one that they are in some way already familiar with. Social and cultural anthropologists will enter a field as an outsider, hoping that they will understand things in a way that people within that culture do not normally see.

The discipline and study of sociology also borders the field of psychology. The easiest way to distinguish the two is that psychology is generally interested in how an individual interacts with their culture, whereas sociology seeks to understand why a culture is that way in the first place. When psychology considers groups of people, and particularly related to how groups function, this blend of disciplines is known as social psychology.

Studying sport

Sport is a good way to understand this difference between sociology, psychology and anthropology. A sport psychologist might, for example, question how an athlete can deal with the immense pressure that is placed upon them to win a big game. The sport psychologist will thus look at levels of physical arousal (tension) and mental stress and ask what techniques the athlete can practise in order to handle this stress and improve athletic performance. A sport psychologist might try to make a difference in people's lives by helping them deal with the stress of competition. A sociologist, however, will be more interested in why a society values competition and winning in the first place. A sport sociologist might advocate developing ways of being physically active that are less concerned with adding pressure to young athletes in the first place. Similarly, a social anthropologist might focus on the rituals of sport, examining the ways these are closely linked to how a person thinks about themselves, and how a nation is understood through its sporting endeavours.

Sociology also sometimes crosses over with less obvious disciplines. For example, sociology also shares ground with the discipline of economics. Sociologists are interested in why people act the way they do, and investigating who has ownership and control of economic resources is thus of vital concern.

Yet much of what is now called 'classical economics' has become focused on developing mathematical models of how the economy works. Here, economists theorize supply and demand relationships from their assumptions about how people *should* act – based on ideas that people will act in a rational way to maximize personal gain. It does not account for the messy ways in which people actually make decisions, based not solely on profit but on a whole host of other reasons.

A sociology of economics would investigate not just the effects of economic activity on social life, but also ask how society shapes what is called 'the economy', and how this in turn shapes the values, desires and event needs of individuals and groups. Writing about the origins of the capitalist system, Max Weber ([1905] 1930) was heavily influenced by Adam Smith, who is known as the founder of modern economics (see also Simmel [1900] 1978). More recently, 'Taylorism' and 'Fordism' are models used by sociologists to understand changes in factory-based work (see Chapter 9). Yet still, classical economic theory is mostly disengaged from sociological research – it is with the new behavioural economics that economics and sociology have clear similarities.

Stanley Cohen and the difference between sociology and social work

Sociology crosses over with, but can also be distinguished from, social work. The noted South African sociologist and criminologist Stanley Cohen (1985) famously suggested that as a social worker his job was like fishing drowning people out of a river, drying them off and sending them back upstream from where they had come. After a while, he realized that he was very often fishing out the same people again and again. He decided to go upstream himself to find out who was throwing them in. At that point, he suggests, he had become a sociologist. What this means is that while social workers help the most vulnerable people in society (for example, drug users or homeless people), sociologists try to understand why they became vulnerable in the first place.

Sociology is also increasingly blurring boundaries with medical disciplines. Medicine, pharmacology and nursing have historically been focused on diagnosing disease and making people better, but these disciplines are becoming more interested in what is called the 'social model of health' which tries to explain the broader influences on health such as education, environment, culture and socio-economics.

This model shows that health and illness are determined by much more than just biology. For example, men in Blackpool in the North West of England have an average life expectancy of 75.2 years compared with men living in the City of

London (London's affluent financial district), whose life expectancy is 83.4 years (Bennett et al. 2015). This sizeable 8.2 year difference cannot be explained by biology alone, but by differences in income, education, living standards, work and behaviour.

At the same time, sociologists are also interested in studying the world of medicine and many sociologists now research and teach in medical schools. Sociologists are interested, for example, in the ways that patients with chronic illnesses deal with everyday life and construct a positive identity under very challenging circumstances. Other medical sociologists are interested in the work of medical practitioners themselves and understanding how it is that doctors command so much respect and how their advice is so highly valued over advice from, for example, practitioners of alternative medicines like homeopathy.

In summary, the social sciences exist as a field between the humanities (philosophy, art, literature, performance and music) and the hard sciences. They involve the study of people in society.

WHAT IS SOCIETY AND WHY SHOULD WE STUDY IT?

Margaret Thatcher, the former prime minister of the UK, famously once said: 'There is no such thing as society.' As sociologists, we know this statement to be false. Indeed, there are *many* societies and the primary concern of sociology is to understand the way in which diverse societies work. But things are not that simple, and defining the term can be difficult. In general, a **society** is defined as a group of people who share common culture, interactions and land or territory. A **culture** is a collection of shared norms, both covert and explicit, and it refers to the way groups of people think and act and their shared common goals. A **norm** is a social expectation that guides behaviour.

Society: a collection of people who share common culture and land or territory

Culture: people's common goals and their ways of thinking and acting

Norm: a social expectation that guides behaviour

Norms and university culture

There are plenty of norms on display in the culture of the university classroom, starting from the very first day of class, when students enter the lecture hall and choose a seat. The initial determination here – deciding which general section of the hall to sit in is largely a personal preference. Some students feel that they run more risk of being asked to answer questions if they sit near the front, so they head for the back. Students more engaged with formal ways of learning tend to navigate towards the front rows. Yet none sit in the very front row; everyone knows this will be interpreted as being 'too keen'. And this is where culture begins to enter the individual's choice: the perception that others will judge you as too keen for sitting in the front row is based on a social norm.

Once the general section of the classroom is chosen, the next factor one considers is whether to sit adjacent to another student or to leave space between. Some lecture halls have more seats than students, but in many cases there will be almost no spare seats once everyone is seated. Given this, would it 'feel wrong' if you are the second person to enter the classroom to sit next to the only other person in the class?

The answer is found in social norms: It is just not done. Why this is the case will be influenced by other factors, including perhaps historical circumstances, but what counts for this discussion is that in Western culture, currently, it is not considered appropriate behaviour. It is one of many norms that the classroom culturally expects.

From our experience in the UK and the US, the first norm is that when you enter a classroom you do not sit directly next to a person in class, unless you know them. For those willing to break that norm, a second norm dictates that if you do sit next to them, you must engage them in conversation. Sitting next to someone in a large and empty classroom and

© Stockbyte

then not saying anything is a violation of cultural norms that would almost certainly be received as deliberate rudeness by the other person. Another classroom 'rule' is that, even once the class is full, students normally remain silent during the minutes preceding the first lecture, making small talk more awkward. Fourth, students tend to sit in the same place each week, meaning that the choice of seats has consequences beyond that first lecture.

These norms have existed across university classrooms for generations. Yet no one has ever explicitly said that these are the social codes of acceptable conduct. No professor ever said, 'you must not sit next to a stranger the first day, and you must sit in the same seat next week.' As such, we call these *covert* or *implicit norms*. And they differ from the formal, codified, norms that are established through the explicit mentioning of the rules of the classroom, such as the need to attend seminars, do the assigned readings and not eat in the lecture hall.

Socialization: the process by which a person learns the accepted ways of thinking and behaving in a particular society

Covert norms are learned from others. While children may be born with predispositions towards all sorts of things, from their personality, artistic, musical and other talents, to their general sexual orientation, they must learn how to engage with a classroom seating scenario. This is the process of **socialization** (see Chapter 6 for more on this phenomenon). This includes how infants learn verbal skills, body language and the multitude of ways that humans relate to each other. This primary socialization occurs by infants emulating the adults around them. It includes being overtly taught rules (such as chew with your mouth closed) and covertly learning by observation (when men pee at the urinal, they do not talk to the guy next to them). Socialization never ends; we are always learning how to better fit in with or contest our constantly changing society.

These covert norms collectively begin to make a culture. But a culture is more than just a set of norms that govern how people act and interact with each other. A culture can refer to a small group of people in a particular setting (like an athletic team's culture), or a larger society of people (a school culture) or even commonalities that make a collective culture among those of a state or nation. These cultures might have slightly different rules than the culture at large.

Cultures may be geographically bounded. This is to say, they have borders that are inclusive not only of types of people, but of places. Countries have different cultures that are in part a result of where they are situated. Spain, for example, traditionally has a 'siesta', an afternoon sleep, because (before air conditioning) it was too hot to work at that time – this cultural norm does not exist in England for obvious reasons. Now, many people in other Western countries will have 'power naps' or sleep after lunch. Yet it is in Spain where businesses close because of the heat. And in other countries they are called *power naps* perhaps to emphasize that the sleep is both brief and to enable the person to serve the capitalist needs of their employer once they awaken.

Research also shows how the way cities are built and organized, in part due to the geography of the area, impacts on how people live their lives (Lefebvre [1974] 1991). Those living in Manhattan, London or Tokyo will have a public transport (subway) culture and accompanying conventions that Californians, the Scottish and those in rural Japan just do not understand (such as not striking up conversations with strangers, and running between trains even if you are not in a rush).

The infrastructure of a university will affect its culture as well. Even with online learning courses, the cultures of universities are rooted in their campus, in their buildings and the layout of their teaching rooms. Campus-based universities are often called 'bubbles' because of the introverted culture that develops within a geographically bounded environment. Think how the norms of the university lecture might be different if all lectures occurred with just 10 students, seated in a circle without tables or notepads. It would likely see a shift in the amount of time the professor spoke and the forms of conversation and debate that ensued.

Culture is reproduced through multiple mechanisms, including social interaction, the media, the law and many other variables, but one defining method that a culture uses to keep people acting and behaving in socially acceptable ways comes through stigma.

> Stigma: a social attribute, behaviour or reputation that is discrediting in some way

In his 1963 book *Stigma: Notes on the Management of Spoiled Identity*, sociologist Erving Goffman (1922–1982) provided a groundbreaking argument about how stigma is used to police norms in society. While stigma could relate to physical deformities, individual character flaws or tribal stigmas, such as nationality, the crucial component of Goffman's argument was that stigma was not ultimately located within the individual, but in the failure to measure up to what society deemed socially acceptable and legitimate.

Key to stigma is that it is used to discredit someone. Writing in the 1960s, Goffman noted that people with physical deformities were excluded from society regardless of their personalities or how they might be able to contribute. And because stigma is based on norms (and in some cases prejudice), it does not have to be logical. This is why taking drugs can be stigmatized, while alcohol consumption maintains social approval when done according to social norms, even though many illegal drugs are less damaging than alcohol.

It is the fear of being stigmatized that often keeps people acting within the mandates of a culture's prescription. One does not even need to commit the stigmatized activity, either; one only needs be associated with it. This is one way in which homophobia was perpetuated in the 20th century – if one said that homophobia was wrong, or supported equal rights for sexual minorities in the

1980s, that person would often be labelled gay regardless of their sexuality. This kept straight people from standing up for gay rights. The effectiveness of stigma is noteworthy, and often permanent. In short, stigma sticks.

Another mechanism for the reproduction of culture comes through **tradition**. Unlike a norm, a tradition has been passed down within a group that has significance and meaning beyond the mechanics of the act. Somewhat strangely, tradition alone often becomes the only reason given to perpetuate negative acts of a culture. Women are 'given away' at weddings by their father to their husband, just as women are expected to take the surname of their husband. Both these practices date back to patriarchal times, and there is now no 'need' for them *except* tradition.

Tradition: a belief or ritual passed down within a group, with meaning imbued to the act

Research on sport shows the danger of tradition as well. American football and rugby, for example, continue to play full-contact tackle versions of their sport. This is despite the fact that, every year, some young players contract chronic traumatic encephalopathy which results in a painful, miserable and shortened lifespan. Yet high schools continue to play tackle football instead of tag football for no better reason than 'tradition', and in full knowledge that such behaviours can lead to concussion and ultimately significant brain trauma. Similarly, in many countries where gun ownership is legal, people fire bullets into the air to celebrate the New Year, despite the fact that those bullets, if not shot directly upwards, arc and come back to the earth with deadly force.

Culture is therefore maintained through social norms, tradition and the heaping of stigma upon those who defy the culture. It is for this reason that 'cultural deviants' often create their own **subculture**, existing within, and to some degree at odds with, the dominant culture. We often think of stylistic trends related to music when discussing subcultures (goths, punks, emos), which are often related to class groups, but subcultures can refer to people who share a disability (like a wheelchair basketball team), religious perspective (like Muslims living in a Christian nation) or sexual interest.

Subculture: a group of people who share common interests that vary from the dominant culture

Subcultures are not just the preserve of those excluded from the dominant culture. Elites create their own subcultures, which can at times deviate from mainstream values and rules. However, it is sometimes the case that dominant groups seek to impose their culture on everyone else, something that sociologists call 'hegemony'. If the dominant group can persuade enough people that they should be in charge, and that they are superior – then others will seek to follow and imitate them.

Power: a contested term, fundamentally about the ability to produce intended effects

This raises the wider sociological question of **power** in society (see Chapter 7). Why are some groups more powerful than others, in economic terms (employment, ownership and earnings), political terms (most leading politicians went to a small number of elite universities and share very similar family and school backgrounds) and culture? Despite the claim that modern Western societies are 'democratic', such institutions as elections have certainly not dislodged powerful economic, political and cultural elites from the key positions of power in society. Sociology is tasked with understanding this disparity.

The difference between a culture and society can be difficult to distinguish. In many cases, they serve as legitimate synonyms. When there is a difference, the easiest way to understand it is to think of culture as the *traits* of a group – the community, behaviours, values and fashions – while a society exists when such traits become formalized to the point where values and norms become rules and even laws. This shift has to do with levels of enforcement, the extent to which disapproval is organized and by which 'authorities' are appointed to exercise discipline and punishment. The relationship between cultures and societies is always open to question. America, Japan, England and France are, for example, all societies – and they have different cultures that determine the ways they interact, their laws, their religious and ethical values, among other areas.

Emile Durkheim and the study of suicide

Written in 1897, **Emile Durkheim's** (1858–1917) book *Suicide* is one of the founding texts of sociology. It was important because it examined a topic that most people at that time believed was entirely personal. Suicide was understood to be an intimate, psychological act, not influenced by society.

Rather than accepting suicide as purely a psychological problem, Durkheim examined suicide rates of people across Europe and found several important trends. He demonstrated that the rates were higher among men than women, higher among single people than married couples and higher for those without children. Most important to the study of sociology, however, is that Durkheim also showed that suicide rates were higher among Protestants compared to Catholics.

© Bettmann/Contributor/Getty Images

It was this finding that put sociology on the academic map as an important social science discipline. This is because of structural differences between the Protestant religions and the Catholic religion, most notably in relation to how they contend that one's sins can be forgiven. The doctrine of the Roman Catholic church required confession to and absolution by a priest, whereas Protestant doctrine promoted the view that a person's relationship to God is more direct and individual – through prayer, reading the Bible or through good works. Thus, Protestants had to seek individualistic routes to salvation, but Catholics believed it was attained through community membership – their Church.

The reason why this matters is precisely the notion of community membership. At the time when Durkheim was writing, church attendance was a key way of providing community cohesion and providing a social network of like-minded people. Protestants had much less integration and more isolation, which Durkheim called **anomie**. In short, feeling like one belonged and having friends to care for you was an important guard against suicide.

Durkheim used statistical analysis of suicide rates to show that Protestants had a far higher suicide rate, arguing this was because Protestants did not have the sense of community that Catholics did. For Durkheim, individual **human agency** did not explain suicide. Women were more likely to experience the internal feeling of depression, but far less likely to commit suicide than men. As such, it was not the individual's internal state that determined their action, but rather the **social structure** in which those feelings were located. Social integration and regulation, or their absence, led to recurrent patterns of different actions (what Durkheim called 'social facts'). We discuss the theoretical debate about structure and agency in Chapter 3, and examine social structures in Chapter 6.

Anomie: a condition felt by people in societies where there is an absence of norms or values

Human agency: the capacity of individuals to act independently and make their own choices

Social structures: ways society is organized that constrain how an individual can act

APPROACHING SOCIOLOGY

While we have defined sociology, a better understanding will emerge if we think about the ways in which we can view sociology. Sociology is not an abstract degree programme, but a mode of thought that can transform how we see the world. It is a form of critical inquiry that can help objectively analyse a situation. Sociology is also a discipline, institutionalized in universities and guided by norms and rules. It is also personal, and influenced by our own lives and perspectives. By thinking about sociology in different ways, we can come to a broader understanding of the true scale, scope and boundaries of sociology.

Sociology as a mode of thought

Whereas some subjects are defined by the area of study, sociology is characterized to some extent by its *way of thinking* about problems. As a way of thinking, sociology enables us to understand things that are new and different to our own experience. As such, it is able to *make the strange familiar*. Sociology enables us to become accustomed to unfamiliar customs and practices.

Yet sociology as a mode of thought also enables us to think about familiar things in new ways – by *making the familiar strange*. We suspect that after reading this introduction, you will think about the lecture hall in a different way – whether remembering the social norms of choosing where to sit or thinking about spit on a spoon, your thought processes will be at least somewhat different. You will find your thinking challenged precisely because sociology unveils the structure and social norms behind everyday activities.

The notion that sociology is a way of thinking is best captured by the phrase, the **sociological imagination**. Developed by famed sociologist C. Wright Mills (1916–1962), and also the title of his book published in 1959, a sociological imagination is not a theory, but an awareness of how people and culture interact. It is a way of thinking that incorporates not only major structural differences, like social inequalities, but also everyday life. Mills argued that the sociologist needs to examine how a person's biography connects with history, writing that 'the sociological imagination enables us to grasp history and biography and the relations between the two within society. ... No social study that does not come back to the problems of biography, of history and of their intersections within a society has completed its intellectual journey' (p. 6). If you have answers to questions about why people act the way they do, you are at least on the path to having a sociological imagination.

For example, do you ever wonder why people refrain from carrying on a conversation in an elevator, but will talk loudly on their cell phone in crowded public transportation? Do you ever ask why it is that some people spend more time and money fixing up their car than playing with their own children? Do you question why some couples express love and affection publicly on social media, even as they are in the same room? Sociologists conduct research to explain these everyday conundrums.

A sociological imagination promotes one's ability to be self-aware and socially aware in order to make decisions that are not swayed by unjust social norms. Thus, Mills envisioned that the sociological imagination could help move society from

Sociological imagination: the awareness of the relationship between personal experiences and broader society

GOOD SOCIOLOGY The Sociological Imagination

A person with a good sociological imagination is likely not to take culturally normative matters for granted. To have a good sociological imagination is, in many aspects, to be a contrarian – to look at what others take for granted and ask critical questions. For example, whereas many people might blindly accept the notion that things are illegal for a good reason (known as the normativity of the law), someone with a good sociological imagination might first evaluate the social context in which the law was made and query its effects based on evidence. The person with a good sociological imagination is far more likely to ask whether, for example, the criminalization of prostitution is wrong and based on sexual stigma than someone who has only read about the issue in popular newspapers.

One might also question why sex between a brother and sister is so culturally condemned that it is criminalized. The incest taboo, long studied particularly in psychology, suggests that this cultural prohibition exists because, historically, intermarriage between different families improved the ability for both groups to thrive through the birth of healthy children, and cemented the bonds of an extended familial support network. But when there is access to high-quality contraception, the censure of incest has less empirical validation. Sex between two sisters is also illegal in many countries, even though there is no risk of procreation.

One with a sociological imagination might ask where these taboos come from, why they emerged and seek to understand whether they are valid. This is important to understanding the sociological imagination because Mills proposed that sociology was unique in that it could teach people the intellectual skills to both expose social injustices and provide new ways of structuring society to alleviate them.

the irrational reproduction of cultural norms, to cultural norms based in reasoned values. Mills believed that teaching a sociological imagination to the citizens of a society could thus promote equality.

We agree. The sociological imagination still plays an important role in modern societies. Sociologists tend to question the status quo, challenging prejudice and assumptions about social norms and unequal opportunities and outcomes. Few sociologists seek to reproduce existing social structures of inequality. Thus, for the majority of sociologists, we are interested in teaching our students to think sociologically, so that they will promote social progress, even if they do not always agree what progress might mean. While C. Wright Mills' idea has failed to resonate culturally – schools do not formally teach sociology in the way they do history, geography and other social sciences – his ideas are central to what sociology is about and an accessible way of seeing the relevance it has.

Sociology as critical inquiry

Part of a sociological imagination is the ability to think critically about society. By thinking critically, we do not mean moaning or stating what is wrong with an issue. Thinking critically means, rather, to think analytically and as objectively as possible about a social issue. Yet to say that sociology is a form of critical inquiry is to go beyond the notion that it is (hopefully) objective and analytic. It is to recognize that sociology has a distinct, scientific approach to understanding society.

This distinctive approach is necessary because society is itself 'self-critical'; with actors able to question their positions and beliefs, and with social structures (see Chapter 6) riddled with conflicts and contradictions. As such, sociology does not just ask how society is now, but also how else it might be, and what changes are both possible and desirable given the alternatives that either already exist or could exist if society were organized in a different way. Sociology is as much about social change as it is about explaining how things are now.

Central to sociology as a mode of critical inquiry is that it is a practice framed by theory and method. To say that sociology has a method means that there are better and worse ways to critically examine a topic. For example, if we wanted to know how climate change is influencing people's consumption patterns, we could talk to our friends about the issue and ask them how much they recycle – this would tell us more than nothing about the topic, and potentially even some interesting observations. But we could also undertake a detailed survey and recruit participants from across the country, of different ages and with varying incomes. The questions could include information about attitudes towards climate change and participants' consumption patterns. The scientific method of sociology means that we can state that the second method is better than the first, and will provide more useful information for making public policy concerning recycling (see Chapter 4).

The notion that theory is central to sociology is also vitally important (see Chapter 3). Without theory, it is possible to say that something is happening in a particular context at a particular time, but it does not address *why* that is happening. We might collect data that shows lesbian, gay and bisexual youth are coming out at a younger age and having better experiences than previous generations, but it is only with theory that we can connect this finding with broader ideas about decreasing homophobia, the impact of the internet and other social trends that have led to this current phenomenon. A theory *explains* a phenomenon.

For sociology, a good theory helps us understand the social world on a larger scale. But a good social theory must be testable, for, as Christopher Hitchens said, anything that can be asserted without proof can be dismissed without proof. That is why sociology has an accompanying method – to ensure these theories are based in evidence. So important are theory and method to sociology that we have dedicated Chapters 3 and 4 to examining them in more detail.

In order to carry out the theory and method of sociology, it is necessary to be as *objective* as possible. Objectivity can be defined as an approach where personal values and beliefs do not influence one's findings. The importance of objectivity is in protecting from bias: thus, objectivity enabled Durkheim to make his arguments about suicide and religion without being critiqued for his own religious faith. There are great debates about how truly objective sociologists can be, as we discuss in Chapter 4, but the key point is that sociologists must minimize the impact of their own beliefs on how they analyse and interpret data.

That sociology is a mode of critical inquiry means that it can be applied to a variety of issues. In this book you will encounter a range of 'sociology of's. We discuss the sociology of class, the sociology of race, the sociology of deviance, among others. At our respective universities, we lecture modules on the sociology of gender and sexuality, the sociology of sport, the sociology of work and professions, and digital sociology. The beauty of the method and theory of sociology is that it can be applied to any issue in which humans are involved.

PAUSE FOR REFLECTION

Sociology is an approach to studying society that can look at a huge diversity of issues and problems. British sociologist Ben Fincham (2016), for example, studies the sociology of fun. Take a moment to think of what you would be interested in studying – 'the sociology of ...' what?

You can study that.

What kind of questions might you be interested in asking? Have they been asked already? Why are you interested in this topic?

Currently, you will likely have broad answers to these questions. That's fine. Make a note of them. We'll ask you more about them in Chapters 3 and 4.

Sociology as a discipline

We have already discussed the ways in which sociology is distinct from psychology, philosophy, anthropology and other fields of study. A more formal way of making this point is to say that sociology is a discipline – a branch of knowledge. This is not to give it institutional credibility, or to enable people to claim professional respectability by saying, '… As a sociologist …' – although it surely serves those purposes. Rather, recognizing sociology as a discipline formalizes the notion that it is bounded by intellectual norms. This means there are ethical procedures that sociologists should follow, and rules that guide how we work – not least that we should not falsify data, hurt our participants or betray their confidence (see Chapter 5).

Sociology is also a discipline in the sense that it has been institutionalized in a number of ways. The most obvious is in the way in which it is studied at universities: in Departments of Sociology, for degrees in sociology and as a general education course. There are also professional associations for sociologists (including the American Sociological Association, the Australian Sociological Association, the British Sociological Association, the European Sociological Association, the International Sociological Association). While sociologists clearly lack a creative imagination in naming their general associations, there are specialized sociological organizations, too. One can, for example, attend a large sociological conference on just the sociology of race, or a conference on the sociology of medicine, consumption, science and technology, or media. These groups organize conferences across the world where academics meet, present papers and share their knowledge.

Sociologists also have various jobs: often working for charities or think tanks, analysing data or employed in jobs which aim to improve society. They also work in advertising and market research, management, international development and urban development.

There are also formal rules and social norms that govern the practice of sociology. Fundamentally, these are concerned with sociology being *ethical*. While sociological research can be undertaken in ways that harm people or support injustice, sociology as a discipline harshly condemns such research and sees ethical practice as a core component of the discipline. It is for this reason that we dedicate Chapter 5 to thinking about ethics and looking at case studies of social science research whose ethical components are complicated or troubling.

Sociology, as a discipline, means all these things. In other words, being a discipline gives sociology respectability and privilege. As academic sociologists employed at universities, we gain from this. But that does not detract from the fact that, fundamentally, sociology is about thinking critically about the social world. Far more important than being a discipline, sociology is also distinctly personal.

Sociology as personal

At the same time that the sociological imagination demands that we think beyond our individual experiences of events, sociology can also be very personal. Many sociologists study issues that are close to them. It is not surprising that a great many sociologists of colour study racial inequality; that gay and lesbian sociologists study LGBT issues and cultures; that many female sociologists study patriarchy and issues related to gender inequality; and that women of colour have influenced the field to study the intersectionality of race, gender and sexuality. Of course, many female academics study issues independent of gender, just as many people of colour study areas not associated with race. Nonetheless, personal experience of social oppression is one motivation to study a social issue.

To make this point – that sociology is personal – is to recognize that it is not always purely objective, but instead often somewhat subjective. Some argue that the greater the level of subjectivity, the less rigorous the study. This is certainly true in some cases: someone motivated to find a particular result to prove their own beliefs has to guard strongly against confirmation bias (where a person focuses on the evidence that supports their argument). Yet to recognize subjectivity and take measures to deal with it can be a stronger course of action than claiming complete objectivity.

In this spirit, it is important to recognize our own influences in sociology – and we have shared these on pp. xiv–xvi in the front matter of the book. Other academics, with other influences and other stories, would have written this textbook differently.

The use of sociology

In our discussion so far, we have highlighted that sociology helps us understand society in a range of ways. Perhaps from this it is implicit that sociology should be useful, although some would argue that sociological studies can be excellent even if they have no practical application. That may be the case, but our version of sociology is one that is fundamentally useful to society. We discuss the complexities of this statement elsewhere in the book, but highlight some key arguments here.

Sociology is useful in multiple ways, but principally because it can effect change. For us, sociology is truly meaningful when it improves society. Some would call this **public sociology**. For example, the sociology of health and illness has helped

Public sociology: a style of sociology that seeks to inform and engage with the public

explain why people do not seek medical attention when needed, and offered ideas to improve the ways in which people engage with medical professionals. The second half of this book, looking at the application of sociology to various issues, is also guided around the notion that sociology should be useful.

Of course, sociology can have influence even if change is not causally related. Sociologists have the opportunity to influence debates and, particularly, social policy through providing a rigorous evidence base to inform decisions (see Chapter 10). When deciding which education system is best, or what the most effective strategies are for reducing crime, sociology provides a framework to gather this evidence and influence debates. It may also be the case that sociologists do not gain influence in their lifetime but their ideas become influential later on (see Chapter 2).

All this brings us to *the task of sociology*. We hold that there are four key tenets here. It is the task of sociology:

- To assess
- To understand
- To challenge
- To change.

Not all sociology has to do all of these, but it is not sociology if it does none of them.

VOX POP Sam Jones

Studying for a degree in sport at the University of Winchester, UK

Before coming to the University of Winchester, I only understood sport in terms of how a sport is played, who plays the sport, which teams are winning and when I can play my sport (volleyball). At first, when I began my course I was sceptical about why I needed to learn about sociology as I only wanted to study sport, and how I can play it to the best of my ability and coach or teach it in the future.

To me, sociology was learning about human societies and why they acted in a certain way in different environments. Nothing about sport or my interests. Yet once I started learning about sociology and how it affected sport in so many ways, I began to look at it in a whole new way. I started to learn that sport has substantial sociological details, including education, leisure, race and gender issues. I knew some of these issues were

© Sam Jones

there but I never thought about them in detail or thought they mattered much to me. By studying sociology, I have learned so much more about sport in detail, both historically and today. I feel now when I look at sport, I ask questions like why and how. I don't just take sport at face value. I feel the need to dig deeper to see why certain teams, societies, athletes and spectators act in the way they do in social issues, behaviours and values.

Sociology has helped me in other ways throughout my course. In sports coaching, I am now able to take a step back when coaching players and ask myself why are they acting in a certain way and how can I coach them to become better athletes and better myself as a coach. I also study sports development, and using sociology has helped me learn more about social and cultural structures, patterns, organizations and groups participating in a sporting activity.

» How does Sam's understanding of sociology match with your own?

» What core elements seen in the section 'Approaching Sociology' (p. 12) does Sam ascribe to in his narrative?

» How else might sociology aid a student studying sport at university? What about people playing sport in their daily lives?

» How might your experiences differ from Sam's?

CONCLUSION

Sociology is about understanding society. Whether you are more interested in individuals' experiences of personal life or the broad social structures that constrain how people act, sociology has the tools to understand these issues. We have shown the ways in which sociology is different from other disciplines, but perhaps most importantly that it is a way of thinking, and a way of thinking *differently*.

HOW WOULD...?

» How would Erving Goffman (see p. 9) have interpreted your school life?

     » Think about the sociological imagination. What norms were present in your school? What was the point of the formal rules? Did you have a uniform, and until what age?

     » Make a note of the key issues, and then discuss with a friend and see what similarities and differences there are.

» How would a sociologist write about your class?

     » Think of the last class you were in. What were the norms of that class? Are they all of similar importance?

     » How might you contest the norms of the class? Which norms are more serious to follow and why?

     » How might you find out the reasons why particular norms in your class exist?

STRUCTURED FURTHER READING

Mills, C.W. (1959). Chapter 1: The Promise. *The Sociological Imagination*. New York: Oxford University Press.

The first chapter of this classic book is an essential read for students of sociology. The way in which C. Wright Mills argues that people experience their lives as a series of traps that sociological thinking can help them overcome will resonate for many people today. He also connects people's personal troubles with broader structural issues of society.

Burawoy, M. (2014). Public sociology: The task and the promise. In K. Gould & T. Lewise (eds.), *Ten Lessons in Introductory Sociology*. Oxford: Oxford University Press.

An accessible chapter by a sociologist who has argued for a form of public sociology across his career. This chapter provides some related arguments as to why sociology, and public sociology in particular, matters. It provides further examples of social problems that can be addressed by developing a sociological imagination.

Bancroft, A. & Fevre, R. (2016). *Dead White Men and Other Important People (2nd edn)*. London: Palgrave.

This is an unconventional textbook that introduces you to sociology, but written in the form of a novel. It is an engaging and accessible introduction to sociology and offers a different perspective to some of the arguments we develop here.

Visit the companion website at www.macmillanihe.com/mccormack for further learning and teaching resources.

Chapter 2
A BRIEF HISTORY OF SOCIOLOGY

INTRODUCTION

This chapter explores the history of sociology as a way of understanding what sociology is today. We chart the historical context in which sociology emerged – as old worldviews were being critiqued by scientific and philosophical arguments at the same time as industrial and political revolutions saw marked social change. We examine the foundational texts of sociology, including the work of Karl Marx, Emile Durkheim and Max Weber. Yet we also examine the contributions of women sociologists and people of colour, and critique the way the history of sociology has traditionally been told. We use these arguments to look at contemporary sociology and survey the key debates today. In our Provocation, we draw on foundational sociological theories to argue that inequality and unemployment are not aberrations but necessary characteristics of capitalism.

THE ORIGINS OF SOCIOLOGY

Sociology has a history. While this may seem an obvious statement, it has significant implications. It is not just the observation that people have been writing about sociology for many years. Rather, recognizing the history of sociology is to understand the ways in which it has developed over time. Sociology is determined by the social, dependent on political and historical conditions for how it is practised. And as a result, sociology will change in the future. It is not static but constantly evolving in response to social changes.

In this chapter, we discuss the ideas of key sociological thinkers (such as Emile Durkheim, Max Weber, W.E.B. Du Bois and others) alongside information about the historical period in which they were writing. It is important to combine these components: To discuss pioneering sociologists without understanding the context in which they lived would be like reading a biography that did not mention a person's family, friends, country of residence or world events. Unsurprisingly, given the topic of sociology, historical context is vital to understanding sociological writing about society.

This chapter is not an exhaustive or entirely chronological undertaking of the history of sociology. Rather, we discuss the ideas of sociologists who have been integral to how sociology developed as a discipline. This includes writing about sociology itself – what type of sociology we should be doing – as well as research on social issues or social problems. We will move beyond the traditional **sociological canon**, recognizing the important scholarship of women and people of colour from the inception of sociology as a discipline.

The power of sociology is far easier to understand by considering concrete examples of empirical studies. It also reflects the fact that sociological knowledge is cumulative in a real sense: by understanding the development of sociological concepts and ideas, it is easier to think about contemporary issues from a sociological perspective – which theories to apply (Chapter 3), what methods to use (Chapter 4), and what prior research and knowledge is most useful (Chapters 6–9).

By situating the origins of sociology in its social context, and discussing some of the core theories and debates about how it should be practised, we hope to equip you with a better understanding of how to approach sociology: both in this book and in your broader intellectual development.

> **Sociological canon:** classical works of sociology that are seen as foundational to the discipline

Thinking critically

In Chapter 1, we provided a number of definitions of sociology and a call to arms for the necessity and also joy of practising sociology. A central component of this is an understanding that sociology is not just theoretical, but also *critical*. It is not the job of sociology simply to *describe* what is occurring, although that can be a valuable endeavour, but to *analyse* what is happening and examine inequality or injustice that is observed. Sociology does not just describe society or social trends but seeks to understand and explain them. Once this is done, it is also possible to develop strategies for improvement – implemented by sociologists, activists, politicians or others (although not all sociology will seek to do this).

This criticality is embedded in sociology degree programmes. In Year 1 of a sociology degree, students might be expected to describe theories or arguments, yet by the third year they will be expected to *critically analyse* these theories and evaluate them through comparison with other related theories, and drawing on relevant empirical evidence. Such analysis requires greater intellectual capabilities, and it is this *critical* component that is the hallmark of contemporary sociology.

The centrality of critical thought can be traced back to the emergence of sociology at a time when religious dogmas were facing increasing challenge. Ongoing in the 19th century, religion's authority started to be challenged in the 1500s.

Martin Luther (1483–1546, pictured on the next page) was a German theologian, writing at the start of the 1500s when the Roman Catholic Church exerted great influence and power in Germany. Luther contested many religious orthodoxies, arguing against 'indulgences' where rich people could pay the Church for their sins to be forgiven. He published his '95 Theses', famously nailing them to the doors of an important church in Germany. As a result, Luther was excommunicated from the Roman Catholic Church, which decreed he could be killed without punishment. Even so, he continued to pit himself against religious authority by challenging the power of the Pope.

© iStock/GeorgiosArt

Martin Luther

While Luther sought to contest religious power from within the Church, a considerable challenge came from the emerging disciplines of science, not least astronomy (as opposed to astrology, which was influential at the time). It was commonly believed, and insisted by the Church, that the Earth was the centre of the universe – and that the Sun, Moon and planets all revolved around it. This thesis was challenged by mathematicians and astronomers who argued that the Earth revolved around the Sun (known as the heliocentric argument).

Nicolaus Copernicus (1473–1543), a Russian mathematician, was one of the first people in the modern era to challenge this dogma. He wrote a manuscript that argued for heliocentrism. Although he shared it with friends, he did not publish the book while alive because of fear of retribution from the Church. When it was published after his death, it did not have a significant initial impact. His arguments only gained increased fame and influence when they were picked up and developed by the astronomer and intellectual, Galileo Galilei (1564–1642). Part of the reason for this newfound credibility was the empirical evidence that Galileo developed in his work.

Working in Italy in the early 17th century, Galileo had built a telescope, based on descriptions of a basic model that only magnified objects by a small amount. His own improved design had significantly enhanced magnifying power, enabling Galileo to observe the night sky in unprecedented detail. Through analysis of this data, Galileo found proofs of the heliocentric model. Even though he tried to minimise publicity of his research, Galileo was accused of heresy and the Church banned him from teaching or advocating these theories. After publishing his book *Dialogue Concerning the Two Chief World Systems*, Galileo was tried by the Inquisition and sentenced to house arrest for the rest of his life. He was also forced to publicly withdraw his support for Copernican theory.

These events were the basis for two important concepts that would come to underpin sociology: 1) critical thinking that challenges conventional belief structures; and 2) the move towards empiricism (see textbox on p. 30 in this chapter), where information and evidence is gathered through our senses. These tenets coincided with the development of the scientific method. It is in this dynamic and exciting period of human history that the origins of sociology can be found.

Sociology in a changing society

Sociology emerged against the backdrop of important changes in society. The challenges made by scientists such as Galileo occurred at a time when European trading ships were returning from the New World bringing news of different civilizations and diverse religions, challenging the assumption of the period that European models of life, religion and society were inevitable, natural and perfect.

It was during this period that European society entered the **Age of Enlightenment**. This movement dominated intellectual life in Europe from the 1700s and has formed the basis of liberal democracies in the West ever since.

The scientific challenge to religious orthodoxies, such as that made by Galileo, accelerated as significant technological advancements occurred. These included the invention of the steam engine and major discoveries in the laws of physics. This scientific revolution occurred alongside new political theories about the organization of society (such as supporting democracy), growing criticism of religious dogma and the expansion of the social sciences into areas such as economics.

Sociology emerged during this time not because of the abstract development of these intellectual ideas, but as a result of the palpable changes society was undergoing (Craib 1997). The scientific revolution led to massive technological and economic changes, including important developments in transport and medicine. This has been called the **Industrial Revolution**. These social changes essentially resulted in the emergence of **capitalism** as the ordering structure of Western societies, alongside economic growth, rising populations, improving communications and increasing urbanization. A capitalist society is one in which, rather than being run by the State, trade and industry are privately controlled by owners who seek to maximize profit for themselves.

Before this time, society was described as **agrarian**. It is perhaps difficult to imagine this kind of society. When we study history, be it the Ancient Egyptians or of our own country, the focus tends to be on those who had power and money. While this is partly because those in power tend to leave more of a record of their lives, it also reflects the interests and values of those in a position to write history. Indeed, Winston Churchill described history as being 'written by the victors'. One effect of this is that it is much harder to imagine life before most people lived in towns and cities.

In agrarian cultures, a small land-owning class had great wealth and power, while the vast majority of people lived and worked on farms. Most people were peasants: They were illiterate and very poor. Rather than society being organized by a range of civic bodies, religious institutions controlled most of the social organization, education and social (or moral) discipline. Police forces run by the State did not exist, and would not for several centuries. Likewise, there was no such concept as weekends, as a person's 'job' was the constant work of making sure crops grew and protecting oneself against the ravages of the weather. Husbands, wives and children worked together with little differentiation in gender roles (Cancian 1987).

Age of Enlightenment: a period where rationality and logic became the way in which societies were organized

Industrial Revolution: the societal transition where technological change saw the economy transformed from an agricultural one to one based on manufacturing goods

Capitalism: a society whose trade and industry is owned by private citizens or corporations who seek to maximize profit through competition

Agrarian society: a society whose economy is based on producing and maintaining crops and farmland

Technological change brought in a new era where people moved en masse from agrarian living to dwelling in towns and cities. The allure of industry, and the better life it promised, influenced such a migration that the percentage of people living in cities rose from just 25 per cent in 1800 to around 75 per cent in 1900 (Cancian 1987). The key driver for the move to the cities was the availability of waged labour, mostly in factories. This **industrialization** had many benefits in society, not least that new machines enabled mass production of items which boosted jobs and enhanced trade. It was during this time that European societies became organized in ways that we recognize today (see Chapter 9 for further discussion of the characteristics modern societies).

> **Industrialization:** the process by which the economy changes from a reliance on agriculture to manufacturing and the production of goods

Trade grew during the Industrial Revolution for several reasons, one of which was the emergence of mass transportation. Whereas travel was limited to walking for many, and transport of goods to what a horse could pull, the development of the steam engine and subsequent creation of a rail network made it significantly easier for businesses to move goods around and reach a larger part of the population, and for people to move to towns and cities. These changes had great benefits for many citizens, particularly the middle classes and those who ran the factories. In the UK, the legal process of 'enclosure' also saw a small number of prosperous landowners buy large amounts of land that entrenched wealth inequality by using public land for great private financial benefit (Thompson 1963).

Of course, not everyone benefitted from this change. Slums were a central feature of most of the cities that sprang up across Europe. Here, the workers, who were frequently paid a pittance, suffered illness in unsanitary living conditions. Crime was high, sewerage did not exist and the health of the general populace declined.

During this period, it was not just religion that was challenged. While landowners and factory owners became wealthy, the more traditional aristocracy came under increasing threat. One aspect of this threat was the growing clamour for democracy in many countries, which was achieved relatively peacefully in some cases (such as the UK, whose civil war had occurred earlier in history) but with more violent uprisings in others (such as France and the US). What is clear is that alongside the Industrial Revolution came profound shifts in how countries and nations were organized. It was in this context of massive social change that sociology emerged.

FOUNDATIONAL SOCIOLOGICAL THINKERS

Karl Marx and a social theory of society

One of the great intellectuals whose writing provided a foundation for sociology was the German thinker and revolutionary **Karl Marx** (1818–1883). While many are aware of his political impact, not least with his book *The Communist Manifesto*, published in 1848, fewer realize his influence on sociology. This is partly because Marx is often perceived to be a purely ideological and political figure. This

© Johan10/iStock Images
Karl Marx

fails, however, to recognize the way in which he developed critical social theory (see Chapter 3) (Ritzer 2015). Marx believed in a scientific approach to understanding society that could critique inequalities in the social system and offer ways to improve the situation for individuals.

Central to Marx's thinking was the concept that one could comprehensively explain the social world through an examination of the prevalent material conditions – known as **historical materialism.** Importantly, Marx did not see people as independent actors able to go about their lives as they wanted. He referred to individuals as **social beings** and argued that their actions and beliefs were dependent on the social conditions around them. Marx famously wrote in the Preface to *A Contribution to a Critique of Political Economy*: 'It is not the consciousness of men that determines their being, but on the contrary, their social being determines their consciousness.' This was a bold, radical argument for the time and one that logically demanded a focus on, and study of, society to understand human lives.

Crucial to understanding Marx is that he was writing about, and in response to, the changes occurring around him. Marx was alive precisely at the time that capitalism was becoming the dominant force in Western society.

Marx developed a profound and overarching critique of capitalism (Marx [1867] 1965). He based this on a historical approach that argued society evolved through several economic stages. These societies differed by their **mode of production**. In hunter-gatherer societies, for example, food is shared between the group. The mode of production determines the types of materials that are valued in the society. In capitalist societies, factories and other industrial buildings that produce goods are valued.

For Marx, the problem under capitalism was that trade and industry were being run for profit rather than for the betterment of society. This meant that the resultant benefits were unequally and unfairly divided. In capitalist systems, economic activity is geared towards making profit, not equality or the social good: those who have control of the means of production – those who own the factories and the land – keep the profits. Factory owners also had the power to pay the workers as little as possible, maximizing their profits while hurting the workforce. Marx called this exploited group the **proletariat.** The wealthy owners of land and property were called the **bourgeoisie.**

Historical materialism: the belief that the social world can be explained through material conditions

Social beings: the understanding that human beings' actions and beliefs are dependent on their social conditions

Mode of production: the way in which people's needs for shelter, food and protection are met in any given society

Proletariat: a term used by Marx for the group of workers in a capitalist society who were exploited by the bourgeoisie

Bourgeoisie: a term used by Marx for the class in a capitalist society who own the means of production and most of that society's wealth

Marx argued that the bourgeoisie and the proletariat's interests were fundamentally pitted against each other. Consider this famous passage:

> The history of all human society, past and present, has been the history of class struggles. Freeman and slave, patrician and plebeian, baron and serf, guild burgess and journeyman – in a word, oppressor and oppressed – stood in sharp opposition each to the other … More and more, society is splitting into two great hostile camps, into two great and directly contraposed classes: bourgeoisie and proletariat. (Marx & Engels [1848] 1967)

Marx argued that while workers were technically free (they were not compelled to work), the social context meant that they had little choice but to accept the very poor pay and conditions offered by the factory owners. This was for several reasons: 1) there were no trade unions or legal protections for workers; 2) there was no broader social security or 'safety net', such as healthcare or minimum wage; 3) there were far more available workers than jobs.

All this meant that workers desperately needed the very low wages offered by the factory owners, who could fire them at will. The owners enforced long hours of dangerous work, for very little pay. It was a situation where the owners exploited the workers, and made great profit from doing so. Marx could not see any solution to this problem other than for the workers to come together and unionize in order to contest their situation. It is in this context that he called for revolution of the workers.

Different ways of sharing profit from business

Consider a business owner who makes $2,000 from his company. One option is that he keeps $1,900, and pays his 10 workers $10 each. He knows this is enough for them to survive, but that their conditions are of great poverty and insecurity. Marx would argue instead that the business owner should split the profits equally, so that the 10 workers and the owner each make just under $182. With this idea, none would be rich, but most would be significantly less poor. Marx maintained that workers could and should each continue with their occupational roles (i.e. one man might be better at selling products, and another at making them), but no one should be valued (paid) less. This contrasts with the principles of capitalism, which encourage larger financial risks for larger financial rewards and assume that highly skilled people are more valuable for profit generation and thus deserve to be paid more than other lesser-skilled workers. We discuss some additional problems of the capitalist approach in our Provocation in Chapter 9.

Communism: a theory of society in which all property is owned by the community

The clash between those supporting capitalism and those advocating **communism** has included major political events, and multiple catastrophic wars. Whereas some might have hoped that Marxist or communist politics would lead to positive and benevolent leadership, this has yet to occur in practice. Communist leaders have been as prone to dictatorship as right-wing leaders. Tens of millions have died over competing capitalistic and communistic ideologies: from revolutions within nation states (as led by Lenin in Russia), to wars against other countries.

Today, while political regimes, and entire nation states, can still be classified as capitalist or communist (and most usually somewhere between the two), changes in modern economic systems have complicated matters. The factory owner of the 19th century was replaced by the corporation of the 20th century. With this, the means of production can be 'owned' by any number of people – millions of people in fact. Most retirement packages are based in the stock market. This means, for example, that even though the authors of this book work for universities, our financial future is invested in countless corporations that we are mostly unaware of – including ones that we may ethically strongly disapprove of. The corporation has not changed the fact that workers sell their labour for a living (so the proletariat still exists) but today even these labourers can buy stock in the company they work for.

These issues speak to the ways in which societies are divided – and we dedicate Chapter 7 to examining how divisions in society exist according to class, gender and race. These theories of **class** are an important backdrop to thinking about broader approaches to sociological theory – with Marx's theorizing being the foundation of a critical approach.

Class: a way society is divided based on social and economic status

PROVOCATION 2: Capitalism requires unemployment and inequality to function

Unemployment is a feature of capitalist countries across the world. Politicians regularly talk about their plans to reduce or 'drive down' unemployment, and the fewer people out of a job, the more likely a governing party is to be re-elected. Jobs matter, and unemployment is seen as a problem to eradicate as far as possible.

But what if unemployment is not about a particular social policy, or a side effect of a temporary economic trend, but is in fact a *necessary effect* of capitalism?

To think about this, imagine you live on a farm with a partner and two children at the turn of the Industrial Revolution. The owner of your farm has just purchased modern, industrial farming machinery. The work of many hands – the hands of your family and others – can now be accomplished by one machine. In this example, we are going to use British pound sterling but substitute whatever currency you wish.

In need of a living, you and your family are forced to leave the farm and head to the city in search of employment. Here, you find that there is massive unemployment. There are factories in this city, but not nearly as many jobs in those factories as the number of people who have been displaced from the farms. When you call at a factory, there is one job available, yet there are 50 other people who also need the money from that job to feed their family and pay for accommodation.

The job available involves screwing the tops onto filled beer bottles.

Would you do this job for £15 an hour?

Most people would. It's boring work, but there is a family to feed and no other job available. In Western countries during the Industrial Revolution, there was no social support system either – no economic support (or healthcare, or education) provided by the State. And this was the only job available. Almost everyone would take this job, knowing it was their only option.

But here is the problem: The employer knows his job is the only option, too. The employer thinks, 'Why am I paying this person £15 an hour for a job literally anyone could do?' He – and it would have been a male employer at that time – decides to reduce the amount he pays.

At what point would you no longer take the job?

Our experience in the UK is that the British minimum wage is the point by which most students have declined the job. But is this realistic? Remember, in this scenario, your family is starving, there are no other jobs and, while a few pounds an hour might not be much, it will keep your two kids alive. You can at least afford bread to eat and a hovel to live in. Are you sure you would be willing to let your kids starve because you think your labour is worth more than £5 an hour?

In this situation, we are confident you would take the job. You would take £3, probably less. The employer is in control.

The point of this exercise is that the employer can only drive down the 'minimum' wage in this way if there is unemployment. Therefore, for factory owners, unemployment is a good thing. Marx (1867) calls this a 'reserve army' of labour. This army is important for another reason as well – should owners want to open more factories, they know they have that reserve to fill the job vacancies.

Consider if unemployment was not integral to capitalism. If there is more work to be done than workers to do the job, the workers maintain the power. They can negotiate for higher pay. This goes against the capitalist drive of making profit. Unfortunately for workers – the vast majority of us – the owners of factories (or corporations) have more power in society and, as Marx argued, the capitalist system is structured to benefit the owners, not the workforce.

This example is, of course, not complete because it does not recognize the key power that the workers do have – the power to unionize. Joining a union is the process by which workers come together to *collectively* argue for wages. Thus, the employer cannot drive down the wages of any one person because he is in effect negotiating with all his available workforce. If employees have formed unions, they can take strike action (cease working) when their demands of the employer are not met; then the employer would lose much of their fortune because their production lines would stop.

While unions are an effective strategy for workers in helping them secure higher wages, better job security and, more recently, better health insurance or retirement benefits, they have limited power. Capitalism also means that any given factory owner is in competition with other factory owners; and as one's competitor lowers their prices for the same goods, workers will have to choose either to accept lower wages or risk being out of a job entirely (if their factory shuts down because they cannot compete with another factory's lower prices).

It is also the case that unions regularly come under attack, and their power has ebbed over the past several decades. They are attacked in the media precisely because they are effective at supporting workers' rights (see Chapter 6): increasing workers' pay and reducing profit, and thus challenging the rationale of capitalism. With the threat of technological innovations and a potential third industrial revolution (see Chapter 9), people have less job security now than in the recent past, and a new class of workers have been described as the 'precariat' (Standing 2014) based on the low pay and poor job security found in contemporary work.

The failure of unionization to spread across all forms of work, and the way in which it is challenged and undermined, is not the result of selfish individuals, but a structural effect of capitalism.

Provoked? Read further:

Holt, J. (2013). *The Social Thought of Karl Marx*. London: SAGE.

Marx, K. & Engels, F. ([1848] 1967). *The Communist Manifesto*. London: Penguin.

Standing, G. (2016). *The Precariat: The New Dangerous Class*. London: Bloomsbury.

Auguste Comte and a science of society

Karl Marx was focused on the exploitation of workers in newly emerging capitalist societies. The social revolution he experienced was related to the mode of production and the economic ordering of society. Nascent sociology was also influenced by other revolutions – not least, the social and political revolution in France that challenged the rule of the monarchy and established the country as a republic. Indeed, a pivotal figure in the development of sociology as we recognize it today was the French philosopher **Auguste Comte** (1798–1857).

© adoc-photos/Corbis Historical/Getty Images

Auguste Comte

Born just after the French Revolution, Comte was fascinated with understanding how and why people rose up against the French aristocracy, and he looked for rules within society to explain this. Like Marx, Comte argued for a science to understand society. He viewed society to be similar to nature in that, in his view, it operates under its own set of laws and thus deserves similar forms of study (Comte 1896). In 1838, he introduced the term *sociology* as part of his call for the scientific study of social behaviour.

Comte and Marx shared some fundamental beliefs. These were primarily around the need to understand society from an intellectual position, and the notion that societies evolved through stages.

Yet they had very different aims for sociology: Marx wanted to change society to improve people's lives, whereas Comte argued that it was people who needed to change, to abide by societal norms, which sociology could identify. While Comte's work occurred in the Age of Enlightenment, religious doctrine was still very powerful. Comte hoped that the study of society would develop a base of scientific 'social knowledge' that would guide society into positive directions, not just those based on religious dogma. This is a core value of modern sociology.

Yet Comte did not view sociology as a tool for progressive values (Swingewood 2000). He sought to protect the existing social order beyond religious values, and argued for sociology in part to try and counter the revolutionary factions that were advocating for greater democracy. He is reported to have said, 'there is no democracy in mathematics' and believed that societies followed unchanging laws that could be discovered in the same way physics describes the natural world. Believing that the inarguable truth of these laws was more valuable than majority opinion, Comte hoped that sociology as a science of society could counter emerging democratic tendencies.

More important than Comte's theories, which are overly generalized and now discredited (Swingewood 2000), is his framework for how to understand society. In addition to coining the word 'sociology', Comte made an influential call for **positivism**. He argued that sociologists should theorize and hypothesize about society, and then conduct experiments to provide evidence for this position. He even offered four methods of sociology, which are still in use today: observation, experimentation, comparison and historical research (see Chapter 4 for more on sociological methods).

Positivism: the scientific search for fixed laws that govern social and natural worlds

Distinguishing empiricism and positivism

Both empiricist and positivist approaches in sociology hold that the collection and analysis of data is very important. **Empiricism** is the idea that knowledge can only reliably be based upon what our senses tell us, rather than our thoughts and feelings. It is the basis of all science. Empirical sociology is thus the view that sociology should be based on data which is gathered from our senses, rather than purely abstract theory.

Empiricism: the idea that knowledge is derived from our senses

Positivism can initially seem remarkably like empiricism as, at one level, it is the belief that social issues should be studied using the methods of the physical sciences. However, the positivist sociology of the 19th and even 20th century also conceived of society as driven by a number of natural laws which sociology could discover, in a similar way to the natural sciences (Swingewood 2000). The great problem with positivism as it has been used in sociology, then, is that it placed too much belief in abstract and unchanging laws to determine how society operated, not allowing for the unique and unpredictable ways that human agency influences society (see Chapter 1) – nor does it recognize the importance of human interaction in the development of meaning (see Chapter 3).

It is Marx's theories, rather than Comte's, that have had lasting influence in sociology and society. Comte's importance to sociology is not found in his theories but for giving us the outlines of a method for sociology, alongside its very name. For these reasons, he is a key figure in the development of sociology

(Ritzer & Goodman 2003). It fell to another European, Emile Durkheim, to combine belief in rigorous social science with high-quality empirical theories about society.

Emile Durkheim and becoming a discipline

If Karl Marx can be attributed as a precursor to sociology as we consider it today, and Auguste Comte gave us the name, Emile Durkheim is perhaps the most famous of a number of early sociologists who sought to consolidate the disparate individuals interested in studying society into an identifiable and distinct group. While earlier thinkers had developed the intellectual space to think sociologically, these other scholars sought to establish sociology as a discipline within universities.

Durkheim is one of the central figures in the development of sociology as a unique and distinct discipline. In Chapter 1, we discussed Durkheim's study of suicide as a pivotal piece of empirical sociology because it demonstrated how something so personal and psychological was deeply influenced by society. The empirical component of that book was vast, and particularly extraordinary given the technology and other resources available to him.

Our focus on Durkheim in this chapter is centred on his book *The Rules of Sociological Method* ([1895] 1982), in which he set out his view of what sociology was and should be: his manifesto for sociology.

Durkheim started from the position that sociology should be a science, and the sociologist should approach the study of society in the way a physicist examines their field. For Durkheim, society is the object of study for sociology.

A key argument for Durkheim was that society is **sui generis**. This means that not only is it unique, but it cannot be reduced to its components; Societal influences interact creatively with the people exposed to them to form a unique society. If you take people out of one social context and put them in another, they will not act in the same way; nor will the social context stay the same. This was crucial for Durkheim's argument about the need for sociology because it meant that neither psychology nor biology could explain society or the actions of humans within it – there was a need for sociology as a distinct discipline.

Sui generis: a term Durkheim used to say that society is unique and cannot be reduced to the sum of its parts

A key component of Durkheim's study was the examination of **social facts**. He defined these as:

> A category of facts which present very special characteristics: they consist of manners of acting, thinking, and feeling *external* to the individual, which are invested with a coercive power by virtue of which they *exercise control* over him. (p. 52; emphasis added)

Social facts: norms and values that do not have objective reality but exist beyond a single individual and exert influence in society

The first part of the definition to highlight is that social facts are *manners of acting, thinking and feeling*. This means that social facts are not 'real-life things'. Buildings, clothes and motor vehicles are not social facts because they have tangible existence.

And yet social facts exist beyond people's consciousness. An individual's thoughts are not social facts on their own because only that person knows them.

Instead, a social fact must exist in society in some meaningful form. Think of the language you speak, or the norms of the culture in which you live. Neither of these are made of real materials, and both exist beyond your own thoughts ('*external* to the individual'). They will both continue even if you die or change your view on them. They are both social facts.

In addition to this, social facts must exert some form of *control* or constraint over people. With language, this might be in the forms of words that people speak, or it may refer to more constraining forces, such as moral prohibitions against, say, casual sex or drug use. The constraint can be normative (we do not do it because we 'know' we should not), there might be legal prohibitions against it or it has become habituated in our behaviours (we have become accustomed to not doing it).

Durkheim also located sociology as a science that followed a rigorous method (see Chapter 4). For Durkheim, this method must be empirical and objective – albeit, for him, it was also rooted in positivism and its search for cast-iron laws of society. While he drew on observation and interpretation, Durkheim's sociology was also quantitative – using statistics to make claims and arguments about social facts and thus society. Durkheim was central to establishing sociology as a serious form of study, and part of this was providing an intellectual framework that people could engage with – and challenge. Perhaps the most important early challenge came from German sociologist Max Weber.

Max Weber and becoming a dialogue

Max Weber (1864–1920) (pronounced Vey-bur) was a sociologist who engaged with and developed the work of Durkheim and Marx, and helped advance the

© Hulton Archive/Getty Images

Max Weber

discipline by proposing theory that interacted with other sociologists' work. With Weber, sociology became more explicitly a dialogue about understanding society. This is because, while he supported the idea that the core aim of sociology was to understand society, he had a markedly different view of what sociological knowledge looked like.

Weber defined sociology as 'a science which attempts the interpretive understanding of social action in order thereby to arrive at a causal explanation of its course and effects' (Weber 1947: 88). In doing so, he did not fully concur with the positivism of Marx and Durkheim. Weber did not believe in pre-existing rules of society that individuals had to follow. Rather, he viewed individuals as the key to understanding society, with society being the product of individual actors and sociology the science of understanding how people behave. Weber was interested in studying the motivations and meanings behind these actions.

Weber and class

Max Weber developed a more complicated understanding of class by talking about **stratification**. Weber ([1921] 1968) argued that there were three dimensions of social stratification: class, status and power.

Weber saw *class* as a component of a person's life that had the power to influence their life chances. He argued that this influence had to be entirely the result of economic interests and wealth and that it occurs in the conditions of labour and commodities. In other words, the material resources that one has (money, property and possessions) will directly affect one's standard of living. Weber also argued that it was the ownership of property that was the key determinant of class – an argument which still holds strong today in capitalist and socialist countries.

Weber added **status** as a key component of stratification. He distinguished class, which was primarily about economics, from more social aspects – and it is status that addresses these elements. So, for Weber, class is not about community and social contacts, but status is. Status includes lifestyle differences, leisure activities and broader issues such as marriage patterns as well.

Weber also discussed power as the third element of social stratification. He defined power as the ability to get what you want even if others want something different. This can include physical force, but also involves economic power (being able to pay people to do things), political power and social power (social influence) as well. (See Chapter 7 for more discussion of how to theorize power.)

What both Marx and Weber's definitions of class have in common is a social stratification that can occur within groups or between groups. Marx and Weber, for example, lived within and thus reflected intergroup stratifications of people who were otherwise similar in their white, Protestant perspectives.

Stratification: Weber's way of understanding social class, consisting of three elements: economic, status and power

Status: the social aspects of class, such as lifestyle and leisure activities

Weber made a pioneering contribution to the discipline of sociology. His works on capitalism ([1905] 1930), religion ([1922] 1965) and the methods of sociology ([1904] 1949) are rightly hailed as classics that have had a lasting influence on the discipline. Perhaps Weber's ([1905] 1930) most famous and influential book is *The Protestant Ethic and the Spirit of Capitalism*, where he argued that both religion and the economy were becoming increasingly rationalized in European society. **Rationalization** refers to the replacement of traditions or non-logical rules for behaviour with calculated, rational ones (see Chapter 9 for a discussion of rationalization in modern societies). It is perhaps easier to see the rationalizing process at work in capitalism – the factory line is almost the perfect image to capture the increased order and rationality of that mode of production. Yet Weber also looked at rationalization in other spheres. For example, religion became increasingly structured through various reformations that sought to impose order on individuals within society.

Rationalization: the replacement of traditions, emotions and superstition as motivations for action by rational, calculated decision-making

However, rather than just occurring at the same time, Weber argued that capitalism emerged at least in part *as a result of* these changes in religious practice. Weber was seeking to explain why capitalism only emerged in Western Europe and not in other parts of the world, rejecting Marx's argument that capitalism is a natural result of economic laws. In *The Protestant Ethic and the Spirit of Capitalism*, Weber argued that changes in religious practice supported the growth of individualism – where the liberty of individuals is privileged over State control or collective good. It was Protestant reformers, such as Martin Luther (see p. 21), who advocated that individuals must try to live Christian lives that please God – rather than the prior view under which priests could perform rituals to absolve a society of its sins, or absolve the sins of a particular rich individual (the 'indulgences' discussed earlier).

These new arguments were developed by John Calvin (1509–1564), who maintained that it was not enough for individuals to submit to God (through prayer and confession) but that they actively had to work for his glory. Yet, given that God's will was difficult to know, it was believed that those who were rich and successful had been blessed by God. The Calvinist position then argued that since those who had been 'blessed' with financial success and security had obviously been rewarded for pleasing God by their labours, it followed that continued hard work was clearly what God wanted and expected from his flock. This ethic of Protestantism (working hard to please God) provided a framework for the spirit of capitalism (the idea that pursuing profit is a virtuous goal in and of itself).

As such, Weber argued that capitalism and Protestantism shared an 'elective affinity' in that they are closely related even if there is no explicit causal relationship. While avoiding any simple causal relationships, and cautioning that his account was incomplete, Weber argued that the Protestant ethic that enabled the spirit of capitalism was then *supplanted* by capitalism.

Alongside these changes, Weber also examined how societies were becoming increasingly 'modern'. This notion of **modernization** has a number of characteristics, including the creation of institutions separate from the State, the increasing drive towards rationality away from mysticism, the growth of bureaucracy, secularization and the separation of public and private spheres. Weber addressed all these issues in his sociology.

Modernization: the changes that occur as a society transforms into an urban, industrial society

Weber displayed some nostalgia for prior societies, writing that modernization had led to the 'disenchantment of the world' (Weber [1919] 1958: 139). He was also concerned about the way in which rationalization was a compelling force, famously describing it as an 'iron cage' that 'forces the individual ... to conform to capitalist rules of action' (Weber [1905] 1930: 54). His research on bureaucracy has had lasting influence within sociology, and has spurred important sociological debates that continue to this day on the effects of bureaucracy and rationalization in contemporary societies. As such, Weber extended Marx and Durkheim's sociological approach both in the range of topics addressed and also the methods employed.

Historical sociology

Much of Weber's work is today described as a form of historical sociology, as was the case with much early Western sociology (Connell 1997). Historical sociology seeks to understand how societies have developed through history. It was of particular interest to the early pioneers of sociology such as Weber and Durkheim, and has gone in and out of fashion as a methodology and sociological approach. One important trend in historical sociology has been the move away from a focus on European cultures to one that engages with, and poses questions about, societal development in places such as China, Eastern Europe and the global south (Adams et al. 2005).

EXPANSION AND CONSOLIDATION OF SOCIOLOGY

The early history of sociology was broader and more eclectic than we have described. Thorsten Veblen, for example, studied the purpose of leisure in Western societies, while Georg Simmel (see Chapter 9) discussed a huge diversity of topics, not all of them about the 'big', 'serious' issues like the economic order of society or rates of suicide. Nonetheless, it is accurate to state that sociology expanded in the first half of the 20th century as it became established in universities and as the formation of sociological associations consolidated the discipline.

However, as the discipline developed it did not just expand but changed its focus and scope of inquiry. Perhaps one of the key shifts was from investigating the ways in which modern societies emerged and comparisons between different countries on universal issues such as religion or the family, to examining a range of social problems and conflicts *within* these countries.

One of the leading proponents of this scholarship, and certainly the most famous, was the Chicago School.

The Chicago School

The Chicago School of sociology holds an exalted place in the history of sociology (Bulmer 1986). It is often seen as the first 'school' where a group of sociologists came together to develop a distinct sociological outlook and connected body of work. The Chicago School produced the first major journal dedicated to sociology (*American Journal of Sociology*), provided the first textbook of sociology, supported a great number of doctoral studies and established many research centres in sociology (Plummer 1997).

The Chicago School produced a wide-ranging body of sociological research that examined issues and problems within Western and, particularly, American society. Many of the academics in the early years of the School used the city of Chicago, their place of residence, as the arena for study. While adopting a range of methods, there was a preference for qualitative studies of observing people, interacting with them and interviewing them about their lives (see Chapter 4).

British sociologist Ken Plummer (1997) suggests that one of the most important books of the Chicago School is *The Polish Peasant in Europe and America* (1918–1920), written by W.I. Thomas and Florian Znaniecki. Immigration was a contentious issue even 100 years ago, and one of the biggest migrant populations in the US at the time was from Poland. Providing a comprehensive social and cultural overview of life in Poland and America for Polish peasants, Thomas and Znaniecki found that the Polish community in Chicago was shaped less by the policies of US government and more by its own imported culture and social history. They argued that immigrant Poles did not become American but formed a new Polish-American ethnic group.

In addition to developing rigorous qualitative methodologies, the Chicago School pioneered research into urban life alongside the study of deviance. For example, one of the key figures of the school, Robert Park (1922, 1928, 1952), examined the experiences of individuals within neighbourhoods, gangs and formal institutions such as schools and workplaces (see Chapter 9). These can be seen as studies of various subcultures within Chicago.

Perhaps the Chicago School's longest-lasting contribution to sociology was through the development of **symbolic interactionism** as a theoretical framework by which to understand society. With its antecedents in Weber's focus on the individual, rather than social structures, symbolic interactionism as pioneered by George Herbert Mead (1863–1931) and, later, Herbert Blumer (1900–1987) privileges the interactional processes of individuals within society. It does this by focusing on the symbols and signs that people use in communication with each other – whether these be verbal, behavioural or more implicit. That is, rather than just analysing the content of what people say and do, symbolic interactionists look for the meanings behind these actions.

Symbolic interactionism: a theoretical framework that studies how people communicate with each other to understand the meaning of actions, focusing on the symbols and signs of their communication

Identity: one's sense of self or how one gives meaning to self in a group

Distinguishing the 'I' from the 'me'

George Herbert Mead, one of the founders of the symbolic interactionist tradition in sociology, is famous for his suggestion that we come to see ourselves through interaction with other people – both real and imagined.

Mead argued that there were two components to **identity** – the 'I' and the 'me'. Think about the grammar of 'me' and 'I'. I see you, but you see me, and if I look in the mirror the person I see is me. Mead noted that the active 'I' becomes the passive 'me' when they are the object of another subject's attention. The way I see myself is shaped by the way you see me. Children learn to see themselves as others see them through interaction, play and then games. Socialization is the process by which I and me emerge in relation to others.

It is the 'me' that is interesting sociologically. Mead argued that there is a component of the self that is learned through interaction with other people and the local environment. People *internalize* their experiences with others to develop a sense of self.

Mead's ideas were important in developing a sociological understanding of identity – through the symbolic interactionist perspective.

There is a significant amount of sociological research that is deeply influenced by symbolic interactionism even if not labelled as such. Think back to our discussion of the lecture hall in Chapter 1: we implicitly adopted a symbolic interactionist approach to understand what it means when you leave one or two empty seats between yourself and another person.

PAUSE FOR REFLECTION

Think about the individuals we have discussed so far in this chapter. What similarities do you see between them? Why might that be?

CRITIQUING THE CONSTRUCTION OF THE HISTORY OF SOCIOLOGY

Women's contributions to early sociology

You may have noticed some similarities between the three individuals we have based our discussion on thus far: aside from parallels in sociological perspective, they are all from Europe and all men. This observation has become so familiar with regards to the sociological canon that it has been critiqued as being about 'dead white men'. Without undermining the central importance of these scholars, in the rest of this chapter we investigate a history of sociology that moves beyond these figures. We first focus on the contribution of women at the time of sociology's formation.

During the 18th and 19th centuries, the time in which sociology was formed as a discipline, women occupied a marginalized position in Europe, America and beyond. Denied the right to vote, women were not allowed to own property or access higher education. Despite these considerable obstacles to engaging with sociological debate, a number of women made important contributions to the development of sociology. Sadly, this was downplayed throughout the 20th century, and still is today (Delamont 2003).

In her book on feminist sociology, British sociologist Sara Delamont (2003: 78) discusses the 'founding mothers' of sociology. Her list of women who made vital contributions to early sociology includes Mary Wollstonecraft, Harriet Martineau, Beatrice Webb, Simone de Beauvoir, Jane Harrison and Hortense Powdermaker.

However, Delamont argues that championing particular women sociologists is less important than recognizing that they contributed to sociology and have been excluded from the discipline. Supporting this, she points out that any list made of specific founding mothers will vary significantly by country, by the interests of the researcher and by how sociology is defined. She continues, 'What is absolutely clear is that each generation of women sociologists has to rediscover the founding mothers, because they are not being … reinstated in the malestream history of the discipline' (p. 79; see also Chapter 7). While we concur, it is also important to discuss individual women sociologists to highlight the broader contribution they have made.

© iStock/GeorgiosArt

Harriet Martineau

Harriet Martineau (d.1876), born in England in 1802, has been identified as the first woman sociologist (Pichanik 1980). Martineau became a professional writer due to social circumstances, including relative poverty and the death of both her father and fiancé. Writing before Marx, Durkheim and Weber published their sociological research, Martineau made an exceptional contribution to knowledge related to society. She translated the writings of Auguste Comte, and also wrote a sociological analysis of American life, based on two years living in the US. It was this book, *Society in America* (1837), that really demonstrated Martineau's sociological orientation.

Martineau critiqued many aspects of the American economy, including the oppression inflicted by slavery. She also highlighted the exclusion of women from public and civic life, arguing that married women, who could not own property or vote, had similar experiences to Southern slaves in the denial of their humanity. In this and her other work, Martineau developed a sociological approach to understanding society and, in contrast to the male theorists we have already discussed, she noted the importance of gender in the organization of Western societies.

Another sociologist who has not received due attention is Charlotte Perkins Gilman, an American feminist writer, most famously of *The Yellow Wallpaper* (1892). Gilman sought to explain the ways in which gender inequality developed in society and how gender roles emerged (Appelrouth & Edles 2012). Gilman's sociological approach recognized the importance of economic and political norms in gender inequality, while also appreciating the ways in which gender differences are strengthened through social interaction and structural norms (ibid.). She argued that the divide of the male breadwinner and female home-maker exploited women and was inefficient in terms of work and labour (see Chapter 7). As such, Gilman focused on *stratification* and inequality in society, and laid out a powerful sociological framing for understanding the social world.

Gilman's contribution to sociology was considerable. Not only was she recognized as a sociologist by others at the time, she taught courses on sociology on college campuses and published articles in the influential *American Journal of Sociology*.

Furthermore, the Chicago School did not, as might sometimes be believed, consist solely of male academics. Several women worked at the School, and perhaps the most influential was Jane Addams. In her book *Democracy and Social Ethics*, Addams ([1902] 2002) argued that diversity was a central factor of healthy democratic societies.

She believed it was a moral obligation to seek diverse experiences that would help one understand others' perspectives and thus be better able to challenge either their perspectives or one's own. She led advocacy in urban reform and women's suffrage (right to vote) and made substantial contributions to the growth of social work as a discipline. Her synthesis of research and activism made important contributions to the Chicago School and, while she did not publish with her male colleagues, her voice was a vital one in the development of the School's sociological tradition (Deegan 1990).

The contributions from women sociologists we have discussed thus far does not include many forms of labour that also tend to remain hidden. This often took the form of devaluing work undertaken by women (see Chapter 7). Consider the following example: Bruce Holsinger, a professor of English, recently highlighted on Twitter the erasure of women's contributions in academia. Reading the acknowledgement sections of old academic books, written on typewriters before modern-day computers existed, he found male academics had thanked their wives for typing the entire book from the author's handwritten work, often multiple times. Consistent across these acknowledgements, the women were never named, only referred to as 'my wife'. While these books were in English Literature, it is emblematic of an experience in much of the 20th century where women's work was undervalued and not given due recognition (Delamont 2003).

In summary, while men form the traditional canon of sociology, it is clear that this is not because of some inherent greater ability or because women were not producing quality sociology at the time in the locations where sociology was valued – they were. Rather, the way women were valued in sociology and broader society meant that their work was structurally and systematically *de*valued compared to men's. As we shall see, this problem in early sociology was not limited to gender.

VOX POP Professor Betsy Ettorre

Lesbian feminist sociologist

My career began after I completed the first sociology PhD on lesbians in the UK (1978) and subsequently published a book, *Lesbian Women and Society* (1980). It has been challenging because I do not separate my personal life, work and activism.

December 1978

I begin my career. I am totally out, sexually harassed, bullied and called a 'pervert'. As I experienced being 'unacceptable', I explore what it means to be a 'deviant body'.

© Betsy Ettore

April 1984

I am relieved to leave my first workplace to go to one where colleagues accept me as I am. I am no longer treated badly or called names as an out lesbian.

March 1999

I ask myself, *'What meaning is there to being a lesbian academic? How do I address my continually emerging lesbianism as I engage in sociology?'*

December 2007

I give a public lecture on my career at my university. My lesbianism is very central to my lecture. I think, *'I do not plan on feeling proud as a lesbian academic, but I am. It is about time.'*

November 2009

When a colleague asks, *'What do you want, Betsy?'* I answer, *'I hope my work, my story, will be able to help other LGBTQIA* [lesbian, gay, bisexual, transgender, queer, intersex and asexual] *scholars now and in the future.'*

January 2011

I retire happily to live in Finland with my long-time partner.

December 2016

I feel a sense of relief when pondering the above. I think, *'Perhaps, my story is important.'*

» **If Betsy was starting her career today, do you think she would encounter the same issues? Can you think of examples supporting or against your position?**

» **How do you think Betsy's experiences differ from the earlier female sociologists discussed in the chapter? What reasons are there for this?**

William E. Du Bois and theorizing 'race'

The other significant omission in the traditional sociological canon is the contribution of people of colour. Emblematic of this has been the exclusion of an African American sociologist **William (usually known as W.E.B.) Du Bois** (1868–1963). Based in Atlanta, Georgia, Du Bois was in charge of the sociology department at the University of Atlanta between 1897 and 1914 – the same time as the Chicago School was producing its groundbreaking research. The Atlanta School organized conferences, attracted several sociologists and had a prodigious output of sociological research.

Du Bois adopted a broadly positivist approach to his sociology, and his most important theoretical contribution was the recognition of race as a social construction rather than a purely biological reality.

© *Underwood Archives/Getty Images*

W.E.B. (William) Du Bois

Du Bois ([1903] 2008) argued that race was 'the problem of the twentieth century' and he wrote multiple empirical case studies showing race as a key way of structuring society. An important concept he developed was that of **double consciousness**, whereby African Americans had to adopt two different identities because of their race.

Here, Du Bois was developing an argument about race as a force that negatively impacted upon the lives of African American men. Writing in the era of the Jim Crow laws – State laws that reinforced racial segregation after slavery was abolished in America – Du Bois argued that 'Negroes' (as was the nomenclature at the time; we shall use the label 'black' from here) were forced to continually think about how they were perceived by white people, who maintained far greater power and held racist attitudes. The conflict of maintaining a sense of self that was markedly different from the perceptions of a white racist culture led to great internal turmoil and conflict. He wrote:

> A world which yields him no true self-consciousness, but only lets him see himself through the revelation of the other world. It is a peculiar sensation, this double-consciousness, this sense of always looking at one's self through the eyes of others, of measuring one's soul by the tape of a world that looks on in amused contempt and pity. One ever feels his two-ness – an American, a Negro; two souls, two thoughts, two unreconciled strivings; two warring ideals in one dark body, whose dogged strength alone keeps it from being torn asunder. (Du Bois 1897, cited in Hancock 2008)

Vital to Du Bois' theorizing was that race was not the result of biology, but of social context (see Chapter 7 for greater discussion of this). He also recognized a diversity of experience among American blacks at the time, again challenging dominant racist ideology of one (inferior) black experience.

African American sociologist Aldon Morris (2015) highlights the truly innovative nature of Du Bois' scholarship. He argues that Thomas and Znaniecki's book *The Polish Peasant in Europe and America* (see p. 36) should not have been hailed as the first great empirical study of American sociology, as such a claim ignored Du Bois' (1899) earlier empirical study of *The Philadelphia Negro* – a study that drew on personal interviews with black householders in Philadelphia, as well as basic statistical analysis of census data, to make a sociological critique of race and racism in the city. Indeed, it is necessary to examine more closely how the history of sociology has been constructed.

> double consciousness: the notion of having two conflicting identities, in this case because of racism in society

Recognizing exclusionary practice in the history of sociology

We have discussed in this chapter the contribution to sociology of a diverse group of people, including pioneering women and people of colour as well as the early giants such as Durkheim and Weber. And yet the traditional canon of sociology still taught in the majority of university courses focuses primarily on the dead white men. There are a number of reasons why this is the case. It is important to recognize that the scholars included in the traditional canon deserve to be there. They wrote pioneering, important work that enabled sociology to become a thriving and important intellectual discipline. The question is not why are these individuals there, but rather why is that canon overwhelmingly white and male?

In some ways, this phenomenon merely mirrored broader gender and racial inequalities. Quite simply, a component of the exclusion of women and people of colour from sociology is that they were excluded in society, and the sociological organizations adopted many of the prejudices of broader society. A significant factor in the establishment of sociology as a discipline was the development of associations and conferences across Europe and America where sociologists could meet and discuss their craft, codify rules and launch journals and other scholarly publications related to sociology. The overwhelming majority of women and people of colour did not have the means or opportunity to get involved in these key early steps, nor was their participation often sought, enabled or encouraged by the white male attendees who did.

There were also gendered and racial reasons for these exclusions.

Men at the time tended to write theoretically and for sociology publications, whereas women were more active in applied and field-based research. The organization of sociology, privileging theoretical publications over applied research, led to the segregation of women from elite sociological positions in the academy into more applied fields such as social work. Deegan (1990) writes:

> Sociology had a sex-segregated system. After World War I, … the profession split into social work as female-dominated and sociology as male-dominated. Almost all the women trained in Chicago Sociology prior to 1918 were ultimately channelled into social work positions. Discrimination against hiring women in academic sociology departments was rampant. (p. 8)

Deegan also highlights how the ways in which sociologists are evaluated professionally (through publishing books and articles) also served to privilege men. Discussing the way in which Charlotte Perkins Gilman's role was discounted in the Chicago School after her death, Deegan (1990) highlights that although she was having daily conversations about sociology, theory and the social world, she did not publish with her male colleagues and focused more on social activism. Thus, while there is strong evidence her contributions to the Chicago School were substantial and worthy of explicit recognition, the impact of her work is far less tangible in historical records than that of male colleagues.

In addition to issues of gender, a considerable number of scholars now critique the way in which the history of sociology has been represented as fundamentally white in Western countries.

Du Bois is perhaps emblematic of the exclusion from sociology of research that did not fit the fundamentally white canon. As discussed above, his sociology at the Atlanta School made serious contributions to understanding race in society, and was trailblazing in its development of empirical methods in America. So why was Du Bois not recognized as central to the growth of American sociology in the 20th century?

In a powerful book that provides a biography of Du Bois' work in the context of American racism, Aldon Morris (2015) argues that the exclusion of Du Bois was planned and strategic. Morris discusses how Du Bois was excluded from the early sociology association meetings where the rules and codes of American sociology were decided. Similarly, racist views meant that white sociologists at the time discounted the work of the Atlanta School. Morris describes a pattern where 'because of race marginalization, the Du Bois–Atlanta school had performed the heavy lifting, only to have the intellectual credit given to white scholars occupying prestigious positions in elite universities' (pp. 197–198).

And so we return to the problem of thinking of the canon of sociology as that of 'dead white men'. To label it such, even humorously, is to ignore the ways in which women and people of colour made important contributions to the discipline of sociology. These contributions are being increasingly recognized, and the diversity of sociology is improving so that sociology more accurately reflects the diverse contributions that have made it the discipline it is today.

 Visit the companion website at www.macmillanihe.com/mccormack for a discussion of decolonizing university curricula and reading lists.

CONTEMPORARY SOCIOLOGY

As we conclude this foray into sociology's history, we reflect on what it means for contemporary sociology. It is important to note the centrality of establishing *theory* in sociology (see Chapter 3) and also the focus that early sociologists had on defining a scientific *method* to collect and analyse data (see Chapter 4). These tenets of early sociology remain as fundamental today.

Similarly, sociology has always been firmly grounded in its social context. Whether this is critiquing dominant ideology, explaining massive social change or understanding the city in which one lives, sociology has evolved – necessarily – in constant engagement in the social world around it. This means that sociology today needs to be engaged with what is happening now – sociology *has* to be topical because it is all about social context.

In addition to this, sociology is engaged with the real world. Just as sociologists like Jane Addams sought to have impact in society, so too does a progressive sociology seek to enhance society and social life. It may still be the case that social theory or quantitative empirical studies are privileged in some aspects above more applied research, but the notion that sociology should be applied to people and situations is widely accepted. Furthermore, it should be accessible to those people and even co-produced by them – people are not just the *subject* of public sociology but active participants in its creation.

While we have also discussed the serious and profound ways in which sociology has lacked diversity, the discipline has always been more diverse than is sometimes thought. Perhaps now it is more diverse than ever imagined, with scholarship on race, class, religion and methods being joined by a panoply of topics including sexuality, ability, music, sport, fun, to name a few. Importantly, scholarship has sought to highlight the exclusions that prevented sociology from being as diverse as it could have been earlier (e.g. Deegan 1990; Morris 2015).

Even so, the demographics of sociologists in academic institutions in the West continue to be markedly more white and male than the general populations of those countries.

We have not focused on sociological research beyond Western society: in our history of early sociology, we have drawn from scholars from across Europe and America. Partly this is because the sociologists we have discussed highlight powerfully the racial and gendered nature of the exclusions that occurred *within* the countries in which the canon became established – these cannot be explained through cross-cultural differences or the difficulty of international collaboration. Yet it is still important to recognize sociological work that was occurring outside these countries, and we draw on examples from across the world in this book (e.g. pp. 84, 222, among others).

Sociology has become a truly global discipline, practised across the world. For example, Connell (2007) calls for greater consideration of social thinkers from the global south, known as 'southern theory', and a more democratic recognition of the global nature of sociological theory. She highlights that there are important theories and perspectives to be considered from Africa, Australia and Latin America, among others, reflecting the experiences of both their dominant postcolonial societies and indigenous peoples. Connell argues persuasively that Western sociology is diminished by not incorporating these theories. In Chapter 9, we also discuss globalization and how different countries are connected in ways never imagined during the early history of sociology.

Despite many positive trends, sociology remains divided. This includes between leading sociologists: The authors all know of prominent academics who work in the same area at the same universities yet who refuse even to talk to each other because of intellectual differences. Similarly, profound differences on how we should understand the social world exist between empirical and abstractly theoretical approaches (see Chapter 3). There is a serious argument that sociology continues to be biased in favour of the global north (Bhambra & Santos 2017), and that sociology mirrors the divisions in broader society in some of the ways in which people are marginalized (see Chapter 7).

PAUSE FOR REFLECTION

To what extent do you think that sociology has become more diverse? How might you investigate this?

And, finally, sociology is, of course, a living, dynamic discipline that will change as society around it changes. How might it evolve in the future?

Have a look at your own social context. If you are at university, does your sociology department have a diverse group of academics in terms of their gender, ethnicity, age and background? How broad is the range of topics taught? If you are not enrolled at a university, have a look at the website of a university near you, to examine the make-up of its sociology faculty.

There are many sociological associations, including: American Sociological Association, Australian Sociological Association, British Sociological Association and the International Sociological Association. Take a look at their websites: who is on the managing committees of these associations? How does the current constitution relate to the issues discussed in this chapter? Many of the associations have 'streams' or 'subsections' where themes and topics are discussed. Have these expanded from the early focus of sociology? Are there differences between groups?

CONCLUSION

This chapter has introduced key sociologists and their thinking, all of whom have had a lasting effect in sociology. Karl Marx's legacy is that the study of class conflict is an enduring central component of sociology; Emile Durkheim codified many of the rules of sociological method and provided exemplary quantitative studies for the time; Max Weber argued for an interpretive sociology and wrote foundational texts. Similarly, the Chicago School and the Atlanta School developed qualitative research that developed interactionist perspectives and highlighted the importance of race, among other issues. We also highlighted the contribution of women sociologists and the work of du Bois, and critiqued the ways the history of sociology has been constructed. We finished by looking at how contemporary sociology is influenced by this sociological history.

HOW WOULD…?

» How would Marx analyse contemporary society today?
  » What constraints would Marx identify as being placed on social beings?
  » What is the prevalent mode of production?

» How would Weber critique Durkheim's notion of society as *sui generis*?
  » In what ways does Weber see society as different from Durkheim?
  » How might this have affected the way in which they practised sociology?

» How would Du Bois develop a different critique of capitalist society than Marx?
  » How might the focus be different?
  » Would Du Bois' theories of 'race' be as relevant in Europe?

STRUCTURED FURTHER READING

Craib, I. (1997). *Classical Social Theory: An Introduction to the Thought of Marx, Weber, Durkheim, and Simmel.* Oxford: Oxford University Press.
A classic introduction to the sociology and theory of Marx, Weber and Durkheim. The book goes into more detail than we have the scope for here and is a good reference for more extended introductions to each of these theorists.

Frankopan, P. (2015). *The Silk Roads: A New History of the World.* London: Bloomsbury.
This engaging and engrossing history of the world starts from the premise that civilization began not in the west but in the region that covers eastern Europe, Central Asia and into China and India. Focussing on the the silk roads that formed the connections for communication and trade, the book can help you think about society and the world in a new way.

Delamont, S. (2003). *Feminist Sociology.* London: SAGE.
A comprehensive and accessible discussion of the role of women in sociology. Delamont covers a range of issues in the book, including women's contribution to sociology; how a feminist sociology is different to earlier practices of sociology; and important empirical and theoretical arguments about feminist thought and women in society.

Visit the companion website at **www.macmillanihe.com/mccormack** for further learning and teaching resources.

Chapter 3
SOCIOLOGICAL THEORY

INTRODUCTION

This chapter examines the role of theory in sociology. It explains what theory is, why it matters and how theories are created. Theory can be a difficult element of sociology and so we break it down to its vital components, as well as highlighting three core forms of sociological theory: functionalist, conflict and interactionist. We then critique bad theory – particularly that which is written inaccessibly. In the Provocation, we ask whether it is more important for a theory to be interesting than true.

WHAT IS THEORY AND WHY DO WE NEED IT?

Theory is vital to sociology because, at its heart, theory is the way in which a social problem or issue is explained. Theory enables us to make sense of what is happening in the world.

Consider the following set of findings. Researchers have shown that the ice caps are melting at the North Pole. Others have found rising carbon dioxide in our atmosphere. Marine scientists show that the temperature of the world's oceans is rising. Others have found that the coral in the Great Barrier Reef is dying.

These events do not seem independent to us because we already know the theory that explains them: climate change. Climate change is the theory that makes the connections between the events. Thus, theory gives meaning to events by explaining why they occur and how they are related.

Theory can also be predictive. With our climate change theory, we can predict that as global temperatures rise, more coral will die. Furthermore, now we know about climate change, we can test other areas of the world. We might hypothesize that areas with the greatest amount of pollution will suffer the worst effects from climate change, or the theory could be used to suggest ways that climate change could be halted if not reversed. Of course, our scientific understanding of climate change is not one theory but a massive conglomeration of theories and evidence about human-influenced global warming (Oreskes 2004).

Similar to a theory of global warming around phenomena in nature, sociologists develop theories to explain *social* phenomena. **Sociological theories** are statements of how and why particular facts about the social world are related. Climate change

> **Theory:** a proposition or a number of propositions that explain why or how something is happening

> **Sociological theory:** abstract propositions about society that can be tested and have empirical support

is not a sociological theory because its focus is on non-human events, even if it has been caused by human activity. Sociological theories about climate change exist, of course, and they focus on how people understand or reject its reality, how individuals and groups might contribute to climate change, or how people can engage in reducing it (e.g. McCright & Dunlap 2011). We return to this subject in more detail in Chapter 9, pp. 235– 237.

Theory is vital to both sociology and society by giving meaning to our world and helping predict future events. Without theory, we just have lots of things happening at once.

Theory, concepts and hypotheses

A theory is a complex thing. Good sociological theory will have been developed over many years with huge amounts of intellectual thought exerted by both the theorist and the people whose work they have drawn upon. Before we look at complex theories, both in this chapter and the rest of the book, it will be helpful to think about what elements make up a theory.

To do this, consider a simple example. Say we have a sociological theory: that men are more violent than women because of social upbringing. We are not going to explore the veracity of that statement here, but instead use this example to think about what is needed for a theory.

First, theory needs **concepts**. Concepts can be considered the building blocks of a theory and they are abstract ideas. Consider our theory of violence and men: 'violence' and 'men' are both concepts. In the theory, they are abstract ideas (definitions) of particular behaviours (for violence) and particular characteristics (for men and, separately, for women). There is necessarily some generalizing here, in the sense that we have to pretend (for this basic theory) that men are a homogenous group (i.e. they are very similar as a group) and that they are distinct from women, who are also a homogenous group.

> Concepts: abstract ways of defining particular issues

To form a concept is to develop a definition of a thing. So, if we have violence as a concept we must know what this means or entails. We have the verb *conceptualize* to describe the process by which we determine a concept. For our theory, we would have to decide what counts as violence. Probably, for example, 'punching someone' is violence, whereas 'not holding a door open for someone' is not.

We then also need a hypothesis. The hypothesis is an educated guess at what one expects to find about the outcome of an event or action. The guess is 'educated' because it is based on knowledge of prior events. If a hypothesis proves true in a particular context, it may become a theory; but if it cannot explain enough phenomena, it might not. Theory is, basically, *a set of connected hypotheses*.

Our theory includes the hypothesis that men are more violent than women. But this is not a theory on its own – it only becomes a theory when we include a suggested reason *why*. Our theory might be that men are more violent than women because of social upbringing. Without the hypothesis, we do not have a theory, but a hypothesis on its own is not a theory. Theory needs a 'because'.

A crucial part of a sociological theory is that it has empirical evidence to support it. In Chapter 4 we discuss the ways in which sociological data can be collected and analysed. For now, we will accept that useful sociological data can be acquired. This is vital as it means theory is then testable and can potentially be found to be wrong – what Karl Popper (1902–1994), one of the greatest 20th century philosophers, called falsifiability. The data obtained through this testing is then analysed and the results used to support or critique the theory.

Now we know the elements of a theory, we consider the breadth of its scope and how it can be applied in a range of contexts.

GOOD SOCIOLOGY Bowling Alone

A classic example of a sociological theory that both explains diverse findings and can be used to make predictions is the message of Robert Putnam's (2000) book, *Bowling Alone: The Collapse and Revival of American Community*. Here, Putnam proposed a theory that he describes as the decline of civic engagement. Civic engagement is the idea that people within a community work together to better that community, and Putnam argued that Americans' involvement in civic life had declined over the past 60 years. This included engagement in community organizations, religious participation, voting and many other activities. While he highlighted several factors that contributed to this decline, the most salient issue in his theory was increased television consumption.

© Getty images

Putnam therefore proposed that the more television people watch, the lower their involvement in civic life. He titled the book *Bowling Alone* because this image exemplified the loss of community: rather than bowling in a sociable manner, reaching out to the strangers in the next lane, in towns across America people went to bowling alleys and played on their own. This theory was designed before the advent of social media like Facebook, and before the impact of the internet had truly been felt. But, at least at its time, it made for a good theory because it explained several social phenomena.

To say that *bowling alone* is a good example of sociological theory is not to disregard the critiques it has received – critique being a vital part of sociological theory, and sociology more broadly. Writing about an earlier essay of Putnam's on the subject, Ladd (1999) argued that rather than civic disengagement, community involvement still existed but was taking different forms: interest may shift from sports to church groups as one ages, or to environmental organizations dependent on social trends or local concerns. The point is that a good theory *can* be critiqued and may even be wrong. Putnam's theory clearly illustrates the basic purpose of sociological theory because it proposes a relationship between two or more concepts, and can be used to predict that the more people watch television the less civic engagement will occur.

Drake and Harvey (in press) argue there are five components of good theory. These are:

» evidence: there is empirical data to support the argument
» explanation: it explains a complex issue
» applicability: it can be applied beyond one setting
» testability: it can be tested
» predictability: it can be used to predict a future event or outcome.

If a theory combines these components, it has the potential to be of value in understanding societies and social problems. In Table 3.1, we apply these components of good theory to Putnam's *Bowling Alone*.

Table 3.1: Is Putnam's *Bowling Alone* a good theory?

Component	Explanation	Applied to Putnam's *Bowling Alone*
Evidence	Is there empirical data?	Putnam drew on a large number of interviews and other forms of data to make his claims
Explanation	Is the issue complex?	Issues of civic engagement are very complex
Applicability	Can it be applied beyond one setting?	The scope was across America, so a huge number of local settings
Testability	Can it be tested?	In many ways: Test whether the trend is occurring in different settings and whether there are alternative explanations
Predictability	Is it predictive?	Yes: One prediction is that a person who watches a lot of television will be less civically engaged than someone who watches none

Levels of theory

We tend to think about sociological theories as relating to particular topics, such as climate change, or being in a particular theoretical tradition, such as Marxism. Yet it can also be helpful to think about the 'level' of theory or the *scale* of its focus. In this context, sociological theory includes broad philosophizing and grand theories that explain social trends and shifts in society, alongside very contextualized and specific micro theories that examine how people act together and focus on the detail of everyday life. Of course, there is a vast array of theories in between, which we call middle-range theories.

Mills (1959) contends that the levels of theory are determined by the amount of abstraction. The more abstract an idea is, the less detail it has about a particular social context. Let us return to our hypothetical theory that men are more violent than women. This is a very abstract theory in its current form. If we wanted to make it less abstract, we would need to add more detail: in what countries is this true? What kind of violence are we discussing? Are there differences by class, age or religion? The more of these kinds of detail we have, the less abstract (and more concrete) the theory. Table 3.2 describes the types of theory and the level of abstraction they have.

Mills (1959) critiques grand theory as being 'a level of thinking so general that its practitioners cannot logically get down to observation' (p. 33). He argues that it loses historical and structural context in the process. The related problem for the micro theorists, he contends, is that they get so lost in observation that there is not enough

Table 3.2: Types of theory and level of abstraction

Type of theory	Definition	Level of abstraction
Philosophy	The study of reason and values and does not concern itself with empirical study. Sometimes philosophy that is applied to social matters is called social theory	Near-total
High Theory or Grand Theory	Generalisations about big ideas, based on observation, so there is some semblance of empirical argument, but the ideas are difficult to measure or test	A significant amount
Middle-range Theory	Although the term 'middle range' is not a recognized phrase, we use it here to explain theories that are testable, and explain why a social phenomenon occurs	Some (and it varies)
Micro-theory	Theories that explain small-scale phenomena or interactions between individuals. They tend to be less interested in structural causes but focus on interaction	Little

abstraction to develop concepts and theories connected to broader structural ideas. Mills maintains there is a need to move between these levels, arguing, 'the capacity to shuttle between levels of abstraction, with ease and with clarity, is a signal mark of the imaginative and systematic thinker' (p. 34).

Any sociologist who seeks to develop theory has to carefully balance the extent to which they generalize versus keeping their arguments within the context of their data (Mills 1959). Make no generalizations beyond that immediate context and the theory lacks importance or interest; make grand claims of generalizability and the theory will be critiqued for not paying attention to detail. The author might even be critiqued for lacking intellectual humility or rigour. The sociologist must therefore ensure their theories connect with broader social issues, but also acknowledge the limitations of their data and arguments.

Getting this balance right is important. Yet, sociologist Kieran Healy (2017) contends that an excessive fear of overgeneralizing in sociological theory may actually stifle the generation of new and important theories. This comes from what he sees as a flawed demand for 'nuance'. He writes:

> When faced with a problem that is hard to solve, ... the nuance-promoting theorist says, 'But isn't it more complicated than that?' or 'Isn't it really both/and?' or ... 'Aren't you leaving out [something]?' ... This sort of nuance is, I contend, fundamentally antitheoretical. It blocks the process of abstraction on which theory depends, and it inhibits the creative process that makes theorizing a useful activity. (p. 119)

In other words, resist discounting a theory merely because it does not account for every example or context. The job of sociology is to generalize: obviously this must occur within specific confines, paying attention to issues that realistically will influence social dynamics. But being trapped by nuance can stifle theory development – and that is probably worse because explanatory theories are central to sociological thought.

BAD SOCIOLOGY Nuance Traps

Healy (2017) argues that nuance can be bad for sociology, in three specific ways.

The first trap is to give ever more detail about the topic of study. This trap is to give so much literal description of what is occurring, there is never any scope to develop theory. Similar to Mill's critique of micro theories (see p. 50 this chapter), this is encapsulated by the English idiom 'can't see the wood for the trees'.

The second trap is the opposite end of the nuance spectrum: to argue for ever more complex explanations and caveats that do not have an understandable, testable theoretical proposition. This kind of nuance fails Ockham's razor (see p. 66). It is just more complex than it needs to be.

The third trap is nuance as a pose. Unlike the first two traps, this is not a serious but flawed attempt to develop good theory. Rather, it is to request nuance of others as a way of appearing sophisticated and better than the author of the theory.

The importance of these traps might seem somewhat abstract for you as readers relatively new to sociology. Yet people who read sociology can fall into these nuance traps at any stage. We have all been in seminars and lectures where a student challenges a theory because it lacks a focus on a particular issue or area (the first trap): this critique is good as far as it goes, but it is not a full evaluation of the theory. While you are less likely to fall into the second trap, it is a good critique and one you might seek to apply to some theories discussed later in the chapter. As for the third trap – of asking for nuance to look good – it is, we believe, generalizable beyond sociology and something to avoid throughout your life.

PROVOCATION 3: It is more important for a theory to be interesting than true

Throughout this chapter, an underlying assumption has been that accuracy is important. A theory is better if it is true. Or, to be more accurate, if it has not yet been shown to be false. And if a theory is false, we have to discard it for another one.

The majority of us would have an instinctive, positive reaction to this position. As sociologists, whether novice or experienced, we would not knowingly advocate a theory we knew to be false. For example, no one can argue that the world is the centre of the universe because astronomy has disproven the theory. We obviously want our theories to be interesting as well, but that is a secondary concern to it fitting the available data.

But what if, deep down, our preference is for interesting theories?

Consider the following: if we were to tell you that later in this chapter there were five pages of empirically rich theory about why food satiates hunger and then another five pages about why water does not actually quench thirst, but then insisted that you could only read one of them, which one would you choose?

We think it likely the majority of people would want to read the section about why water does not quench thirst. Even though you think it is going to be wrong, you are probably interested to see what the argument will be. Besides, you already know food makes you less hungry; unless you have a particular interest in the science of hunger, you will not want to read five pages of worthy writing about a notion you are pretty certain is correct from your own experience.

Sociologist Murray Davis (1971) highlighted the importance of theory being interesting in 1971. He opened his article with these important words:

> It has long been thought that a theorist is considered great because his theories are true, but this is false. A theorist is considered great, not because his theories are true, but because they are *interesting*. Those who carefully and exhaustively verify trivial theories are soon forgotten; whereas those who cursorily and expediently verify interesting theories are long remembered. In fact, the truth of a theory has very little to do with its impact, for a theory can continue to be found interesting even though its truth is disputed – even refuted! (p. 309)

It does seem that we have confirmation bias towards theories that are interesting – we *want* them to be true. Think about some of the theories we have discussed already in this book. Durkheim's notion that suicide is not an individual phenomenon but a social and cultural one is so powerful, we *want* it to be true.

Perhaps the greatest living popularizer of sociology alive today understands this well. Malcolm Gladwell (pictured) has written five bestselling sociology books that deal with the unexpected implications of social science research. He made famous the notion that it takes 10,000 hours of practice to become an expert in his book *Outliers*, and his podcast *Revisionist History* uses counterintuitive occurrences to examine broader sociological issues. We are not arguing that Gladwell is regularly wrong, but rather that Gladwell is so successful because he manages to present theories in exciting, interesting ways.

Supporting our argument of interest over accuracy, we have plenty of evidence that theories have staying power even when we know them to be false. Let us consider psychology for a moment. The theories of Sigmund Freud are no longer considered to provide an accurate model of the human mind by professional psychologists or therapists. Yet cultural and social theorists still use his theories as ways to interrogate contemporary norms – not because Freud was correct but because he asked questions in interesting and significant ways.

© Jerome Favre/Bloomberg via Getty Images

Theories tend to be interesting when they challenge our own assumptions and everyday routines. In this regard, then, interesting theories are also inherently sociological, in the sense that the sociological imagination seeks to make us think differently about society. It is also what we are doing with these Provocations – presenting an argument in a counterintuitive and, thus, provocative way.

And yet this preference for the interesting theory has negative effects. It is one reason why conspiracy theories survive – we like them because they interest us and they make the mundane seem more exciting. This means that falsehoods have staying power beyond the time they have been shown to be false. It also explains why we let untruths be retold. As satirist Mark Twain said, 'A lie can travel halfway around the world while the truth is putting on its shoes.'

Of course, people will not believe anything. Developing a theory that we are ruled by aliens will see you labelled a 'crackpot', and arguing against established facts without evidence will see you ridiculed in many contexts – although there is a worrying trend in the US regarding the phenomena of 'alternative facts' and 'fake news' which may suggest an increasing openness to conspiracy theories (see Chapter 10 for more on this). Even so, Davis (1971) is still accurate in his warning:

> There is a fine but definite line between asserting the surprising and asserting the shocking, between the interesting and the absurd ... Those who attempt to deny the *strongly held* assumptions of their audience will have their very sanity called into question. They will be accused of being lunatics; if scientists, they will be called 'crackpots'. If the difference between the inspired and the insane is only in the degree of tenacity of the particular audience assumptions they choose to attack, it is perhaps for this reason that genius has always been considered close to madness. (p. 343)

Provoked? Read further:

Davis, M.S. (1971). That's interesting! Towards a phenomenology of sociology and a sociology of phenomenology. *Philosophy of the Social Sciences*, 1(2), 309–344.

Gladwell, M. (2009). *Outliers: The Story of Success*. New York: Penguin.

Connecting the micro and the macro: The strength of weak ties

It can often seem that the macro theories of sociology are disconnected from the micro theories that focus on everyday interaction. This is certainly an issue that sociologists continue to battle with, as combining the two is difficult theoretically and methodologically – like trying to focus on what is directly in front of you and what is visible in your peripheral vision at the same time. One way this issue can be addressed is through thinking about social networks.

Consider John, a middle-aged man who has lived in his community for many years and gains emotional support and comfort from his close friends, who all live nearby. He does not socialise much outside of this group because he gets all the social support he needs from them, and his preferred method of socializing is to have his friends over for dinner. John has one acquaintance, Juan, whom he sees very occasionally but never invites to his house because he does not consider him a good enough friend.

Compare this with Juan, who has far fewer close friends than John, but many more acquaintances. Rather than dinner parties, Juan much prefers to go to a bar and meet new people. He does not have the same social support networks with these friends, but he finds he has far more opportunities for work and leisure activities than John. Why is this the case?

One of the key studies that addresses this issue is Mark Granovetter's (1973) seminal article in the *American Journal of Sociology*, 'The strength of weak ties'. Here, Granovetter argues that it is the people with whom we are least connected that offer us the most opportunities in life. Granovetter theorizes that the intensity of the connections between people matters. He conceptualized this into 'strong' and 'weak' ties, defining a tie and its intensity as 'a combination of the amount of time, the emotional intensity, the intimacy (mutual confiding), and the reciprocal services which characterize the tie' (p. 1361).

The basic argument (as illustrated in Figure 3.1) is that our close friends (*strong ties*) are more likely to know each other than our acquaintances (*weak ties*) are. Weak ties tend to be only loosely connected to our networks, which is why they remain weak ties. Yet we tend to already know our close friends' close friends. As such, the strong ties network becomes a relatively closed circuit. Thus, John meets very few new people. The greatest potential for him to meet new people and gain new opportunities is through his social butterfly friend, Juan. Weak ties are strong, in the sense that it is these connections that provide new opportunities in life.

A key word here is *opportunities*. It is weak ties that give us the prospect of new challenges and breaks, but this does not mean they are inherently better. Strong ties give us more emotional support and are much more consistent over time, particularly in life's emergencies.

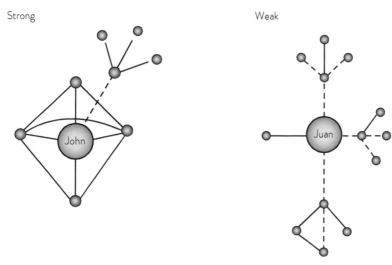

Figure 3.1: Strong vs weak ties

An important aspect of this theory is how it connects the micro with the macro. The study highlights how personal (micro) experience of opportunities in work and leisure are deeply connected with and reflect (macro) observations of how social networks are structured. Insulated groups, such as close friendships and families, have often been studied with micro theories, and Granovetter's work enables these groups to be brought into macro discussions of social structure.

How is theory developed?

We have provided examples of theory – including bowling alone and the strength of weak ties. But how do sociologists move from an idea or some data to constructing a good theory? There are two broad ways to develop new theory: deductively or inductively.

Deductive theory works from the more general to the more specific; sometimes this is informally called a 'top-down' approach. Its longer formulation is 'hypothetico-deductive' and while this may sound more confusing, it can be helpful to remember as it is based on hypothesis testing.

The process of developing a deductive theory generally involves the following steps:

> **Deductive theory:** a theory that is developed from a set of hypotheses that are then tested

- Specify the topic

- Specify the range of phenomena the theory seeks to address

- Identify and specify major concepts and variables

- Find out what is known about the relationships between those variables

- Reason logically from those relationships to the specific topic

- Then develop a research question and conduct an empirical study of the topic to test the hypothesis (see Chapter 4, pp. 70–71).

The first step in constructing a deductive theory is thus picking a topic and then identifying the range of phenomena to be examined (i.e. limiting the scope of the examination). After conducting a review of the literature to determine what is already known (see Chapter 4, pp. 71–72), one identifies patterns which lead the theorist to develop their theory to explain the interrelated phenomena. One can thus state a hypothesis, test it and prove its validity as a theory.

Field research, in which the researcher observes the events as they take place in the field first, is often used to develop **inductive theory**. Developing an inductive theory generally follows the following steps:

> **Inductive theory:** a theory that emerges from analysis of data

- Define broad research questions based on a social issue or topic

- Collect data

- Analyse data to look for patterns, connections and significant findings

- Develop a theory

- Compare the theory with existing literature.

The reality of theory generation, however, is that rarely does one follow purely either the inductive or deductive approach. The generation of theory often happens organically, as a scholar conducts research, revisits old theories, determines what can no longer be explained by existing theories and creates new theory. There is no singular formula for the creation of a theory.

PAUSE FOR REFLECTION

How do these types of theories appeal to you? Why is that? What benefits might inductive theory have over deductive, and vice versa?

HOW DO WE THEORIZE 'PEOPLE'?

A central goal of sociology is to understand how people behave, and then to examine why. It is not possible to predict with certainty how people will act – individuals behave in different ways, even in seemingly identical conditions or when given the same 'instructions' (Freese 2008). This is where the social sciences differ from the hard sciences (as illustrated by the Neil deGrasse Tyson quote we saw in Chapter 1). Computers are programmed to operate in a particular way and can be relied upon for consistency of action, yet this is not true of people. Human beings interpret and react to the instructions they are given, and do not just 'follow' them in the way a computer does.

Sociologists recognize two key influences on people's actions. First, people are influenced by their own internal ways of thinking that motivate them to act in order to achieve certain outcomes. Sociologists call this human agency (see p. 11), and it is the idea that we act of our own accord and even have free will in doing so. Agency refers to the ability to act upon one's interpretations and motivations, and not just to react in a mechanical way to social stimuli.

These social stimuli are the second influence on people's actions: sociologists call this the **structures** of society. These structures condition what actions might be possible (see Chapter 6). A society's structures include its laws, norms and institutions (in education, family life, health services, sport, religion, entertainment, etc).

> **Structures:** ways society is organized that constrain how an individual can act

The question is what is the key influence on how people act – is it their own ideas and initiatives or the context of their lives?

Of course, social structures like families socialize their members. For example, they use stigma to generate feelings of guilt and disgust in relation to transgressions of their values and rules. As such, many values and beliefs are 'internalized', making the relationship between agency and structure far more complex than just being inside or outside a person's mind. Nevertheless, people are not zombies. They do not simply internalize social norms in the way computers receive coded instructions; nor are social structures entirely rigid or lacking in contradiction and conflict.

A central sociological question about understanding how people act is to work out the balance between agency and structure. This does not mean it is possible to determine the precise influence of each, but rather to recognize that both agency and structure combine so that individuals are a product of their culture but are still able to resist, contest and change the norms of the society in which they live. Indeed, there has been a movement away from seeing structure and agency as oppositional or even discrete categories, as sociologists have developed theories that incorporate both components in a grander theoretical framework.

Many sociologists examine both social structures and individual agency in their work. Máirtín Mac an Ghaill (1994), for example, looked at school as an institution that structured how schoolboys behaved and the identities they took on; yet he also examined the agency they had in contesting these norms. Mac an Ghaill's work is an example of sociological research that recognizes the need to focus on both structure and agency, does so to an extent, but does not address the underlying theoretical tensions about the influence of each.

Anthony Giddens (1984) is one sociologist who has attempted to theorize how structure and agency can be considered simultaneously. Giddens places great value in the agency of individuals and recognizes that how people act often has an imperceptible influence on social structures that, over time, can change them. These structures can also change much faster if there is concerted action by many individuals collectively. The rule of law holds, for example, because people in general believe in it. If everyone, or a large majority of people, were to stop believing in the right to own property, the social structures of society would change radically.

Giddens theorized this relationship as **structuration** – the idea that structure and agency are inherently related and cannot be separated. How people act has an influence on social structures, yet people can only act in ways that are allowed in the structures in which they live.

Consider the example of being gay. A gay person living in Britain today has legal equality with heterosexuals and has practically the same social freedoms. This person can be open about their sexuality, marry their lover and raise children. Yet some people with same-sex desires will remain closeted and not disclose their sexuality. Two people within the same social structures will act differently, because of human agency.

How these individuals act will influence the social structures. For example, an important middle-range theory of sociology is contact theory (Allport 1954): that the greater contact people have with people who are different from them, the more positive their attitudes towards them will be. Thus, the more people who decide to come out, the more likely it becomes that the social context for sexual minorities will further improve, including legal changes and greater inclusion in various institutions (Weeks 2007). Thus, if more people choose to come out, within the confines of their social structures, they will affect those structures – as structuration theory argues.

Giddens' (1984) theory of structuration is complex and draws on a long history of writing in this area, and it is important to introduce it here as an example of how sociologists have attempted to move beyond the view of structure and agency as distinct and exclusive influences on people.

Structuration: structure and action are necessarily related to each other and cannot be disentangled

THREE CORE APPROACHES TO SOCIOLOGICAL THEORY

Whatever theories sociologists use, they tend to be bound up in a broader framework of how to understand the social world. There are three core approaches in sociology, and these are functionalism, conflict theories (also known as critical theories) and interactionism.

Functionalism is an approach to studying society that holds that societies operate the way they do for a reason, and that changing society is therefore a risky endeavour. Some functionalists, like Durkheim, believe that society operates in much the same way as our bodies. Here, functionalists maintain that if something exists, it must exist because it has a function in the normal operation of that body. A functionalist thinker would therefore suggest that our institutions are like organs, in that they all work together to produce the smooth running of society (like organs ensure the body survives). Accordingly, functionalists warn that even if you see a problem with one particular institution (organ), you should be careful in extracting it or modifying it, as doing so might negatively affect another institution (organ) that you did not intend to change.

> **Functionalism:** the theoretical perspective that all aspects of society serve a function necessary for the survival of that society

This approach is also known as *structural functionalism*, in which the role of the sociologist is to objectively describe the structures of a society and explain their functions. The value of the research is determined by the accuracy and quality of the description it provides.

This approach contrasts with sociological thinking that is framed as conflict or critical theories. **Conflict theories** largely stem from Marxist thinking, and generally hold that individuals are in competition with each other for financial gain or social reward, and that this results in power and wealth being disproportionately obtained and maintained by some groups over others. Conflict theories tend to be critical of society and how it is organized, and the sociologist in this context looks for social *problems* or *issues* that can be addressed.

> **Conflict theories:** theories that are critical of society and seek to contest oppressive social norms

Conflict theories also tend to view society as being held together through coercion. Understanding power in society thus becomes a central question, focusing on how power is wielded over the less powerful and the ways in which rebellions are quelled or critical voices are silenced. We discuss conflict theories in detail in Chapter 7 as they are applied to class, gender and 'race'.

The third core theoretical approach is known as *symbolic interactionism* (also referred to as interactionism). Interactionist theories focus on how people act together in groups as well as focusing on the actions of individuals. Here, the focus is on the symbols and signs that people use in communication with each other – whether this be verbal, behavioural or more implicit. That is, rather than just analysing what people say about their intentions and behaviours, symbolic interactionists look for the meanings behind actions. The signs and symbols, and their meanings, are liable to change over time, as well as being dependent on the context in which they occur (see Chapter 2, p. 36).

Interactionists hold that symbols and signs are unique to humans, and are subject to change dependent on context. Wearing gym clothes, for example, can be a purely instrumental action when at the gym as they best facilitate intensive exercise. Yet wearing gym clothes elsewhere can be a sign of that person's values and beliefs – around fitness, health and a 'body project' (see Chapter 8). Crucially, people are able to purposely change the meanings of symbols both individually and collectively. This might be a change that occurs over time, just as once-fashionable accessories become distinctly untrendy, or it can be through active subversion.

Symbolic interactionists believe that it is the combination of these ideas that means the symbols we use are the basis of how societies are interpreted and experienced.

Table 3.3: Theoretical approach and related sociologists

Theoretical approach	Core ideas	Famous sociologists
Functionalism	Societies operate as they do for a reason and social change is risky. Society acts like a body: institutions are like organs that ensure the body runs smoothly.	Emile Durkheim (Chapter 1) Talcott Parsons (Chapter 6)
Conflict Theories	People are in competition with each other for money or status. Examines social problems and issues in society.	W.E.B. Du Bois (Chapter 2) Patricia Hill Collins (Chapter 7) Gayle Rubin (Chapter 8)
Interactionism	Focuses on how people interact in groups. Examines symbols and signs people use to communicate. Less interested in macro issues.	Erving Goffman (Chapter 1) Howard Becker (Chapter 10)

How would a sociologist theorize the Roman Games?

The Ancient Romans regularly held public games that featured chariot races, sacrifices to the gods and battles between gladiators, often to the death. It is widely accepted that these events, paid for by the emperor, were used to keep the poor and the working classes entertained and, as a result, reduce the threat of rebellion.

© Duncan Walker/iStock

Yet how would sociologists interpret this?

A functionalist is likely to view the ancient Roman Games as functioning to appease an unruly Roman citizenship. They might describe these games as a unifying event, a sporting entertainment spectacle to please and thus control the masses of citizenry. They might argue that this was a positive event as it removed any need for harsher forms of control. It could thus be seen as providing help for the poor before any form of social welfare as we know it today was tenable.

A critical sociologist would probably accept the crowd-pleasing rationale for the games, but would critique them in a number of ways. They could be understood as the exploitation of the working classes – regardless of how it entertained the crowds, it helped keep a form of unfair and unequal governing elite in place. Animals were made to fight too, and they might critique this form of abuse. In addition, women were often barred from attending these events, and thus the Games can be seen as reproducing male privilege. Perhaps most significantly, the critical sociologist might highlight who the participants in the gladiatorial fights were: normally poor people convicted of minor crimes, as well as opponents of the regime, sent to these events to face near-certain death.

A symbolic interactionist would be likely to focus on the meanings and signs of the event itself. They might examine the ways in which the emperor consolidated his power through the Games, and how this was done. They might study the value of the animals in the events, and why people were sent to fight them: death by animals was a very stigmatized way to die, reserved for people convicted of particular crimes. Likewise, interactionists might be interested in how the crowd reacted to the events and the symbols and signs they used to show their emotions – the ways in which they celebrated or condemned particular behaviours.

The Frankfurt School and critical theory

While we are focusing on sociological theory in this chapter, it is important to keep in mind the influence of social theory (see textbox, below) in sociology. Not to be confused with conflict theory, so-called **critical theory** is one of the influential set of social theories that developed in the early 1900s that rejected the positivist approaches of the emerging discipline of sociology, seeking to develop a more critical account of the social world. Critical theorists used the techniques of literary and philosophical criticism in order to both challenge the way society was ordered at the time and argue for a more optimistic future. The point was not to gather arguments from empirical data, but to imagine better futures through critical argumentation.

> **Critical theory:** an influential set of theories that critique the social world from a philosophical perspective

Distinguishing sociological theory from social theory

There are great similarities between sociological theories and social theories. Sociologist Kenneth Allan (2006) provides a useful distinction. He states that sociological theory is characterized by abstract propositions about society that can be tested. It aims for objectivity and collects data according to rigorous sociological methods. He contrasts this with **social theory**, which is characterized more by social critique and commentary. It is less concerned with objectivity and does not base theories on empirical studies. Social theories are like grand theories of sociology, with less concern for empiricism and a greater interest in intellectual critique.

> **Social theory:** intellectual critiques of society that are connected with sociological theory but more located within philosophy

Critical theory became established as a movement through work at the University of Frankfurt, known as The Frankfurt School. Unlike the Chicago and Atlanta Schools of sociology, the Frankfurt School incorporated scholars from a range of disciplines, including psychoanalysis, cultural studies, philosophy and political economy. Here, scholars developed an important critique of how positivism was practised within sociology at the time (see Chapter 2). As Inglis (2012) writes, critical theorists believe that 'positivism is not neutral … By collecting superficial data that only depict the *surface* aspects of society, positivism cannot penetrate underneath the surface, in order to reveal the true *essence* of that society' (pp. 69–70). He contends:

> Critical theory must reject the ways of thinking that are more common in society. It must be utterly sceptical of *everything*. Critical theory must therefore reject people's own understanding of the world, as these are thoroughly shaped by ruling class ways of thinking. (p. 70; emphasis in original)

This perspective is fundamentally different from some of the tenets of much empirical sociology. The extension of critique beyond observable data is thus one of the core distinctions between social theory and sociological explanations of the social world. Yet many sociologists still use critical theory because it can help them think differently about issues where dominant norms are particularly entrenched, especially related to culture, oppression and marginalization (e.g. Ettorre 2007; O'Neill 2010).

Theodor Adorno (1903–1969) was one of the more sociological of the critical theorists. Along with Horkheimer, Adorno (1996) focused on the importance of entertainment, leisure and the media in the operation of society. Conceptualizing this as the **culture industry,** he argued that rather than enabling people to enjoy their free time, this industry commodifies these activities for the benefit of the powerful in society.

The culture industry provided mass-produced activities for people to consume, yet this had the (intended) effect of keeping them in a state of passivity – rather than engaging in a Marxist revolution, people stayed at home watching films and listening to music instead (see Chapter 6 on the media). Adorno distinguished these forms of entertainment from 'better' forms of art and literature that enabled people to think critically about the world around them. This argument extends Marx's contention that **commodification** tends to downgrade the quality of the thing in question. For example, viewing a painting as a product to own results in people buying art not for its inherent quality, or how it makes a person feel when looking at it, but because of the value it has in a capitalist marketplace.

Adorno's writing on culture has spurred a sociology of the media and a critical engagement with leisure activities that is important in contemporary sociology (see Chapter 6). While we have distinguished between social and sociological theory, and critical theory is clearly within the social theory classification, it has had significant influence within sociology. This is true of the sociology of personal life, which we examine in Chapter 8.

Culture industry: the notion that culture is the commodification of activities that reproduces power inequality by rendering people passive

Commodification: the process of treating something as a commodity

Paradigm: an established theory or way of thinking that acts as a framework in sociology

The plural of theory is ...

One of the more confusing things for people first encountering theory is how the word can be both singular and plural at the same time. When sociologists discuss particular theories of class or gender, we happily use the plural *theories*. Yet when talking about a subdiscipline of theory or a **paradigm** of sociological thought, sociologists tend to use the singular. So there may be a range of different theories of gender, but we also discuss 'gender theory'; Adorno, Horkheimer and Marcuse devised a range of critical theories, but we refer to them all as 'critical theory'. If you are studying the media and television, you will likely engage in 'cultural theory' and use many different theories at once. The plural of theory depends on the context: *theories* when discussing multiple theoretical ideas, and *theory* when referring to a set of related theories or a paradigmatic approach to an issue.

VOX POP Professor Maggie O'Neill

Professor of Sociology

My entrance to academia as a working-class woman was not the standard route and, when I look back at my academic journey and trajectory, what stands out is a love of theory that is not just about seeking to understand the complexity of our lived lives, relationships and the cultural structures we are born into and help reproduce, challenge and change, but above all about engaging in critical, creative work that makes a difference.

The relationship between critical theory (for me, feminist critical theory influenced by the Frankfurt School), lived experience (the importance of ethnographic and participatory research,

© Maggie O'Neill

working with people and not just for them) and praxis (purposeful knowledge) became central to my own work and biography. This is motivated by a strong impulse for us – as academics, as thinkers, as educators – to both support and do social justice.

The role of art in all this is, for me, crucial and I can still remember vividly the moment when this became clear, in one of my final-year undergraduate extended essays – on the liberating transformative potential of art. I have enjoyed working with artists ever since and really enjoy the creative, productive sparks that happen in collaborative work with artists.

I had an inspirational lecturer called Dr Conrad Lodziak who created the space and conditions for us to think critically and creatively and who introduced us to the history of ideas in sociology and psychosocial theory. As part of his course he introduced us to critical analyses of society and culture and feminist thought, the many ways that we can explore our lifeworlds as contested sites of meaning while never giving up hope for the possibility and operation of social justice, of challenging and changing sexual and social inequalities.

In many ways his course ushered in the turn to cultural studies. I am grateful for his support and encouragement as well as the role model he provided. His classes were a proving ground for the kind of academic I wanted to be and hope I became and will continue to be.

> » How does Maggie's perspective on theory connect with the key arguments in his chapter?

>> » How does Maggie's perspective on critical theory fit with its aim to improve society?

> » Have you had theory connect with you in the way Maggie describes?

>> » What theories have you most enjoyed in this chapter or in the book so far?

>> » What areas do you think might connect with you most? Why?

The poststructural critique

The roots of sociology are based in the idea that there are scientific ways of understanding society. A central tenet of sociology is that there is a *method* to sociology and that this method is systematic, testable and yields results that stand up to scrutiny (see Chapter 4). As discussed in Chapter 2, sociologists of the 1800s and 1900s developed a field of scholarly work proposing that society was bound by structures; social facts or even social laws that a society operates by. The work of Durkheim and others was characterized as **structuralism** – the notion that society ran according to a set of laws and social structures, almost as a train that is compelled to run along tracks that are laid out in advance.

Yet a paradigm of sociological theory, known as **poststructuralism**, emerged in part to contest these ideas about preordained rules and structures that greatly limit individual agency. There were important contributions to knowledge that enabled us to study language, context and social change more clearly and with greater sophistication (e.g. Foucault 1991).

Yet poststructuralist ideas have also moved far beyond this. Many are opposed to the idea that social facts exist, questioning the value of empirical evidence because they maintain that all evidence is subjective because people have to interpret it (Derrida 1976). Poststructuralists are thus sceptical about academic claims to have found empirical truths; and they question 'grand narratives' or high theory that seek to explain broad social trends. They believe that the Age of Enlightenment, and the rationality that it is widely perceived to have brought, is founded on false principles.

Like any group, poststructuralists vary in their degree of scepticism. Some just ask us to question and reflect upon the researcher's position and impact in the collection of social data, and are very clearly located within the empirical sociological tradition; others are sceptical of even the truths that scientists generate (see Davies 1999).

Poststructuralists contend that the real-world context in which scientific research is conducted means that it is subjective and deeply flawed, highlighting assumptions that it contains, including pre-existing relations of power and privilege. They might, for example, argue that science is inherently biased because it is mostly an enterprise dominated by men (e.g. Harding 1986). Others, like Michel Foucault, emphasize that science has often been misused by those in power to promote control over people. There is a history of racism within science where so-called 'scientific facts' have been used to protect racist views. For example, in 1851, a paper in *The New Orleans Medical and Surgical Journal* claimed that slaves ran away from their masters because of a fictitious disease, drapetomania. Craniometry is another notorious example, where scientists measured internal skull sizes to argue that racist laws and norms were justifiable on the grounds of inherent physical differences between 'racial types'.

Poststructuralists contend that rather than an objective reality, our perspectives of the world are created by the **discourses** we use to talk about them (Derrida 1976). Foucault (1984) most famously discussed this in relation to sexuality, where the ways in which people could talk about sexuality served to limit the possible sexualities in society. Exemplifying this, in the *Diagnostic and Statistical Manual of Mental Disorders* (*DSM*), psychiatrists have historically determined that homosexuality, transgenderism and paedophilia were mental disorders, only later to decide that

---

Structuralism: a set of theories that contend that society runs according to a set of laws and social structures

Poststructuralism: a set of theories that critique structuralist notions and also contest the core tenets of Enlightenment beliefs about science and empirical research

Discourse: an institutionalized or societally condoned way of speaking that controls the ways in which a topic can be discussed

each was not. In each of these cases, what was observed were behaviours, which individual social scientists then moralized upon to create a fact that was not, actually, true. Poststructuralism remains influential in sociology, particularly in areas such as gender and culture (e.g. Butler 2004).

Poststructuralism is prone to inaccessible writing. Consider the writing of one of the most famous poststructural authors, Judith Butler. Her work is difficult to comprehend, and the following excerpt won an award for bad writing in philosophy:

> The move from a structuralist account in which capital is understood to structure social relations in relatively homologous ways to a view of hegemony in which power relations are subject to repetition, convergence, and rearticulation brought the question of temporality into the thinking of structure, and marked a shift from a form of Althusserian theory that takes structural totalities as theoretical objects to one in which the insights into the contingent possibility of structure inaugurate a renewed conception of hegemony as bound up with the contingent sites and strategies of the rearticulation of power. (Butler 1997: 14)

BAD SOCIOLOGY Bad Writing

Sociological theory deals with complex issues. Understanding and explaining the ways the world works is intellectually demanding. The Neil Tyson deGrasse tweet we quoted in Chapter 1 really has value – sociology is not physics, it is harder than that. Unfortunately, there is a tendency to extend that argument to maintain that if it's difficult, like rocket science, we should write it up like it is rocket science; complex and inaccessible, even intimidating, to the non-expert.

Some sociologists contend that the complex language of much theory really is necessary to properly engage with important social issues – and that some level of jargon can be found in any other discipline or profession: a technical code to the theory that one has to get to grips with in order to have a serious conversation in this area. It is also true that some theoretical arguments will be harder to grasp than others – theory certainly deals with complex ideas that need careful thought.

However, while we recognize some truth to this position – for example, it is not really possible to talk about sociology without terms such as theory, method and concept – some theoretical writing is a style, a pose or even just a bad habit. Writing about theory is complex, but this means that we should work even harder for accessibility. This is an argument that C. Wright Mills (1959) also made in his book *The Sociological Imagination*, which we discussed in Chapter 1, where he critiqued the writing of high theory for its inaccessibility, focusing on the work of Talcott Parsons.

The final problem associated with some sociological writing, particularly related to high theory, is that many scholars are concerned with sounding like they belong to the 'in-crowd' (see Healy's third nuance trap, p. 52). Using dense or convoluted language is not just about trying to explain ideas as precisely as possible; it is partially, or sometimes even primarily, about demonstrating one's own intellectual worth to a particular crowd. If you can write in that style, you must understand that style. We do not believe this truism is true.

Feminist philosopher Martha Nussbaum (1999) denounces Butler for her writing. She argues it is not just the use of complex language, but an attempt to 'dazzle the reader into submission'. The problem is not just the particular words used, but how they are strung together, and how long sentences are preferred over short ones. Some of Butler's sentences are very long indeed.

This is one of the primary complaints about poststructuralism: the language in which it is often written is close to indecipherable. Whereas science is supposed to be clear, so that it can be reproduced and tested, poststructural writing often does not seek this clarity.

The flaws of this difficult writing style were highlighted in the 1990s with what has become known as *The Sokal Affair* (see Sokal 2010). Here, physics professor Alan Sokal submitted an article to a poststructural journal, *Social Text*. The journal was highly regarded in its subdiscipline, but Sokal believed that too much of this prestige was based on a 'highbrow' style of writing rather than intellectual contribution or rigour. To test his theory, he submitted an article about theories of knowledge that was, to his mind, gobbledegook. In it, Sokal argued that reality did not exist, and he called for a 'post-modern science' that would provide a 'transformative hermeneutics of quantum gravity'. Even so, the article was published in the journal – at which point Sokal announced he considered it a fake and meaningless. Whatever your perspectives on the value of social theory – we urge you to think about clarity of meaning in your writing.

GOOD SOCIOLOGY Writing Well

Poststructuralists are perhaps the most notorious culprits for inaccessible writing, but sociologists operating from any theoretical disposition stand accused, too. Indeed, sociologists are regularly critiqued for writing poorly, and the credibility and influence of sociology in the world is negatively impacted as a result. Some of this is a natural consequence of writing in an area in which one specializes. We strive for accessible writing yet sometimes are critiqued for use of jargon, or we reread a phrase and think, 'we really wrote that?' It is difficult, sometimes, to remember what it is like to be a new reader in sociology, or whatever specialism we inhabit.

Writing simply is also incredibly difficult. Writing simply is *harder* than writing in complex language. It is easier, for example, to use the term 'neoliberal capitalist economy' than it is to explain clearly and concisely the particular issues one has about the way the economy is organized.

An important concept here is *Ockham's razor*. William of Ockham was a monk in medieval England. His Latin razor, devised to evaluate competing theories, is '*Entia non sunt multiplicanda praeter necessitate*', which translates as 'more things should not be used than are necessary'. His argument is, essentially, that among competing hypotheses, it is best to choose the one that accounts for all the details in the simplest way possible. To 'account for all the details in the simplest way possible' is superb advice for writing on sociology, or any potentially technical subject. Albert Einstein's version of this is that 'Everything should be kept as simple as possible, but no simpler'.

Our contention is that the over-reliance on phrases or labels like neoliberal, epistemology, ontology, hermeneutic and others beyond their appropriate use is in contravention of Ockham's razor. In other words, to use 'neoliberal capitalist economy' as shorthand would, for Einstein, be 'simpler than possible'. Do not write the 'buzzwords' that seem to fit and make you look clever; *actually make the argument yourself*. This will include using lots of shorter words to explain your position and what you believe.

The American writer Mark Twain encapsulated the difficulties of writing simply and concisely when he said, 'I didn't have time to write a short letter, so I wrote a long one instead.' Whether it is writing essays for class, or books on sociological theory, always take the time to write the short letter, and not the long one. We realize we are making ourselves hostages to fortune in arguing this, but it is something we passionately believe. (In other words, go ahead and critique our writing!)

CONCLUSION

This chapter has explored sociological theory. What can be seen as an aloof and abstract idea is, in fact, a vital component of sociology because it is the thing that explains the social world. Without theory, we just have seemingly unrelated facts. We have distinguished sociological theory from other scientific theories through its focus on people and society, highlighting how it differs from social theory in its emphasis on empirical methods. Some readers will enjoy the abstract writing of high theory, and we encourage you in this endeavour and hope it inspires you as it did Maggie O'Neill in our Vox Pop. We focused on sociological theory, and encourage you to write as clearly and accessibly as possible – and to take the time needed to do this. Finally, even if theories are more valued if they are interesting rather than right, we encourage you to take the time to be as right as possible.

HOW WOULD...?

» How would you approach theory?
  » Do you see yourself as a functionalist, interactionist or conflict theorist?
  » Do you prefer inductive or deductive approaches? Why?
  » What about critical theory and poststructuralist approaches?
» Think about the study you considered doing in Chapter 1. How would this study connect with these theoretical approaches? Explain why you would use or discard each of them.

STRUCTURED FURTHER READING

Sears, A. (2005). *A Good Book, in Theory: A Guide to Theoretical Thinking*. Ontario: Broadview Press.
A brief and fun introduction to many of the leading social and sociological theorists. The book is refreshingly free from jargon and provides a further introductory exploration of theory as a way to think critically about society. If you are tempted by theory, but still not sure, this might further whet your appetite.

O'Byrne, D. (2011). *Introducing Sociological Theory*. London: Routledge.
This book provides an accessible and more detailed introduction to sociological theory. As well as covering topics such as functionalism, critical theory and Marxism, it will also introduce you to theoretical traditions we do not cover here. This includes exchange theory and ethnomethodology. The book has lots of real-life examples to help contextualize the complex theory in the social world.

Inglis, D. (2012). *An Invitation to Social Theory*. Cambridge: Polity.
If you have been interested by the more abstract theoretical discussions in our chapter, and want to engage more fully with *social* theory, Inglis' book is an engaging and comprehensive introduction to a range of theorists, their ideas and their influence in understanding the social world.

Scott, J. (2012). *Sociological Theory: Contemporary Debates*. Northampton, MA: Edward Elgar.
This book examines contemporary issues in sociological theory. It follows up on some key theorists we have not had space to discuss, such as Talcott Parsons and Jurgen Habermas, in an engaging and accessible text.

Visit the companion website at **www.macmillanihe.com/mccormack** for further learning and teaching resources.

Chapter 4
THE METHOD OF SOCIOLOGY

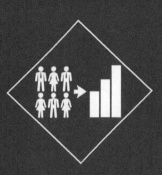

INTRODUCTION

This chapter will address the *method* of sociology. Sometimes this subject is seen as 'dry', 'difficult' or 'boring' by sociologists in training; either too mathematical or too detached from the human actions it studies. Yet, methods enable us to answer questions about society. Consider how a sociology module on sexuality might be seen as sexually 'explicit'. It *is* explicit, but only to the same extent that a module on health must explicitly be about illness, or one on crime will explicitly discuss breaking the law. You have to discuss the substance of the issue. A key substance of sociology is method. We cannot do sociology without method; otherwise, it becomes philosophy at best, opinion or conjecture at worst. Discussing method in a sociology course, then, is the same as covering sex in a sexuality lecture – fundamental to the aims of the project. In our Provocation, we question whether pornography really is bad for you.

THE METHOD OF SOCIOLOGY

A set of rules about **methods** exists to ensure that sociology is a social science. Yet while methods are an integral component of sociology, they are often taught in isolation, compartmentalized into a module within a degree programme or a separate textbook. This is problematic as it tends to marginalize the importance of methods in sociological understanding. As we discuss later in this chapter, the improper use of methods can lead to bad results and bad sociology. As such, one must always be aware of the methods that have been used and how these affect the way we should view claims made in sociological research.

> **Methods: the techniques of data collection and analysis**

This chapter is not a 'how to' manual. If you think of methods as a set of tools, this chapter will not tell you which tool fits which problem; rather, it will explain why particular tools are useful in certain situations. Just as it is inappropriate to use a sledgehammer to crack a nut, so we need to be careful in the tools we use in sociology. As such, the aim of this chapter is to ensure that you can approach the subject of methods with an understanding of the issues around them.

This means that we are not just talking about methods but also about **methodology**. It is one thing to know what a method is; it is a completely different

> **Methodology: the principles that guide how methods are used in the attempt to generate valid results**

issue to know when to use it. The reason why one method might be more appropriate than another is the realm of methodology.

Yet we are also going to talk about methods in relation to the key ways to collect data and analyse it. After all, obtaining useful, accurate and relevant data, and being able to analyse it in ways appropriate to what we are trying to find out, is the whole point of having methods.

In order to think about all these issues, we have organized the chapter into five sections: Before Choosing a Method; Research Design; Types of Method; Data Collection; and Data Analysis. First, we shall think about the issues involved in designing a research study before moving on to research design and which specific methods to use, how we gather data via these and, after that data is collected, the various methods of analysis. Of course, eventually, for more experienced researchers, all these stages will come to inform each other. For instance, you must be thinking about your analysis at the design stage of a study. Answering your research question requires that the data collected can be analysed in a way that will answer the question posed, and hence must be the right data to fit the analysis technique you believe will work best. Such interlinkage is difficult to represent here: The research process is cyclical, but a chapter in a book is not.

BEFORE CHOOSING A METHOD

In Chapter 3, we examined how theory is developed, including inductive and deductive approaches to theory generation (pp. 56–57). In that discussion, we assumed that empirical research existed that gave us the information to guide our thinking. The theory-making process in that discussion did not include the real sociological work of data collection and analysis. Now, we are going to take that step back and think about building the evidence base. Or, in other words, we will take you through the process of conducting an empirical study.

What is a research question?

If sociological methods are to be used to answer a question, we must first be clear about how to formulate that research question. Fundamentally, a question should address a problem in need of a solution. This problem may be intellectual – a gap in our understanding of the world – or it may be more practical, such as a specific social, political or economic difficulty to be solved or improved. As such, research is always driven by values in choosing what to study.

Forming a research question is a skill. Some questions have no meaning. To ask 'what is it like to be a stone?' falsely implies that stones have some capacity to know what being a stone is like. Other questions cannot be answered because there is no way we can get to the **evidence**. We will probably never know what colour dinosaurs were, or with what accent the Ancient Egyptians spoke.

The questions we are interested in are those that we can answer if we had the evidence, and where that evidence is possible to collect. A research question must then, in principle, be a question that can be answered. Rhetorical questions that

Evidence: the data required to answer a particular research question

stimulate the imagination but cannot realistically be answered can have value, but they do not count as research questions. So, asking about the accents of Ancient Egyptians might spark our thinking on class, geography and the evolution of language – but it would still fail as a research question.

We should also let the question itself push us forward in searching for possible sources of evidence. We should not fall back on questions that existing, readily available evidence can answer. There would be less need for method if we did so, as the evidence would already be available to us; instead, methods are the tools that enable us to answer new questions that demand new data or evidence.

Questions can also vary in levels of focus. For example, 'What is going on in everyday classroom interactions?' is very open-ended. 'Why do some children do better at school than others?' is more focused. 'Does the sex of the teacher impact on the relative performance of male and female pupils?' is even more specific.

The level of focus that your research question needs will depend on what 'gaps' you encounter in the body of past relevant research. The greater knowledge you have of an issue already, the more precise your question has to be. There is little point, for example, asking broadly whether class impacts on educational performance when there is a raft of evidence showing that it does (e.g. Reay 2017). To usefully research this area, you will need to find a focus not covered in as much detail – whether that be about the topic itself (e.g. class and education) or a particular demographic (maybe the evidence is not as strong or complete for a particular group of people). As such, formulating a research question will depend upon carrying out a review of past research.

Indeed, before formulating a question, the researcher should look to see what previous researchers have done *and how they have done it*. Doing a literature review is as much about doing a methods review as it is about simply recording what other people concluded from their research. We can see what earlier researchers have found out from reading their books and articles, but while doing so we should also be asking *how* these researchers came to their conclusions. When was the research carried out, by whom, where, using what collection techniques and who with (what was the sample?)? These 'when, who, where, what and how' type of questions should then structure a comparison between the different studies that have already been carried out (see 'Populations and samples' on p. 90).

Nicola Green (2008: 47–49) suggests six dimensions to a 'good' research question, as shown in Table 4.1. Thinking about these dimensions can help evaluate the quality of a research question.

Searching the literature, doing a literature review

As we have seen, deciding what to research will require an examination of prior research. A literature search involves systematically searching archives – once on paper and in libraries, but now usually online using digital archives and databases. Here, you use keywords to find books and articles on the topic of interest. Such keyword searching will usually involve cross-referencing – using more than one keyword and selecting only those books and articles that feature all, or the most

Table 4.1: Six dimensions of a 'good' research question

Interesting	To the researcher
Relevant	To the wider research community or to other interest groups
Feasible	Within the constraints the researcher finds themselves under
Ethical	In relation to the choice of topic, the research to be conducted and in the way results are disseminated
Concise	Being the most efficient way of addressing the issue at hand
Answerable	In actually being able to produce a true answer

Source: authors' own, based on text of Green (2008)

significant, of these key terms. Whatever library, archive or database you use will have its own systems for such searching, so you will have to learn how to use them. It is tempting to just rely on Google Scholar, but using a range of databases will yield the richest results.

A literature search requires that you have some initial idea of what to look for, but as you progress, you may become aware of new terms that will help you to refine your search for further literature. This is when a literature search starts to become a literature review. A literature review involves *reading* the works that the search identified, and identifying their key characteristics. This 'reviewing' will enable an understanding of what has gone before, and allows a researcher to identify what might be useful to do in the future.

A simple guide to doing a literature review is to ask six basic questions of any piece of research you find: what, when, where, how, whom and why? *What* did the researchers research, *when* did they do it, *where* did they do it, *how* was the data

Deduction and induction

Just as theory development can be deductive or inductive (Chapter 3), so too are the styles of questions you can adopt. If your question can be reformulated into a prediction to be tested (such as 'boys do better with a male teacher'), this allows for a theory-testing (*deductive*) research design. Here, the researcher sets out a theory in advance, and develops a **hypothesis**, with data collected in such a way as to 'test' whether the hypothesis is valid or not.

If you are not starting with a statement that is to be (dis)proved, or if you do not feel such 'closure' is possible or useful, you will want a more exploratory (*inductive*) design. Here, you will collect lots of data and build a theory from it. *Grounded theory* (Glaser & Strauss 1967) involves constantly analysing your data as you collect it, developing an initial theory early on and continually 'testing' and revising that theory against new data as you collect it. This continues until the researcher arrives at what they consider to be a robust theory of the phenomenon. See Chapter 3 for our discussion of inductive theory generation.

Hypothesis: a specific statement or prediction that can be tested empirically

collected, from *whom* was the data collected and *why* was the data collected? By comparing different pieces of research on these questions, it is possible to identify where researchers agree (across exact question, time, place, sample, method and purpose), and where there are differences. It is in the gaps and differences highlighted in such a review of the literature that a new research question emerges.

A key question to ask in a literature review is 'Where did everyone else go wrong?' Well, perhaps they didn't. If all prior studies, in all the places and times, using all sorts of different methods and samples, came to the same conclusion, then it is unlikely that you will find something different. Still, if all those studies were carried out a long time ago, or in very different locations from yours, you may still want to see if what everyone else found applies where you are now.

However, if different researchers, using different designs, sampling, collection and analysis methods, in different places and at different times, generated different results from each other, you have reason to ask WHY? These differences, once you have studied them, will help clarify possible reasons for such diversity, and hence focus your own research question. Having set out with a vague research question, a study of prior literature should allow you to get a little more focused. Looking at what has been studied already, and how, should help to answer in more detail: 'What needs to be studied and how can you study it?'

Methods and what it means to be human

Social scientists often seek to understand the internal beliefs of actors, and not just the external conditions within which people act. In Chapter 3, we discussed one of the key divides in sociology: whether an individual's agency or the power of social structures has the greater influence over social problems and the dynamics of society. Another way of framing this discussion is to think about whether we should study people's beliefs or the context in which they live (known as their conditions). And just as we found with structure and agency, beliefs and conditions are not two discrete categories. People are influenced by their surroundings, but the individual is not a passive, mechanical product of circumstances; people's actions also contribute to creating those surroundings. Actions are also shaped by beliefs. People in very similar conditions can hold different beliefs and act in different ways. The study of this interplay is what social research seeks to achieve.

In this chapter, we move from a theoretical discussion around structure and agency to a methodological discussion of how structure and agency, and beliefs and conditions, affect how we can study people. In their approach to this key question, sociologists tend to be divided into two camps.

One school of sociology says, 'Look, the one thing we, the researchers, know that we have in common with those we study is our ability to form understandings of what it means to have beliefs and values – to make meaning of events in our lives. Let's go from there.' That is, as humans, we have the unique ability to think; to have an inner life of the mind. As researchers, we can use that ability to try to comprehend the inner lives of others. This approach is known as **Verstehen**, translated as 'understanding' or 'interpretation' (Weber 1922). In terms of the previous chapter's theoretical debate, it is the same approach as deciding to focus on agency.

Verstehen: an approach that tries to comprehend the meanings and motivations of human action

The Verstehen approach uses a focus on meaning in two ways. First, the focus of research is on meaning – the beliefs and meaningful actions of others. Second, meaning-making is the way of achieving that focus – reconstructing other peoples' meanings through the researcher's interpretations of them.

A second school of sociology, more in line with 'traditional' scientific methods, says 'Well – that sounds nice, but while we *might* be able to interpret what drives the actions of others, it is better to record what people actually do and the conditions in which they do it, and see if there are externally observable patterns that can then be used to formulate theories about cause and effect.' In other words, we cannot be sure of the intention behind an act, so let's focus on the act instead. The patterns of such observable actions – recurrent trends, associations and sequences – are what Durkheim (1895) called social facts (see p. 31). This is more like studying structures, although structures are not of themselves observable actions, so there is a real difference between observing conditions and the analysis of structures.

One approach looks for meanings as drivers of action, while the other looks for patterns of association that predict effects. Those who look for meanings usually employ methods that highlight how language constructs and structures peoples' experiences, and how meaning is composed through language and social interaction. Those who look for external causes generally favour methods that are sensitive to how patterns can be measured, and this usually requires the collection of numerical data to see how often some things happen in relation to other things. Disputes rage over how far these two approaches overlap or diverge, but broadly speaking, this can be described as a divide between qualitative research (focused on meanings) and quantitative research (focused on numerical relationships).

Most sociologists are more comfortable with and specialize in one approach or the other, and, to varying degrees, they can become attached to that way of thinking. However, given that qualitative and quantitative methods have different strengths in different contexts, the choice of which to use should depend on the problem you are addressing and your research question.

Causality and correlation

We routinely invoke the idea of causation – that one thing *causes* another. C. Wright Mills (1940) describes what he calls 'vocabularies of motive', the way people learn to invoke causes that other people will accept as 'excuses'. 'I was too drunk to finish my essay' does not tend to work as a reason for requesting a deadline extension, but if I was drowning my sorrows because my goldfish died, that just might.

The excuses we find socially acceptable change over time. Sociologists are not directly in the business of judging excuses, but the idea that an outcome was caused by prior events or circumstances, rather than by a 'free' choice, implies that we cannot simply attribute the action to the person concerned. As such, studying causes, and evaluating the claims behind them, has implications for many political, social and legal questions.

When two things routinely go together, we might think their coincidence is not a random accident. Perhaps one is making the other happen (more education improves employment prospects); perhaps both things are the product of a hidden cause (maybe instead, high family income causes better educational results and increased employment prospects). To say that two things tend to go together is only

BAD SOCIOLOGY Causation, Everywhere

There is a real human tendency to see causality in things that are around us. Indeed, there is a famous Latin phrase that captures the logical fallacy – the flawed thinking – of when people attribute causality to something without evidence: *post hoc ergo propter hoc*. Translated as 'after it therefore because of it', it highlights the desire we have to attribute causal relationships simply because one happened after the other. It is imperative that sociologists do not fall into this trap. See Provocation 4 for an example of how a correlation can be taken for causation, and how thinking sociologically can help us examine the validity of this cause–effect paradigm.

to observe a correlation, a pattern of *association*. A correlation can be positive (as one thing increases, so does the other) or negative (as one increases, the other falls), but this pattern is just a description of events. It does not prove a causal relationship exists. To claim a causal link requires not just that a pattern exists, but that the supposed cause preceded the supposed effect; and that an explanation can be given for what is going on (sometimes called the mechanism at work).

In order to examine for causality, experimental research tries to obtain *controlled conditions*. Controlled conditions and a clear sequence of before and after allows an experimenter to be confident that a change in outcome was the result of the change in input they introduced. This is best exemplified by the science laboratory, where everything can be controlled, from the temperature of the room to the duration of the experiment, to a matter of milliseconds.

However, experimental conditions may not reflect real-world situations and the complexity of social life cannot be reproduced in a laboratory. This has led sociologists to adopt alternative non-experimental methods, such as surveys, interviews and ethnographic observations (see pp. 81–84). These methods seek to address the problems of the experimental method, but each has its own limits in terms of **generalizability** (can what is found in the study group tell us about the whole population) and **validity** (does the data truly show what is going on). The term 'external validity' is sometimes used to mean generalizability, and how we have used validity is called 'internal validity'.

Generalizability: the extent to which the findings from a sample can be said to be true of the population that the sample is assumed to represent

Validity: validity refers to how far data collected captures the true nature of the things being measured

PROVOCATION 4: Watching pornography is probably good for you

It is often argued that exposure to sexually explicit content has a harmful effect on viewers. Indeed, radical feminist writing in the 1970s and 1980s developed a critique of pornography that claimed social problems, such as rape and gender inequality, were perpetuated through forms of pornography that were equivalent to violence against women (e.g. Dworkin 1979). A substantial body of research has since focused on potential negative effects of pornography. So overwhelming is this focus on the harms of porn in research that McCormack and Wignall (2017) describe it as a 'negative effects paradigm'.

There is a significant amount of research on pornography that argues it has causal effects, and that these effects are bad both for the person viewing it and society as a whole. For individuals, the theory is that people act out the 'scripts' they see in pornography and that, because these scripts are damaging in some way, pornography has negative effects (Wright 2013). Hence, if porn has become more violent, sex between consenting adults will become more violent. Or, because porn objectifies women, women will be more objectified in society (the objectification of men in porn is seen as less important). It is also argued that watching porn that depicts rape will lead to increased acceptance of rape myths and increase violent sexual fantasies (e.g. McGlynn & Rackley 2007).

But is this an issue of causality or correlation? What do you think?

Let us assume for now that people who watched porn were found to show increased sexual objectification of others compared to those who do not watch it, and that they also repeated rape myths to a greater extent. Is it the case that porn *caused* this difference, or is it merely a correlation? Perhaps, instead, people who sexually objectify others are more likely to watch porn because it is a medium that depicts sexual objectification. The prior attitudes and desires may have caused the viewing pattern, rather than the viewing causing the attitudes and desires.

The crux of the argument that porn *causes* negative effects necessarily rests on experimental studies that show increased negative attitudes or behaviours after viewing pornography – in particular, the finding that viewing pornography containing violence leads some people to engage in violent behaviours in their lives. Unfortunately, there are systematic methodological flaws in the experimental studies on porn consumption (McCormack & Wignall 2017).

These experimental studies necessarily occur in laboratories to enable controlled conditions, yet the settings are nothing like how people consume pornography in their own lives (McKee 2007). In the experimental studies, participants do not get to choose the pornography they watch; they have to watch it for a designated amount of time (often 30-plus minutes); and they are not allowed to masturbate. These studies thus lack ecological validity; they do not reflect 'real-life' porn consumption. As such, they do not speak to porn consumption more generally. Negative effects from laboratory studies likely reflect the *context* of the consumption and not the *content* of the pornography.

The only time research has shown that watching porn has damaging effects is for a small subset of the population who have very problematic relationships with sexual behaviour already (Malamuth 1984). However, this involves a very specific group of men with a particular set of circumstances (the findings are not generalizable).

It is also important to consider the theoretical issues related to this. Those espousing the causal argument have tended to apply a simplified form of sexual script theory. Sexual script theory has been a valuable tool for understanding how people experience sex (Simon & Gagnon 1986). The core idea is that people do not experience bodily (sexual) sensations without connecting these to broader social meanings of sex and sexuality in the culture and society in which they live. People adopt a script which helps them process their physical and emotional feelings related to sex. This is particularly important given how sex is imbued with great meaning in society (see Chapter 8). Sexual script theory is quite sophisticated, and sexual scripts are not passively learned and recited, like an actor learns a movie script, but they are *actively* interpreted by individuals in complex ways involving agency (Frith & Kitzinger 2001). People change and even challenge sexual scripts through their own experiences of sex.

Yet scripting theory in the negative effects paradigm of porn research assumes a simple causal relationship between the scripts in porn and the person watching it (Wiederman 2015). The consumer is assumed to accept and adopt the scripts in the porn they watch, uncritically. As such, the negative effects paradigm does not explain pornography consumption satisfactorily, and further research is needed to develop a more accurate understanding of how people consume pornography.

Given all this, there is simply not the evidence to prove a *causal* relationship between watching pornography and negative effects in general.

We have shown how it is not fair to say watching porn causes harm (the dominant cultural narrative) – but can we say it might actually be good for you? A growing body of research is starting to explore this possibility.

Australian media scholar Alan McKee has called for pornography to be conceived as a form of entertainment. He argues this would establish a different research agenda than one which is focused on potential negative effects. Clarissa Smith, a Professor of Sexual Cultures, and colleagues have shown that young people consume porn for a variety of reasons, including: as a leisure activity in its own right; as an erotic experience; out of boredom; and to explore sexual identity (Smith et al. 2015).

In a study on how non-heterosexual young men consumed porn, McCormack and Wignall (2017) found no support for ideas of harm or negative effects. Instead, there were a number of potential benefits:

1. Some participants appeared to delay their first sexual experience because they could explore safely through watching porn.
2. Several participants stated that pornography helped them understand their sexual identity.
3. Participants spoke about the *enjoyment* and sexual satisfaction they got from watching porn. It made them feel good, gave them a good orgasm and was, for most, a pleasurable leisure experience.

Research into the positive effects of pornography is not developed enough to prove that watching porn has positive effects. Yet the harms of watching porn appear to be restricted to a small subgroup of men. It might be the case that porn does not have very much effect at all, other than momentary pleasures. If this is true, it still stands in sharp contrast with the dominant attitudes in society about porn and the harsh laws that criminalize a raft of pornographic films (Attwood & Smith 2010).

Perhaps it's time society shifted its view on porn.

Provoked? Read further:

Rubin, G. (1993). Misguided, dangerous, and wrong: An analysis of antipornography politics. In Assiter, A. & Carol, A. (eds.), *Bad Girls and Dirty Pictures*. Boulder: Pluto Press, 18–40.

Comella, L. & Tarrant, S. (eds.) (2015). *New Views on Pornography*. Oxford: Praeger.

McKee, A. (2010). Does pornography harm young people? *Australian Journal of Communication*, 37, 17–36.

RESEARCH DESIGN

As the tools of the sociologist's trade, methods do not just enable research but also guide and restrict what research is possible. A research question directs the researcher towards constructing a research design, but issues of data collection and data analysis may also influence your formulation of the research question.

The first issue to decide is whether to test a theory or develop a new one. If the intention is to develop a hypothesis that corroborates or challenges existing theory, this is a deductive approach. It will likely use quantitative methods. While one could interview people to do this, it would be an inefficient, time-consuming process compared to sending out a survey or **questionnaire**.

However, if the intention is to develop a new theory about a social issue, adopting an inductive approach, where the theory development comes from data analysis, then qualitative research is better suited to the rich data needed. Table 4.2 gives some suggestions as to what method best suits different types of research question.

Questionnaire: a written set of questions

Longitudinal research: research where change over time is the primary focus of attention

Cross-sectional research: research design that collects data at one point in time

Comparative methods: research focused on at least two locations to identify similarities and differences between them

Case study methods: in-depth investigation into individual cases rather than comparing variables from multiple cases

Table 4.2: Research questions and appropriate methods

Research question focus	Example	Appropriate method
How one or more variables impact upon an outcome variable	How does gender impact upon a particular educational qualification?	Quantitative questionnaire/survey
Why people behave in a particular manner	What are the motivations for the photos one posts to Instagram?	Qualitative interview
What the dynamics of a particular context are	Why does bullying occur in school cultures?	Ethnography
Examining why a particular event occurred	What social issues were relevant to the emergence of the Black Lives Matter protests?	Archival research

A second dimension of research design relates to the focus of study. Are you looking at change over time (**longitudinal research**) or differences within a group at one point in time (**cross-sectional research**); differences between locations (**comparative methods**), where comparisons can be made between large cross-sectional data sets or between in-depth cases, or in-depth exploration of a particular place and time (**case study methods**). If your research question best fits one or other of the above types, your design and method should follow accordingly. However, in large measure these designs still employ the methods outlined below, just in a variety of different manifestations. Longitudinal research might compare quantitative causes and effects (parental education and a child's achievement) and use survey data collection methods, as it is usually interested in causal relationships between prior states and outcomes. Similarly, a comparative project looking at educational results in different countries might also use surveys, but the focus is on correlations, even though causes can sometimes be tentatively suggested. Alternatively, biographical interviews might be used to explore changing experiences of ageing over time, or for measuring attitudes to marriage in different countries. In-depth case study research might draw on interviews, observations, archives and/or questionnaire data (even though the latter is less common), and might even have comparative or longitudinal elements – at the level of individual lives or whole institutions (see David 2007).

A research question addresses what you seek to study. Research design engages the question of what sort of approach would be best suited to answer the research question:

- What balance should be struck between qualitative and quantitative data, induction and deduction?

- Is the question best answered by looking at patterns over time, in many places, in one place but through many cases, or by studying just one or a very small number of particular cases?

Once the question of research design is settled, the actual detail of what methods to use must be addressed.

TYPES OF METHOD

Now that we have touched upon many of the issues related to method within sociology, it is important to discuss what these methods are and some of the issues related to each of them. We start by discussing *observation*, in the traditional sense of observations in the laboratory. We then examine ways in which sociologists can observe people in their everyday lives. Sociological methods extend beyond observation, however, and we discuss the power of asking questions through interview and survey (questionnaire) methods. These are all ways of collecting *primary data* – directly from participants themselves. Next, we examine the possibilities of using archival data and secondary data. We then look at how methods have evolved, including the use of digital and mixed methods.

Observation by experiment

If sociology followed the hard sciences, sociologists would undertake experiments all the time, fixing the conditions in which people act.

Any experimental design requires that the researcher first identify what they believe to be the cause and what effect they want to test. However, given that all sorts of things are happening all the time to all sorts of people, it is hard to pin down patterns unless the researcher takes some control over the situation. As such, in experimental research, it is essential to create controlled conditions – where there is no 'outside' interference with the things we want to study.

The experimental laboratory is designed to give the researcher maximum control over all the conditions in the participants' environment for the duration of the research. **Sampling** (discussed in more detail in the 'Sampling theory, myths and reality' section) is a component of this, as it enables the researcher to avoid bias and distortions that might arise from simply measuring unrepresentative and divergent groups.

The results of a well-controlled experiment will allow the researcher to be confident that any difference in outcomes between the groups can only be due to the differences the researcher introduced, and not ones that already existed in the

Sampling: the process of selecting units within a population

groups being studied, or other conditions in which they were studied. Experiments are therefore useful for showing causes, not just correlations.

However, problems with 'the lab' method lie in the fact that people do not behave normally when they know they are being studied. It is also very difficult to recreate complex social situations in laboratories, so the creation of controlled conditions very often relies on simplifications that do not reflect real life.

This issue was originally labelled the Hawthorne effect. It referred to research undertaken at Hawthorne Works in Illinois, where a study showed that focusing on workers' needs would lead to improved productivity (Mayo 1949). The study was critiqued, however, and it was argued that the real reason for improved productivity was that the workers were enthused by being the focus of empirical research (Landsberger 1958).

One solution to both the problem of distortion and that of simplification is not to try and recreate laboratory conditions at all, but rather go out looking for *naturalistic experimental* conditions. If two locations are in all respects the same, except for the one variable you are interested in studying, you can use those two locations as a pseudo-laboratory to see if the presence and absence of that thing (i.e. the variable of interest) makes a difference. For example, the introduction of a new school examination in one location would allow comparison with results in other (comparable) locations where the new exams have not been introduced.

The major criticism of the experimental method is that the experimental environment itself has too much of an effect on the participants over and above any actual effect of the independent variable being tested. As such, most sociological research is non-experimental. Before moving on to discuss non-experimental research, it is worth noting that while experiments are often criticized because of the bias they introduce by their impact upon participants, 'researcher effects' can bias non-experimental research as well. We discuss some of the ethical issues around the role of the researcher in Chapter 5.

Observing people in their own worlds

Most observational research in sociology is carried out in naturalistic settings, looking at people going about their everyday lives. Such **naturalistic** observation has the advantage of being less complex to set up than a laboratory experiment. Naturalistic observation also allows the researcher to experience 'real life' in all its complexity, while having less biasing effect on those they observe than occurs in experimental conditions. Nonetheless, exposure to the complexity of 'real life' has its drawbacks as the researcher cannot be fully aware of all the factors that are impacting on those they study, and cannot control, prevent or even fully know these factors when trying to determine what is influencing what.

Naturalistic observation may be purely detached or participant-based. A detached observer may simply observe, and actively avoid interaction with those they observe so as not to 'disturb' their normal routines. If they were interested in how children interact in classroom settings, a researcher may sit at the back, or record interactions, whether by audio or visual recorder, without being directly present. However, passive observation may be insufficient for gaining an understanding of what is really going on when people do the things they can be seen doing (see Thorne 1993).

Naturalistic: a form of observation that observes people in their 'natural' settings rather than in a lab or interview conditions

Participant observation is a technique where the researcher gets involved in the routines of those they study, in order firstly to observe their activities more closely, but also to combine observation with practical experience (and dialogue). An anthropologist going to live as part of a hunter-gatherer village, or a sociologist who gets a job in a call centre to study working conditions are both carrying out participant observation.

Participant observation is a name that sociologists coined to refer to what anthropologists call *ethnography* (a term sociologists now also regularly use) – the practice of living within the community you want to study. Sociological research on friendship has frequently used ethnography as a way to understand the social dynamics of this relationship – see Chapter 8 for a detailed discussion. However, there is a huge variation in degrees of involvement, from engaging in the community for a sustained period of time to full immersion in the life of those being studied. Traditionally, ethnographers observed but did not participate; but various modes of participation have now become the standard.

Much controversy exists as to just how far it is possible to know another culture even by living within it. For sociologists, the use of participant observation raises similar questions, but in addition there is the fact that many of the groups, communities and subcultures that they study are linked to the researcher's existing life. Some forms of participant observation involve members of a particular community studying other members of their own community, such as teachers researching teaching. These issues are discussed in Chapter 5, particularly in relation to the research of Laud Humphreys and his much-debated book *Tearoom Trade*, and Alice Goffman's more recent book *On the Run*.

This may make it easier for the researcher to get involved and be accepted, but it also raises issues of *bias* as the researcher may come to share unconscious attitudes or taken-for-granted behaviours with those they study, and so not perceive these as 'interesting' and in need of investigation. The openness of ethnographic observation may also create information overload, and the researcher needs to be aware of how they make their choices about what to follow up and what to set aside.

The *ethics* of sociological research is a key issue (see Chapter 5). Experiments are unethical if they inflict harm through manipulation of participants, and also if participants are not being told what is being done to them. Naturalistic observation avoids the ethical problems of manipulation as the researcher does not tend to manipulate those they observe.

However, naturalistic observation creates different ethical problems around consent and deception. Here, the sociologist might be observing people who do not know data is being collected from them. Gaining access to people's 'real' lives may enhance the quality of the data, but it also increases the risk of exposing the secrets of those being observed. There is also concern that sociologists can be voyeuristic tourists – dropping in to glean data about sensitive topics, affecting the lives of their participants and then leaving, never to be seen again as they write up their research and publish it in academic journals.

Naturalistic observers may choose to tell those they observe exactly what they are up to. Not to do so is called *covert observation*. This has been justified by some as it allows researchers to find the truth about groups who might hide their true activities

> Participant observation: where the researcher participates in the activity along with participants and observes them simultaneously

if they knew they were being watched. Covert observation is ethically controversial, and many argue it is simply unacceptable (see Chapter 5). Some maintain it leads to invalid results anyway as the researcher cannot verify their interpretations of what they see. If the researcher is covert, they may find it hard to ask the people they are studying to clarify any issues that arise, so covert research may limit the scope to actually ask people what they are doing and why. Of course, if you are researching covert activities (deviant activities that many others disapprove of and which might also be illegal), participants might respond dishonestly if asked directly what they are doing. If this is the case, a researcher might decide they themselves need to be covert as well, but this scenario raises so many ethical concerns that such research might not be a good idea for a trainee student (again, see Chapter 5). The researcher must also protect themselves from harm, both in where they go and who they spend time with.

Asking questions

The advantage of observation-based research is that you can record people's actual activity, which may be the very thing you are interested in. What they think and say may be deceptive, not just to you, but to themselves (people lie to others and themselves about many things). However, many things are not easily observed (such as how people voted), cannot be observed (past actions) or can best be identified by asking (attitudes and beliefs). For all of these reasons, it may be better to ask people about such things, rather than observing them.

Asking questions is a unique research method in the social sciences as it is only human beings who can answer in words. The capacity of human beings to use language means their actions are meaning-based: people act on intentions that are shaped by the meanings they hold and are geared towards achieving future outcomes the individual can conceptualize. People have some capacity to recall past actions, and they have the ability to communicate these things to others – including researchers. People spend a lot of time thinking about the past, the present and the future, and this makes them very valuable sources of data.

Asking questions can take different forms, and the two most important are **interviews** and **questionnaires**.

Interviews: a form of data collection where the participant is asked a set of questions by the researcher

- Interview: An interviewer asks the interviewee a set of questions, giving the interviewee time to answer each question before moving on to the next one. This is most typically carried out face-to-face and with the questions asked and answered verbally. Depending on the format, follow-up questions may be asked and the interviewee may have quite a lot of control over the interview. Answers are recorded either through recording device or note-taking.

Questionnaire: a written set of questions

- Questionnaire: A questionnaire is a written set of questions. The respondent is asked to write down their answers (these are now most often in a digital form) and return the questionnaire to the researcher.

While this is the simple and fundamental difference between interviews and questionnaires, many subtleties exist. Interviews are commonly associated with questions that are more qualitative, while questionnaires are usually associated with more quantitative data collection. Speaking in person and filling out a paper form respectively lend themselves to these different forms of data collecting. However, this does not have to be the case, and the forms of both questions and answers vary greatly within and between interviews and questionnaires. The term 'survey' is strongly associated with the conduct of questionnaires. A survey is the systematic collection of the same data from a specified sample or census. This is most often collected in the form of questionnaires. Both the Chicago and Atlanta Schools of Sociology, discussed in Chapter 2, drew significantly on interviews as a way to collect data. These groups were pioneers of the interview method, and qualitative research became firmly recognized as a legitimate method within sociology as a result.

Interviews cost more to set up, and they take more time for the interviewer (who may have to travel to the interviewees). Sending out questionnaires is easier. However, questionnaire response rates are often very low, leading to potential sample bias (see our later discussion of sampling) as the people who actually return the questionnaires may be unrepresentative, usually being the most 'opinionated' individuals. Telephone interviews can help overcome travel, cost and sampling bias issues, and online options further develop this potential (David & Millward 2014).

Not all interviews and questionnaires are the same. Interviews range from 'structured' to 'open' formats. Structure here refers to the wording and sequence of questions in an interview schedule. A fully structured interview is one where the wording and sequence of questions remains fixed so all interviewees are asked the same questions in the same order. This makes responses more comparable, but limits the scope to explore in detail particular things that each interviewee says. A fully structured interview is very similar to a questionnaire, as the sequence and wording of questions on a page cannot be altered once given to the respondent.

A semi-structured interview is one where the interviewer retains some level of flexibility in how they ask and sequence the questions. Depending on the interview, the sociologist may want to explore some issues in more depth, link questions to previous answers in a distinctive way for particular interviewees, and may even decide that some questions can be merged together or even deleted if they are clearly not relevant. The sociologist is also free to follow the thread of the interviewees' answers, reordering the sequence of questions to follow up interesting points. These techniques can be particularly useful in inductive research where the sociologist is interested in a particular issue, but wants to be guided by the person they are interviewing. This form of interviewing requires preparation and experience to do well, and is far more complex than simply 'asking questions'.

A fully unstructured interview might have no prior set of questions, and is more like a conversation that an ethnographer might strike up in their fieldwork – when the opportunity arises or when there is a question they want to explore with someone at that moment.

In addition to structure in the sequence and wording of questions, there is also an issue with openness or closure in the answers to be given. A fully closed question is one where the answer is prescribed within given options (Yes/No; on a scale of 1–5; one of a given set of 'multiple choice' options, etc). Closed questions enable the collection of quantitative data because responses are either already numerical, or they can be easily converted into numerical variable values. Open-ended questions allow the respondent to answer 'in their own words' and as such offer more scope for qualitative data collection. There is a wide spectrum between fully closed questions and fully open-ended ones.

Both the Chicago and Atlanta Schools of Sociology (see Chapter 2) drew significantly on interviews as a way to collect data, and qualitative research became firmly recognized as a legitimate method within sociology as a result of their pioneering work.

 Visit the companion website at www.macmillanihe.com/mccormack for a discussion of additional practical issues that arise when the subjects of study are children.

Individual or focus groups

The classic interview has one interviewee and one interviewer, but focus groups involve more than one interviewee to create a more dynamic dialogue. They are more flexible than questionnaires because the researcher maintains agency to add and change questions during data collection. Focus groups – usually of between 6 and 12 participants – seek to bring together experts (in what is called a 'Delphi Group'), members of a particular category of people (where different focus groups would be used to study other types to allow comparisons) or members of different categories (to study their interactions in generating responses). Putting similar people together may allow patterns to emerge through the group's dialogue with itself. Putting diverse people in the same group can provoke reactions and hence insights, but might also inhibit interviewees saying what they might say among those they think are 'like-minded'.

In focus groups, the interviewer becomes a facilitator for the group to talk among themselves, not just responding to the interviewer's questions one by one. Jenny Kitzinger (1994) notes that interviewing a group does not constitute a focus group if the research just collects an answer to each question from each person; a focus group needs to generate dialogue within the group.

 VOX POP Dr Elham Amini

Researching the experiences of menopausal Iranian women

My interest in the sexuality of menopausal women started with my background as a midwife. My professional work saw me spending time with many different women, from different age groups and social backgrounds. I frequently heard about the most hidden and private parts of their lives.

Most of the women who were more than 35 years old thought of the menopause as 'dysfunction' or 'disease'. They also thought it was inevitable and a biological consequence of the ageing process; yet they felt guilty that they could not be a 'good wife' and 'satisfy their husbands'.

© Elham Amini

They also carried within themselves a fear of losing their husbands due to not being able to 'fulfil' their 'marital duties'. My feelings as their midwife were both of concern for the women and of frustration of how the menopause was understood.

When I interviewed menopausal women in Iran, it was no surprise that these interviews were full of emotional feelings. My participants cried, sobbed, shook with emotion and raised their voices. Several of the women said I was the first person they had ever talked to in depth about issues of sexuality.

Their feeling of exposure was very strong, which always brought a lump to my throat. At these times, I showed my empathy by taking their hands, giving them a tissue or glass of water, and tried hard not to cry in front of them. I thought the participants would feel burdened by my crying, and I did not want to interrupt their stories. I only cried when I returned home.

After returning to England, I transcribed the interviews into words so I could analyse them. Listening to these stories for a second time was emotionally difficult again. While this was taxing for me, it was a chance for me to listen to women's lived experiences and move understanding of the menopause, sexuality and gender from the abstract to one based in Iranian women's realities.

» How does Elham's story influence your opinion of qualitative research?

» Do you think her experiences of emotionality strengthen or hinder the validity of her research? What are the benefits and disadvantages of this emotional engagement?

» You will read more about the influence of social structures that constrain women's lives in Chapter 7.

Using archival data and/or secondary data

Some of the expense and ethical troubles associated with collecting your own data can be reduced if the data you need to answer your research question has already been collected by someone else. Sometimes it is not possible to collect new primary data. Past events cannot be repeated, but records may exist documenting them. Observations from the past might have been captured on film or in photographs.

Archives are therefore a very useful source of data. Archives come in many forms – as primary or secondary source archives and as public or private ones. Many archives store materials that are generated in the course of their keepers' work and/or life, not for the particular purposes of research. Newspaper groups archive their newspapers. Schools archive their pupils' performance reports. Individuals keep diaries and photo albums to record their lives and, of course, there is lots of information about our lives on social media. All of this material can be of use to a sociologist.

Historical records have formed the basis for much archival research, where it is not possible to research historical events directly. Just as there is discussion regarding the degree to which interviews and questionnaires can get to the truth of people's actual behaviour, so it is that archives must be 'read' with critical attention to the distinction between what they say and what they claim to be talking about.

What people wore in old photographs, their posture and group composition tell us a lot about what those people wanted to say in these images, but that is not the whole truth. Old photographs can provide glimpses of how people wanted to be seen and to see themselves, but perhaps less about what they actually looked like, and less still about what they were really like as people.

Consider the image we have of Victorians in England. The perception is of dour, serious people. There are few photos of people laughing from this time. Many might think this is a result of living in what is widely seen today as a stern and repressed culture. Or perhaps they see this dourness as reflecting a difficult era, where work was hard, most families knew people who had been in a war and there was little leisure time.

The reality, though, is that the process by which photos were developed, and the amount of time it took, meant that photographers told people to stand still and not move. It was very difficult for people to keep a smile so long in the same position, and so they simply did not smile (see Figure 4.1).

Figure 4.1: A Victorian couple enjoying themselves

The field of **visual methods** grapples with this issue. The study of selfies (Robinson 2007) raises very similar questions about what such images tell us about society, even in the various acts of revelation and concealment being practised in making these digital images.

Visual methods: methods that enable the study of images and non-textual data

Funny faces

Look at Figure 4.2. From the 'about the authors' information on the back of this book and in the front matter before Chapter 1, can you tell which author is which? Some of these images are 'selfies', but each has been selected by the author to say something about themselves. We saw in Chapter 2 (textbox, p. 36) how the early 20th-century sociologist George Herbert Mead ([1934] 1967) argued that humans actively identify themselves through the way others see them. The 'selfie' is just the latest manifestation of this sociological phenomenon. How do you think each of these 'authors' is 'writing' their 'self' in their image? In the language of symbolic interactionism, how much are they 'giving out' (on purpose) and how much are they 'giving away' (perhaps by accident)? If people are active in the images they present, we cannot assume that 'the camera never lies', but when people are trying to tell stories with the images they present, those images can tell us something about the 'myths' people want us to believe. The 'myths' we create about ourselves reflect the 'mythology' our society creates about itself. Roland Barthes (1973) pioneered the 'semiotic reading' (see Chapter 3) of visual 'texts' as ways of studying the myths we live by.

© the authors

Figure 4.2: Images of this book's authors 'found' online

Another parallel between archival data and other forms of data is the problem of sampling bias. Who leaves behind a trace and whose lives are forgotten or were never recorded in the first place? The phrase that history is the story of the winners is quite well known, but to what extent is it the case for sociology? The diaries of 17th-century farmers' wives will be biased in favour of the better off – the authors of those diaries, those who were literate – just as the volume and popularity of selfies on the internet reflects today's 'digital divides' – between those with and without access, faster and more reliable access, and more knowledge and confidence in using the technology (David & Millward 2014). When investigating records, what you are studying is how the world was being represented by dominant groups, not how everyone saw the world, and certainly not how the world was. Some archives are more inclusive than others, so it is important to ask how representative any archive is, when assessing what data from that source can tell you.

Evolving methods: Digital sociology and mixed methods

The rise of the internet means more and more people are leaving a trail of self-representation for researchers to collect. As such, the internet creates huge opportunities for sociologists to study the here and now by means that were once reserved mainly for the study of the past. Of course, the 'digital divide' means not everyone is equally represented.

The rise of what is called the 'network society' is not just confined to the internet and the practices of networked individuals (see Chapter 9, p. 238). Institutions – from governments, schools, universities, police forces and private companies – make it their business to collect ever more information about their citizens, pupils, students, users and customers. Some refer to this as the rise of 'big data' (Savage & Burrows 2007).

Supermarkets, states and insurance companies know vast amounts about you, sometimes exceeding what you know about yourself. Whether this data is available to social researchers to use is a different matter. The ethical issues involved in such a 'surveillance society' (Lyon 2001) are very significant, as they are when a social researcher seeks to use such live archives to study people online. In online research, the researcher may blend archival research with non-participant observation, as the archive materials are often records of ongoing activity.

Alternatively, researchers may engage directly with participants of online archiving communities (such as blog sites, Twitter and e-fanzines) in a form of *online ethnography* (David & Millward 2014: section six). The researcher may be just 'lurking' in the margins of online public space, but such observation and asking questions should be treated with the same ethical consideration as would apply to other interview-, questionnaire- and observation-based research. Researching public records of past events raises fewer ethical concerns than online participant observation of active archives (Snee et al. 2016).

Mixed methods means different things to different people, some of which are not new. Preparing for an experiment or questionnaire, a researcher might do some preliminary observations, secondary data analysis or interviews to hone their questions. Such qualitative exploration may then develop into 'piloting' the themes that will be developed in the later quantitative work. Alternatively, after a survey, a researcher might choose to carry out smaller-scale interview research to enable

Mixed methods: a research design using more than one form of data collection. How far the methods are integrated together is a source of much discussion. Sometimes called multi method

a better interpretation of the statistical results. More recent advocates of mixed methods reject this linear add-on model for a more integrated interaction between methods. Jennifer Greene et al. (1989) suggest five forms of mixed methods research, each seeking to combine different data-collection strategies in particular ways and to particular ends: Table 4.3 explains these components.

Table 4.3: Mixed methods research formats

Form of mixed methods	Explanation
Triangulation	Involves parallel research methods designed to test whether different approaches confirm the same result
Complementarity	Sequential, and one method is used to clarify prior findings
Developmental	Builds upon the results of one method to 'fine-tune' a subsequent method
Initiation	Allows one method to develop results that subsequent approaches might challenge, highlighting alternatives and contradictions
Expansion	Explores different aspects of an issue that singular approaches would miss

John Cresswell (2014) rejects mixed methods as a bolt-on pre-test, post-test addition to one main method. He argues that mixed methods ought instead to be the default approach, reflecting how the 'true' interpretation of any issue is complex and often contradictory. Different methods must be given equal weight because what is discovered by different methods can never simply be added up into one overall result.

Is sociological method in crisis?

Social changes during the 19th century related to the growth of organizations and institutions (see Chapter 9) saw the collection of large amounts of data about people. Durkheim's method of comparing statistics on different rates of suicide between different groups (discussed in Chapter 1) drew upon such data, and subsequent generations of sociologists developed the means of analysing such data. Similarly, an increasingly literate society left behind written records which can be analysed, and the Verstehen tradition in sociology combined personal and bureaucratic records of human lives and their meanings. The telephone, the tape recorder and now the computer have aided the development of interview techniques, as still- and moving-image recording devises have in the development of visual methods (Pink 2014).

However, the emergence and expansion of the internet has resulted in digital records of our lives that would have been unimaginable a generation ago (Savage & Burrows 2007). As well as these records kept by the State, this 'big data' is generated by corporate and networked systems that record communications, purchases, viewing habits and lifestyles. Large amounts of interpersonal and institutional interactions are being recorded digitally in a way that verbal and even handwritten communications never were. As such, the old methods of surveys, questionnaires, interviews and localized observations may come to seem rather antiquated. This is why some sociologists consider there to be a crisis in sociological methods because it is argued that few sociologists have access to the new forms of data, nor the tools to analyse them (ibid.).

While Google and Facebook's algorithms, 'crawlers' and 'bots' claim to be capable of mapping our beliefs and desires faster even than we can recognize them, they are also limited. Working out how to measure and analyse all the tweets about a particular issue might be interesting and valuable, yet it will supplement rather than replace what traditional methods continue to tell us about these practices. Human beings are not computers and the 'language' they use is not the clearly defined and structured 'command language' of machines. Instead, human beings interpret words and commands in ways that defy simple prediction. As such, interviews and observations allow us to build up a picture of people's beliefs and attitudes in ways that algorithms have yet to do convincingly.

How sociologists, using new forms of network analysis combined with older (often slower) research methods, might be able to research beyond the priorities and the biases of commercial- and state-generated 'big data' collection and analysis remains to be seen. In part, the explosion of 'big data' is a challenge to sociology. At another level, it opens up previously unimagined possibilities. And the analysis of a range of questions, concerning our beliefs, interpretations and private practices that are not fully captured and reflected by the new kinds of 'big data', will still rely on the traditional methods discussed in this chapter.

DATA COLLECTION

The following sections provide the reader with some key ways of thinking about the interaction between research design and data collection, and how data can be analysed. It should be noted here that data collection must always be designed with a view to how that data will subsequently be analysed; so keep in mind that choices being considered under collection should always be made in the light of what is discussed in the subsequent sections.

Populations and samples

In order to answer a research question, we need to decide who (or what) we are talking about. This is deciding on the **population**.

A population is every member of a category. We often think of countries, towns or villages as having populations, but the sociological meaning of the term refers to the membership of any group. A population is not simply 'everyone' but rather everyone in the group of interest. If you are interested in current students in your

Population: all members of the category under investigation

university or college, then that does not include all students ever or everywhere, let alone all adults. All the pupils in a school are the population of pupils at that school. If you are interested in the total population of a school, you will include teachers and other staff.

For most research methods, sociologists need a **sample** of participants to take part in the study. It is sometimes possible to study the whole population if it is small (e.g. all the clubs in a particular sporting league). Such studies do not need to worry about sampling. Most of the time, however, the population is too large for all members to be studied.

The importance of defining the population lies in the fact that research can only be representative if it is clear who (or what) it is about, and when there is a clear relationship between the cases being studied (the sample) and the group such results are claimed to be about (the population that sample seeks to be representative of).

Opinion poll organizations try to predict election results based on samples, but if they sample people by telephone they should only claim that their population were telephone owners, not the general population. Those who have lived in the same home for many years are more likely to be selected (identified, contacted and included) by opinion poll companies; such sampling represents only the population of stable residents and so often excludes many. Far fewer young adults have access to a landline phone compared to older people. Opinion polls that try to select a sample that is representative of the whole population, in the sense of every adult eligible to vote in a territory, may also be unrepresentative if the actual population of those who do vote excludes many less secure citizens.

These issues help explain why there have been some notable polling failures in recent years. Approximately half the opinion polls predicted the British referendum vote to leave the EU (known as Brexit). In this case, the polls predicted a 'remain' vote when telephone polling was used, whereas online polls found greater support for exit. The issue here was that telephone polls tend to oversample graduates, which skewed the data.

| Sample: a subset of a population |

Sampling theory, myths and reality

It is always important to start the sampling process by clearly identifying the relevant population. The question that then arises is whether all members of that population can be identified – that is, whether a **sampling frame** can be produced. If a sampling frame can be produced, it is possible to select a subset of the population in a way that would allow each member of the population an equal chance of being in that sample.

Next, a selection method whereby all members of the population have an equal chance of being selected should be designed. This is called a *random sample*. If this is not possible, a non-random sample will have to suffice. The problem with non-random samples is that you cannot generalize to the entire population from such samples. See Table 4.4 for an overview of different sampling methods available.

| Sampling frame: the list of every person or thing in a population that can be sampled |

Sample size

The final element in this brief discussion of sampling is sample size. The answer to the question 'how big must my sample be?' depends on two things. First, the variation

Table 4.4: Types of sampling

Type of sample	Explanation
Random	No bias exists in influencing who gets into the sample. It does *not* mean spontaneous or unpredictable.
Stratified random sampling	Selects proportions of different subpopulations in advance, and those subpopulations are then sampled randomly. Allows for small populations to be compared with large ones.
Quota sampling	A non-random sample. Subpopulations are identified in advance as in stratified random sampling, but these subpopulations are not sampled randomly. The primary concern is to fill the quota rather than eliminating bias.
Cluster sampling	The researcher recruits from a number of locations. This can be a form of random or non-random sampling, depending on how participants are recruited from each location.
Convenience sampling	Select the first (or easiest) people you meet. This is non-random because where and when you select them has a biasing effect on who is selected.
Snowball sampling	Initial participants identify others to participate in the research. This is non-random, and justified where a population is hard to access, difficult to identify or hidden.

observed in the population. A population that is highly diverse in relation to the things being studied will require a larger sample. A more similar (or homogenous) population will require a smaller sample. One French person might be all you need to gain a working knowledge of the French language, but you would need a much larger sample to study French political attitudes, which are much more diverse.

Second, sample size will depend on the mode of analysis being undertaken, with more complex forms of analysis requiring greater amounts of data.

Qualitative studies tend not to collect numerical data, and so do not allow for statistical tests. A small sample of very detailed interviews may generate very fascinating data, but the sample size will make the results hard to generalize from. Some qualitative researchers simply suspend the issue of generalization in favour of small samples studied in detail, while others argue that theory can be developed from this data, which can then be tested quantitatively.

The question of sample size for qualitative research is also a challenge. Very little qualitative research has more than 100 participants because the amount of data from that many interviews or observations would be overwhelming, and only manageable by a large team of researchers. Additionally, some qualitative researchers start out with an intended number of participants which they think will allow them to gather enough data to answer their research questions but will also be flexible regarding this. For example, a researcher might hope to gather interview data from

40 participants but stop data collection after 34 interviews. This decision to stop might be because of *theoretical/ data saturation* – where a researcher feels that the data they are gathering is not offering any new findings or insights. Deciding when you have reached this saturation point is very difficult and requires researchers to have an extremely detailed knowledge of their data.

What happens when sampling goes wrong?

Sampling is difficult, and can be flawed for a number of reasons, including implicit biases and cultural norms. For example, the Nuffield 1980 class study used men's earnings for household income as the baseline against which to see whether children's outcomes in health, school and employment were predicted by such a background factor. It did not include women's income in determining this. The choice of the father's earnings was supposed to be 'better' than using 'total household income' because it was considered difficult to compare dual-earning households with 'breadwinner' households. This idea has become increasingly redundant as more and more women go out to work, and as family forms diversify. It is also seen as a failing of the study based on outdated gender norms (see Delamont 2003: 53–54). We discuss the exclusion of women from sociology in Chapter 2, and look at gender as a form of social division in Chapter 7.

Sociologist of education and inequality, Vikki Boliver, notes that, in the UK, black and minority ethnic (BME) 18- to 25-year-olds are more likely to be in higher education than their white peers (Boliver 2016). However, at the same time, black men in that age group are more likely to be in prison than to be in higher education. To combine black BME men and women into one group is therefore potentially misleading. Likewise, talk of 'South Asian' students obscures more than it reveals; while 18- to 25-year-olds with Indian heritage are more likely to be in higher education than their white peers, those from Pakistani and Bangladeshi backgrounds are less likely. Boliver (2016) also notes that the term 'higher education' is rather a broad category, as participation rates by class and ethnicity are very different for 'old' universities and newer institutions (see Chapter 7 for discussion of race).

The question of when it is useful to sample gay, lesbian, bisexual and transgender individuals as a group, or as distinct groups, is similarly complex. It is sometimes appropriate to group together experiences of sexual minorities, yet there are distinct differences in other dimensions (Worthen 2013). For example, research has found bisexuals have worse experiences than gays and lesbians in education settings (Robinson & Espelage 2011). In this case, combining gays, lesbians and bisexuals into one block is problematic – inflating problems for gays and lesbians while simultaneously underplaying those for bisexuals.

DATA ANALYSIS

Once a sociologist has collected data, it is then their task to analyse it to produce meaningful results. This process of turning a large amount of data into results requires *systematic* analysis to identify valid patterns. Here, we give a simple outline of what you can do. We begin by looking at textual (qualitative) data analysis and

BAD SOCIOLOGY Bad Sampling Leads to Bad Research

Bad sociology is often the result of poor methods. Bad research can produce misleading results that can be used to promote false claims about society. For example, a comparison between children raised by same-sex and different-sex couples (Regnerus 2012) claimed research showed that children raised by same-sex couples performed less well in education and other measures of life-success and wellbeing. This was a provocative claim, not just because it contradicted other research but because of the *political* effect such a result could have, given the existence of homophobic attitudes in society.

However, many more of those in the same-sex parenting group were divorced or separated from a previous heterosexual partner. As such, it could not be demonstrated that the research was showing any 'effect' of same-sex parenting, instead of and distinct from the impact of parental separation on children. Sociologists have a responsibility to ensure that their methods are as accurate and rigorous as possible.

Whether divorce harms children is equally controversial. Research has shown that children of single parents are more likely to be unemployed, in prison or to drop out of school (McLanahan & Sandefur 1994). However, becoming a single parent is more likely for those who are poor and discriminated against in society. As such, once you control for class, employment, ethnicity and parental education, it turns out that disadvantage explains the harm these children experience, far more than family form (Ni Bhrolchain 2001).

Similarly, children are 100 times more likely to be killed by a step-parent than by a biological parent. However, Rose (2000) points out that adopted children are no more likely to be killed than biological offspring. It is not biology that makes the difference. Rather, it is the stigma by which step-parents are not considered 'real' parents in the way that biological and adoptive parents are.

Given that sociological research addresses social problems and issues in people's lives, great care needs to be taken with method. Whether intentionally or not, methods used poorly may well lead to incorrect results that can have real, material effects on people's lives and perceptions. Research (as noted above) that falsely suggests certain types of people are 'bad parents' will reinforce stigma against them and harm their lives, as well as those of their children.

then at how to analyse numerical (quantitative) data. While analysis takes place after data collection, data collection should have been carried out with a clear view of the data analysis that is to be undertaken.

Qualitative data analysis

Qualitative data analysis treats data as *text*. By text we mean anything that can be 'read' for its meaning. Qualitative data analysis searches for patterns of meaning within text: within and between individual texts – interview transcripts, newspaper reports, radio broadcasts, songs, diary entries, films or photographs, etc. Visual material can be 'read' as text! The conduct of analysis involves three basic steps: *coding, content analysis* and *discourse analysis.* Some research only combines the first two steps. Others jump directly to the third.

Levels of coding

Coding means going through textual data and highlighting each time a particular theme or idea recurs and giving it a label. Each instance of this is a **code** and each time it recurs the sociologist *codes* it. For example, in an interview transcript a participant might repeatedly refer to their pet dog. In this case, the sociologist would highlight every time this happened, labelling each instance as something like 'dog'. Coding may be conducted with a computer software package or using coloured pens. Once data is coded, it is possible to look for patterns; how often codes arise, where they do and in what combinations with other codes.

> **Code:** a word or short phrase that characterizes a larger amount of text in order to undertake analysis

The question then arises as to how to choose the codes to use. There are various levels of coding, and each performs slightly different kinds of pattern searching. Coding is deductive if codes were selected in advance of beginning the analysis, and inductive if codes are selected by engaging with the text – by reading carefully and making codes for what 'leaps out' at the researcher.

Deductive coding is more appropriate if examining relationships that are already known, while inductive coding is more exploratory.

Qualitative content analysis

Once textual data has been coded, it is possible for the sociologist to search through the content to look for patterns. Simple (deductive) content analysis can be quantitative. If the hypothesis was some newspapers would use terms more frequently than others, statistical tests can measure this. One could look for how many times the term 'fake news' is used, and see whether this depends on the type of newspaper (see Chapter 10). Qualitative content analysis is more inductive and exploratory, and the pattern searching is less concerned with testing prior theories statistically as it is with looking for such patterns in the first place. Qualitative content analysis allows the researcher to look for patterns, but most qualitative sociologists want to go beyond just looking for patterns like the use and non-use of certain key terms (content or codes), and rather want to study what meanings are present and how they are constructed in such content/codes. This leads us to *discourse analysis.*

Discourse analysis

The term discourse is used here to refer to systems of meaning by which representations of the world are constructed in language (including visual 'text'). These may be media discourses or medical discourses, legal discourses or many other forms besides. For example, some groups of people are more likely to be reported in connection with crime than others. Qualitative content analysis can help identify what elements recur in such stories, what language is repeated, what images are used and what other links are routinely made. That sort of pattern identification is what qualitative coding allows us to explore. However, once we have identified that pattern, it is possible to ask not just *what* elements are routinely deployed, but *how* and *why* these elements are put together. This is where content analysis shifts into discourse analysis.

There are at least 13 different types of discourse analysis (see David & Sutton 2011), but some simple commonalities exist. The basic approach is to identify how particular meanings are constructed, not how often they recur (something that quantitative content analysis can establish for you in advance of your selection of what to analyse discursively). Through the study of grammar, metaphor, equation, myth, narrative, thematic construction, omission, framing, network links and various other linguistic devices, the researcher seeks to identify how particular constructions in language work to present 'discursive figures' – seemingly real characters, patterns, sequences, events and relationships that tell a version of events that appears true because they close down alternative versions of reality.

Content analysis can only give us a sense of the objects in play (the vocabulary of the text). Discourse analysis examines how the grammar used puts these words into place to create meaning (see David & Sutton 2011: 338–387 for an extended account of the various terms and vocabularies used to describe forms of qualitative data analysis).

Quantitative data analysis

Quantitative research collects data as numerical values within specified variables. Large volumes of such data can be collected and, as with qualitative data analysis, the issue for the researcher is how to extract patterns from such a mass of data. Quantitative data analysis looks for patterns of graphical and statistical relations. Such patterns can take many forms.

Undertaking quantitative analysis can be complex, with mathematical steps required. We do not provide an instructional manual of how to undertake each form of analysis, but we discuss the broader issues about which sort of analysis is relevant, and how to choose the right one. To do this, one must first consider how variables are recorded numerically.

Levels of measurement

A variable varies in a way that can be recorded numerically. The values of such variables are numbered, but some variable values are more numerical than others. There are three basic *levels of measurement: nominal, ordinal* and *interval/ratio* (see Table 4.5). These levels relate to how numerical each measure is.

Nominal and ordinal variables are called *categorical* data as their values are in the form of categories, whereas interval/ratio variables have real numbers and not categories. Scale and ratio are numerical data.

The first step in analysis is to examine your individual variables. This is called *univariate analysis*. This includes producing graphic displays and carrying out basic statistical measurements. These displays and measures allow you to identify problems and patterns that might be obscured in later, more sophisticated forms of analysis.

Recall the levels of measurement. For a nominal variable, a *pie chart* (see Figure 4.3) is best. You can also calculate the *modal* value – the most popular value in that variable.

Table 4.5: Types of data and levels of measurement

Level of measurement	Definition	Example	Notes
Nominal	A variable whose values have no sequence or scale	Degree subject studied Country of origin Hair colour	These numbers are just labels or identifiers
Ordinal	A variable whose values have sequence but no scale	Olympic medals Satisfaction surveys	It is the order that matters. It is not possible to say how much better a gold medal is to a silver one.
Interval	A variable whose values have sequence and scale, but not a true zero	Clothes sizes Temperature	The lack of a 'true zero' (where 0 means an absence/lack of value) means that ratios are not meaningful in these scales. Size 0 is not an absence of size, and Size 6 is not half the size of Size 12.
Ratio	A variable whose values have sequence, scale and a true zero	Speed Distance Age Height Weight	'Fully' numerical data. This is the best kind of data, in the sense that a lot of quantitative analysis can be used on it.

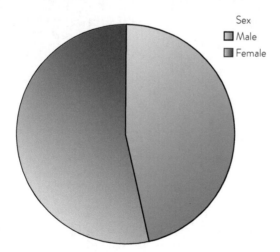

Figure 4.3: A pie chart showing the nominal sex variable in overall population

For ordinal data you can plot a *bar chart* (see Figure 4.4), and calculate the modal value and the *median* value. The median value is the value of the middle case; that is, if all cases were lined up sequentially (from lowest to highest value) the value of the middle case would be the median. In an even-numbered sample, the median is the value shared by the middle two cases, and if these are different, then just split the difference.

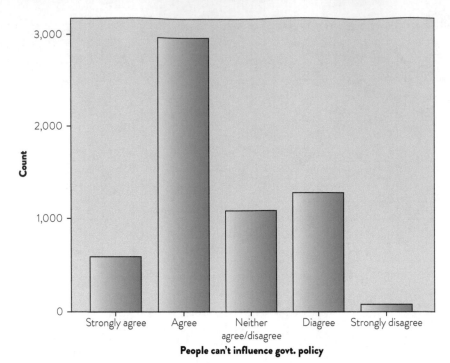

Figure 4.4: Ordinal variable of belief in political efficacy

If you have interval or ratio data you can use a *histogram* (see Figure 4.5) and calculate the mode, the median and the *mean*. The mean is the *average* – the sum of all the case values added up and divided by the number of cases.

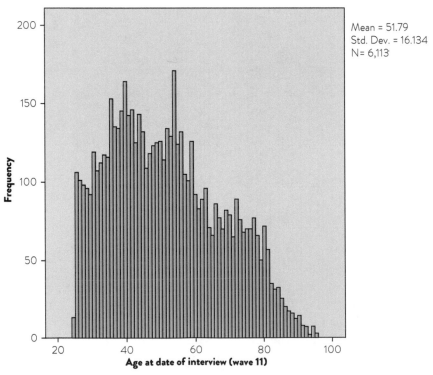

Figure 4.5: A histogram for the interval age variable

The mode, median and mean are known as the *measures of central tendency*. This is a more formal way of describing the 'average' of a set of data, and these measures are ways of describing a set of data with one value that offers some form of 'central' position. Only fully numerical variables can use all three measures (and others).

It is also possible to calculate the *range*, *variance* and *standard deviation* for interval and ratio variables. These measure how widely the data is distributed. The range is just the gap between the highest and lowest values.

The variance measures how far either side of the middle value the values in a data set actually are. Variance is calculated by working out the mean, and then calculating the distance from the mean to each value. Because some values will be above the mean and some below, each such value is squared to make all these differences positive values. The sum of all those differences will vary depending on how far the values disperse from the mean.

Taking the square root of the variance removes the exaggerating effect of all those squarings, but keeps the overall effect of all the positive values, and gives the *standard deviation* – a useful measure of how narrow or wide the sample distribution really is. Computer software does the number crunching these days. However, most statistical tests for relationships with interval variables use the properties of standard deviations to work out how far things actually go together, so be aware of that.

Example: Groups with the same average are not the same

Univariate analysis is helpful in showing broad trends or highlighting any obvious problems with data.

Ten people all earning £20 an hour for work will have the same (mean) average wage as a group of ten people where five earn £40 and five earn nothing. We only know, in this context, that this difference exists if we also take the range (0 vs. 40).

If we add a third group where two people earn nothing, three people earn £10, three people earn £30 and two people earn £40, the average and the range is the same as the second group. It is only through finding the standard deviation that you see the differences between these groups.

For examples with this kind of small sample size, it is easy to see that differences exist by looking at the raw data. But if you are doing similar analysis with thousands of cases, these tests are needed to acquire this information.

Bivariate analysis

Once univariate analysis has looked for interesting results related to individual variables, it is possible to search for interesting relationships between two variables. This is done through *bivariate analysis*. Clustered and stacked bar charts graphically display relationships between two nominal or ordinal variables (see Figure 4.6).

A scatterplot represents the relationship between two interval variables (see Figure 4.7).

If you wanted to look at how the distribution of values in an interval variable distributed for values within either a nominal or ordinal variable, you could use

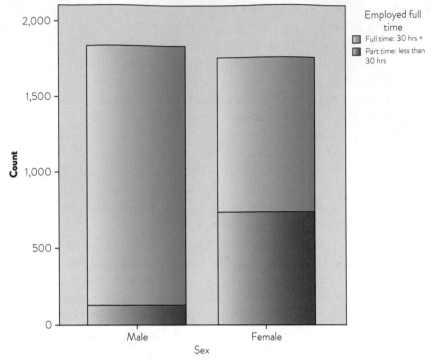

Figure 4.6: A stacked bar chart for two categorical variables

multiple histograms. Once plotting graphical representations, you should ask whether there is a statistical relationship present. The most important statistical measures are *association*, *significance* and *regression*.

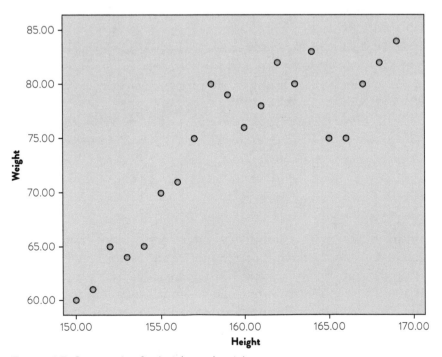

Figure 4.7: Scatterplot for height and weight

Association

Does change in one variable coincide with change in another? With categorical (nominal or ordinal) data, this association is called *cross-tabulation*. Between interval/ratio data, association is called *correlation*. If you are using two variables of different levels of measurement, always use the test appropriate for the lower level of measurement (nominal being the lowest and interval/ratio being the highest). Table 4.6 shows the statistical tests for association depend on the levels of measurement involved.

Table 4.6: Association tests appropriate for different levels of measurement

	Nominal	Ordinal	Interval/ratio
Nominal	Cross-tabulation (*Cramer's V, or if both are binary, Phi*)	Cross-tabulation (*Cramer's V*)	Comparison of means (*Eta*)
Ordinal		Cross-tabulation (*Spearman's Rank*)	Comparison of means (*Eta*)
Interval/ratio			Correlation (*Pearson's r*)

All the statistical tests generate a result on a scale of 0 to 1 (though variables with sequence can vary between −1 to +1). Zero means there is no association between variables, and one shows absolute association.

- If all men had short hair and all women had long hair, that would produce an association value of one.

- If the distribution of earnings had no association with age, the result would be zero.

- If the pattern between sex and hair length, or between income and age, was mixed, the result would be somewhere in between.

Usually, an association of less than 0.2 is considered weak, and above 0.4 as strong, with a result above 0.6 as very strong. Where both variables have sequence (ordinal, interval and ratio data), association could be positive or negative (where a minus sign shows). If ageing associates with worsening health, we would see a negative association (assuming the health variable was measured from low health [1] to higher levels of health [a higher number]).

Still, you should take such results for what they are, simple measures of association. The way a variable is coded can lead to confusion, so always be careful when interpreting results. Other things should tell us how much importance we can place on such outcomes.

Significance

If you produce a measure of association, that result is a measure of the association *within the sample you have analysed*. All results that measure patterns within a sample are called *descriptive statistics*. *Inferential statistics* are claims that what was found in a sample can be generalized to the wider population from which the sample was drawn. Assuming you drew a random sample (see above), it is possible to gauge how likely it is that the result in your sample could have come about by random fluctuation in the composition of the sample relative to the population. Fortunately, there are tests to assess this. The bigger the sample and the smaller the variance in the sample, the lower this risk is. Measures of *significance* offer an indication of this risk.

Significance tests produce a *p. value* which indicates the *probability* (on a scale of 0–1) that your result was a sampling accident; the higher the p. value, the less confidence you can have in the generalizability of the association result. The simplest significance test is called the *Chi Square test* and was designed for nominal data. Other significance tests (such as the *T-Test* and the *Anova*) build on the Chi Square test, but they are all based on similar principles of working out a balance – the bigger the sample and the association result, and the smaller the variance in each variable, the lower the risk. A p. value of less than 0.05 is commonly taken as acceptable in non-experimental research designs as it means there is less than a 5 per cent chance that the association in your sample came about in a population where association was zero. Experimental designs usually use a 0.01 (1 per cent) level of acceptable risk.

Regression

If you found an association between your two variables and that association in your sample is statistically significant, you can ask yourself a third question. If years of education associates with higher earnings, how much does an additional year of a person's education tend to increase their earnings? Not everyone with more education earns more. Likewise, if there is a significant association, this does not tell us whether more education leads to a lot more earning power or just a little more. A strong association simply means education and earnings tend to rise together. Even if everyone with more education earned more than everyone with less (a perfect association), it might still be the case that each additional year of schooling only led to a small amount of extra money. The association was strong but the 'effect' might still be small. Regression measures the strength of this 'effect', not the strength of the association.

Importantly, it is only worth measuring the size of an effect once it has been demonstrated that a link exists between two variables that is not there by chance (that is, that there is a significant association between variables). Only when this is the case do you then examine the size of the effect – by running a regression test.

Simple linear regression looks for straight lines between two interval or ratio variables (see Figure 4.8). A measure of association between interval variables looks at how close cases are to the line of best fit. Linear regression asks what the angle of that line is. By how much does the effect alter when the cause alters? *Logistic regression* allows you to measure effects for categorical variables. The usefulness of regression is that once you have started with a simple linear regression, it is possible to add in multiple variables to measure how a number of inputs predict an outcome. A *multi-variate regression* test might look at how earnings could be predicted by a combination of sex, ethnicity and years of education; the result would show how each of these predictors maps earnings relative to each of the others. Multi-variate regression is very useful for building *models* that delve into several layers of complex interrelationships, and they are used to check whether apparent predictors are in fact just proxies for other factors.

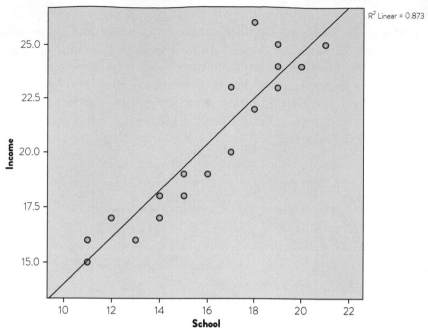

Figure 4.8: A scatterplot for two interval variables – current income and years spent in formal education (with line of best fit)

For instance, length/level of education achieved may correlate with earnings, but is itself predicted by parental earnings. Putting both parental earnings and years of education into a multi-variate regression to predict earnings might show that – once you control for background – those with similar parental earnings do not earn different amounts depending on their own years of education. However, if we then add in sex, we might find that sons of rich parents tend to get well-paid jobs irrespective of their own education, whereas daughters find that education does matter in accessing well-paid jobs (Egerton & Savage 1997). Egerton and Savage conclude that education is more important for daughters than for sons in turning background advantage into career success.

CONCLUSION

This chapter has examined the methods of sociology. We have explained why particular methods are useful in certain situations, and provided the information needed to understand why that is the case. In doing so, we have examined the methodology of sociology. Thinking about methods starts before you choose a method, and requires consideration of the type of method, the collection of data and how that data is analysed. We also examined some of the issues in methods, including the question of bias.

In conclusion, methods involve a degree of technical skill, and technical skills can become mechanical if practised in isolation from the craft of knowing when and where to apply them. Nevertheless, a sociologist who does not learn the broad range of available methods is constrained. Methods must be used to answer the questions a sociologist wants to ask, not to dictate the questions they can ask. Some questions cannot be answered empirically and, as such, become rhetorical, or the answers given remain purely speculative. An awareness of the limits of sociology is an awareness of the limits of method. Methods need to be respected, but we must never let ourselves become subservient to method in isolation. There is no single correct way to research society, but there are many things to think about and many ways to get it wrong if you do not choose the most appropriate approach for the question you want an answer to.

HOW WOULD...?

» Think about your ideal subject for study, such as we discussed in Chapters 1 and 3. How would you design your own research study on this?

   » What might your research question be?

   » How might you address this using inductive and deductive approaches? Using Green's criteria as shown in Table 4.1 (p. 72), have you developed a 'good' research question?

» How have other people studied this issue?

   » Find two studies that have investigated the topic (or one closely related). What methods did they use? Are they appropriate? Why?

   » If you could improve these studies in terms of methods, how might you do it?

STRUCTURED FURTHER READING

David, M. & Sutton, C. (2011). *Social Research: An Introduction*. London: SAGE.
An introductory textbook that provides those new to social research with a comprehensive introduction not just to research methods, but also the theory and logic of qualitative, quantitative and mixed methods.

Pink, S. (2014). *Doing Visual Ethnography*. London: SAGE.
An accessible and engaging introduction to doing research with images, video and the internet. The book provides a foundation for thinking about visual ethnography and introduces the practical and theoretical issues related to using visual and digital technologies.

Cancian, F. (1992). Feminist stances: Methodologies that challenge inequality. *Gender & Society*, 6(4), 623–642.
An important article that makes the case for a feminist approach to methods and methodology. It calls for participatory methods where more agency is given to the participants and less power is given to the researcher.

 Visit the companion website at www.macmillanihe.com/mccormack for further learning and teaching resources.

Chapter 5
ETHICAL SOCIOLOGY

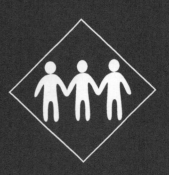

INTRODUCTION

This chapter examines what it means for sociology to be ethical. Ethical practice is vital to sociological research, and social science more broadly, and so it deserves careful consideration as a core aspect of sociology. We look at the different dimensions of ethical research practice, and explore some examples of past sociological research that some people consider unethical. We highlight that ethics is not just important in conducting research – although this is where the most harm is likely to occur – but that there are ethical considerations for the way research is written, and even ethical questions about what should be researched at all. In our Provocation, we ask whether ethics panels in universities are damaging novel sociological research.

ETHICS IN SOCIOLOGY

Sociologists must think about ethics in every study they undertake. There are formal guidelines and codes of ethics in place to help determine if practice is ethical. Indeed, for any sociological study undertaken at a university, the proposed research must be presented to an ethics board or committee and receive permission. But what do we mean by ethics? Banks (2012) defines **ethics** as follows:

> Ethics is about matters of right and wrong conduct, good and bad qualities of character and responsibilities attached to relationships. Although the subject matter of ethics is often said to be human welfare, the bigger picture also includes the flourishing of animals and the whole ecosystem. (p. 58)

There are great philosophical debates about ethics, yet we are not directly concerned with these abstract arguments about living a moral life. Instead, we are interested in the ethical practice of sociology and will approach the topic by considering examples, arguments and theories developed by sociologists.

So what might ethical sociology include? Well, just as medical doctors swear the Hippocratic oath to 'first, do no harm', so too sociologists have a duty to minimize the possibility that our practice may have negative effects on people. In thinking about sociology being ethical, this instruction not to harm others is a good first rule.

Ethics: moral principles and a code of conduct that govern researcher's behaviours when doing their jobs

Perhaps the most obvious group of people sociologists are required to protect are the participants in their studies. It would not, for example, be ethical to physically strike people in the face and then measure how their reactions varied by age, gender or any other characteristic. The issue of putting participants at harm is a serious concern in several of the case studies examined later in this chapter (see pp. 109–112). Sociologists must also minimize harm and the threat of harm to themselves and their co-workers, as well as other research stakeholders (see Provocation 10, p. 250), and the general public. But the interests and protection of these groups do not always align, and ethical sociology can be a complex endeavour.

Dealing with ethics in sociology usually requires thinking about the impact of methods within the context of their use. While some studies are inherently unethical, and others present few or no ethical issues (for example, studying how many times certain words occur in newspaper articles), ensuring ethical practice normally requires careful consideration. In other words, few methods or research designs can be quickly summarized as 'ethical' or 'unethical'. Instead, they tend to be located somewhere along a continuum that is dependent on a range of variables and contextual factors. This is one reason why universities require all research with human subjects to undergo analysis from an ethics board.

In this chapter, we are going to draw out some of the key questions that ethical sociologists must ask of research studies. These include:

- Who should be protected in a study? At what expense to quality of data?

- How much responsibility does a researcher have for negative effects of their research?

- What harms are sociologists concerned about?

British Sociological Association's ethical guidelines

Sociological associations provide ethical guidelines and codes of conduct for sociologists. Many of these guidelines concern the broader role of being a professional sociologist, including maintaining professional competencies. Some guidelines also directly relate to engaging in ethical research. The British Sociological Association (2002), for example, provides the following:

'*Relations with and Responsibilities towards Research Participants*

Sociologists, when they carry out research, enter into personal and moral relationships with those they study, be they individuals, households, social groups or corporate entities.

Although sociologists, like other researchers, are committed to the advancement of knowledge, that goal does not, of itself, provide an entitlement to override the rights of others.

Members [of the BSA] should be aware that they have some responsibility for the use to which their data may be put and for how the research is to be disseminated. Discharging that responsibility may on occasion be difficult, especially in situations of social conflict, competing social interests or where there is unanticipated misuse of the research by third parties.'

These are overarching points that guide ethical conduct. Given these indicators, how might that influence your arguments about our opening example of a potential research topic and method?

CONCEIVING, CONDUCTING AND DISSEMINATING ETHICAL RESEARCH

As sociologists, we must consider multiple factors to ensure that we are acting ethically. This includes considering the impact of the research, in all capacities – on participants, on wider society and on oneself. In this section, we highlight the stages that a sociologist goes through in conducting research, and ethical considerations that need to occur along the way. In all of this, it is important to remember that ethics is not just a one-off checklist to be satisfied, but an ongoing *active process* that is considered at each part of any sociological study.

Ethical considerations in choosing a research topic

The first question of ethics is whether a topic should be researched or not. We should always approach this answer with an open mind and a desire to enable research wherever possible. Knowledge often advances through surprising means, with unforeseen and unexpected discoveries. Teflon is perhaps the most famous example of this idea: the non-stick coating for cookware was discovered by accident during research into possible substances to use in refrigeration.

Yet there are also potential studies we know to be unethical. Some of the most notorious experiments were those the Nazis performed on Jewish people in the concentration camps. These horrifying experiments sought to examine how human bodies reacted to toxic chemicals, torture and other extreme conditions. They were unanimously condemned after the war and a 10-point Nuremberg Code was devised that laid out key principles for research with human subjects as a mechanism to stop such studies ever happening again (see https://history.nih.gov/research/downloads/nuremberg.pdf).

Within sociology, one might consider whether questions that sought to prove a bigoted perspective were worthy of study. The underlying motives might matter here, including whether the research questions were based on reasonable empirical evidence or whether they were based on prejudice (see Chapter 4).

We should also consider whether our research is *a waste of time*. For example, if we know that a Master's student is never going to become an academic, and that their research is for the sole purpose of getting a degree (never to be published), is it ethical to ask participants to give their time without financial compensation? This raises questions about whether researchers need to inform their participants about what will become of the research. If participants are led to believe that their participation will contribute to a study that has some palpable benefit in the world, but the researcher in fact has no intention of using this data in any such practical way, that is unethical. However, if the participant knows that this research is purely theoretical and gives their time anyway, that would be ethical.

This highlights a crucial point: the same investigation or act can be both ethical or unethical. What determines its ethical status is what the participant is told or, in other words, how the sociologist has addressed ethics *in their practice*.

Ethical considerations in choosing a research method

How we design our research – the methods and analysis we use – will determine whether our study will help or hinder the participants or society, or have no effect.

A poor research design will often harm the sociologist: by failing their dissertation, being unable to get their research published or damaging their reputation. Yet when inaccurate results and flawed conclusions are published, the effects can be worse and may well harm people beyond the study participants.

In Chapter 4, we discussed the work of sociologist Mark Regnerus and his research on the 'outcomes' of gay parenting. He used poor research methods in determining that children from gay households fared less well than children from heterosexual households (Regnerus 2012). The methodological design was flawed because it used unequal samples. The children from heterosexual families came from non-divorced families, whereas the children studied from the gay families came from a background of divorce.

This design flaw was likely intentional. The issue is an obvious one, particularly to trained sociologists, and the 'error' unsurprisingly yielded results that supported Regnerus' prior opposition to same-sex marriage. Over 200 sociologists, led by Gary Gates of the Williams Institute at the University of California, Los Angeles, wrote a letter to the journal editors who published the article critiquing many aspects of the study, focusing on its deeply flawed methods.

The reason so many people were motivated here was the fact that this issue is deeply political, and the study was used to sway politicians into denying same-sex couples the right to adopt. Regnerus also touted the study as proof of why same-sex marriage should not be legal. He thus used sociology as a tool to limit the rights of sexual minorities, going against the ethical code of the American Sociological Association.

But what if Regnerus had conducted the study using an appropriate comparison; by comparing samples of children from straight and gay households that were otherwise alike? Would it have now been ethical to examine whether gay parents provided worse outcomes for children than heterosexual ones?

This is certainly more complex, but many people would still say no. This is because lots of external structural factors affect childhood outcomes; divorce is just one variable. At the time of Regnerus' research, gay and lesbian couples did not have the same legal rights as heterosexual couples. This should also factor into a study on the issue. Choosing on the basis of one's own social concerns to examine a group that is already legally discriminated against is to (advertently or inadvertently) use the discipline of sociology to encourage the prevention of equality for same-sex couples. The ethics of this would then depend on whether the methodology was sophisticated enough to uncover and compensate for these other forms of discrimination: if not, the study is quite possibly not ethical.

Another research design ethical issue concerns the deception of participants. **Covert research** is when participants are not told they or their actions are being assessed as part of a study (see Chapter 4, pp. 81–82). In general, this is acceptable if it is in a public space, and unacceptable in other contexts. **Deceptive research** refers to where the participants are told they are being studied for one thing, but are actually studied for another.

For example, some researchers wanted to know if the processes of group identification affect how people will react to others involved in another group on issues of medical intervention. In this case, they told sport fans they were to be tested on something unrelated to what they were actually testing (Levine et al. 2005). After filling out a questionnaire, they were told to cross the courtyard for an interview. On

Covert research: research where participants are not told they are part of a study

Deceptive research: research where participants are told the study is about something other than its real aims

the way, an actor wearing a replica shirt of either the participant's favoured or most disliked NFL team feigned a jogging injury in front of the participant. When the 'runner' was wearing the shirt of the participant's favoured team, they were more likely to help than when the runner was wearing the shirt of a rival team. Had the participant known that this 'random' interaction was the heart of the research, they may not have exhibited such preferential behaviour.

Ethical considerations in conducting research

After choosing a topic to study and determining an appropriate method to conduct the study, the next level of ethical concern in the research design regards the emotional and physical safety of those we study. This first comes through the concept of *avoiding unnecessary harm* (emotional harm as well as physical harm). This is easy for most sociologists: few sociological studies directly involve the possibility of creating bodily harm, the way studies in drugs, exercise, medicine or nuclear technologies might. Yet the risk of physical harm is still an issue to consider, particularly in the fields of medical sociology or sport sociology, where collisions might occur.

Still, humans are capable of committing violence towards each other. Hence, alongside the principle of avoiding unnecessary harm, researchers must ask questions about risk. Ideally, researchers *do not take risks* (physical, emotional or otherwise) with their participants, research team or themselves. We thus ask you to consider whether it is ethical for a white academic who conducts research on a group of men who are white supremacists to ask one of his black graduate students to join him in interviewing them? Or if conducting a group interview on rival gang members simultaneously is acceptable? In both cases, the research design puts people at unnecessary risk and thus should be avoided.

Apart from these (hopefully obvious) ways of avoiding physical harm, the next issue to consider is emotional harm. This can pertain to emotional or psychological trauma that could result from completing the study. Such a risk does not mean that research cannot take place, but that care must be taken to deal with the issue.

Consider, for example, a study on asylum seekers. One might ask participants to recall painful memories of leaving family behind in their country of origin. This could quite possibly cause emotional harm in that it may bring forth painful memories; but that does not necessarily mean the study should not take place, as the outcomes of the research have the potential to positively influence policy or understanding of the issue. If, conversely, the research is not intended for publication, and is only a learning exercise for students, then this might not be deemed ethical. Why should someone have to revisit painful memories just so a student can gain practice in interviewing?

Another important issue here is that the participant should agree to take part in the research. Unless you have good reason to undertake covert research (most likely, you are observing in a public place), you have to gain the **informed consent** of your participants. This means that not only do they agree to participate, but also that they have been provided with enough information to give that consent with a full understanding of what is involved.

Informed consent: refers to participants agreeing to participate in the study having been informed of its aims

Ethical considerations related to the researcher

Our ethical obligation to consider what and who we study also extends to our own **positionality** within a group and whether we are the appropriate researcher to study this topic. This means that we should examine how our own perspectives influence the data we collect.

Perhaps the most important way to do this is to reflect on any personal bias: racist people should not research issues of race and ethnicity; misogynists should not research issues about gender inequality. Here, the bias is so great that the results will not be trusted by others.

We should also ask ethical questions about whether our positionality has the impact of unduly influencing results. This might be because of personal friendships in a setting, it could refer to previous experience or even political allegiance. One way we deal with this is through **reflexivity** – where the researcher critically reflects on their position.

Consider the following example:

A 60-year-old professor, who is well known on campus for her opposition to excessive drinking, enters a college nightclub to research a group of 21-year-old students and their rate of alcohol consumption. Given the academic's intellectual beliefs and her position of authority in relation to her students, it is very likely that the participants will consume *less* alcohol because of the presence of the researcher. This could bias her results, making her research less valid. This is something we call the **preacher effect**: people act differently around religious (or other) authorities.

The same effect might be true in the opposite direction in a different context. If the professor was studying drugs and was rumoured to take drugs herself, perhaps students might be likely to overestimate their consumption of drugs. We call this a **coach effect**. So, a sociologist who is known to be an avid runner, in studying middle-aged men and their exercise habits, might find that participants over-represent the amount of running they do. In both cases, participants may well alter behaviours or conceal feelings if they fear being judged.

Given these issues, a researcher must, at a minimum, reflect on their personal identity and how that could affect the data they gather, including their potential influence on participants. If the results of the exercise or alcohol consumption studies were to be used for policy purposes, for example, it is particularly important that the findings of the research be accurate.

Finally, in ethnographic work, researchers become thoroughly embedded within the culture or community they study. Sometimes they do this by travelling to foreign shores, and sometimes they conduct ethnography in communities they are already a part of, something known as an insider ethnography. The risk with both forms, but particularly the latter, is that if the researcher gets too close to those they study, for too long, they begin to understand and even interpret the world through their lens. This can have value, but it can also lead the researcher to be biased in their account of events. This is known as **going native**. While this does not hurt those you study, and is really more of a research methods consideration, if this loss of objectivity biases data that is then used to make a policy argument, or is otherwise used to influence people's lives, there may be ethical considerations.

Positionality: the researcher has a position in the research process and that this may affect the data collected

Reflexivity: thinking critically about one's positionality and its effect on data or society

Preacher effect: where people underestimate a claim because of the presence of the researcher

Coach effect: where people exaggerate a claim because of the presence of the researcher

Going native: when a researcher adopts the views of their participants without realizing, and loses an objective perspective

Ethical considerations in writing research

Ethical risks extend to how the researcher portrays their participants in writing up research. In much qualitative and all ethnographic research, the author gives details of the participants' lives, views and experiences. This could lead to a range of negative effects if made public, from social embarrassment to employment termination or family break-up. Consider conducting research on illegal drug consumption, for example, or studying how corporate executives break laws to promote financial gain. If one is to present research on these topics, participants must be protected from harm – otherwise they would lie about their data. Thus, all participants in research must be assured **anonymity** by the researcher. This means that when anyone else reads the research, identifying the participants is impossible.

The first step in doing this is to make participants' names anonymous by using pseudonyms, instead of real names. Still, sometimes the description of the participant is enough to identify them to others familiar in the setting. Ellis (1986) researched fishing communities and published her findings. Yet in later follow-up research (Ellis 1995), she found that her participants were angry over the way they had been portrayed in her book, and that they believed others in the (small) community could identify them. Sometimes it is necessary to exclude, or even slightly change, data to ensure anonymity is protected.

Participant anonymity must also be protected via **confidentiality** when discussing participants with each other. Much like a therapist cannot share details of one client's sessions with her other clients, researchers are required to keep other participants' data and stories anonymous (Tolich 2004). In general, this confidentiality is kept unless the researcher feels there is a genuine risk of serious and immediate harm to the participant or another person – and only then would the researcher break confidentiality by telling relevant people.

The British Economic and Social Research Council offers some useful guidance in this regard. They argue that confidentiality should be breached only when a 'participant or another person identified in the interview is in significant and immediate danger'. They also argue that confidentiality will be 'preserved as far as the law permits', but this is a statement nebulous enough that sociologists can interpret it in several ways. Hiriscau et al. (2014) argue similarly, stating: 'Circumstances under which it may be permitted or required to disclose confidential information include situations where a legal obligation exists to do so or where there is an immediate risk of harm that can only be averted or prevented by disclosing information.'

There are also questions about when a sociologist is 'wearing their sociological hat', because as an academic, they are held to a higher standard for what they casually express. In other words, it asks questions about *professional status*. A blog, for example, may sometimes be academically informed, but it is not peer-reviewed. It is important for a sociologist to distinguish between when they are merely offering an opinion and when they are directly citing sociological research or theory.

There are ethical questions about *defamation*, too. What if a sociologist interviews people, appropriately lays out their participants' views and then criticizes those views in their analysis? What if they have actively gathered data, treating their participants respectfully while doing so, but then used that data to socially damage the participants in writing about them. What is the ethical approach to doing this?

Anonymity: the guarantee given to research participants that they will not be identifiable in any publications about the research

Confidentiality: the requirement that information about a participant that cannot be shared without their express consent

PAUSE FOR REFLECTION

Does the mere fact that the commentator is, or even used to be, a sociologist mean that they have a moral duty to carefully and intellectually consider what they blog, tweet or post about? Should they always have to speak as a sociologist when engaging with the public?

You may have seen academics' profiles with 'Tweets are personal opinions' or similar disclaimer text added, but does this absolve them of all responsibility? What if a sociologist uses the same Twitter account to tweet to their students about a class?

↗ Pg. 250

Some of these concerns are discussed in Provocation 10, where we ask whether sociologists should 'pick a side' in their research.

Finally, there are ethics concerned over *whether to publish* data collected in research. For example, consider a sociologist who collected ethnographic data on a stigmatized group of people. Her intentions were to shine light upon a misunderstood community. Contrary to expectations, the data strongly supported the negative stereotypes of the group. Is it ethical to publish the data? Doing so would be an accurate representation of her participants' perspectives, but it would have the effect of further reproducing social stigma against the group she studied. What would you do?

 Visit the companion website at www.macmillanihe.com/mccormack for a discussion of how Eric Anderson dealt with an ethical issue that occurred after he had an article from his study accepted for publication.

GOOD SOCIOLOGY Framework for Ethical Consideration

When thinking about designing a research project, the following steps should help ensure that the project is ethical.

Choosing a Topic to Research

 » Should the topic be studied?
 » Is it possible the results of the study could harm a community or grouping of people?

Choosing a Research Design

 » Is the design objective and are comparisons appropriate for objective investigation?
 » Do participants need to be made aware that they are being studied?
 » Is the research a waste of the participants' time?
 » Will the research design harm anyone in physical or emotional ways?

Procedures

 » Have the participants given full and informed consent?
 » Have they been told that they can drop out of the study?

» Does the collection of this data harm the participants in any mental or physical way?

» Is there a possibility that they will regret their participation later on?

» Does this research expose the participants to any criminal repercussions?

» Is anonymity provided, including assuring that there is no way the participants can be revealed?

» Has your research been approved by an appropriate ethical body?

Analysing and Writing the Research

» Will the presentation of the data cast social stigma onto any particular community?

» Is the analysis fair to the participants' perceptions of what the research is?

» Should this research be published?

VOX POP Dr Kim Jamie

Member of a university ethics committee

Ethics is fundamental to the research students and staff undertake in universities. Doing ethically sound research is one of the things that differentiates rigorous academic research from journalism and simply asking people a few questions about their lives.

© Kim Jamie

All research that involves human participants at universities has to be reviewed by an ethics committee, and that's where I come in. Members of the ethics committee will receive an overview of a research project, copies of all material which participants will receive and a description of what will be 'done' to participants (e.g. if they'll be interviewed or observed or asked to be photographed). We then review this to make sure research participants are being treated well, that they are fully informed about the purpose of the research and they are able to consent to taking part. Sometimes research deals with sensitive topics and vulnerable participants. In these cases, upsetting participants may be unavoidable or it may be difficult to obtain consent. This doesn't necessarily mean, though, that the research shouldn't be done. In fact, this type of research is some of the most interesting, with the capacity to change society's perspectives.

Ethics committees are also there to look after the wellbeing of researchers. Setting out to do fieldwork can be dangerous, so ethics committees provide support to minimize the risks to researchers and help identify to keep safe in potentially dangerous research fields.

An ethics review can often be seen as a barrier to research as you have to get ethics approval before you can begin collecting data. However, I think it should be seen as a way to improve research design and open up conversations about how to actually *do* research. I also think conversations about ethics should be broadened out to issues of positionality (how you as a researcher are positioned in the field) and reflexivity (how you will deal with this position), which can be challenging and are vital.

Although reviewing lots of research projects can be very time-consuming, I feel privileged to be able to read about researchers' fascinating and diverse research projects.

» What are the key ethical issues that Kim looks at in proposals? How might Kim's expertise as a sociologist help her in this task?

» Many ethics boards have members of the community or other non-experts on their panels. How useful do you think this is?

EXAMINING ETHICAL DILEMMAS

Ethics is a process. As such, you will encounter many ethical dilemmas. And it is most important that you think carefully about how to address them. In the rest of this chapter, we want to learn about ethical practice through engaging with studies that are known for their ethical dilemmas. In the four research studies that follow, we will describe the study and some of the debate. In thinking about ethics, we ask you to consider the four key issues:

1. the topic;

2. the research design;

3. the implementation of the research; and

4. how participants were treated in the writing of the research.

At the end of the chapter, we will highlight key issues to consider with each of these studies; but we will not supply a definitive answer as to whether the research should have taken place or not: we leave that for you to think about and discuss.

The cases we feature here come from the US. This is not a deliberate choice but reflects what we consider to be the best examples for discussion. Not all of the cases are based in sociology, but all are from the social sciences and adopt methods that could be used by sociologists.

Case 1: Laud Humphreys and Tearoom Trade

In the 1960s, American sociologist Laud Humphreys wanted to know more about men who had sex with other men in public restrooms of city parks in the US. This was a time when homosexuality was illegal and incredibly stigmatized, and so understanding these practices was a way of investigating gay culture. Men seeking an outlet for their sexual desires resorted to 'cruising' – going to secluded public places to have sex with other men. Restrooms provided shelter, and protection from being accidentally discovered by others passing by – or, indeed, being arrested by police.

These restrooms were known as tearooms to those who used them for this purpose and, unlike in most European countries, the practice was and remains illegal in the US. As such, recruiting participants was difficult. Humphreys got creative: he joined the groups of men by acting as 'watch queen', playing lookout to warn others if anyone was coming. The men involved did not know he was a researcher.

In addition to recording the sexual activities of over 100 men, Humphreys wanted to find out more about the relationship between their anonymous sex lives and their public identities. He knew that the men would be unwilling to discuss matters with him near the restroom; there was a no-talking rule in cruising spots that still exists today.

As such, Humphreys recorded their licence plates as they returned to their cars and, through the Department of Motor Vehicles, found out their addresses (this is no longer possible). A year later, with a different hairstyle, clothes and car, he knocked on the door of 50 of these men. He portrayed himself as a social health researcher and elicited information from them about their marital status, sexual orientations and occupations.

In his subsequent book, *Tearoom Trade*, Humphreys (1970) found that men who had sex with other men in public restrooms defied cultural stereotypes. First, they came from diverse social backgrounds. Second, it was not just gay and bisexual men partaking in bathroom sex with other men, but also men who identified as heterosexual and were married. Many of the men he studied lived otherwise conventional lives; they were family men and respected members of their communities. He found that their sexual activities posed no danger of harassment to straight males, or anyone else. His study thus provided new evidence about anonymous male–male sexual encounters in public places, and the lives of men with same-sex sexualities in America at that time.

PAUSE FOR REFLECTION

- Identify the important findings of Humphreys' research.
- Identify what ethical issues were present in his research.
- How might one use the internet to perform this research today?
- What if Humphreys performed a similar study today on how people who sexually molest children operate? If he were to do covert research on this topic, should he report the perpetrators to the police?

Discussing the ethics of Tearoom Trade

Humphreys' research into same-sex sex had many benefits, helping dispel myths about gay people and same-sex sexuality. His research design was a result of laws that criminalized same-sex sexual activity and because of the way homosexuality was stigmatized. One can argue that, given this context, Humphreys' approach was the least emotionally harmful way to collect the data, and possibly the only way to do so. Most social scientists agree that observing people in public spaces is ethical, regardless of the legality of the behaviours – as long as people are not identified in the research.

Yet the major flaw with his method is that there was a high risk that his study could have resulted in imprisonment for his participants, or ruined their lives and reputations in several other ways. All that needed to happen was for his notes to have been found. There are many ways this could have happened: he could have lost his notebook, had it stolen or even been subpoenaed by the police. These were not risks for Humphreys, but for his participants – who did not even know they were being studied.

This has been the key critique of his method: that there were not sufficient measures to secure his data (Israel & Hay 2006). The logic is that the research would have been acceptable had there been better controls in place. He could have, for example, used a code for identifying information about individuals that only he knew. The research would still be deceptive, but ethical because the risk to his participants was minimized.

Humphreys' work is generally accepted because he was researching an unfairly stigmatized group – and helping to reduce oppression. Indeed, his research contributed to the body of evidence that led to the decriminalization of same-sex sex and the removal of homosexuality as a mental disorder by the American Psychiatric Association.

Yet this raises a further important question: Humphreys was studying a behaviour that was then both illegal and culturally condemned. We approve of it now in part because the social change in many countries has been such that we overwhelmingly oppose homophobia and decry laws that criminalize sexual minorities.

But what if Humphreys had been studying an activity that remains illegal and condemned? That is why we asked about how these methods could be applied to studying people who abuse children. Should our views on how we study such people be compatible with how researchers have studied homosexuality in exceptionally homophobic cultures? To what extent should contemporary social norms influence or limit research that might provide greater knowledge, and even in time alter those norms?

Case 2: Philip Zimbardo and the prison experiment

In 1971, Philip Zimbardo was interested in how good people can end up doing bad things. As part of a research design intended to explore this, he paid 24 male university students to participate in his prison experiment. Depending on the flip of a coin, the students were randomly assigned to take the role of either prisoners or prison guards (Haney et al. 1973). A Stanford University basement was turned into a makeshift prison to facilitate the experiment. The 'prisoners' were first collected by 'police car', stripped naked, 'decontaminated' and placed in gowns with no undergarments. Zimbardo says that this was designed to 'effeminize' the men, suggesting that they began 'to walk and to sit differently, and to hold themselves differently – more like a woman than like a man.' The men's heads were shaved, and shackles placed around their feet. As happens in real prisons, their names were replaced with identification numbers.

The guards were given no instructions, other than to 'keep order in the prison'. They were given uniforms, along with whistles and billy clubs (also known as truncheons or batons). At 2:30 a.m. on the first morning, the guards woke the prisoners for 'count', and forced the prisoners to repeatedly recite their ID numbers. At this stage, the dynamic was quite playful: there were jokes and banter, as neither the prisoners nor the guards took their new role too seriously. But this playfulness quickly dissipated, and the guards' level of control soon escalated, as the men began to inhabit their social roles (see the discussions of structure and agency throughout Chapter 3).

The experiment, originally designed to last two weeks, was cancelled after just six days, as the guards began to wield power over their 'prisoners' in problematic ways. First, the guards gave push-ups as punishment, and this escalated to

© Getty Images/Image Source

Prisons are designed to remove people's individuality and agency.

degrading, homophobic and power-laden guard-to-prisoner discourse. The tactics of interrupting prisoners' sleep and humiliating them provoked a rebellion among the prisoners, who blocked the door and removed their prisoner hats. The guards then sprayed the prisoners with a fire extinguisher, stripped them and increased the verbal humiliation. Although the men adopting these roles had not studied prisons, or received any guidance on how they should behave, Zimbardo (1972) highlighted that these are the same tactics that real guards utilize to quell resistance.

Then, borrowing a tactic used to discourage workers from forming unions, the guards gave privileges to some prisoners, and not to others. Prisoners who continued to rebel were starved. The guards then reversed the 'privilege', which further set the groups of prisoners against each other. Soon all prisoners stopped rebelling. Perhaps most illuminating, on the fifth day, when a new prisoner was brought into the scenario, he rebelled against the treatment of the prisoners. But this was no longer a favoured tactic of the longer-term prisoners, who viewed him as an unwanted troublemaker.

When one prisoner broke down, crying and shaking, he was chided by the guards for not being 'man enough'. He was asked how he would make it in San Quentin (a notoriously dangerous American prison). When this prisoner said that he wanted to quit the experiment, he was told by the other prisoners to suck it up and stay put. And, when visiting parents complained about the condition of their sons, the guards chided them.

But Zimbardo did not cancel the experiment. He was given pause to think about the issue when a colleague observed his study. On his website (Prisonexp.org), Zimbardo writes:

> I was sitting there all alone, waiting anxiously for the intruders to break in, when who should happen along but a colleague and former Yale graduate student roommate, Gordon Bower. Gordon had heard we were doing an experiment, and he came to see what was going on. I briefly described what

we were up to, and Gordon asked me a very simple question: 'Say, what's the independent variable in this study?' To my surprise, I got really angry at him. Here I had a prison break on my hands. The security of my men and the stability of my prison was at stake, and now, I had to deal with this bleeding-heart, liberal, academic, effete dingdong who was concerned about the independent variable! It wasn't until much later that I realized how far into my prison role I was at that point – that I was thinking like a prison superintendent rather than a research psychologist.

However, this intervention from a colleague did not stop the experiment immediately. Zimbardo dismissed the concerns using problematic language.

As the study continued, several other young men broke down, crying uncontrollably. One requested medical assistance, and others asked to speak to lawyers.

Zimbardo ended the study early because the behaviour of participants was becoming more dangerous, and because of another colleague's outrage regarding the issue.

The finding of the research was that the prisoners had adopted their roles so well they essentially forgot they were only involved in a college experiment. Although, according to the contracts they had signed, they were free to leave at will (losing only their pay), they had seemingly lost their agency. They had developed a form of self-imprisonment.

PAUSE FOR REFLECTION

- Identify the important findings of the research.
- Identify what ethical issues were present in both the design and execution of the research.
- Could this experiment ever be performed ethically today? If so, how might it be possible?

Discussing the ethics of the prison experiment

Zimbardo's prison experiments are well known both for their findings – of role adoption – and the ethical issues they raise. This study is infamous even beyond the world of social psychology to this day; as recently as 2010, a Hollywood movie (*The Experiment*) was based on it. The men (both prisoners and guards) learned to conform to authority and to act according to their preconceived perceptions of the roles they were assigned. Even Zimbardo was swept into overly associating with the role of warden. Clearly, role adoption is a real component of human nature and Zimbardo theorized about this from his findings. His study also resulted in changes to the way US prisons are run.

Yet Zimbardo's research is widely viewed to be *un*ethical because the students were mentally abused, and somewhat physically hurt (Fitch 2005). It is important to consider how far conditions had deteriorated by the end of the study. Zimbardo writes on his website: 'First, we had learned through videotapes that the guards were escalating their abuse of prisoners ... Their boredom had driven them to ever more pornographic and degrading abuse of the prisoners.' To use the language of abuse, and for this to be pornographic and degrading, seems to go far beyond what can be considered ethical practice.

Indeed, the academic who expressed outrage declared, 'It's terrible what you are doing to these boys!' According to Zimbardo, she had witnessed 'our prisoners being marched on a toilet run, bags over their heads, legs chained together, hands on each other's shoulders'.

It is unlikely that there was any *informed* consent about the study. Arguably, there was no outright deception at play. The students knew in theory what they were getting into, and were given the right to drop out at any time. They were also paid for their labour. Perhaps adults should be able to make such choices, and these events were probably less damaging than regularly participating in 'acceptable' activities that cause physical harm, like boxing.

Yet how free were the participants to withdraw? They were students at university, and Zimbardo was a professor. Given the power and authority context of the prison – and of Zimbardo as their 'Governor' – did the students really feel able to leave at any time? This issue may seem a more genuine concern once you have read the next case study. Similarly, how were they reminded about their option to leave, if at all?

Another issue to consider is the longer-term effects on participants. When they were reunited with Zimbardo years later, the prisoners still harboured deep emotional pain and anger from the experience. Many had attended counselling because of their participation; not only prisoners but also the guards, who felt guilt about how they had acted.

One thing that almost all people will agree upon, however, is that Zimbardo lacked significant researcher reflexivity and failed to account for his own positionality. If the research was about the adoption of roles, it is salient that he ought to have assumed people might indeed adopt their roles to a dangerous or harmful extent – including himself. It was therefore unethical to place himself into the role of warden. Had he not, he may have stopped the experiment earlier.

Case 3: Stanley Milgram and his behavioural study of obedience

In the wake of World War II, and specifically the horrors of the Holocaust, social psychologist Stanley Milgram of Yale University set out to determine if convicted war criminals, Adolf Eichmann and other Nazi officers, could argue with any justification that they were simply following orders. This would make them accomplices to these crimes rather than the instigators. His study was designed to see if a layperson would obey the commands of an authority figure to the point of violating their moral conscience.

Accordingly, while telling participants they were participating in a learning experiment, Milgram instructed an actor to pretend he was being electrically shocked. The actor was concealed from view but clearly audible to the participant. The participant asked the actor a question and, when they gave an incorrect answer, the participant was to administer what they thought was an electric shock – provoking a scream from the actor. The participant would then be instructed to continue with the experiment. With each wrong answer, the participant was told to systematically escalate the level of electric shock. Milgram (1974) summarized the experiment in his article 'The perils of obedience', writing:

> The legal and philosophic aspects of obedience are of enormous import, but they say very little about how most people behave in concrete situations. I set up a simple experiment at Yale University to test how much pain an ordinary citizen would inflict on another person simply because he was ordered to by an experimental scientist. Stark authority was pitted against the subjects' strongest moral imperatives against hurting others, and, with the subjects' ears ringing with the screams of the victims, authority won more often than not. (p. 62)

As the intensity of shocks increased, so did the actor's screams, even begging for the experiment to stop. The actor would even complain about a heart condition. Most of the participants at some point asked Milgram (the experimental scientist in the white coat) if they could stop the experiment. Milgram would respond to each request: The first time, he simply said, 'Please continue.' The next attempt to stop was met with, 'The experiment requires that you continue.' Followed by, 'It's absolutely necessary that you continue.' Finally, the participant was told, 'You have no other choice. You must go on.' If the participant again asked to stop the experiment, it was halted. Otherwise, it continued until the participant thought they had administered 450 volts (a potentially fatal shock) three times in a row.

© Photoalto

Doctors' uniforms are a sign of authority that people often do not challenge.

In the original experiment, none of the participants stopped before administering 300 volts, and 65 per cent went on to the final stage of 450 volts, three times each. Many continued to administer the shocks even though the actor had ceased to scream (as if he had died). Since the original experiment, it has been replicated and altered in numerous ways. In one study, the wall between the actor and the participant was removed, so that the shocker could see the (acted) pain the other person was experiencing. Nonetheless, the consistent finding remains that approximately two-thirds of people will administer the lethal dose of 450 volts (Blass 1999). And, of those who refused to go on, none demanded that the whole experiment be stopped altogether, and none bothered to check on the health of the person they thought they were shocking.

Milgram's shocking experiments clearly complement Zimbardo's study, but instead of studying how people adopt roles, it examines how we submit to authority.

His study shows that when people believe they are simply the instrument for carrying out another person's wishes – in particular, an authority figure – they no longer hold themselves responsible for their actions. Once this critical shift of viewpoint has occurred, people become obedient to the person who has that authority.

The findings led Milgram (1974) to develop his *agency theory*, arguing that when we receive commands from authority figures, we lose our sense of responsibility because it is diffused by others: that we lose our capacity to make our own choices because of the influence of others. Essentially, we enter an agentic-free state where we become agents of a higher authority, feeling 'responsibility to authority' but 'no responsibility for the content of our actions that the authority prescribes' (Milgram 1974: 145–146).

Many individuals who hold little institutional power or authority assume that they are supposed to carry out orders without question (Hamilton & Sanders 1999). They no longer believe they are in control of their own actions, and so become willing cogs in the group machine, carrying out the authority's orders without considering their implications or effects (ibid.). Milgram (1973) is quoted as saying:

> This is, perhaps, the most fundamental lesson of our study: ordinary people, simply doing their jobs, and without any particular hostility on their part, can become agents in a terrible destructive process. Moreover, even when the destructive effects of their work become patently clear, and they are asked to carry out actions incompatible with fundamental standards of morality, relatively few people have the resources needed to resist authority.

Later variants of the experiment show that the closer a person is to the damage they inflict, the less likely they are to comply with authority. When participants were told to place the hand of the 'learner' on the electric shock plate, conformity rates dropped to just 30 per cent. Interestingly, although women showed more distress at having to administer electric shocks, they complied equally with men. Also, when other researchers encouraged the participant to apply the shocks, compliance improved.

PAUSE FOR REFLECTION

- Identify the important findings of the research.
- Identify what ethical issues were present in the research.
- How might this experiment be performed ethically today? Is it possible?
- If the participants were forewarned that they might experience extreme psychological distress in the experiment, would that make it acceptable?

Discussing the ethics of Milgram

Like the Zimbardo prison experiments, the Milgram shocking studies have achieved iconic status (Haggerty 2004). First, they have significant findings about obedience to authority. Latane (1981) argues that Milgram's results can be interpreted through social impact theory. This theory contends that the influence of an authority figure on a person is determined by three main factors: First, the strength (or importance) of the influencer (a professor compared to a stranger on the street); second, the number of influencers; and third, the immediacy (or closeness) of the influencer. As each of these increase, levels of conformity also increase. Social impact theory can account for a large body of experimental research on conformity, compliance and obedience (Latane & Bourgeois 2001), all of which offer useful insights into the explanations of multiple social situations, including, for example, the abuse athletes are subjected to by their coaches. They are a clear example of the use of deception to achieve the study aims.

The first criterion of the need for deception is clearly met: if participants were to know the study was about when they would stand up to authority, they would be much more likely to do just that. So to get the answers, deception was seemingly necessary. But was it justified when one balances the need for deception with the possible damage to participants?

While the study did not cause any physical pain, it quite possibly created significant long-term anxiety for the participants who had provided enough electroshocks to kill another human being. Baumrind (1964) made this point, arguing that the participants were deceived into highly distressing situations.

It is likely that most of you reading this think that you would not do such a thing: that you would have the agency to say, 'No. I'm not going to shock him anymore,' or to realize that shocking someone for the sake of learning is inhumane in the first place. This could be a comforting illusion – a method of protecting one's sense of self – because 65 per cent of those Milgram studied *did not* exhibit this agency. Those individuals must now live with the fact that they lacked the resolve to stand up to authority not to kill another human being.

The study has been adapted in many ways, and one easy response would be to *lessen* the effects – not killing a person but disadvantaging them in a much less damaging way. Slater et al. (2006) have also developed a virtual experiment where participants are not dealing with real people, although the fictive nature of these experiments might harm the validity of the results. But, as they argue, few if any universities would allow the experiments as run by Milgram today – ethical practice means that alternative plans must be developed.

Beyond the unethical canon

We have started our practical discussion of ethics with these three cases because they are widely attributed as being key factors in the introduction of mandatory ethics panels for the social sciences in universities (Librett & Perrone 2010). In our experience, it would be impossible to replicate these studies today because of these ethics panels. It seems likely that these panels have helped reduce the number of unethical studies that can occur. In the next case, we discuss a contemporary ethical issue in sociology and explore its complexity.

Case 4: Alice Goffman and On the Run

Alice Goffman, daughter of the esteemed American sociologist Erving Goffman, wrote an ethnography of inner-city life and how African American communities are subject to police activity and high levels of surveillance. Published in 2015, *On the Run: Fugitive Life in an American City* details her six-year study of a poor black community in west Philadelphia, US. She embedded herself with those she studied, moving into an apartment with her participants, studying them and their social networks. They were aware she was writing her doctorate and then a book and that they were research participants, so there were no issues of consent. Goffman chronicled their lives, including their regular interactions with law enforcement. She promised them anonymity, and kept this promise.

Goffman's participants were almost constantly subject to arrest for outstanding warrants related to failure to pay fines, missing court dates and parole violations. Fearing arrest, they even had to avoid important social institutions and venues, like hospital emergency rooms, driver's licence facilities and even their own children's schools. Burdened by prior convictions, they also could not obtain jobs, forcing them into an underground economy of bartering, drug dealing, loan sharking, stealing and other illegal matters for survival.

© iStock/Tupungato

Goffman's *On the Run* demonstrates some of the challenges of doing ethnographic work related to questions of crime and criminality.

Goffman also reported a great deal of police surveillance. The people in her study were regularly subject to stop-and-search procedures, the searching of their homes and a constant state of police monitoring. She also documented police violence; she 'watched the police punch, choke, kick, stomp on, or beat young men with their nightsticks' (p. 4).

For bringing all this to light, *On the Run* has been highly praised by both the sociological community as well as the literary world. However, her work drew criticism, too. Firstly, people have cast doubt on the accuracy of some of her reports. Several incidents seem implausible, or highly embellished. One example is of an 11-year-old being arrested for riding as a passenger in a stolen car – something that is not illegal in Philadelphia.

However, there may be a larger problem: Goffman appears to indicate that she participated in a major crime in the course of her fieldwork. In an appendix, she discusses the murder of one of her closest participants. Placing herself at the scene of his death, she then writes, 'the hunt was on to find the man who had killed Chuck' (p. 261). Her other participants believed they could identify the killer. Armed, they drove around the city looking to enact their revenge. Goffman took notes on this and also described driving the car:

> We started out around 3:00 a.m., with Mike in the passenger seat, his hand on his Glock [pistol] as he directed me around the area. We peered into dark houses and looked at license plates and car models as Mike spoke on the phone with others who had information about [the suspected killer's] whereabouts.

One night, Mike thought he saw his target:

> He tucked his gun in his jeans, got out of the car, and hid in the adjacent alleyway. I waited in the car with the engine running, ready to speed off as soon as Mike ran back and got inside. (p. 262)

Mike decided that he had the wrong man, and nobody was shot that night.

PAUSE FOR REFLECTION

- Identify the important findings of Goffman's research.
- What ethical issues were present in her research?
- As a sociologist, would it be acceptable for her to engage in a serious crime?
- Had Goffman refused to drive the car, should she also have called the police to tell them that she had reason to believe the men she was studying were looking to commit murder?

Discussing the ethics of On the Run

On the Run is one of the most controversial sociology books of recent years. It is important to recognize how well received Goffman's book was by many people. Respected academics reviewed it very positively for the critique it developed of how police surveillance damaged the lives of African American communities – an issue that was particularly topical, exemplified by the Black Lives Matter movement (see Chapter 9, p. 232). Her call for criminal justice reform was viewed positively by many experts in the area.

Yet the book has also been criticized in relation to ethical concerns. An academic, Steven Lubet, published a critique of *On the Run* (http://newramblerreview.com/book-reviews/law/ethics-on-the-run), arguing that Goffman had admitted to committing conspiracy to murder. After contacting several law officials, he quotes a former prosecutor from the Philadelphia District Attorney's office saying, 'She's flat out confessed to conspiring to commit murder and could be charged and convicted based on this account right now.' Lubet also questioned the accuracy of some of the claims in the book, arguing that some were logistically very improbable.

Reminiscent of Zimbardo, an issue appears to be that Goffman adopted the role of participant too much – she went native. Goffman wrote, 'I did not get into the car with Mike because I wanted to learn first-hand about violence. I got into the car because … I wanted Chuck's killer to die' (p. 263). She added, 'Looking back, I'm glad that I learned what it feels like to want a man to die – not simply to understand the desire for vengeance in others, but to feel it in my bones' (ibid.). That, Lubet argues, is an alarming confession from an ethnographer.

Goffman provided a revision of this episode that characterized the activity not as a hunt for revenge but a ritual of mourning for a dead friend. This opens up a related critique: that the seeming factual errors in *On the Run* are not the result of ethical problems, but of a writing style that sacrifices some elements of truth for a more powerful narrative.

This issue of writing style is at the heart of some of the debate about *On the Run*. Quoted in a *New York Times* article about the debate (Lewis-Kraus 2016), sociologist Victor Rios critiqued Goffman for writing too much for a public audience rather than a sociological one. He is quoted as saying, 'How much do we sacrifice to become public intellectuals? … At the end of the day, we have to be careful about how much pandering we do to the masses.'

Yet perhaps Goffman has a legitimate claim to write a different form of sociology than that preferred by Rios. Perhaps a journalistic style has the power to draw attention to systemic, racist inequalities in the criminal justice system. The balance between total accuracy and telling a story that is honest to the broader context is an ethical issue with no easy formula. What do you think the answer should be?

The question is whether total accuracy is more important than developing the power of an argument. If we opt for total accuracy, how is that squared with the accepted technique that sociologists should change data somewhat to protect a participant's identity? A behaviour could be unethical if related purely to the form of the sociological argument, but ethical when related to the bigger-picture ethical process. Is that appropriate?

Others have argued that the flaws with *On the Run* are not the fault of Goffman but of an ethics process that requires anonymity and confidentiality for participants. Following the issues raised by Humphreys' *Tearoom Trade*, Goffman also had to destroy her fieldnotes – making it more likely that, over the course of writing a book, errors might creep in. Keeping track of fieldnotes and pseudonyms is difficult, and Goffman's period of data collection lasted six years. Some errors are to be expected, and some of the strongest critiques have come from non-sociologists who might not be aware of these practical complexities.

Undoubtedly, *On the Run* is a provocative book about complex issues. Research on criminal behaviour is often more difficult to evaluate ethically. A key question concerns the ethics of reporting crimes to the police. Goffman witnessed many crimes, and never reported them. This was approved by her ethics committee and is standard practice in criminological research. But are there limits to this? At what stage should an individual's safety trump the data collected? And what should Goffman do in such a situation?

PROVOCATION 5: University ethics panels are damaging novel sociological research

Following the ethical issues raised by our first three case studies, all universities now require their researchers to undergo an ethics approval process for every study that involves human beings. These are called Institutional Review Boards in the US, and Ethics Panels or Committees elsewhere. There are clearly several reasons for this: one is legitimately to protect participants and researchers; another is to protect universities from litigation.

There are benefits, undoubtedly, to a mandatory ethical process. But the existence of these boards may not be entirely beneficial to sociological research (Lincoln & Tierney 2004; Reed 2010).

Most disciplines involve some ethical dimensions to consider: some have huge implications for society. Research that seeks to splice genes for the betterment of the human condition, but could also in theory lead to the creation of designer babies or super-humans, clearly has profound philosophical questions at its heart. Similarly, medical research can present life-changing opportunities as well as dangers – and participants may well face severe risks from these studies. Ethics panels here have a great deal to discuss and bear significant responsibility.

While sociology engages with important questions, we cannot think of many issues that are on a par with even the standard cases of medical research. For the most part, sociological research is fairly benign.

Consider this: even the most egregious examples of ethical violations we highlighted in this chapter were committed decades ago by psychologists who may have caused some harm. But, in the end, nobody died or was gravely injured. Society was not irreparably damaged. Haggerty (2004) concurs, writing, 'notwithstanding the iconic status of the early examples, the harms that social science ethics committees routinely try to mitigate are generally of a considerably lower magnitude' (p. 400).

It also seems obvious that the types of things a sociologist might do that are seriously unethical are likely covered – and prohibited – by law, anyhow. In the case of Goffman, the ethics of her situation are pretty much guided by the law – with the sociological practice that she need not report minor crimes or those that are specifically related to her research activities.

But why does this matter? If the relatively minor inconvenience of filling out some paperwork makes a sociologist think twice about ethical practice, isn't that a good thing? Well, that is a positive aspect certainly, but it does not include the negative issues involved with ethical review.

While ethical review processes were primarily developed to protect the welfare of participants and defend universities from litigation, ethics review panels today have actually evolved to wield significant power over the types of methods and topics sociologists can pursue (Hammersley 2010). The review process normally includes assessing proposed interview and survey questions – meaning the panel has the power to exclude types of questions and dictate how participants should be recruited.

This all means that ethics panels can and do restrict the autonomy of academics in designing research and its methods (Jamie 2013). This is because the structure and make-up of these boards has largely taken the control of methodological decisions away from academics with expertise in the specific research area under investigation, shifting it towards bureaucrats whose primary concern is minimizing risk for the institution (Boden et al. 2009) rather than pushing the boundaries of scholarship.

Haggerty (2004: 291) describes this as the 'creep' of institutional review processes, arguing that academics in the social sciences are 'currently witnessing the emergence of a host of new fetters on our knowledge production endeavors' (see also Hammersley 2010). This is of especial concern for topics that boards often deem 'sensitive', including sexuality. Here, the conservatism of bureaucratic institutions can stifle research. The retelling of the same issues that we covered in this chapter, like Zimbardo and Milgram, has contributed to this creep. This is because they build up fear in novice ethics committee members, socializing them into an exaggerated concern about reproducing these worst-case scenarios, while simultaneously legitimizing the entire ethics review process. Thus, when institution review boards, or ethics committees, are in place, sociologists may be limited in the topics they can study because of squeamish institutional review board members who are usually not experts in the subject area that the researcher is working in.

There are many ways this can occur. We have direct experience of ethics review panels asking for more revisions in studies on sexuality than in other areas. In one study on pornography consumption, it was demanded that we have a full plan in place in case any participants disclosed watching child pornography – this was not the topic under discussion and child pornography represents a tiny proportion of porn.

You might argue that this is a perfectly acceptable request given the criminality of watching such material. The problem is the uneven application of rules: if this query is applicable for pornography consumption, a study on driving should demand that the researcher consider what happens if the driver discloses a hit-and-run crime in their past; a study on student athletes should demand that the researcher consider what happens if they disclose physical, psychological or sexual abuse by coaches. Yet these requests tend not to happen. It is an uneven application of the same guidance.

The question becomes: do ethics panels allow sociologists to conduct research into sensitive issues? The sociologist may be researching undercover crimes or marginalized groups. An ethical review process that is overly concerned about the threat to the university, and not sufficiently focused on the need for the study, can have a chilling effect on sociological research.

Another reason that ethics review panels have hurt sociological research is that social science research often needs to adapt methods *in situ*. Some scholars have thus argued that there is limited potential for methodological innovation from research that needs to be pre-approved (Taylor & Coffey 2009). In short, researchers often do not feel able to respond to events as they unfold because they are scripted by their prior ethics approval for what they can do. This means that novel methods are difficult to trial, and the less structured a study is, the less 'safe' it is considered to be (cf. McCormack et al. 2013).

Ethical review boards protect against unethical practice. But they do so at a cost to methodological innovation and the autonomy of academics to pursue research that may be deemed sensitive or provocative. Sociologists must ensure that their research and practice is ethical. We are not convinced, however, that ethical review boards as they currently operate are the best way of ensuring this.

Provoked? Read further:

Boden, R., Epstein, D. & Latimer, J. (2009). Accounting for ethos or programmes for conduct? The brave new world of research ethics committees. *The Sociological Review*, 57(4), 727–749.

McCormack, M., Adams, A. & Anderson, E. (2013). Taking to the streets: The benefits of spontaneous methodological innovation in participant recruitment. *Qualitative Research*, 13(2), 228–241.

Guillemin, M. & Gillam, L. (2004). Ethics, reflexivity, and 'ethically important moments' in research. *Qualitative Inquiry*, 10(2), 261–280.

CONCLUSION

This chapter has explored what it means for sociology to be ethical. Laying out a framework for thinking about ethics within sociological research, we highlight that this goes far further than being ethical when collecting data: thinking about ethics is important when identifying the topic right through to disseminating findings – or even, in some cases, deciding not to publish them at all. We then explored ethical sociology by discussing studies which have been deemed *unethical*. Examining the reasons why individual studies were unethical in some areas enabled us to think more critically about how we may all be ethical in our own research.

HOW WOULD...?

» How would you ensure that your sociology is ethical?

   » Go back to Chapter 4 and think about your answer to the study you would design in that chapter's *How would ...?* section.

   » Are there aspects that were unethical? How might you change these? Could thinking about ethics improve your study?

» If you are based in a different discipline, how would your own subject area think about ethics? Are there key differences? Is the emphasis different?

» Do you have concerns about how you can be ethical in your academic practice in the future? How might you address these?

STRUCTURED FURTHER READING

Israel, M. & Hay, I. (2006). *Research Ethics for Social Scientists*. London: SAGE.
This book encourages knowledge of research ethics in practice. It interrogates the practices that have contributed to the adversarial relationships between researchers

and regulators. Finally, the book hopes to encourage both parties to develop shared solutions to ethical and regulatory problems.

Tolich, M. (2014). What can Milgram and Zimbardo teach ethics committees and qualitative researchers about minimizing harm? *Research Ethics,* 10(2), 86–96.

This article highlights that neither Zimbardo nor Milgram set out to be unethical and that modern ethics reviews would prevent the problems associated with each study if they were to commence today. The second aim is to examine how sociologists, including the authors of this book, routinely demonize these classic psychological studies, but fail to identify a number of recent examples of ethically dubious qualitative research from their own fields.

Calvey, D. (2017). *Covert Research: The Art, Politics and Ethics of Undercover Fieldwork.* London: SAGE.

We have discussed the issues with covert research in this chapter. However, they remain an interesting source of data as well as a contested methodology. This book argues for covert research, drawing on interesting sociological studies to make the case.

 Visit the companion website at www.macmillanihe.com/mccormack for further learning and teaching resources.

Chapter 6
STRUCTURES AND INSTITUTIONS

INTRODUCTION

Social life is highly organized and standardized in many ways. But it is not always clear *how* this organization occurs because much of it is implicit and taken for granted. Sociologists are interested in uncovering this hidden organization of society and a key way of doing so is through researching social structures and institutions. This chapter will begin by defining social structures and institutions before examining four important institutions which shape our behaviour and help to organize our social world: family, education, media and work. In our Provocation, we question whether Western societies are really meritocratic or whether the term itself fosters inequality.

THE STRUCTURES OF SOCIETY

Ever since the work of Marx, Durkheim and Weber, sociologists have approached society from two different perspectives (see Chapter 4). One group has tried to understand how and why individuals act, looking at their agency and the meanings developed in social interaction (a Weberian approach). The other perspective, the one we focus on in this chapter, interrogates the social structures of society – invisible frameworks which organize the social world around us and our interactions with each other (the approach of Marx and Durkheim).

A structural perspective contends that these structures exist outside of, and have primacy over, the individual. Individuals are constrained to act in the limited ways that are available in society (we discussed the *structure-agency debate* in Chapter 3). Social structures are supported, maintained and reproduced through social institutions, which we now turn to look at.

What is an institution?

When you hear the word 'institution', what do you think of? Perhaps a place or building, possibly an old hospital for people with mental health problems. Yet when sociologists discuss institutions, they are most often talking about social institutions, which sit within the wider structures in society. Social institutions can be defined as 'systems of established and embedded social rules that structure social interactions' (Hodgson 2006: 18). In other words, they embody the 'rules of the game' (North 1990: 3), determining how to behave appropriately in a particular society.

Some of these rules are upheld by **formal institutions**, such as the law, and are enforced by official agencies such as police, prosecutors and the judiciary. Formal institutions will often have buildings or places associated with them – we can think of courthouses that relate to the judiciary; prisons that relate to the police; and schools that relate to education. Yet the buildings themselves do not make the institution, they just consolidate it. Formal institutions are comprised of expectations and conventions, while the buildings are the physical spaces where these expectations are enforced.

Other rules are learned through **informal institutions**, like cultural customs and taboos, where rules are not written and enforced by agencies but are taken for granted and important to fitting in. These norms, usually unwritten, are created, communicated and enforced outside officially sanctioned channels.

Think about driving a car. Driving has many rules and conventions, some of which are upheld by formal institutions and others by informal institutions. Adhering to the speed limit and not driving while drunk are examples of conventions that are transmitted by the formal institution of law and enforced by agencies like the police. However, raising your hand to thank another driver who waited for you is a convention that is transmitted informally – by word of mouth and observation. These kind of actions are not enshrined in law but you might face social reprimand if you do not follow these informal rules.

Both formal and informal institutions can constrain and enable individual behaviour. The influence of institutions and the conventions they transmit means that individuals are pressured to act consistently with the dominant norms and expectations of their society. This is inherently constraining because it places limitations on people's behaviours. But, institutions and conventions can also give us choices and make life easier and safer. Take again the example of driving: traffic lights force us to stop in particular places where we might not want to, but this also means that traffic flows more freely and safely.

Organizations are important parts of social institutions, although they can be conflated. For example, a university is an organization which sits within the larger institution of higher education. There are lots of universities (organizations), but only one overarching institution of higher education that educates adults to a particular standard.

Yet some sociologists will refer to organizations, such as an individual university, as an institution. This is because although the organization is part of a larger social institution, the organization itself might have its own particular norms and rules. This makes it an institution itself, while also being an organization within a larger institution.

Organizations and institutions tend to develop particular cultures which are unique to them, known as *institutional* or *organizational cultures*. These cultures can range from benevolent to exclusionary, which means that they purposefully or unknowingly exclude certain groups of people. This exclusion can be symbolic, where a group is made to feel unwelcome, or literal, where certain people cannot be a part of an organization because of some characteristic (like age, gender or race). We discuss issues of social exclusion and division in Chapter 7.

> **Formal institutions:** rules, such as the law, that are enforced by official agencies

> **Informal institutions:** cultural customs and taboos, where rules are not written and enforced but are important to 'fitting in' in a culture

> **Organizations:** physical entities that consolidate the norms and values and do the work of a particular institution

Consider the example of high finance. McDowell (2011) draws attention to how this institutional culture disadvantages women. Explicit forms of exclusion include overt sexism (e.g. overlooking women for promotion) and the prevalence of a masculine culture wherein demeaning or inappropriate actions are excused as supposedly harmless jokes. Covertly, the organization of work tasks, such as timing work hours and events that make balancing caring responsibilities and paid work challenging, has a greater impact on women because more women are in caring positions than men.

These covert and explicit issues do not only impact on those women who already work in the sector. They can also discourage women from wanting to work in high finance because of this institutional culture. Thus, the highly masculine culture is self-perpetuating, and will continue to dominate these workplaces, meaning that women will continue to be effectively excluded from participating in this highly paid and high-status profession.

TYPES OF SOCIAL INSTITUTION

We now turn to look at four key social institutions that shape our behaviour and our interactions with other people – family, education, media and work. These institutions are a vital part of social life in the modern era, but they are still culturally and historically located. That is to say, although the four institutions we examine in this chapter are universal to almost all societies now and throughout history, the way they look and work is dependent on time and place. The Western concept of family, for example, is notably different now from 200 years ago because we live in a different economic, social and technological time. Similarly, the family in nomadic tribal communities today are quite unlike those in the Western world. The nature of the institutions we describe below have all only very recently emerged in their current forms in Western societies following the industrial revolutions there during the 18th and 19th centuries.

FAMILY

The word 'family' can evoke many images: one's own parents or guardians; a friend's parents; imagined future children; or maybe a fictional family from TV or a novel. The dominant Western cultural image of family is what has been called the '**nuclear family**' – a married heterosexual couple and their two biological children who live together in one house. Despite the many different forms that families take in the Western world, this is still the most common representation.

Nuclear family: a heterosexual couple and their genetically related offspring

The small nuclear family unit has traditionally been assumed to be the most emotionally and economically stable model, and to provide children with a balanced upbringing by having two parents of different sexes. Non-nuclear family types have always existed, and these include same-sex parents, families headed by a single parent, reconstituted families with step-parents and stepchildren, families in which children have been adopted, among many others. We are much more accepting of these diverse family forms today than in the past. Historically, people whose family

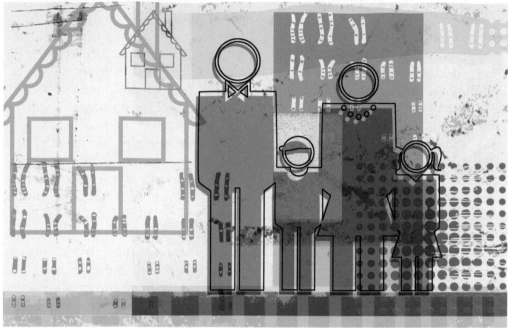

© Photodisc/Getty Images

In what ways might the idea of a so-called 'nuclear family' be unhelpful and even unhealthy?

circumstances did not conform to the nuclear family model were highly stigmatized and some, particularly single mothers, experienced a great deal of ill-treatment (see Keating 2009).

Sociologists have extensively researched the family, its role in society and the ways that families are changing. The family is understood as a key informal social institution supporting the broader social structures of society. It is understood as an informal institution because it is not an officially sanctioned or organized body, though, as we will see later, it occupies an ambiguous position, being simultaneously public and private. The primary role of the family is the socialization of children (see p. 8), which teaches children the appropriate ways to behave, ensures social order and, thus, maintains the broad social structure.

Types of socialization

Socialization is an important concept in sociology of the family. As we saw in Chapter 1, socialization is a learning process where people learn the norms and expectations of a particular society. It is often split into *primary* and *secondary* socialization. Primary socialization occurs early on in life and is usually led by a child's family. During primary socialization, children learn from their parents or carers the attitudes, values and actions that are appropriate in a particular society. Secondary socialization occurs after the initial learning through the family unit and involves children learning to behave appropriately around people with whom they do not have an emotional connection – for example, at school. As such, secondary socialization entails a degree of negotiation and decision-making by children as they learn to participate successfully in society. Socialization is not just limited to childhood, it is a lifelong process in which we are constantly learning the most appropriate ways to successfully be part of a society.

Functionalism and the family

Talcott Parsons (1902–1979) is perhaps the best-known sociologist of the family. As a structural functionalist (see Chapter 3), he was interested in describing the ways in which institutions work to maintain the structure and function of society. For Parsons, the nuclear family unit evolved to fit the economic and social needs of industrial capitalist societies (Parsons & Bales 1955). Within this ideal nuclear family, men took on the 'instrumental' role of breadwinner and family leadership, while women became responsible for the emotional wellbeing and domestic work in the family through their 'expressive role'. Though many women also worked outside the home, men tended to have the higher-paid jobs while women still bore the responsibility for all the domestic work. According to Parsons, these gendered roles were complementary and enabled the nuclear family to fulfil its two main functions – primary socialization (see textbox) and the stabilization of adult personalities.

The gendered division of labour meant that the family had become a sanctuary for men from the stresses of work, one in which they were looked after by their wives. Through this care, men's emotions and personalities stabilized, supposedly making them better workers and reducing the amount of conflict in society in general. This understanding is referred to as the **warm bath theory** because the family unit is thus like a soothing warm bath that men can relax into after a day at work.

Notably, the family is not seen as a sanctuary for women. Instead, women are expected to create and maintain a supportive physical and emotional environment within the family, not to benefit from it. Here, the family is a site of gender inequality (see Chapter 7).

For many years, the nuclear family was regarded as the 'ideal' family form. Other types of family were stigmatized and discredited, and this oppression was often hidden within moral ideals. Homophobia, for example, was frequently phrased in terms of the immorality of homosexuality, with much of this framed as concern that gay relationships would undermine the nuclear family. Indeed, the political aims of these claims are apparent when one considers other similar prejudices: such as, for example, that having children with someone from a different racial group (known as **miscegenation**) was illegal in the US until 1967.

Functionalist perspectives on family endorsed the nuclear family model, but they have been widely critiqued. David Cooper (1971), a Marxist scholar, argued that the idealized functionalist image of the nuclear family ignores the true purpose of the socialization of children, which he contends is to indoctrinate them into their role within the exploitative capitalist system. Furthermore, Parsons' understanding of the family is outdated, failing to account for the diversity of family forms that exist today (Scott & Schwartz 2008), particularly mixed-race couples, same-sex couples, single parents and adoptive parents. It also ignored the harm caused to these groups of people, when such families were heavily stigmatized and censured.

Perhaps the most pervasive critiques of the functionalist perspective have come from feminist scholars, who argued that the traditional nuclear family reproduced patriarchal norms. Part of this was because of a different focus on the family (Delamont 2003): while functionalist approaches examined the structure and role of families within society, feminists investigated the relationships and interactions *within families*. As we discuss in Chapter 7, second-wave feminist scholars of the 1970s drew attention to the limitations that traditional gender roles placed on women's

Warm bath theory: used by Parsons and Bales (1955) to compare the nuclear family to a warm bath which men could relax after a long day working outside the home

Miscegenation: having children with someone from a different racial group

employment opportunities outside the home and the financial power that this gave husbands over their wives (Greer 1970). Anne Oakley (1974) drew attention to the unrecognized value of the domestic work that women in traditional gender roles performed. Others argued that women who worked outside the home had to undertake a 'triple shift' of paid labour, unpaid domestic work and **emotional labour**: taking care of the family's wellbeing, such as the emotional stabilization of men (Duncombe & Marsden 1995). This can be read as a critique of the warm bath theory in functionalist approaches. Indeed, for functionalists, the nuclear family was thought to reduce conflict in society, but, for feminists, the family itself was understood as the site of conflict.

> **Emotional labour:** work that involves emotions rather than just doing activities

Children, families and emotion

Children are often considered to be a central part of families. Family gatherings are frequently characterized, certainly in cultural representations of them, as having young children as the centre of attention. And yet the notion of children as central to family is not without its problems. Not everyone has children; not everyone *can* have children and not everyone *wants* to have children. We have asked some lecture classes how many students want children, and the great majority raise their hand. Yet when one or two say they actively do not want children, there is often a gasp from some of the other students – the thought of not raising children is that shocking to them. Indeed, there is a lot of societal pressure on people, particularly women, to have children and those without children often find themselves subject to negative stereotypes and stigma (Park 2002). Given this, the term 'child-free' has been suggested for use instead of 'child-less' as the latter attaches negative connotations to a life without children (see Gillespie 2003).

However, the emotions around having children are not restricted to whether to have them, but *when* to have children if you do. There are many negative stereotypes about young parents, particularly mothers (Yardley 2008), but women who have children later in life are also subject to negative stereotyping (Whitley & Kirmayer 2008). This, again, involves not just the parents deciding to have children but also wider society: for example, if people have children too young, it is widely assumed that the State will have to support them, through benefits and welfare packages (Brown 2015).

No matter the age of parents when their children are born, the experience of being a parent is also emotionally charged. Children are assumed to be future citizens and, therefore, how they are raised is deemed public business – even before they are born. Given this, Longhurst (1999) draws attention to the scrutiny that pregnant women often find themselves subjected to, particularly receiving unwanted comments on their behaviours and unwelcome touching of their stomachs. You can also see this kind of public interest in action if you think about guidance for pregnant women on what not to eat, drink and do; although the guidance is about what *mothers* should (not) do, the intention is the wellbeing of the foetus.

Policy debates and the family

Although families are usually seen as private, they are subject to a great deal of public scrutiny. This does not mean that every family unit will be highly scrutinized, but

VOX POP Becoming a young mother: Holly's story

© iStock/Halfpoint

I found out I was pregnant when I was 16 and I had my son at 17. It wasn't planned and I wasn't prepared for a baby at all, but I decided to keep it. My family were pretty upset when I told them I was pregnant and my dad didn't speak to me for about a month. I think they thought I'd ruined my life, but after my son was born, they fell in love with him.

I took a year away from college and then started doing my qualifications part time because I get financial help with the nursery fees. I'm starting university this year, so I don't feel like I'm doing anything different to my friends that didn't have babies young. I just feel like I'm doing it a few years later but the whole pregnancy and babies thing is out of the way for me now.

There can be lots of negative attitudes about young mums and you do get comments from people about it. When you first have your baby, you're really worried about being a rubbish mother and I stayed at home for months because I was really not confident. But then you realize that everyone has that no matter what age you have your babies. Now I just don't care. My son is fed and happy and that's all that matters. If people comment, I just ignore them or tell them to mind their own business.

(Note: 'Holly' is a pseudonym, and neither she nor her child are shown in the accompanying photograph.)

Reflection

» What do you think about Holly's story?

» Do you agree that there are lots of negative attitudes about young mothers? If so, what are these? How are they spread?

» If adolescence is criticized as a 'bad' time to have children, and so is waiting 'too long', do you think there is ever a societally acceptable 'good' time to have children – and if so, why is that time deemed 'better'?

that the notion of 'family' is subject to a great deal of debate. Take the example of *in vitro* fertilization (IVF), which is the technique of fertilizing a woman's egg outside the body. The process involves harvesting eggs from a woman's body, implanting sperm directly into the egg in a laboratory and then re-implanting the zygote (the cells which form when an egg is fertilized) into a woman's womb with the intention of establishing a successful pregnancy. IVF is used by couples who are unable to conceive naturally either because of fertility problems or because they are a same-sex couple. IVF has been heavily debated for several reasons.

There are debates about who should pay for IVF (see Chapter 10 for discussion of social policy). In countries with nationalized healthcare systems, the crux of this debate is whether having children is a lifestyle choice (so the health service should not pay to help people have children) or a right (so the health service should pay). It seems that the policy answer is somewhere in the middle. In the UK, for example, the National Health Service (NHS) pays for two or three cycles of IVF (this varies by region) and then couples have to pay for additional attempts themselves – the success rate of IVF for under 35s is around 32 per cent, though this declines as women get older. However, given that IVF is very expensive, some couples will be unable to pay and so may look to adoption, which in itself involves a great deal of policy debate about personal life.

Secondly, there are policy questions about who should be able to access those IVF services that are paid for by national healthcare services. Before 2008, in the UK single and lesbian women were unable to have IVF paid for by the NHS. Today, same-sex couples and single women can use NHS IVF services, though there are still criteria governing who is eligible: only women under 40 and those who are still not pregnant after 12 months of unprotected sex or 12 attempts at artificial insemination (directly inserting sperm into a woman's womb without having intercourse) are able to apply for IVF through the NHS; everyone else has to pay.

There are often additional criteria, such as being a non-smoker and a healthy weight. Although these are positioned as being for clinical efficiency reasons (because IVF is less likely to work for unhealthy people), there is also arguably a moral imperative to this which could be read as an attempt to ensure only 'well-behaved' people are supported in having children.

Extreme rules around children and families also exist. For 36 years, from 1979 until 2015, China enforced a law that mandated that couples were only allowed to have one baby, in order to curb overpopulation – known as the 'one-child policy'. While there were exceptions, particularly for ethnic minorities and parents whose first child was a girl, this law meant that the Chinese government enforced coercive birth planning that caused considerable human suffering (Whyte et al. 2015). This provides a radically different image of the family, and social policy related to the family, than that in many Western countries.

Yet regardless of how the family is framed – whether it focuses on parents, grandparents or children, or brothers and sisters to aunts and uncles, nephews and nieces, pets, or close friends who are not blood relations – the family is a place where people are supposed to care for each other beyond State intervention. It is likely that a family member will be your next of kin as well as your emergency contact number on your phone. Even so, families occupy an ambiguous position in society. As an institution, they are simultaneously isolated and private, but yet are charged with enormous responsibility for bringing up the next generation of citizens and workers, which necessitates some degree of public and policy involvement. Of course, the first time where families recede in importance in a child's life is when they start school and enter the institution of education.

EDUCATION

Education socializes children into the norms, values and expectations of the society in which they live (Boronski & Hassan 2015). Although upper-class boys, historically considered to be the future leaders of society, have always been educated in one way or another, universal and compulsory education was not established until the

19th century in Western societies. In the UK, the Elementary Education Act of 1880 made schooling compulsory for everyone. In the US, education was made compulsory between 1852 and 1917, and in Australia, this happened between 1830 and 1870. Prior to compulsory education, the teaching of children had been provided in an ad hoc manner, with schools established by churches, private philanthropists and industrial organizations. Provision was variable across different areas and countries.

There was significant resistance to compulsory and universal education because many people believed that educating the poor would lead to revolution. In the UK, for example, in an 1807 debate about compulsory education, British Conservative Member of Parliament Davies Giddy commented that

> giving education to the labouring classes of the poor ... would, in effect, be found to be prejudicial to their morals and happiness; it would teach them to despise their lot in life, instead of making them good servants in agriculture and other laborious employments to which their rank in society had destined them; instead of teaching them the virtue of subordination, it would render them factious and refractory. (cited in Chitty 2007: 15)

Giddy was concerned that educating the poor would alert them to the injustice they suffered and awaken a desire to be more than servants to the upper classes. He was not necessarily wrong in this prediction; it's just that most of us would see this as an argument *for* education, not against.

A Marxist (see Chapter 2) would argue that Giddy was worried that the poor would become aware of their **false consciousness** and rebel against the upper classes, potentially overturning the entrenched class structure. We might suspect that not only was Giddy concerned about disrupting existing social structures more generally but also directly concerned about his own position given that he was a very wealthy member of the classes oppressing the poor.

Despite such opposition, calls for universal education increased and included individuals and groups with privileged social status, such as church leaders and education activists. Voices of opposition were soon in the minority and eventually universal education became the norm across the Western world. Education was constructed as a way through which poorer children would be able to improve their lives and enter into a social class above their parents (Morrish 1970). We return to this idealized goal below.

False consciousness: the state of mind where the proletariat are unaware of the inequality of their situation because class and wealth stratification is thought to be the natural order of social life

Theorizing education

Sociologists have analysed education as a social institution from a variety of perspectives. For Durkheim ([1925] 2011), school not only instilled shared common values that ensured a functional society, such as hard work and respect for authority, but also taught children the skills needed for highly specialized roles in the labour market. Whereas in pre-industrial societies these roles would have been learned within the family unit, where work occurred, in industrial societies Durkheim believed that school provided this socialization.

Parsons also saw school as important for the socialization of children to ensure the functionality of society. For Parsons, schools instilled the value of achievement which cannot be learned within the family because of the fixed nature of a person's status within that unit (Parsons & Bales 1955). In other words, you cannot work hard and achieve your status as a son or daughter in a family – that is set from birth and cannot be changed – but you can work hard in school and achieve higher status in later professional life.

Marxist scholars have also understood education as an agent of socialization but have highlighted how schools have trained children to become the right type of workers for capitalism. Bowles and Gintis (1976) argued that there is a 'correspondence' between the routines and structures of school life and the routines and structures of working life; listening to teachers and following their instructions is markedly similar to listening to bosses and following theirs. Schools, therefore, do not just provide students with the right knowledge and skills to be productive future workers but also train children in personality, personal appearance, self-presentation and social class identification.

An important addition to debates in education came from the 'new sociology of education' that emphasized the socially constructed nature of the curriculum, arguing that what counts as knowledge in schools is the result of power relations that benefit the State (see Brooks et al. 2013). There was a call for significantly more qualitative research that could foreground meaning and experience in school while also recognizing that such knowledge is constructed through individuals' interactions and interpretations (see Chapter 3).

In this model, sociologists have argued that there is a *hidden curriculum* in education which trains children to accept the status quo of how the world is. Proponents of this perspective argue that as well as overtly teaching students knowledge about particular subjects, school implicitly teaches children the norms and expectations of the class system and their place within it. Through school, children are taught to 'know their place and to sit still in it' (Illich 1971: 41).

This hidden curriculum is not just taught through the lessons themselves but also implicitly through other elements of school like the teacher's power, the architecture of the school, the use of language and the use of school uniform. Think about this last example in terms of the hidden curriculum. Firstly, school uniform reproduces a gender status quo. It is, generally, culturally unacceptable for boys to wear school skirts and might even be against school rules. This reproduces the idea of a fundamental difference between boys and girls which is made visible through their clothes. There is often concern in schools about the length of girls' skirts, with occasional sensationalist media reports of skirts being measured and girls being sent home for wearing them too short (Ahlum & Fralley 1976). This perpetuates the idea that from an early age women's clothing is subject to public scrutiny and even punishment when it does not match expectations of propriety.

PAUSE FOR REFLECTION

Did you wear a school uniform when you went to school? What did you feel about wearing it? Why do you think that the great majority of schools make pupils wear a uniform?

It is often argued that school uniform can make social class differences invisible as all children are required to dress the same (Craik 2003). But is this really true? The uniforms are also only the same within each school. Consider how uniforms differ between elite, fee-paying schools and the poorer schools that are free to attend and run by the State. Not only are the uniforms at elite, fee-paying schools far more expensive, they are often more tightly governed and carry connotations of wealth, power and status. Some schools require uniforms to be bought from a specific (expensive) shop; they may also require a sport uniform as well, increasing costs further. In this context, school uniform reproduces class inequality.

© Christopher Furlong/Staff/Getty Images

A closer inspection of the pros and cons of school uniforms is a great example of the sociological imagination in action.

And think about how it felt when you went from wearing a uniform to not wearing one. In the UK, uniforms tend to be mandatory between the ages of 5 and 16, but for the ages 17 to 18 many students can wear their own clothes. This is about more than class, also signifying a shift to adulthood and self-dependence. In these schools, you are also expected to do more independent work. The logic would suggest that uniforms also confer the notion of childhood and implies – or encourages – a level of docility in the wearer (as also indicated during the Zimbardo prison experiment that we examined in Chapter 5, p. 116).

Education and social mobility

Social mobility:
the change in
social status
that a person
achieves over
the course of
their lives

Social mobility almost underpins stated education policy. **Social mobility** refers to the change in social status that a person achieves in a set period (Roberts 2011), or the difference between an adult's income, professional standing and social class position relative to their parents. For example, a barrister whose parents were unskilled or low-skilled workers we would define as being socially mobile.

Sociologists have largely disputed the claim that education is a vehicle for social mobility. Working-class children tend to do worse in education than their middle-class counterparts. Yet most concur that working-class children are no less intelligent than their middle-class counterparts. Why then do working-class children, generally, achieve lower grades and have lower attendance at elite universities?

Most sociologists agree that this is because we do not live in a **meritocracy**. Instead, sociologists have shown that structures of inequality which exist in society (between genders, socio-economic classes and ethnicities) are reproduced through the education system at all levels.

Lampert (2012) has compared the education system to **social Darwinism**, where inequalities are justified as the 'natural' result of a meritocracy. Borrowing from Charles Darwin's natural selection theory (famously summarized by English philosopher Herbert Spencer as 'the survival of the fittest'), Lampert argues that the notion of meritocracy is used to justify the relative underachievement of some students as purely the result of their lack of ability or hard work. This justification, he contends, masks other factors and inequalities (such as material deprivation) which impact on student achievement and leave certain groups of students 'behind'. Sociologists and educationalists have demonstrated that children from lower socio-economic groups get 'left behind' in education at a very early age and never catch up (see Jackson & Marsden 2012; Reay 2017).

> **Meritocracy:** a social system in which people succeed and are rewarded based on talent and ability alone

> **Social Darwinism:** the theory that individuals and groups are subject to the same Darwinian laws of natural selection as plants and animals (i.e. survival of the fittest)

Radical alternatives to formal education

Radical philosopher Ivan Illich (1971) argued that societies need to move away from compulsory education altogether, a process he called 'deschooling'. Illich was a staunch opponent of industrial capitalism, which he saw as eroding people's capacity for creativity and self-reliance. Instead, Illich thought that capitalist society had become increasingly dependent on 'expert' knowledge (that of doctors and teachers, for example), which primarily served to further capitalism. He argued that compulsory education indoctrinated children into an uncritical acceptance of the dominant social structure through messages and ideologies hidden in school curricula and routines. Instead of compulsory school education, Illich advocated for the development of peer-to-peer creative learning models where children would use technology to connect with others and learn the material most relevant to them in the most appropriate way. Though Illich's deschooling thesis has been widely critiqued for not being well thought out and not proposing realistic alternatives (Gintis 1972), the increase in home schooling and 'alternative' models such as Montessori schools (where pupils' freedom and creativity is encouraged as a mode of learning) in the West certainly chime with his calls for more creativity and freedom in education.

PROVOCATION 6: We do not live in a meritocratic society

A meritocracy is a society in which citizens are rewarded by merit. In the US, this is known as the 'American dream' and it holds that the rewards of society – normally, becoming rich – can be yours as long as you work hard enough and are good at your job.

The notion of moving from poverty to great wealth exists in stories and folk tales across cultures and time. This notion of 'rags to riches', where someone progresses from a lowly or poor position in life to one with great power or wealth, is normally attributed to hard work, natural skills and great talent. But do we really live in a meritocratic society?

The first issue to consider is how success is defined. The way in which educational success is measured is quite limited, largely assessing competency in retaining a great amount of information and being able to recite it on command. Exams are, quite simply, a bad way of measuring an ability to understand or interpret, and yet they remain the primary way children are assessed in schools.

Albert Einstein is attributed as saying, 'Everybody is a genius. But if you judge a fish by its ability to climb a tree, it will live its whole life believing that it is stupid.' So, the way we measure success in education – and part of the way we measure 'merit' – is deeply flawed and lacks validity (see Chapter 4).

Second, we must recognize that success is impacted by economic inequality. Success at school is partly the result of hard work – most children will not succeed if they do not try – but it is also dependent on the context into which you are born and how rich and educated your parents are.

Research has demonstrated a multitude of ways in which children from lower social classes have less access, on average, to resources at home compared to middle-class students. Working-class students have less access to sufficient nutritious food, educational toys, music lessons, and trips to theatres and museums. They certainly have less additional private tutoring. All of these things influence the likelihood of academic success.

So-called meritocratic societies, like Britain, Australia, Canada and the US, also fall short as meritocracies because of how they are stratified by class.

The families who can afford to send their children to private schools buy access to smaller class sizes, better facilities and, often, influential social networks that can last a lifetime. These are the reasons why privately educated people get into elite universities at far higher rates than working-class students (Boliver 2013). New research suggests that even more entrenched class inequalities exist at the postgraduate level, where people from working-class origins are only 28 percent as likely to obtain a postgraduate degree compared with their peers from privileged origins (Wakeling & Laurison 2017).

Educational research has also highlighted, for example, many ways in which working-class students suffer from the way schooling is organized. Working-class children often find it harder to complete homework, not because of the difficulty of the work but of their social context: working-class children frequently have more caring responsibilities or work a part-time job to help support their family. They have less free time outside of school to complete homework – and their home situations can preclude dedicated time and space to do homework away from these other responsibilities.

The problem with the education system is that it does not recognize the other demands on working-class students. The tests that denote educational success benefit those who have had the time and space to complete homework. It does not give any reward to those who have dealt with other issues, and developed significant skills in these areas. Instead, they get lower grades because they had less time to revise.

Meritocracies are also problematic intellectually. Marxist sociologists have developed this argument to suggest that meritocracy is actually a political tool that serves to reproduce class inequality.

A meritocracy can, for example, be used to justify inequality. If it is believed that we live in a meritocratic society, then it can be argued that those who do less well do so because of some deficiency, rather than social context.

Indeed, research has shown that schools reproduce class values. In his famous ethnography of working-class young men in schools, *Learning to Labour*, Paul Willis (1977) argued that rather than providing these 'lads' with the possibility of going to university, the school actually trained them to become good (or obedient) manual labourers. Willis showed the ways in which schooling functioned so that working-class kids got working-class jobs. At the same time, middle-class students were being trained to become managers and to rule over them.

And so we come to the potential reality of what our society really is. Perhaps it is not a meritocracy, where skill and merit is rewarded; perhaps, instead, it is a society which projects the illusion of meritocracy in order to justify and reproduce class inequality, and to keep the workers in their place.

Provoked? Read further:

Alon, S. & Tienda, M. (2007). Diversity, opportunity, and the shifting meritocracy in higher education. *American Sociological Review*, 72(4), 487–511.

McNamee, S.J. & Miller, R.K. (2009). *The Meritocracy Myth*. Lanham, MD: Rowman & Littlefield.

MEDIA

The media has the power to shape how we perceive the world and our place within it. Today, the media is hugely diverse and includes all sorts of tools of communication like TV, music, books and newspapers. Sociologists have studied traditional forms of media like these and are increasingly turning their attention to the internet and social media.

Political economy approaches to the media

Early research into culture and the media came from critical social theorists who saw the media as an institution that reproduced structures of inequality in society. Scholars from the Frankfurt School were particularly important in understanding the role of mass media in society. As discussed in Chapter 3, the School was named after its original home in Frankfurt, Germany. These scholars were forced to relocate to the US during the 1930s because of the rise of Fascism under the Nazi regime in Germany. As a result, they had witnessed first hand the importance of the media in shaping public opinion (Wiggershaus 1994). In the US, the School flourished and important scholars like Theodor Adorno, Max Horkheimer, Leo Lowenthal and Jurgen

Habermas produced critical neo-Marxist accounts of the power of the mass media in entrenching and reproducing capitalism, which benefitted the wealthy and powerful.

One of the most notable ideas to come out of the Frankfurt School was Horkheimer and Adorno's ([1947] 2002) notion of the 'culture industry'. They drew attention to the industrialization of mass-produced culture, arguing that through this process, culture had become just as standardized and commodified as any other industry. They argued this development of a culture industry embedded capitalism as the dominant economic model and induced people to work hard, for the benefit of the wealthy and powerful elite.

Members of the Frankfurt School were particularly concerned about the integration of the working class into the capitalist ideology. In traditional Marxist thought, the working class were imagined to be the instigators of revolution so if they were also duped by mass communications into working hard and consuming goods, there would be little hope of a revolution and an end to capitalism.

These understandings of the mass media as a capitalist industry owned by private interests are often referred to as political economy approaches. Based on Marxian principles (rather than the more political ideology of Marxist views), political economy studies 'the social laws of production and distribution' of goods, recognizing that production and consumption are continual cycles (Lange 1963: 7). To understand mass media from a political economy perspective means recognizing the economic forces behind it.

Central to these political economy approaches is the critique of private ownership of the media, which has tended to be concentrated in the hands of a very small number of international media magnates. The most famous magnate is probably Rupert Murdoch, who owns several global media outlets, including Fox News. Those who subscribe to a political economy perspective argue that this private ownership deliberately excludes particular ideas and people from the mainstream media (Golding & Murdock 1997). Voices which are represented in the media, then, are those unlikely to criticize the inequality of power and wealth in contemporary society (we discuss this in further detail in Chapter 10).

Herman and Chomsky (2002) theorized the importance of ownership of the media with their 'propaganda model'. They argue that

> the media serve, and propagandize on behalf of, the powerful societal interests that control and finance them. The representatives of these interests have important agendas and principles they want to advance and they are well positioned to shape and constrain media policy. (p. xii)

Countries where the media is State-owned also use the media to control the population. In China, for example, until the 1980s, all TV, newspapers, radio stations and magazines were owned by the government. This meant that the government controlled how it was represented and could ensure no dissenters were allowed to reach a mass audience through media. Although the media is increasingly privately owned in China, the government still retains a strong influence, particularly in censoring parts of the internet for fear of dissent and Western influence. There are around 3,000 websites which are currently inaccessible in China (including Google and Facebook), though maintaining this so-called Great Firewall of China is increasingly challenging as the population becomes more computer savvy.

Representation in the media

The mass media *represents* social life, people and events.

Representation has traditionally meant the depiction of an event or a group of people through selected words, images and videos which are implied to capture the 'full story'. That is, representations 'stand in' for actual events and enable us to know about what is happening in the world without actually being there and experiencing it. This clearly gives great power to the media. Events are *re*-presented to us by them, and that retelling is a moment of considerable influence.

If we take a political economy approach, these representations might further the priorities of an individual or organization by showing events and people in one particular way. Sociologists have critiqued media representations of, among others, women and ethnic minorities. Feminist scholars have drawn attention to the ways in which women are regularly cast in roles and positions conforming to stereotypes of them as sexual objects or belonging to the domestic sphere (Byerly & Ross 2006).

© Tim Graham/Getty Images   © iStock/Andylid

Charles and Diana represented as different heights.

Consider this 1981 image of a familiar couple: Prince Charles, heir to the throne of Great Britain, and the soon-to-be-Princess Diana. This couple had huge fame in the 1980s, and there is little obvious to critique about this image. One might note that the stance of Charles is more authoritative (hand placed on Diana's shoulder), whereas hers is more pliant (resting on her own arm). If you search for pictures of them together, you will see many more in basically the same fashion. This representation even extended to the official postage stamps issued of the couple (see right-hand image).

But here's the thing: Princess Diana and Prince Charles were *the same height*. They were both 5 foot 7 inches. Yet in staged photos like this, Charles is *always* taller than

Diana. It happens so frequently that it cannot be coincidence. Given that research tells us that height confers authority (Etcoff 1999; Gladwell 2005), it suddenly makes much more sense: Charles is given authority by manufacturing his stature in a way that reproduces (through re-presenting) gender inequalities. American sociologist Philip Cohen has written about this issue on his blog, familyinequality.com.

Similarly, sociologists have also drawn attention to media representations of ethnic minority groups which reinforce stereotypes about different cultures. These representations have shown people from diverse ethnic backgrounds in a very limited set of social roles. Park et al. (2006) draw attention to the racial stereotyping of blacks and Asians in the 1998 film *Rush Hour* arguing that such stereotypical representations of ethnic groups naturalizes, rather than challenges, racial differences.

While this interpretation of representation allows us to understand the fundamental process and issues with it, cultural theorist Stuart Hall (1997) argued in favour of a view which acknowledges the active role of representation in the way we understand the world. He questioned whether events and people ever have one objectively 'true' version against which media representations and distortions can be measured. Events do, of course, happen, but Hall argued that these events have different meanings for different people depending on who they are, where they are from, where they live and their life experiences, and so on.

Stuart Hall and representation

Stuart Hall (1932–2014) was one of the best-known cultural studies scholars. Cultural studies is an interdisciplinary field which looks at contemporary culture, its historical foundations, defining traits and conflicts. The field developed in the UK in the mid-20th century and probably the best-known cluster of scholars worked at the Centre for Contemporary Cultural Studies at the University of Birmingham. Cultural studies scholars understand culture as fluid and changeable, shifting with wider economic, political and structural changes in society. They also tend to be interested in the ways in which contemporary culture intersects with different power structures like race, class, gender and sexuality (see Chapter 7).

Hall argued that to have meanings, events need to be represented in some way. By this, he does not mean the simple description of an event through text and image after it has happened, but that representation is implicated in the event itself at a base level; that the event is partly constituted as it is happening by how it is represented. Events are classified and described using a shared language; these classifications and words are then used to help us understand the events. In other words, to attribute language to something is to represent what it *is*, which then allows us to use our prior experience to attribute meaning to it.

Think of the various balls used to play different sports. We attribute meaning to different types of balls (i.e. what sport they are used for and what the rules of that sport are) based on the language used to classify them (i.e. whether they are golf balls, footballs or tennis balls) and our previous experiences (i.e. we have seen football, golf or tennis being played before, so we know what they are).

Analysis of this type of representation in the media has, then, focused on language and the process of giving meaning to events, objects and people. Given that the mass media is one of the most powerful ways in which meanings are circulated, meanings cannot easily be separated from questions of power – the question becomes who has the power to define objects, events and people, as well as whose meanings are being privileged when things are represented in the media. For Hall, arguing from a neo-Marxist perspective, the powerful seek to fix meanings to support their own agendas.

Social media

Traditional forms of media are owned by a small number of very rich and powerful people. Yet new forms of **social media** have emerged to challenge this paradigm. Although social media companies like Facebook, Twitter and Instagram are owned by very powerful people, its content is produced by its users. These users come from diverse backgrounds and will not necessarily share the agendas of the company owners. This model of open, collaborative user-generated content, where users produce as well as consume the internet, was known as Web 2.0 (see Beer & Burrows 2007), although this name is seldom used now that this internet model has increasingly become the norm.

> Social media: websites and apps that allow users to create and share content or connect with other people

According to the World Bank (2015), the great majority of people in the West are regular internet users. This includes 92 per cent of people in the UK, 74.5 per cent in the US and 84.6 per cent in Australia. In other developed nations, internet use is similarly high, with regular internet use at 98.2 per cent in Iceland, 93.3 per cent in Japan and 88.5 per cent in Canada. In developing countries, the story is quite different, with only 4.9 per cent, 2.7 per cent and 1.1 per cent of people in Burundi, Chad and Eritrea respectively using the internet regularly.

This ubiquity of the internet in the West has changed everyday life there and revolutionized the ways we communicate with other people. Manuel Castells (2005) argues that we now live in a networked global society where our social networks of friends and contacts are not just limited to those people physically close around us but can also include people in other countries, living in very different cultures, who we may never actually meet face to face.

Perhaps the most visible aspect of such a globally networked society is the increased use of social media and social networking websites. Although social media has often been seen to challenge the monopoly of large media companies and their biased representations, Rheingold (2000) predicts that the internet could easily become dominated by conglomerates as, therefore, just another form of mass media. He also argues that the internet would allow corporations to monitor and, ultimately sell to, the population much more easily. His prediction about corporations monitoring users has indeed come true.

Think about when you go online and are confronted by adverts for all sorts of things from beauty products to video games. The range of goods and services you are offered is not random selection but targeted specifically at you based on what you have searched for previously, what websites you use and what your interests appear to be (see Bakshy et al. 2015). Though the internet was billed as a form of media somewhat free from capitalist forces, it has become increasingly commercialized just as Rheingold argued (Weis 2010). It seems that even new forms of social media cannot escape some of the institutional powers more often associated with traditional media.

Sociologically speaking, this increased use of social media presents interesting questions about what it means to be 'in touch' or 'friends' with someone (Turkle 2011). Consider those people who you went to school with when you were younger and who are your friends on Facebook. You most probably know a lot about these people – whether they are in a relationship, which university they study at and where they went on holiday last summer. But you might not have spoken to them (either in person or online) for a few years, and you might know little about their thoughts, feelings and perspectives on the world. So, are they really *friends*? As we go on to discuss in Chapter 8, the answer to this question is complex because social media *and* friendship mean different things for people at different times (Lambert 2013). Lambert (2013) suggested that social media involves particular forms of intimacy (intense and publicly displayed emotions) which have now spilled over into 'real life' and are changing the ways in which we communicate offline.

Another question for sociologists is about the presentation of the self online. Goffman (1956) suggested that we all have social 'masks' which we use to present ourselves in the most desirable way. Though Goffman was talking about interactions in the offline world, his perspective is relevant when we think about social media. When you post a picture on social media, you are saying something about yourself with that picture; you are presenting yourself in a particular way. Hogan (2010) argues that social media users work hard to curate their images, status updates and friends lists to present themselves in the most appealing way for their friends or followers. Others have questioned whether these carefully curated presentations of the self are damaging as they can perpetuate stereotypes about beauty and set unattainable goals (Lambert 2013).

The effects of social media broadly fall into two categories. On the one hand, positive understandings of social media (and the internet more generally) have advocated it as a platform for the development of new relationships which transcend traditional boundaries such as national borders and subcultural divides. These positive perspectives draw attention to the empowering and emancipatory power of the internet and social media for people who may not have a voice in society (e.g. Baym 2015; Wignall 2017).

Others have drawn attention to social media's potential to enact political change. Eltantawy and Weist (2011) cite the example of the 2011 Egyptian uprising which led to the resignation of the dictatorial leader, Hosni Mubarak. Given that free speech in Egypt was increasingly difficult in the years leading up to the uprising, meeting other disaffected people and organizing protests was incredibly challenging. Social media provided a method through which large groups of people were able to organize quickly and plan protests which eventually ended in positive political change.

However, social media has also been argued to be damaging in contemporary society. The most prominent aspect of this negative understanding is the use of social media as a platform for hate speech and bullying, which tends to be particularly directed at women and marginalized groups. Other scholars argue that the prominence of social media has led to people being connected online but disconnected from meaningful relationships (Turkle 2011).

Technological change and fear of technology

New technologies are frequently the subject of cultural concern that they cause harm or damage the 'social fabric'. Contemporary worries include whether social media means we have poorer relationships with our friends, alongside fears about internet porn and 'sexting'. There may be genuine cause for concern in these areas. But it is also worth noting that very similar concerns have been raised for centuries about new forms of media as they emerge. Barker and Petley (1997) remind us that popular songs were seen as dangerous in the 1500s because they presented criminals as heroes. They write:

> For more than 150 years, moral campaigners have been making wild claims about the effects of media which they don't like. When in the 1830s Thomas Bowdler claimed that the plays of Shakespeare would corrupt young girls' minds, he was doing something no different from Conservative MPs [British politicians] today claiming that *Casualty* [a popular UK television drama] could encourage inner-city violence. (p. 7)

We need to be wary, then, of critiques that warn about these new technologies fostering moral or social decay. The technologies may be new, but these cautionary tales are very, very old.

WORK

Working eight hours per day, five days per week, for the 251 working days a year, we spend up to 22.9 per cent of our year at work. This does not include time spent travelling to and from work, any overtime we do, the weekend time that we spend putting together work for a big deadline on Monday, or the time we spend thinking about work when we are not actually there. It also does not take into account the breakdown of the boundary between work and personal life which has happened as new technologies like laptops and smartphones have enabled us to take our work with us wherever we go (Fleming 2014). Many of us spend much longer than 22.9 per cent of our time doing, or thinking about, our work.

This begs the question as to *why* we spend, at a conservative estimate, a quarter of our adult lives working. There are two ways to answer this question: one is to look at people's motivations and the other is to consider social structures. Personal explanations focus on issues such as gaining a sense of personal identity, striving for 'something better', developing specific skills, connecting to a social network and, of course, earning money.

Yet structural explanations suggest that the nature of work is interwoven with the structure of society – the structure of society dictates the model of work and, simultaneously, work supports the overarching structure of society. If we lived in agrarian or nomadic cultures, our perception of work would be radically different. To examine these issues in more detail, we need a better understanding of 'work'.

What is work?

Defining work is complex. We tend to think of it as an exchange of our time and some form of labour for money. For most of us, this type of work will take place outside the home and under the direction of another person. Part of our work as authors of this book includes sitting at computers at a university, where we also have to apportion our time between teaching, publishing original research and undertaking administrative activities.

But this model of work is relatively recent and specific to industrial capitalism. Prior to the Industrial Revolution in Western countries, work tended to be undertaken in family groups and focused on survival rather than generating surplus capital (Edgell 2012). Indeed, this is still true in large parts of the world today (see Chapter 9).

Yet this modern understanding of work does not capture unpaid labour such as childcare and domestic chores. These tasks are assumed to be less valuable and not recognized as 'real' work, partly because they have no explicit monetary value (although you can, of course, pay other people to do this work for you).

These unrecognized tasks have tended to be disproportionately undertaken by women, which has led to a strain on many women's lives. Studying women who have jobs and a partner, Hochschild (1989) found that her participants would work a full-time job, and then complete a 'second shift' of several hours of unpaid labour in the home. Despite families becoming more egalitarian, with an increasingly common approach to domestic work where men and women more equally share the burden, Bianchi et al. (2012) find that it is still women who undertake most unpaid labour. There has also been some evidence that when men do take on more equal amounts of childcare, they tend to have a larger share of the fun or enjoyable aspects.

There are two main consequences of this. First, it means that significant portions of the work that women do are not recognized *as* work because it is unpaid. A recent article in the British newspaper *The Guardian* (2015), for example, drew attention to the invisible labour that women do in families, such as making and remembering appointments, arranging children's playdates, buying greetings cards, knowing about allergies, remembering household goods that need replenishing, and so on. While individually these tasks are not necessarily notable and not something we would consider to be work, taken together this sort of labour entails a significant investment of time and emotion, little of which tends to be recognized and none of which is economically recompensed.

Second, people who work in these areas as a waged occupation (e.g. cleaners, carers, cooks, early-year professionals) tend to be paid less money than people who work in occupations of equal value. When we say 'equal value' here, we mean a different job which can be said to make the same level of contribution to society. For example, a refuse collector and a care worker do work of equal risk and equal value – both involve shift work, both are 'dirty' occupations (see Ashforth & Kreiner 1999) and both make an equal contribution to public services. Yet, according to the website Payscale.com, a refuse collector earns an average of £16,572 per year compared to £13,920 for a care worker. Occupations which are paid less tend to be predominantly undertaken by women and people from minority ethnic backgrounds, further reproducing inequality in society.

As such, we can see that defining work is complex because the definition is both social and political – how work is defined determines how that work is rewarded, and which groups benefit and which do not.

Why do we work?

Sociologist C. Wright Mills (1973) argued that 'for most employees, work has a generally unpleasant quality' (p. 219). Drawing on a Marxist argument, he suggested that workers in contemporary society are alienated from the content of their work as they have limited control over it. Mills suggested that, for most workers, work is simply a 'sacrifice of time, necessary to build a life outside of it' and argued that, where workers are satisfied with their work, it is not so much the actual *doing* of the work that is the source of this satisfaction but the power, status and money that work provides (p. 228). Why, then, do we bother working at all?

There are several sociological explanations. As discussed in Chapter 2, Max Weber argued that work took on a moralistic meaning in the late 17th century – what he called the Protestant work ethic – where working hard in your 'calling' (the obligations imposed upon an individual by their position in the world) and being disciplined were thought to be ways to become 'chosen' by God. We can see this moralistic framing of work still evident today: being a hard worker is still imbued with positive connotations.

Other scholars have suggested that work provides a framework for constructing a positive identity (Ashforth & Mael 1989). Even when work is stigmatized in some way, workers reframe, refocus and revalue their work in order to present themselves and their work in a positive light (Ashforth & Kreiner 1999). Roberts (2013) has shown this is the case with young working-class men in the **service sector** – men who have taken on jobs that were once deemed solely for women, and adapted them or their perception of them to fit their conceptions of masculinity. In addition to this, sociologists have highlighted the positive social connections, friendships and intimate relationships that work can facilitate (Kakabadse & Kakabadse 2004). Unemployment is also seen to have negative effects on identity (Kelvin 1981).

> **Service sector:** a sector of the economy focused on providing a service rather than goods

The value or otherwise of work may become an increasingly pressing question. As we discuss in Chapter 9, the growing automation of technology we are witnessing, from driverless cars to (artificially) intelligent robots, means that we may be approaching a time when there simply is not enough work to share between people. Indeed, work is changing in a number of ways which means how we currently understand and value it as a society is a pressing sociological issue.

The changing nature of work

In Western societies, work has changed significantly over the last century or so (see Chapter 9). One significant change has been the increase in the number of women working: the so-called 'feminization' of the workforce. Standing (1999) demonstrated that this is a global trend, with 71.4 per cent of developing countries and 72.9 per cent of developed countries showing an increase in the number of women working from 1975 onwards. In the West, women who worked outside the home in the early 20th century tended to be from lower socio-economic classes, were concentrated in domestic and other service work and rarely occupied high-status positions in organizations. Today, women from across the social class spectrum work in a multitude of sectors and there are many women in high-status positions.

However, women are still under-represented both in the most prestigious work sectors (e.g. law, medicine, engineering and science) and at the highest levels of organizations (e.g. in the boardroom). In addition, there is still a significant gender pay gap, with women in the UK and US being paid respectively 13.9 per cent and 20 per cent less than men for the same work or work of equal value. This is despite second-wave feminists drawing attention to the gender pay gap back in the 1970s and several laws that are meant to ensure that women and men are paid equally. Although increased female participation in the labour market is understood by feminist scholars as liberating women and giving them financial independence, inequalities persist.

The *nature* of work has also changed significantly. At the turn of the 20th century, much of the Western world was heavily reliant on manufacturing as a source of income, but today the service sector is by far the largest employer. By service sector, we refer to jobs which are based in the production of services (for business and customers) rather than based on the production of goods. This is sometimes also called *affective labour* (Hardt 1999).

Working in shops, cafes, call centres, transport, hairdressing and sales are all examples of service sector jobs. Working in the service sector requires a very different set of skills from the manufacturing sector – it prioritizes what are often referred to as 'soft skills', such as good communication, looking presentable and emotional labour (Hochschild 1983). These are all skills which women are traditionally assumed to have a 'natural' aptitude for, and therefore, the increased availability of jobs requiring these skills goes someway to explaining the feminization of the workforce. In the Eastern world and developing countries, the nature of work has also changed significantly, becoming increasingly characterized by manufacturing rather than agriculture.

Recently, entrepreneurialism has also become a much more salient feature of Western labour markets. The US Bureau of Labor Statistics (2016) found that 10.1 per cent of the US population was self-employed in 2015. These rates significantly increased after the economic downturn of 2008 and have remained relatively steady. Uncertainty about a country's economic health and in its labour market are key drivers of an increase in self-employment, but sociologists have also looked at more ideological reasons behind increased entrepreneurialism. Richard Sennett (1998) argued that the uncertainty of modern labour markets means that people are unable to form positive connections with, or to fulfil their identities through, work because they have to change jobs so frequently. Instead, they look to self-employment to express their 'authentic' selves. In this way, self-employment can be understood as a way of resisting the capitalist 'rat race'.

Automation: the introduction of automatic equipment (robots, machines and computers) in a manufacturing or other work environment

However, this notion of entrepreneurialism and personal fulfilment can be somewhat romanticized. Self-employment entails a high degree of precariousness and uncertainty, even if such uncertainty has been 'rebranded' through notions of 'freedom' and 'flexibility' to appear much less problematic. This 'flexibility' may be appealing for young, mobile entrepreneurs but is much more challenging for those with caring responsibilities and a mortgage to pay.

The *future* of work is another serious concern for sociologists. Primarily, this concern has focused on **automation** and increased precariousness. Workers have been concerned about the implications of automation since the early 19th century. The Luddites were English textile workers who smashed new cotton mill machinery out of fear that their traditional way of life would be destroyed and they would lose their jobs to new machinery that was quicker and cheaper than manual workers (Thompson 1963). People are still concerned about automation and the effect on jobs, and sporadically articles appear in the media informing us that our jobs will in the future be done by robots (see this recent example from the BBC: www.bbc.co.uk/news/technology-34066941). Braverman's (1974) classic work on deskilling, however, argued that workers' anger and concerns about automation should not be directed at the technologies themselves (as the Luddites did) but at the class and power structures of modern capitalism which focus on companies attaining a monopoly over a particular area of production no matter the cost.

Related to this, sociologists have also drawn attention to the risk of increased precariousness in future labour markets. As machines and computers are increasingly able to undertake work, human workers will be needed less regularly. This means that permanent, long-term contracts will be rarer and people will increasingly engage in irregular work. Guy Standing (2014) has been highly critical of this move towards precarious and irregular labour and argued that a new social class is emerging – the precariat. He argued that the precariat (an amalgamation of the words precarious and the proletariat) is characterized by chronic underemployment (i.e. people work but do not earn enough to make a decent living) and insecurity. While forms of flexible working can be beneficial for people in certain life situations, particularly young people fitting in work around education, the normalization of this type of work is thought to be indicative of just how deep the roots of modern capitalism go (see Chapter 9 for further discussion of organization of work in modern societies).

Autonomist Marxists have theorized the changing nature of work as part of the increased *society of control* that they argue we now live in. Autonomist Marxists are interested in the everyday workplace resistance techniques of the working classes (such as being absent, coming in late and not working as hard as one could) and the changes that such resistance can bring about in the capitalist system outside of traditional organizations like political parties and trade unions. Writing in this tradition, Deleuze (1992) argued that we now live in a society of control in which the boundaries between work and personal life are blurred. As such, while it appears that we have more freedom within contemporary society, we are also subject to more control. For example, many jobs allow work from home but, at the same time, employers now also expect workers to take phone calls or answer emails outside of core working hours. For autonomist Marxists, this tension between freedom and control in work is also evident in forms of workplace surveillance. Whereas previously, workers would be physically watched by a manager while they were at work, we are now subject to surveillance through complex matrixes of information, such as how long we spend online and what websites we visit. This information is not just available to our employers but can also be shared with authorities and even used by and sold to companies to market products to us.

PAUSE FOR REFLECTION

In 2017, the billionaire businessman Bill Gates called for a tax on robots. What is your response to this idea?

It might initially sound preposterous or surreal, but given what we know about automation, alongside Marxist theories of the economy, perhaps it has merit.

A tax on robots would shift the cost of automation from the worker (who would face losing their job to it) to the businesses (who would pay this tax on it). If these tax revenues were then reserved to support people displaced from work by robots, it might help offset the potential impact of automation.

Considering this, has your view of the idea changed?

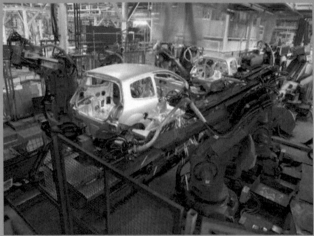

© Getty Images/Marin Thomas

Employability

At school, college and university, you will be encouraged to think about your own relationship with work in terms of what you want to do after you finish education. Your university or college will have services and opportunities that are designed to put you in the best position possible for securing employment when you leave education. These focus on increasing your **employability**: that is, how attractive you are to potential future employers. Over the past two decades, schools and universities have focused much more on supporting students' employability. The intention is to make sure that students are work-ready (that they have skills and experiences employers are looking for) when they leave education, through activities like careers fairs, guest speakers and key skills modules – and you will find that every university has a careers centre.

This increase in support that schools and universities give to students' employability is known in the UK as the *employability agenda* but is not limited to UK universities. Part of the reason for the introduction of the employability agenda in universities was the increase in student numbers, the widening of university to previously under-represented groups and the subsequent upskilling and professionalization that accompanied these changes. With so many people being educated to degree level, there was a concern that having a degree was no

> **Employability:** a measure of how attractive individuals are to employers and, by extension, how easy they will find it to get a job

longer 'enough' – students needed additional skills and experiences which would be valued by employers. The employability agenda can also be seen to be rooted in neoliberal ideas about personal responsibility, whereby being successful in a particular sector of social life lies with an individual irrespective of the wider landscape of that particular sector. As such, having or not having a job is framed as being down to the success or failure of the individual (their own 'employability', or lack of) rather than the wider state of the labour market (i.e. whether there are actually jobs available or not).

While the employability agenda supports students to gain useful experiences and coaches them to present their experiences in particular ways, it fails to recognize inequality of opportunity. Being employable means, in part, having extracurricular experiences such as senior memberships of societies, internships and study abroad opportunities. Yet some of these experiences are more easily secured through personal networks, meaning that students whose networks do not include influential people are disadvantaged. Broadly speaking, students from lower socio-economic groups and minority ethnic students are less likely than their white, middle-class counterparts to have access to people who can facilitate extracurricular activities such as these (see Chapter 7).

Moreover, the employability agenda assumes that all students will succeed in extracurricular activities like internships and memberships of societies. However, these activities rely on a set of skills, knowledge and codes most often part of a white, middle-class *habitus* (Sennett & Cobb 1972).

Consider the following: imagine you are undertaking an internship and are invited out for dinner with senior partners in the firm. As you sit at the table, you notice that there are several sets of cutlery and three types of wine glasses. Then, the person next to you begins to talk about a recent opera they went to see and the person opposite starts to talk about an exotic holiday they are planning. If this situation and the conversations do not reflect your prior experiences, the chances are you will have a rather uncomfortable time, be less able to bond with your colleagues and ultimately less likely to 'succeed' at your internship. This is not because you are incapable but because your habitus does not match.

The benefits of employability

Although we have encouraged you here to take a critical approach to the employability agenda, it is still something you will need to engage with and it is never too early to start. You do not necessarily need to know what you want to do as a career but you should start to think about what kinds of skills employers might be looking for and how you match up against these. When doing this, you should not be afraid to admit if you are lacking skills in certain areas. Where you do see room for improvement, look for ways to improve: join a student society, try to get some voluntary or work experience, enrol on a course.

If you are reading this at university, you should also make sure you do two things. First, start writing a CV and regularly update it as you acquire new skills or experiences. Second, book an appointment with your college or university's careers service to discuss your skills, CV and career plans.

THINKING SOCIOLOGICALLY ABOUT STRUCTURES AND INSTITUTIONS

Social institutions are culturally and historically contingent and are the result of social norms and tangible organizations that enforce these rules. Importantly, today's Western social institutions are relatively recent, emerging in their current forms during the Industrial Revolution. We have examined four of the key social institutions in society – family, education, media and work – and have explored the ways in which these institutions have been analysed and understood by sociologists. We could have looked at many other institutions – from sport and leisure to medicine and health – and the way we have approached them can be applied to other areas.

In each of the four cases, studying the implicit and taken-for-granted norms of institutions yields important and surprising results. For example, when focusing on education, examining the institution of education confounds some of our expectations about meritocracy and the success of education as an institution – education does not necessarily reward the most innately able or the hardest working. Indeed, success is determined in no small part by how well suited a person is to the forms of assessment that are used. Similarly, the sociology of the media tells us that how we enjoy our leisure time and the culture we like may have more negative effects than we realize – are we cultural dupes who waste our time when we could proactively be campaigning for positive social change? The study of structures and institutions is a vital part of sociology precisely because it challenges our preconceived ideas of society, helps route out injustice and inequality, and has the potential to effect progressive social change in the future.

CONCLUSION

This chapter has shown that society is highly organized through invisible social structures. These structures both constrain and enable our individual behaviours and are supported by social institutions, some of which are formal and others informal. These institutions socialize us into particular behaviours and roles in society which allow us to maintain the existing social structures. We have explored the ways in which sociologists have critiqued institutions and the social structures they support, focusing on education, the family, the media and work. Some of the more radical sociological thinkers have even suggested we move away from social institutions altogether, assuming that this would eventually lead to the collapse of some of the more problematic structures which are built on inequality.

HOW WOULD...?

» How would a qualitative sociologist study representations in the media from an empirical perspective?

   » Think back to Chapter 4. What key methods might be used to practically examine the more abstract ideas of cultural theorists like Stuart Hall? What areas would you look at?

» Say you wanted to study the elites in the media who control how ethnic minorities are represented on television. What issues might you examine, and what do you think you might find in undertaking this study?

STRUCTURED FURTHER READING

Morgan, D. (1996). *Family Connections: An Introduction to Family Studies.* Cambridge: Polity. This book introduces family studies and argues it is central to sociological research and theory. Making connections with other institutions such as work, the book also introduces some of the key debates in family studies.

Brooks, R., McCormack, M. & Bhopal, K. (2013). *Contemporary Debates in the Sociology of Education.* Basingstoke: Palgrave. This edited book draws on an international group of sociologists of education to examine key debates in how to understand education in society. Accessibly written, there are empirical chapters on technology and education, the globalization of education policy, the role of fear in education and various forms of inequality, including related to disability.

Hodkinson, P. (2016). *Media, Culture and Society: An Introduction (2nd edn).* London: SAGE. This book examines the issues and debates around understanding the media in society. As well as introducing the elements of the media, it also offers ways to understand the power the media exerts and who controls it. Finally, it examines how the media intersects with race, ethnicity, gender and sexuality to develop an overarching account of media in society.

Grint, K. & Nixon, D. (2015). *The Sociology of Work (4th edn).* Cambridge: Polity. This established textbook provides a holistic examination of work that is accessible and engages with the key debates in the field. Providing a historical and theoretical account of work, the book also draws out key issues related to class, gender and race, as well as thinking about technological change and globalization.

 Visit the companion website at **www.macmillanihe.com/mccormack** for further learning and teaching resources.

Chapter 7
SOCIAL DIVISIONS

INTRODUCTION

Many sociologists are interested in examining inequality in society and how some people gain privilege at the expense of others. One of the primary ways this is studied is through examining social divisions, where these stratifications are the results of both social structures and human interaction. Crucially, these divisions are not fixed and can be changed for the better. In this chapter, we examine social divisions that are based on class, race and gender. We focus on these three areas of sociological study because they are key ways in which societies are structured unequally. We discuss theories that seek to understand inequality and oppression in these areas, and how people have sought to contest them. In our Provocations, we ask why segregation is acceptable in sport, and, in the online Provocation at www.macmillanihe.com/mccormack, contend that the criminalization of selling sex amounts to class war.

SOCIETIES DIVIDED

We are not all treated equally. Yet societies do not have to exist this way. Rather, inequality is the result of how societies are organized; if that organization is changed, things can become fairer. In society, we are set against each other as individuals and as groups. Sadly, societies too often are divided and one social group will frequently find itself discriminated against by another or even by the society as a whole. There are a great many ways we oppose each other and, despite the fact that we tend not to be at literal war with one another, we are nonetheless engaged in conflict. Consciously or not, *you* are part of that conflict.

Social divisions take many forms. There are divisions in society where one group does not directly influence or interact with another. People living in the cities of Melbourne or Sydney will have a different experience and understanding of Australia compared to those in the Outback. These are horizontal divisions, as living in cities is not inherently better or worse than living in rural areas. Yet even if neither group is discriminating against the other, there may still be a very real division because of different life experiences.

The other way people are divided is hierarchically, in what can be thought of as vertical stratification. This is where one group has more of some valued asset than another group. These assets include money, power, social respect and access

© C_Fernandes/iStock

Which social divisions does this image convey to you?

to other resources. This form of social division is often called **social stratification** (see Chapter 3).

The ways we are divided and divide ourselves occur both intentionally and unintentionally. Divisions in society can exist through self-segregation and in-group formation, and these can have positive or negative effects. They also occur as a result of social institutions such as education, health, politics, religion and sport (see Chapter 6). Sometimes these divisions are literally built into cities through architecture and urban planning (see the picture above of a gated community).

One thing uniting the social divisions sociologists are interested in is that they are all social processes. Skin colour, for example, is a biological characteristic, but the values ascribed to that skin colour, and the ways in which certain groups of people experience considerable oppression because of skin colour, is the result of society. Likewise, the sex you are born into is biologically prescribed, but the classification of sex (as a fixed binary) is a social construct, and the experiences you will have as a man or woman (or as trans or intersex) are again structured by society.

Division often occurs because of structural and cultural reasons. Consider the experience of a friend of the second author who taught at a mostly black high school in Southern California in the late 1990s. The school was just eight miles from one of the finest beaches in Southern California, but most of his pupils had *never* seen it or any other beach.

There were structural reasons for this: most of these students did not have easy access to a car to get there and there was no easy route via public transport. Simultaneously, cultural reasons discouraged them. These youths spoke about feeling out of place in white neighbourhoods, and this particular beach was inhabited

> **Social stratification:** the way groups of people are divided unevenly in society

almost entirely by white people. As we shall discuss later, such feelings of being out of place are the result of cultural norms and social inequalities that are structural and deeply entrenched (Bhopal 2018). But the shocking fact remains: just eight miles from amazing beaches in Southern California, the majority of the class had never visited.

Social divisions are rarely about individuals, but about groups instead. Groups of people view other groups of people poorly because of group membership, leading to division. This is the case with class, race and gender. Research comprehensively documents that being middle class, white and male means you are more likely to maintain privilege in your life (e.g. Crompton 2008; Delamont 2003; Feagin 2006). Similarly, not being these things – being working class, a person of colour or female – means that you are more likely to encounter stigma or discrimination. One key reason for this is that power in society is distributed unevenly.

Theorizing power

In order to understand how societies are divided, we need also to think about power. The majority of sociological research has to consider power in some capacity, because power is a key component of how societies are organized.

At its simplest, power is the ability to make something happen – what Russell (1938) described as the 'production of intended effects'. Power is not a tangible artefact, but a set of relations between people. Indeed, Weber defined it as the ability to get what you want even if others want something different. Early theorizing of power – whether explicit or implied – examined how privilege was unevenly distributed and how power was thus possessed by a ruling elite. For Marx, power was located within the economy, with those who ruled the mode of production having power over those who did not (see Chapter 2).

> Discourse: an institutionalized or societally condoned way of speaking that controls the ways in which a topic can be discussed

Yet it is also important to conceive of power beyond social structures and people with authority or privilege in society. Foucault (1991) emphasized that power is not possessed but is diffused around us. He said that power was everywhere, and that it was fragmented. Foucault defined **discourse** as an institutionalized or societally condoned way of speaking that controls how a topic can be discussed. Power operates, in part, by who can influence and steer discourses.

PAUSE FOR REFLECTION

You have probably heard the saying that history is told by the winners. That aphorism is an example of how Foucault thinks of power. Historical knowledge is determined by those who have the knowledge, social positioning and authority to make these claims.

Can you think of any current examples of dominant ways of thinking about an issue in society that might be told differently if different people had more influence on the story?

 – Government : taxes – if both sides oppose why do they exist? This among many relief packages don't help the american people. The influence of the media in society is disturbing

Foucault developed his theory of power when writing about the transformation of societies around the industrial revolutions (see Chapters 2 and 9), and he charted the effects this had on a number of social institutions such as prisons.

Critical to Foucault's understanding of power was that it can be *creative* – not just a negative or restrictive force but one that enabled things to happen as well. There are two ways of thinking about this. First, power makes as well as breaks people: it is not just 'bad' but can be 'good'. Second, if power can be resisted, the 'thing' that is doing the resisting is also 'power'. This is the sense in which power is diffuse – it is present both in the act of resistance as well as in whatever act is being resisted.

In Foucauldian language, we would say that power is constitutive. This means that we are not *forced* to do things, but we end up doing them as we unconsciously adopt as our own those desires that have been shaped by dominant frameworks. We become *self-regulating* subjects as we go about our daily lives.

It is through discipline and being disciplined (e.g. told off or rewarded) that improvement is achieved. Doctors, teachers and prison guards all claim authority to 'discipline' their charges on the basis that they have specialist (disciplinary) training themselves. People can be policed through physical punishments, but also by various kinds of reward designed to make us want to 'get better' (whether physically, medically or mentally).

The effects of power and self-regulation

Airlines talk of passengers as 'self-loading luggage'. Have you ever wondered why you feel so keen to do things expected of you – to join queues, to fit in, to earn lots of money at the expense of seeing friends and family?

In his book *Distinction*, Bourdieu (1984) wrote about the way in which culture enables people to develop an identity and distinguish themselves from others. Through our taste in certain activities, we assert our distinction from other groups of people.

Bourdieu argued this occurred in three domains: culture, food and presentation. Consider the following statements:

» *'She watches these awful daytime soaps. I much prefer going to the opera.'*

» *'He drinks beer. I like red wine.'*

» *'What are they wearing? You shouldn't wear sneakers in a venue like this.'*

In each example here, taste is being used to distinguish a middle-class person from an (inferior or stigmatized) working-class norm. Bourdieu argued that this was the point of taste and culture – to make clear divisions between the classes, and reproduce inequalities between them.

To understand how these notions of taste connect with the body, we need to consider Bourdieu's concept of **habitus**. Habitus refers to the way a person presents themselves: their accent, how they walk, how they stand, as well as their cultural tastes. It also relates to the presentation of your home, the car you drive (or if you use public transport) and the activities you engage in.

Habitus:
the physical embodiment of cultural capital

British sociologist Steph Lawler (2014), describes habitus as 'the ways in which the social is incorporated into the self'. That is to say, while these behaviours and practices seem natural to the individual, they have been shaped and structured by life experiences – much in the way a symbolic interactionist would argue. Somewhere between habits and habitat, habitus refers to that part of ourselves that feels second nature to us, but which would seem unnatural to anyone outside our circle.

The value of habitus as an idea is that it enables an understanding of individuals that does not characterize people as simply cultural dupes to tradition or the latest capitalist advertising. At the same time, habitus also recognizes the influences of society. In other words, people are able to make active choices about their lives, but these choices are made against a backdrop of unconscious norms that have been internalized over many years. These norms will be influenced by modes of power such as class, race and gender. They will also be influenced by the social history of the artefact being considered.

Class, race and gender

When discussing social divisions, issues of class, gender and race are central to these debates in contemporary sociology. There are several reasons why these categories have emerged as core to sociology, but one key factor is that they are dominant ways in which societies are divided, and around which political movements have developed.

There is an interesting geographical split with regards to these issues: while it might be a stereotype that the British are preoccupied with class and Americans are divided by issues of race, there is truth to the idea. This is not to deny issues of race in the UK or class in America, nor to ignore how race and class are closely linked, but it is to recognize how central class and race are to cultural identity and politics in the UK and US respectively.

Class and race are important in many other countries, but will manifest differently in each context. In India, for example, the caste system is a social hierarchy that combines elements of class, race and

© Richard Baker/In Pictures via Getty Images

This early settlers' poster promised friendship and equality of treatment under the law to Australian Aborigines – a promise that did not come to fruition.

religion in a manner distinct from the UK and the US. In Australia, the history of British colonization and the oppression of Aboriginal peoples requires an understanding beyond US theories of race, even though similar racist arguments were used to legitimize horrific oppression. For example, Aborigines faced significant exclusion and oppression and did not have full citizenship rights, and access to these rights was obstructed. When British conquerors arrived in Sydney, they brought with them diseases such as smallpox and syphilis that killed more than half of the Aborigines in the area. They also killed Aborigines and treated them like animals in many cases, and the Aboriginal population was decimated across Australia (Rose 2000).

Class is perhaps the most established of the big three, certainly in British sociology (Savage 2000). Both Marx and Weber developed influential theories of class division, and the ways in which inequality was structured through these divides established class as an important characteristic. Ken Roberts (2011) highlights that unlike race and gender, which were held to be biological characteristics for the early parts of the 20th century, class has long been recognized as a social construction and thus the domain of sociology.

Mike Savage also notes that the study of class became dominant in Britain in the 1960s because it allowed British sociologists to distinguish themselves from American sociologists who had developed functionalist approaches to class (see Chapter 3). It also enabled connections with more established disciplines such as economics. The British have long been preoccupied with class, and issues of status, wealth and power associated with class have captured the British imagination for a significant period.

In America, it is race that is the primary marker of division. While W.E.B. Du Bois developed the first sociological analysis of the ways in which race was a social construct, it took longer for it to be established as a legitimate object of sociological study – not least because of the structural exclusion of Du Bois from sociology's history (see Chapter 2). Yet racism has been a central feature of American social life, from institutionalized slavery to Jim Crow laws that kept African Americans segregated from white Americans, and an approach to interpreting and enforcing the law that unfairly polices people of colour to this day (Goffman 2015). In this chapter, we discuss key components of the sociology of race. This is not limited to American sociology, as racism occurs across the globe, but we do draw on particularly influential American sociologists and schools of thought in this chapter.

Our third area of focus is gender. As discussed in Chapter 2, women made significant contributions to early sociology and their contributions were then erased (Deegan 1990). This was in the context of oppression against women, who were denied the right to vote or own land. Laws also stated that it was the duty of wives to have sex with their husbands, and so it was not legally possible for a husband to rape a wife – meaning that women did not have control over their bodies during this time. Just as with class and race, gender was a core political issue across much of the 20th century – from women's suffrage (the right to vote) to laws around equal pay and accessing abortion legally.

We finish the chapter with a short discussion of sexuality and homophobia, an increasingly important component of sociology. We also focus again on issues concerning sexuality in our discussion of personal life in Chapter 8.

CLASS

The social elements of class

We introduced the basic ideas of Karl Marx's critique of capitalism in Chapter 3. One criticism of Marx's position on class and the economy was the significance he attributed to universal economic rules at the expense of the role of society. Marx described the modes of production and the relations between employer and employee as a 'base structure' that determines all other aspects of society, including culture, institutions, political structures and the nature of the State – what he called the superstructure. While Marx recognized the ability of the superstructure to influence the base structure, the diversity of social, cultural and political life simply is not explained sufficiently by the ordering of the economy.

One of the early attempts to understand the social aspects of class in British society was the work of Charles Booth, a social reformer and researcher. His book *Life and Labour of the People in London* (1889) collected survey data on people who lived and worked in London in the late 1800s and discussed their occupation and the realities of their lives. He developed poverty maps of various areas in London, and his research was influential in developing early forms of welfare for London's poor – particularly the young and elderly.

Moving on from the focus on economic problems, in his book *The Making of the English Working Class* (1963), E.P. Thompson demonstrated the active ways in which class was created through social interaction. He wrote, 'I do not see class as

Poverty and inequality

Poverty comes in several forms, and there is a difference between absolute and relative poverty. Relative poverty means that those who are in poverty today have a different standard of living to those in poverty in Victorian times. Practically all citizens in the West have access to clean water, free education, food that will not poison you and a certain standard of healthcare. The mass production of goods has also dropped the prices of luxury items, meaning that many poor people have smartphones or other forms of technology.

Most Western citizens do not live in absolute poverty. Few Westerners would elect to swap their position to live in a very poor part of the world, for purely financial reasons, and we suspect even fewer would seek to live like the working class of 200 years ago (Pinker 2018).

Yet sociologists highlight the importance of *inequality* in wealth, and why relative poverty matters. In their influential book *The Spirit Level*, Kate Pickett and Richard Wilkinson (2009) demonstrate that more equal societies tend to do better and that inequality in society erodes trust, increases anxiety and illness, and encourages excessive consumption.

Using statistical analysis to compare large data sets across many countries, they showed that all the social problems that are more common at the lower end of the social ladder are also more common in more unequal societies. So, while relative poverty means that poor people are not generally living in the horrific conditions that Marx and others described, the inequality still present in many Western societies means that relative poverty continues to be a pressing social issue.

a "structure", nor even as a "category", but as something which in fact happens ... in human relationships' (p. 9). He highlighted how the working class developed a collective consciousness through working values that included collectivism, mutuality and religious conviction.

It is important to recognize the *social effects* of class beyond determining where one lives and what one can afford. Richard Sennett and Jonathan Cobb (1972) wrote about the 'hidden injuries of class', underlining the ways in which working-class people were marginalized. With resonances of Du Bois' concept of double consciousness (Chapter 2), they wrote:

> This fear of being summoned before some hidden bar of judgment and being found inadequate infects the lives of people who are coping perfectly well from day to day: it is a matter of hidden weight, a hidden anxiety, in the *quality* of experience, a matter of feeling inadequately in control where an observer making calculations would conclude the workingman had adequate control. (pp. 33–34)

This experience runs from stereotyping about accents to the knowledge that many institutions, such as schools, are organized around the norms of the middle class. Diane Reay (2002), for example, discusses the experience of a high-achieving working-class boy in an inner-city school and the social complexities and psychological stressors of maintaining a white working-class masculinity simultaneously with an educationally successful identity.

This is something that is found across countries. For example, Froyum (2007) discusses the identity work that ethnic minority students perform to negotiate their stigmatized class identities in the US. These students would deploy homophobia to mitigate their own low social position, stating that while they may be poor, 'at least I'm not gay'.

As such, while it is vital to recognize the economic components and basis of much of what constitutes social class, we also have to engage with the ways in which class is *social* and influences everyday life. In order to understand this further, we turn again to the work of Pierre Bourdieu.

Pierre Bourdieu and capitals

This social component of class adds a great deal of complexity to understanding how to theorize it. One key reason for this is because class is not fixed. Consider someone who has parents with manual labour jobs, attended a school that had teacher and budget shortages, and grew up in a working-class area. His hobbies were working on his motorbike and playing football with friends, and he spoke with a regional accent. There were very few books in his house. At age 17, he would be accurately categorized as working class.

And yet how would we understand this person if he got accepted to the University of Oxford to study English Literature? Would he still be working class? Probably so, particularly as his experience at Oxford would be very different from those with middle- and upper-class backgrounds. But what if he proceeded to study for a PhD? And then became a lecturer at Oxford? What if he became a professor, and renowned as a leading world authority who regularly appeared on the BBC?

Finally, what if he was made a lord in the British Houses of Parliament? By the time our working-class young man has become a world-leading professor of English literature and a member of the House of Lords, few would consider him working or middle class. Even if he was not part of the aristocracy, most would see him as socially elite and upper class.

The interesting question here is not that he has changed class, nor is it to try and label his current class position, but to understand the *process* of class change. Traditional class models do not account for this – asking about income, job type and other socio-economic questions over the course of this person's life might show a gradual shift in class position (not least, as income changed), but that would not capture the experiences or complexity of this transition (see pp. 140–143 for further discussion of social mobility).

 Read the eVox Pop from Matthew Ripley at www.macmillanihe.com/mccormack/ voxpop/MatthewRipley for a personal account and insight into this kind of social class transformation.

One of the key modern theorists to explore the complexities of this transition is French sociologist Pierre Bourdieu. Bourdieu recognized that class is more than just about money. As with Weber, he argued that class can, instead, be understood as a set of 'capitals' (Bourdieu 1984) – economic, cultural, social and symbolic forms.

Cultural capital: non-financial assets that can promote social mobility

Alongside money and wealth, we all have non-financial assets that can promote social mobility, including education, accent and style of dress. If you own art or play a classical musical instrument, you have different experiences than someone who does not. Bourdieu classified these things as **cultural capital**. Many middle-class people speak of growing up around books – of living with parents who owned books and encouraged them to read; many working-class people speak of growing up watching the television instead. Books in this context are forms of cultural capital.

Social capital: the cultural resources a person has based on their networks and group membership

Social capital refers to the cultural resources a person has accrued via their networks and group membership – the social capital of someone whose main friendship groups are part of a gang is markedly different from someone whose friends sing together in a local church choir.

Bourdieu defines social capital as 'the sum of the resources, actual or virtual, that accrue to an individual or a group by virtue of possessing a durable network of more or less institutionalized relationships of mutual acquaintance and recognition' (Bourdieu & Wacquant 1992: 119). Thus, social capital can be shared childcare support that a group of parents offer one another; similarly, it is the sharing of food and resources that working-class communities develop (Ehenreich 2001).

Symbolic capital: one's prestige in a social group, such as reputation and celebrity

Yet these capitals (or forms of privilege) are not the only forms that exist. *Who* you know is also very important. Think of YouTube celebrities: these people might not make significant amounts of money directly from their Vlogs, yet they will still have benefits from their status. This includes access to events, meeting other celebrities and the possibility of new employment opportunities. Bourdieu calls this **symbolic capital**. This can be used to explain differences in experience between similar groups of people.

These capitals come together to form a *symbolic economy* of class that enables consideration of these different aspects of a person's life beyond the economic. This is important because these forms of capital can be quite closely entwined.

Sometimes these forms of capital can be hard to differentiate – not least in deciding whether something is a cultural or social capital. This is partly because of the complexity of the issue, but also because these capitals become convertible over time.

Consider the earlier example of the working-class kid who became a lord and world-renowned professor of English literature. Undoubtedly, his class position changed. His income will certainly have increased, and place him within the upper-class salary range. His attendance at Oxford and his position in the House of Lords will enhance both his symbolic and social capital. The University of Oxford is a prestigious institution, and so he will gain prestige from that (symbolic capital). It also opens networks and connections that he would not have otherwise (social capital). These forms of capital are intricately interrelated.

Bourdieu's theorizing thus helps us understand how class inequality can take multiple forms. While economic position, not least in terms of salary and inherited wealth, matters greatly, Bourdieu's symbolic economy of class and other similar theories recognize the social and cultural aspects of class inequality (Atkinson et al. 2012).

Sociological thinking about class today

The continued prominence of both the economy and social class is evident from the politics of the past 30 years. US President Bill Clinton, when he ran for election in 1992, stood by the maxim 'It's the economy, stupid', and economic competence is held to be essential to winning elections. The recent prime minister of the UK, David Cameron, based his policies on the oft-repeated phrase 'long-term economic plan' and the need for 'austerity'. And this focus on the economy is centrally linked to class – for example, a core critique of the austerity agenda has been that the 'pain' of austerity was mostly strongly felt by the poorer people in society. In contemporary society and politics, it is still the case that you follow the money to understand who has power.

Bourdieu's theorizing of capitals and a symbolic economy of class enabled consideration of different aspects of a person's life beyond the economic. His ideas and concepts still have great relevance today and are even undergoing something of a renaissance. One particularly newsworthy study was the BBC's Great British Class Survey. Launched in 2011, more than 161,000 people took part, making it the biggest survey of class ever in the UK.

The survey emerged as a result of two key issues in theorizing social class. First, concerns were growing about how the old conceptualization of class – as having working, middle and upper classes – no longer captured how British society was stratified. Not least, how the concept of 'upper class' made little sense as it spoke to aristocracy (lords and ladies, dukes and duchesses, earls and so forth) and did not describe the super-rich who had not inherited long-established family money, lands or status.

The second issue was that while research was starting to recognize that class was far more diverse than employment inequalities (e.g. Atkinson 2010; Crompton 2008), it lacked large-scale quantitative data sets that could help understand the macro-level issues associated with diverse class groups.

The sociologists of the survey published their findings in the journal *Sociology* in 2013 (Savage et al. 2013). They argued that while

> a large 'rump' of the established middle (or 'service') class, and the traditional working class exists, there are five other classes which fit less easily into this conventional sociological framing, and which reveal the extent of social polarisation and class fragmentation in contemporary Britain. (p. 221)

Perhaps most importantly, the authors highlight the role of the most privileged in society – those with average savings of more than £100,000, and with lots of social and cultural capital. They call this group the elite and argue its 'sheer economic advantage sets it apart from other classes' (p. 245). People in this group tend to have had very privileged upbringings as well.

The authors also argue for recognition of a 'precariat' class – about 15 per cent of the population who lack any significant amount of economic, cultural or social capital (see also p. 153 for discussion of the precariat). Often having household incomes of around £8,000 a year, they are likely to rent and live in old industrial areas. Key to the class is insecurity in terms of their jobs, their ability to pay rent and even put food on the table. The authors also expanded the ways of thinking about the middle and working classes, but these additions were not as significant as the focus on the elite and the precariat. Indeed, Savage (2015) argues that one of the survey's most important contributions was to shift class analysis away from working- and middle-class groups to focusing on the elites.

The Great British Class Survey certainly popularized discussions of class, and resulted in many conversations in the media. It also generated a large amount of sociological debate. Mills (2014), for example, critiques the survey on methodological and analytical grounds, arguing that the new formulation is *too* inductive (see Chapter 4) and not built using class theory. Dorling (2014) praises the survey and its associated publications for grappling with how class is changing in contemporary Britain and internationally, but raises concerns – not least that the survey asked for friends' occupations (e.g. social and cultural capital) but not one's own.

PAUSE FOR REFLECTION

Perhaps you should fill out the survey. As of this book going to press, it is still available online at: www.bbc.co.uk/news/magazine-22000973. What did you make of it? How accurately do you think class is captured by the seven categories described in the Great British Class Survey?

Social class in Australia

Based on the Great British Class Survey, Australian academics Jill Sheppard and Nicholas Biddle (2015) surveyed 1,200 Australians about their social class. The authors argue for five classes that included two 'affluent classes' that are similar to the elites mentioned in the Great British Class Survey. They argue that Australia is less divided by class than the UK, and that class is less meaningful in contemporary Australia than it was previously.

You can also take the Australian survey here: www.abc.net.au/news/2015-10-28/social-class-survey-where-you-fit-in-australia/6869864.

For a provocation about whether the criminalization of sex work is a form of class war, visit the book's companion website at: www.macmillanihe.com/mccormack

RACIAL DIVISIONS

The impact of slavery

Race is a major form of social division in society. It is important to note that this way of dividing people has not always been in use. The Ancient Greeks, for example, did not care about race but divided people according to whether they spoke Greek. In many medieval societies, religion was the key way to categorize and differentiate between people. Race was far less important in these contexts.

There are numerous broad (macro) social changes that resulted in race gaining importance, and one of the central, and most troubling, was its use as a concept to legitimize slavery.

While slavery has been a horrific social problem across many different civilizations and eras, it expanded massively in Europe and America in the 16th and 17th centuries as Europeans built better ships and started to explore beyond the European land mass (Rawley & Behrendt 2005). Technological changes meant cheap labour was needed to expand farming and industry – with competition between bordering countries that were regularly at war with each other. One of the solutions to this was slavery.

European settlers in America also introduced slavery to build the country's new cities and infrastructure. The prosperity and wealth of America and European countries today is the result of slavery.

We look upon slavery today as a truly horrendous scar on Western history. Yet there were many people living at the time who did not see slavery as a problem. There are a lot of reasons for this, but fundamental to them was the belief (or ideology) that slaves were not equal to non-slaves – that slaves were not fully human. 'Race' was used to justify the gross inequality in treatment and status between different groups – to explain why people with one skin colour were 'less than' people of another skin colour. In other words, racism or racist ideologies were the way that people justified the horrors of slavery.

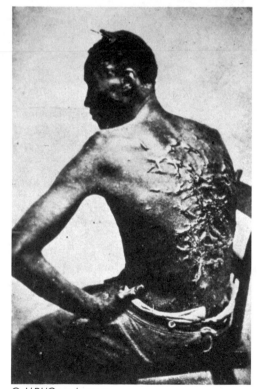

© MPI/Getty Images

The significance of race in American society is inescapable.

It is because of this troubled history that many people do not like to use the term 'race'. However, there are different norms cross-culturally related to the use of the term. Some argue that it is an entirely damaging construct that should never be used; some suggest using quotation marks to recognize the damaged history of the construct ('race'); others discuss *critical* theories of race; while others use the term and distinguish between race as a shared lineage and a presumed shared physical characteristic, with ethnicity relating to cultural characteristics instead (Kivisto & Croll 2012).

Ethnicity is another important concept when discussing these issues. People of a particular ethnicity will often have similar skin colour, but skin colour is not close to being equivalent to ethnicity.

Many of you will have filled out forms, particularly related to jobs or educational institutions, which ask you to choose your ethnicity. In the UK, options will often include White British, White Irish, Asian British and Black British, among many others. The point is that these ethnicities are distinguished by a range of factors, and they do not necessarily pertain to skin colour.

> **Ethnicity: a socially created system of classifying people on the basis of cultural or nationality differences**

Slavery and the US

America's founding fathers adopted a constitution that legitimized slavery in 1776 (although slavery had been part of American culture since 1625). Over the years, the 'land of the free' became a very rich nation through slave labour. Abraham Lincoln finally administered the emancipation proclamation freeing slaves in 1863, but this was done at least as much out of political necessity as social justice: three years into a bitter Civil War, Lincoln needed freed former slaves to fight as soldiers in his war, while simultaneously weakening the slave-powered economy of the rebel South. The agreement that was reached included a commitment that each slave would be given forty acres of land and a mule. However, unlike for survivors of later government-induced atrocities, the promise of reparations was never honoured.

Without access to the means of production – without owning capital, land, factories or resources – newly freed black slaves survived by working for owners of industry or for their previous owners as tenant farmers. They had more freedom in theory, but the Jim Crow laws still discriminated against African Americans, and covert racism made life very difficult. Their lack of resources left them vulnerable to institutional discrimination. Thus, African Americans became ghettoized, living in squalor, paying rent on buildings owned by white people, and working in white people's homes, farms and factories.

In 1968, Martin Luther King Jr referred to this in a speech in Washington, DC:

> In 1863 the Negro was told that he was free as a result of The Emancipation Proclamation being signed by Abraham Lincoln. But he was not given any land to make that freedom meaningful ... And the irony of it all is that at the same time that the nation failed to do anything for the black man, it was giving away millions of acres of land in the west and the Midwest ... [to] white peasants from Europe ... Not only did it give [whites] land, but it built land-grant colleges to teach them how to farm. It provided low interest rates so that they could mechanise their farms ... And these are some of the very people who tell Negros that they must lift themselves by their own bootstraps.

Scholars have also demonstrated that the use of prisons changed markedly at the end of the slave trade (Davis 2003). While the 13th Amendment of the US Constitution prevented slavery, it did not apply to prisoners. After the end of slavery, prisons shifted focus from trying to reform criminals to adopting strategies and punishments once used by slave owners. African Americans continue to be over-represented in the US prison system today, with harsher sentences regularly given to non-white convicts.

In the US today, African Americans ostensibly have full legal equality, but there still exists a great deal of cultural and economic inequality. Much of this can be traced to the fact that white America has been able to pass its wealth, made largely off black labour, down through generations, often tax free.

Sociological theories of race and racism

The sociological study of race started with the work of W.E.B. Du Bois and his Atlanta School (see Chapter 2). Du Bois undertook important empirical work and developed an overarching argument that race is a social construction and that the inequalities of race are the result of social structures, not biology. As Delgado and Stefancic (2012) argue:

> Race and races are products of social thought and relations. Not objective, inherent, or fixed, they correspond to no biological or genetic reality ... People with common origins share certain physical traits, of course, such as skin color, physique, and hair texture. But these constitute only an extremely small portion of their genetic endowment, are dwarfed by that which we have in common, and have little or nothing to do with distinctly human, higher-order traits, such as personality, intelligence, and moral behaviour. (pp. 9–10)

It is important to stress that this does not mean that there is literally no role for biology. As highlighted in the quote, things like physique and skin colour similarities do exist, but they do not account for the important, damaging differences explained far better by racist behaviours, norms and structures.

VOX POP Professor Kalwant Bhopal

Professor of Education and Social Justice

As an academic working on exploring inequalities to do with race, gender and class, I am often defined as someone 'who has an axe to grind'. This is particularly the case in relation to issues to do with race. Many people find the subject of race and racism uncomfortable; and this includes many academics working in higher education. They don't like discussing it, and they don't like to be confronted by uncomfortable truths.

Universities often promote themselves as liberal and inclusive institutions; but quite often if you scratch the surface, you find that your race, class and gender impact massively on how you are positioned in universities. I am deeply passionate about issues to do with equality, particularly race – as an Asian woman, I experienced racism in the playground and remember being called a 'Paki' and told that I smelled of curry.

© Martin Myers

I have continued to experience racism all my life. For several years I was racially bullied by a female, white, middle-class colleague in a university where I worked; other white, middle-class colleagues seemed not to quite notice it was happening. In a liberal and inclusive organization, you expect people to notice.

Racism is something that upsets me terribly and hurts me. It is something I think we should all be aware of and something we should always be fighting against. This attitude led me to focus on trying to use my research on minority ethnic groups to fight for issues of social justice and equity – to create a society that values everyone and not just the few.

I use my research on education to argue that education is a right and not a privilege – every individual, regardless of their ethnicity, gender or social class background is entitled to a quality education. So, we must firstly continue to acknowledge that racism exists and is a feature for some of everyday life. A failure to acknowledge racism results in a failure to address it and act upon it. Secondly, we must ensure that as educators we continue to challenge those inequalities that favour the privileged and fight for a society that values social justice and equity for all.

> » How do Kalwant's experiences of prejudice within higher education connect with theories of gender and race discussed in this chapter?
>
> » In what ways are Kalwant's experiences structural and when are they interactional? How might these be linked?
>
> » Reflect on your own experiences growing up. How have you encountered privilege or prejudice in your life?
>
> > » Has your gender had an influence on your experiences? In what ways?
> >
> > » How do you think your life would have been different if you were not the gender you are? What about your race and class?
> >
> > » Thinking about your own experiences, what concepts or theories discussed above are most helpful in understanding your context?

Critical race theory and black feminist thought

One of the key ways of understanding issues of race and ethnicity has been through **critical race theory** (CRT). CRT began as a theoretical movement within US law schools in the mid-1980s. Its core argument is that society needs to be understood and analysed primarily through a race lens (Bell 1992). Central to this argument is the idea that society is structured to privilege white people at the expense of people of colour. While CRT was developed in a US context, many of its ideas are applicable across the world.

Discussing CRT in the context of law, Roy Brooks (1994) provided an overview of its core aims, arguing:

> It focuses on the various ways in which the received tradition in law adversely affects people of color not as individuals but as a group. Thus, CRT attempts to analyze law and legal traditions through the history, contemporary experiences, and racial sensibilities of racial minorities in this country. The question always lurking in the background of CRT is this: What would the legal landscape look like today if people of color were the decision-makers? (p. 85)

In their comprehensive introduction to CRT, Delgado and Stefancic (2012) argue there are five propositions that define CRT:

1. Racism is *ordinary*. Rather than seeing racism as shocking or an aberration to normal society, CRT holds that racism is a regular, expected occurrence in society. Some sociologists also refer to this as *systemic racism* (Feagin 2006).

2. White privilege and power serves important purposes for the dominant group, and they gain from it.

3. Race is a social construction. It is the product of human interaction and thus changes over time.

4. Dominant society **racializes** different minority groups (see textbox below).

5. People of colour have a presumed competence to speak about race and racism. Within CRT, this includes African Americans telling their stories of oppression under the law as a way to address racism. As Delgado and Stefancic point out, this presumption is theoretically problematic as it assumes an inherent ability based on race; the kind of assumption criticized or rejected in other areas of CRT.

> **Critical race theory:** a set of critical theories that analyse society primarily in terms of race

> **Racializing:** the attribution of particular values or stereotypes to racial groups

> Delgado and Stefancic argue that the ways in which racialization shifts are closely related to the shifting needs of society, not least the labour market. African American men, for example, were portrayed as being physically inferior to white men during slavery, yet are now stereotyped as being strong and dangerous (Hoberman 1997).

An important further component of the study of race is to recognize that white people are heavily implicated in these discussions (Garner 2007). That is, whiteness itself has significant influence on social life. Dyer (1997) highlights that this includes the fact that white people are imbued with the power to determine culturally what counts as racist.

It may be clear that CRT is not a singular theory, as we discussed in Chapter 3, but is a collection of theories, or even a theoretical framework by which to approach social issues.

CRT has made important contributions to knowledge about the issues of race and racism in society. However, it has also been critiqued for its primary focus on race at the expense of other modes of oppression (Collins 2000). Most notably, it was argued that CRT relegates gender as a mode of subordination and assumes race is always the most important form of discrimination faced. This may be true for black men, but it is less likely to be accurate for black women. This critique, by scholars such as bell hooks, Patricia Hill Collins and Kimberlé Crenshaw, has become known as **black feminist thought**, which can be characterized as arguing for recognition of issues of class, gender and sexuality alongside race.

For example, bell hooks (1981) powerfully critiqued the black rights movement historically. She wrote:

> the dominant white patriarchy and black male patriarchy conveyed to black women the message that to cast a vote in favour of social equality of the sexes, i.e. women's liberation, was to cast a vote against black liberation. (p. 185)

Kimberlé Crenshaw (1991) made an important contribution to this debate with her concept of **intersectionality**. Critiquing the sole focus of race in CRT, she argued that debates about which mode of power is most important are pointless. She called for recognition that different forms of power, such as race, gender and class, intersect to form complex, multifaceted oppressions. The experiences of a white heterosexual man are different from a black heterosexual man; but both men's experiences will be different from those of a lesbian woman of any race.

Patricia Hill Collins (2000) developed this further, arguing that oppressions of race, class, gender and sexuality not only intersect but are mutually constituting, meaning that they re-enforce each other. She also included a discussion of the role of sexuality, which had been missing from much of the debate on these issues.

Black feminist thought: a body of writing that argues for recognition of issues of class, gender and sexuality alongside race

Intersectionality: the interconnected nature of social categories, particularly how they relate to oppression

An example of intersecting oppressions

Many black people experience racism as the primary oppression in their lives. Similarly, many gay people experience homophobia as the primary oppression in their lives. But what if you are gay and black? It is not just the oppressions added together – new oppressions form as well. For example, racism in gay communities has meant that gay black men are often excluded from these cultures, and consequently they have less protection from homophobia (Green 2007). Now consider how class intersects with this: A man who is gay, black and very rich will suffer far less than a poor gay, black man. Wealth will serve as a form of protection, while poverty will exacerbate the oppressions. Certainly, being middle class and gay is a very different experience than being gay and black and poor. Some of these issues are explored in the 2016 Oscar-winning film *Moonlight*, which presented three stages in the life of Chiron, a black, gay youth growing up in Miami.

The intersection of race and gender is exemplified by Sojourner Truth (1797–1883), who was born into slavery in New York State. After gaining her freedom in 1827, she became a well-known anti-slavery speaker and in 1851 at a Women's Convention in Akron, Ohio, she gave her famous speech, 'Ain't I a Woman', in which she emphasized that her life as a black woman was impacted by racism, but also that the framing of women as passive and vulnerable was incompatible with the dominant ways in which womanhood was constructed at the time.

 Visit the companion website at www.macmillanihe.com/mccormack for extracts from Sojourner Truth's Akron speech, plus further commentary.

Of course, scholarship on race and racism extends beyond CRT and black feminist thought. Joe Feagin (2013), for example, has made important contributions to understanding race and racism in society. One of his most influential concepts is that of the *white racial frame*. He describes it as a worldview that has 'long legitimated, rationalized, and shaped racial oppression and inequality' (Preface, p. x). It 'includes a broad and persisting set of racial stereotypes, prejudices, ideologies, interlinked interpretations and narratives, and visual images ... [that] imbeds inclinations to discriminate'. He uses the example of a study of black airline pilots who report being asked to call for a taxi (cab) for members of the public. So dominant is the idea of black Americans as serving in lesser roles in society, people mistake the pilot's uniform for that of the taxi rank concierge.

Similarly, Bertrand and Mullainathan (2004) highlight racist hiring practices in the US: they systematically responded to clerical, administrative and customer service help-wanted ads in the *Chicago Tribune* and the *Boston Globe*. They applied using names associated with white people (like Craig) and black (like Jamal), based on naming data for babies born in the 1970s. Their results found that a white name on a CV that was of equal quality yielded 50 per cent more call-backs for a job than with a typically black name: an equivalent advantage to having eight extra years of experience on the CV.

In line with CRT and black feminist thought, Feagin (2013) argues that sustained collective action is needed to challenge systematic and entrenched contemporary racism and make society more equal. This includes exposing and challenging concerted efforts to prevent people of colour from voting, as well as a criminal justice system that punishes and incarcerates non-white people far more than white people.

Our discussion of race has focused on issues within the US. This is not to deny the role that race and racism plays in countries across the world. Paul Gilroy (1987), for example, argues that anti-black racism has been a component of much of British history and is linked with a blurry idea of a 'national culture' that is predominantly white. Drawing on scholarship from Du Bois among others (see Chapter 2), Gilroy argues, as per CRT, that racism is not an aberration, but has been connected with justifying colonialism and wars of conquest that are part of British history. This is true of a number of institutions, not least schooling (Bhopal 2016, 2018). The Vox

Pop in this chapter (p. 172), from Professor Kalwant Bhopal, who has undertaken important research on race and racism in the UK, tells of her experiences of inequality and prejudice in the UK.

Orientalism: a set of social processes by which the global north frame Arab peoples according to a range of damaging stereotypes

Inequality across the globe

Racism is not just a problem within countries, but also an issue that affects nations and continents. One of the key distinctions is between the global north and the global south – known as the north–south distinction. For example, Said (1978) conceptualized **orientalism** as the processes by which the global north framed Arab peoples (from the 'orient') as being uncivilized, backward and dangerous. This book can be seen as the foundation for a branch of social studies known as postcolonialism that seeks to understand the ways in which the West controls how other regions such as the global south are understood and the influence it has in contemporary global politics (see, for example, Spivak 1988).

GENDER

In addition to class and race, gender is another key division in society. Issues of gender equality share much in common with racial and class inequality, but there is also a crucial difference: whereas class and race groups tend to be segregated through broader social structures – like racist laws that literally segregate non-white people away, or economic realities and social structures that reinforce class divides – people are not segregated by gender from birth: heterosexual families are necessarily of mixed genders. Almost everyone has a mother. Thus, to oppress women is to oppress a very member of one's own family: one's mother, wife, sister or daughter.

Patriarchy: a concept to understand systematic gender inequality in society

One of the key concepts used to examine gender inequality has been **patriarchy** (Lerner 1986; Walby 1990). This concept has examined how men are stratified to have more power than women, both culturally and legally.

In her book *The Creation of Patriarchy*, Gerda Lerner (1986) contends that the concept has its roots in family systems organized around the idea of the primacy of the father. Families are institutions in which wealth, prestige and power are passed on from one generation to the next (see Chapter 6 for discussion of the family as an institution). In a patriarchal culture, those goods are passed on disproportionately to male offspring. While most power today is located within politics, religion, corporations, government and education – institutions outside the household – these institutions are heavily dominated by men.

However, patriarchy is a concept that has proven difficult to define, with much debate about its utility (Rubin 2011). It can be seen to reify static notions of gender, and has suffered from ongoing debate about its precise meaning. As such, we find the term gender inequality to be more useful than patriarchy to examine the role of gender as a mode of power in society.

Gender scholars are concerned with understanding how and why the social dynamics of men and women have come to exist as they currently do. Sociologists have helped discredit older biological theories that posited 'natural' differences to debates about gender norms and cultural politics. This is not to say that biology has no influence but, similar to CRT, to argue that the attribution of values, privilege, stigma and power on gender lines is primarily social.

One of the first key moves away from a biological focus on the differences between men and women was scholarship that examined *sex roles*. As Kimmel (2004) comments, 'sex role theorists explore the ways in which individuals come to be gendered, and the ways in which they negotiate their ways towards some sense of internal consistency and coherence' (p. 95). Sex role theory was an important milestone in gender scholarship because it provided an initial understanding of the role of the social in gender.

As discussed in Chapter 6, early functionalist research in sex role theory thought that socialization was necessary for a stable and orderly society (Parsons & Bales 1955). In this view, gender norms existed for a reason, such as women having an important role caring for the family – gender inequalities were seen as natural and right. While feminists used sex role theory to challenge gender norms and argue for expanded roles for women in society, the theory did not sufficiently account for issues of historical context, social conflict and power in society (Stacey & Thorne 1985). The notion of particular roles for men and women seemed to presuppose gender differences rather than examine the production of these differences. This is problematic, as it is through ideas of difference that inequalities are rationalized. Thus, while sex role theory was an important component of gender scholarship, it has been superseded by more contemporary theories.

Sex or gender?

Should we say 'sex' or 'gender'? You may have noticed that sex role theory was used to discuss gender relations. What is going on?

The history of the terms used is complex and has generated much debate. Nowadays, 'sex' is generally used to describe a medical or biological classification: this has traditionally been 'man' or 'woman', but also includes 'intersex' or 'trans'.

Gender refers to behaviours associated with a person's sex ('masculine' or 'feminine') and it can also refer to an *identity* – how you feel as a man or a woman.

Gender at the individual and cultural level

A holistic understanding of gender must include focus at the individual and cultural levels. This involves considering how gender is enacted in social interaction (West & Zimmerman 1987), and also examining the ways gender is structured by institutions and society.

In our daily lives, we classify people to a sex (normally a binary of male or female) almost instantaneously. Yet, the way science actually defines sex – through genitalia, chromosomes and hormones – are very rarely obvious or even known to us. Nonetheless, we readily categorize a person as a man or woman. How is that?

West and Zimmerman (1987) introduced the concept of a *sex category* to explain this. Think about how you judge a person's sex. You will pay attention to secondary sex characteristics, such as facial features, hip size, musculature and other similar things. And you will also notice things that they have some influence over: their voice (pitch, volume, etc), hairstyle and clothing choices. These are the behaviours and codes that people use to identify a person's sex – their sex category.

West and Zimmerman argue that 'doing gender' is the process of behaving in a way that aligns one's sex category with the sex they wish to be perceived as. This means that gender is not an attribute ascribed at birth or determined by one's body, but a social performance and an accomplishment achieved in social interaction. We discuss the body and gender inequality in Chapter 8 (pp. 194–197).

At the macro level, Joan Acker (1990) highlights how gender is a central way in which society is organized. She argues that organizations are gendered, where 'advantage and disadvantage, exploitation and control, action and emotion, meaning and identity, are patterned through and in terms of a distinction between male and female, masculine and feminine' (p. 146). Lorber (1994) stresses that these differences are vital, because without difference it is much harder to justify inequality (as per our discussion of race above).

Risman (2004) contends that thinking of gender as a social structure 'brings gender to the same analytic plane as politics and economics' (p. 431). She argues for a cultural component of a gender social structure that recognizes the doing of gender at the interactional level and engaging with a range of theories about how gender is reproduced in society.

PROVOCATION 7: What's wrong with segregation in sport?

While visiting a university in the American South, a professor of sociology noted that the campus was quite diverse in terms of ethnicity and race. He noted that there was a good mixture of people with different ethnicities socializing together. Walking past the playing fields, he saw several soccer teams competing. Asking who the teams were, he was told that the university teams were playing against a visiting school. However, unlike in the wider campus areas, the playing teams were entirely segregated.

Shocked by this segregation, the professor asked one of the coaches why the teams were split this way. He was told it was for two key reasons: First, the players preferred it that way; and second, most of the players on one team were better than the players on the other. The coach argued that segregation thus best served the players on both teams.

The sociologist was incensed. 'Segregation is a sign of oppression,' he said. 'I'm appalled that you should reproduce decades if not centuries of inequality in how you organize your teams. How can you do this?'

The coach was confused. 'What do you mean?' he asked. 'I don't segregate. Look, I have African American and Caucasian players on the same team!'

'Yes,' the sociologist replied, 'but you have those teams segregated by sex.'

*****

While we have made great improvements in promoting equality in some areas of society, we remain a deeply sexist and gender-segregated society. The sociologist was dismayed by the fact that the teams were split into a men's team and a women's team because of the immediate and long-term consequences of segregating children and young adults by sex.

*****

After this initial exchange, the sociologist asked the coach why we, as a society, endorse organized, competitive team sports. 'They promote health and fitness,' the coach responded. Perplexed, the sociologist said, 'Yes, but we can gain health and fitness through any exercise.

Why do we promote competitive team sport?' The coach produced his answer quickly. *'Sport is useful for teaching students motivation and dedication. It teaches them teamwork.'*

Still dissatisfied, the sociologist asked, 'But learning dedication is not unique to team sports. That can be done with running or cycling. Why do we value team sports in particular? Do they offer students anything that an individual sport does not?' 'Yes,' the coach replied. 'They teach us to learn to work as a team, and that's vital for the world of work.'

The sociologist nodded, saying, 'And that's exactly why segregation by gender is a problem. Segregated sport helps perpetuate gender inequality at work.'

*****

There are a number of ways this argument can develop, not least depending on the points that the person defending gender segregation in sport raises. Yet the sociologist accepted the coach's contention that sport enabled teamwork – a widely held cultural belief. What follows is an exploration of the key arguments for gender integration in sport.

One of the most frequent arguments for segregating men and women tends to be about biological capacities and 'natural' levels of strength, size and speed. For example, most agree that a 300-pound man should not be tackling a 150-pound woman; but fewer people agree that a 300-pound man should not tackle a 150-pound man. The point is that it is dangerous for a 300-pound man to tackle any 150-pound person – gender is not the issue, weight is. Yet even when we divide teams or competitors into categories by weight, as appropriate for safety, we still tend to also divide by sex.

Some people might argue that most men are better at sport than most women, and that segregated spaces facilitate their own abilities. Assuming for now that this is true, it is to privilege winning over the supposed purpose of sport. Yet if we value sport for character building and teamwork, segregating men and women harms this endeavour.

Perhaps your own perspective is that sport is *really* about achieving feats of human excellence, not team building and leadership skills. In this case, segregation is wrong because it limits the best women by not permitting them to play with the best available players (many of whom are men). Just imagine how good the best women could be if they consistently played with the best players. Robert Merton called this the Matthew effect, after the parable of the talents in the Gospel of Matthew, where people who show early skill are rewarded disproportionately compared to others of a near-similar skill level. In this case, gender segregation ensures that men keep their advantage in sport. The skill gap could shrink and possibly disappear if sports were gender integrated.

But let's focus on the primary reason for sport in educational settings: the idea that it develops the ability to work as a team.

If this is the rationale, then it should be the duty of sport to ensure children learn the skills necessary

© monkeybusinessimages/iStock

to work with everyone in the real world workplace – *not just men*. Segregating children in sport suggests, at some level, that men and women should be treated differently at work.

There is significant evidence that this effect is real. First, when boys are socialized into sport for its perceived 'character-building' benefits, they also construct a language specific to sport that they then take with them into the workplace. Boys and men learn to bond, relate to each other, work and solve problems via sport, all without the presence of girls or women.

Because sport is gender segregated, women are excluded from the domain in which this language and way of relating is learned. Women therefore have a harder time acquiring the cultural codes and behavioural conducts deemed necessary to impress masculine gatekeepers in work and other social institutions that are dominated by men.

This is something gatekeepers (those who do the hiring) code as 'skills'. At job interviews for young adults with little work experience, the easiest answer to questions about 'leadership' or 'team building' is to give an anecdote about sporting participation. Because of gender segregation in sport, this is easier for men to answer. The skills, experiences and behaviours learned through sport – part of what Bourdieu called habitus – also means that a male interviewer and interviewee can more easily relate to each other. This later translates to men's advantage in advancement in corporate life.

There are also negative effects for boys. The gender segregation of sport means that young men are not introduced to the athletic abilities or the lived experiences of women. Instead, young men are socialized into an ethos in which women are devalued as athletes or leaders and primarily viewed as sexual objects. Without the possibility of socializing with women in sport, men fail to learn of women's athletic abilities and leadership skills. With this organization of leisure time, they rarely have the opportunity to become friends with women.

Part of the difficulty in recognizing the problem of gender segregation in sport is it has become so normalized in everyday life. If you were to walk by a sports field and see two soccer teams segregated by race (an all-black team playing another all-black team on the left field, and an all-white team playing an all-white team on the right field), you would most likely think that you were witnessing racist segregation. But seeing an all-female team playing an all-female team on the left field, and an all-male team playing an all-male team on another field is not perceived as gender segregation. The same difference would certainly apply if this segregation was codified in rules, institutionalized in sporting leagues, and supported by media and educators.

And that's why we argue segregation by gender is wrong, and team sports should be gender integrated.

Provoked? Read further:

Foddy, B. & Savulescu, J. (2011). Time to re-evaluate gender segregation in athletics? *British Journal of Sports Medicine*, 45(15), 1184–1188.

Joseph, L.J. & Anderson, E. (2016). The influence of gender segregation and teamsport experience on occupational discrimination in sport-based employment. *Journal of Gender Studies*, 25(5), 586–598.

McDonagh, E. & Pappano, L. (2007). *Playing with the Boys: Why Separate is Not Equal in Sports*. Oxford: Oxford University Press.

Feminism

Just as the civil rights movement challenged racist oppression in the US, so too have people fought for equal rights for women. While each culture has its own history of political action in this regard, it is generally known as **feminism**. Feminism has roots that existed long before the label. Historians sometimes label people who advocated for women's equality, or at least protested certain aspects of women's oppression, as protofeminists.

It is often said that feminism is as simple as believing that women deserve equal rights with men. While admirable in sentiment, the reality is more complex: Not just because different groups of people advance different political strategies about how best to achieve equality, but also because differing views exist about what even constitutes equality. So, one group of feminists passionately believe pornography and sex work are forms of oppression against women (Dworkin 1985), while others reject such claims (Rubin 1993). Indeed, the aims of feminism have changed across time, and have been categorized into three distinct waves.

> **Feminism: the intellectual and political movement that seeks rights for women and to challenge gender inequality**

The three waves of feminism

The three-wave model of feminism's development is associated with particular times in (Anglo-American) women's fight for gender equality.

First-wave feminism

First-wave feminism occurred between the late 1800s and the mid-1930s. Emerging from ideals of the Enlightenment, it was focused on women gaining the right to vote and the right to own land, and women collaborated internationally to achieve these aims. The emancipation movement emerged to fight in particular for the vote. This right is referred to as women's suffrage – hence the name of the suffragettes who emerged as a political force during this period.

The suffragettes fought for women's rights in ways that contrasted with the dominant notion of women as compliant and passive. They threw themselves in front of horses at high-profile racing events (English suffragette Emily Davison died as a result of this), entered into physical altercations with police officers and generally demonstrated that the idea that women were not able to partake in political debate was plainly false.

The two world wars that dominated global politics in the first half of the 20th century had important influences on the first wave of feminism. While the suffragettes were campaigning prior to the start of World War I (in 1914), the war meant great numbers of men went off to fight and women took their place in factories and industries where society had previously prohibited them from working. Over a million British women joined the workforce during the four years of war. While many women returned home after peace was declared, significant numbers remained in the workforce and the Sex Disqualification (Removal) Act of 1919 made it illegal to exclude women from a job because of their gender.

More significant and prolonged change for women occurred after World War II (from 1945). During the conflict, women had directly contributed to the war effort,

© Topical Press Agency/Stringer/Getty Images

Women being arrested in Chicago, US, for wearing 'indecent' swimwear in 1922.

in the Women's Auxiliary Airforce, among other organizations and roles. Women worked as spies, in the navy and army, and again demonstrated the falsity of dominant images of passive femininity in society.

While we must be cautious of attributing causal links, the feminism of the 1960s has its antecedents in both first-wave feminism that fought for fundamental rights and the historical events that transformed working practices.

Second-wave feminism

Second-wave feminism has strong connections with the civil rights movement – the social movement in the US that sought to end racial segregation and discrimination in the 1950s and 1960s. The tactics and hopes that this struggle inspired likely encouraged other groups to adopt similar tactics. Second-wave feminism is probably what many people think of as 'feminism': political action that sought to contest legal inequality.

It was also in the 1960s that feminism adopted intellectual arguments from within academia and applied them more generally. For example, French philosopher Simone de Beauvoir wrote an influential book, *The Second Sex* (1949). This included the now-famous phrase 'One is not born, but rather becomes, a woman'. Here, she was arguing for the social nature of gender: that being a woman is dependent on social attitudes and views of femaleness that constrict the possibilities afforded to women. Her ideas fermented into political action and meant that feminism had a strong intellectual foundation alongside its political action.

Influential non-academic books were written during this second wave. For example, Australian feminist Germaine Greer (1970) argued in *The Female Eunuch* that the traditional 'nuclear family' (see Chapter 6, pp. 134–136) served to repress women's sexuality and effectively rendered them eunuchs. A combination of scholarly research alongside polemical writing, Greer presented problems with the way society discussed female sexuality in bold, bawdy terms. Similarly, Betty Friedan (1959), an American feminist, wrote *The Feminine Mystique*, which examined the negative experiences of women in American society at the time. She demonstrated the ways in which women were unhappy, and highlighted the societal reasons for this.

Second-wave feminism also drew wider cultural attention to the social problems of rape, domestic violence, and other social injustices and crimes that disproportionately affect women. Feminists during this period engaged in political actions, from trying to implement new laws to developing new forms of intellectual critique. This latter trend included examining how a narrow and stereotypical representation of women in the media had negative social effects.

Second-wave feminism achieved multiple social gains, at least in the West. Women's rights to reproductive health, to attend schools, to work, to live independent of men, to have a sex life, play sport, drive, and many more opportunities and rights have come from the marriage between academics and activists.

Another feature of second-wave feminism, however, was the emergence of substantial and strident debate *between* feminists. Whereas most women, and certainly all feminists, agreed that women should be legally entitled to vote and own property, debates about the regulation of pornography and sex work are far more contentious. The 'porn wars' of the 1980s were particularly acrimonious and saw significant divides within the feminist movement (Rubin 1993).

Most of these debates centred on issues of sex and sexual desire. However, they also included issues of race. Second-wave feminism was also critiqued for mostly reflecting the views and perspectives of white women, straight women, and women of the middle and upper classes. This led to what some today recognize as third-wave feminism.

Political language and feminism

Much second-wave feminism was intellectually accessible and politically potent. Second-wave feminists developed new terms and concepts to identify oppression. Consider the following:

Malestream: a term used to describe mainstream (or normative) thinking in society that is representative of men's thinking, with no attention paid to gender.

Herstory: the notion that history has traditionally been written by men about men's perspectives. Herstory seeks to address this by writing about women's issues and perspectives in history.

Both of these are effective neologisms that identify serious issues in the treatment of women in society.

Third-wave feminism

As a new generation of women academics, writers and activists entered the feminist movement, third-wave feminism marked a growing dissatisfaction with the way in which second-wave feminism had polarized in the 1980s. Growing from the successes of the second-wave, focus shifted in the 1990s to other forms of discrimination that had not been addressed in such depth and included a diversification of approaches to understanding gender inequality. Key issues here were the recognition of intersectionality and the experiences of non-white and working-class women.

Third-wave feminism thus both attempts to expand feminism to a more diverse set of women's identities – to include the voices of those traditionally excluded – and to focus more on cultural issues of sexual inequality. Debates about the aims and terminology of feminism persist, as do the debates about sex work, and the porn wars are back with a vengeance as some argue that pornography inherently damages women (see Provocation 4 on p. 75).

One component of feminism has shifted from a focus on political action to more intellectual pursuits and queer transgressions. Renowned feminist philosopher Martha Nussbaum writes in *The New Republic* (February 1999):

> Many young feminists, whatever their concrete affiliations with this or that French thinker, have been influenced by the extremely French idea that the intellectual does politics by speaking seditiously, and that this is a significant type of political action. Many have also derived from the writings of Michel Foucault (rightly or wrongly) the fatalistic idea that we are prisoners of an all-enveloping structure of power, and that real-life reform movements usually end up serving power in new and insidious ways. Such feminists therefore find comfort in the idea that the subversive use of words is still available to feminist intellectuals.

It is thus important to understand that third-wave feminism is not united, and it has not erased the factionalism of feminism from the second-wave.

Of course, feminists have always faced opposition that looks to devalue their cause and stall social progress for women. Much of this has been done by stigmatizing the notion of identifying as feminist. Feminists have long been stereotyped as unattractive, humourless, man-hating single women; modern feminism is stereotyped as being obsessed by political correctness. This is not to say that feminists have given up the fight for quality education, reproductive rights, and improved living conditions for women and children, but that the quest for gender equality has faced many challenges.

Men and masculinities

An important sub-branch of the sociology of gender is the study of men and masculinities. It holds men as the core focus of analysis, explicitly recognizing them as gendered beings. This scholarship has developed understanding of how men benefit from patriarchy, but it also discusses the ways in which men lose out from their gender.

© Reimphoto/iStock

In recent years, the study of men and masculinities has become a buoyant subfield.

One of the core problems with masculinities is that they are often defined in opposition to a highly stigmatized femininity. As Kimmel (2004) argued, 'the antifemininity component of masculinity is perhaps the single dominant and universal characteristic' (p. 97). Men have also had to be macho and tough. In the UK, Máirtín Mac an Ghaill (1994) discussed the three Fs of masculinity: football, fighting and fucking. Pollack (1999) showed that from the time they are very young, boys had to act like little men, including the idea that 'boys don't cry' – even though expressing emotions is an important component of being human and suppressing them can be detrimental to mental health and wellbeing.

This machismo was accompanied by a pervasive homophobia. As a result, men went to great lengths to avoid being perceived by others as gay. The most effective way of doing this was to deploy homophobia. Accordingly, masculinity became not just a show of physical strength and emotional stoicism, but also an expression of anti-gay attitudes.

Australian sociologist Raewyn Connell (1995) introduced the notion of hegemonic masculinity to theorize the ways in which privilege and damage were distributed between men. Importantly, she argued two core ideas: 1) that masculine hierarchies existed *between* men; and 2) that dynamics of masculinities perpetuate gender inequality.

In terms of hierarchies between men, Connell argued that there were four archetypes into which groups of men fit. There is one masculinity that is the dominant, *hegemonic* one in society: This is the masculinity that men aspire to, although it may be different in different cultural contexts. Within each context, though, there was only ever *one* masculinity that maintained this dominance.

Anderson (2005) named this *orthodox masculinity*, in part because Connell did not provide a name for it: it tended to be macho, sporty, violent and homophobic.

Connell identified three other groups of men and their masculinities: *complicit*, who benefitted from patriarchy but did not conform to the hegemonic (or orthodox) ideal. *Marginalized* described working-class men and people of colour who might gain some benefits from masculinity, but these are outweighed by the issues they encounter because of their class and race. *Subordinated* referred to gay men and other sexual minorities, who were excluded from masculine contention because of their sexuality: so homophobic was the 1980s that gay men were not considered masculine *because of* their sexuality (Plummer 1999). Many of the men in these groups, particularly those with complicit masculinities, believed in the right to rule of those at the top, and they desired to embody orthodox masculinity themselves – hence the hegemony of the system.

Connell also argued that these stratifications of masculinities served to reinforce gender inequality between men and women. We have no doubt that many men who embodied orthodox masculinities also reproduced gender inequality, but there is scant evidence that the hierarchies of masculinity are the core issue in how gender inequality is perpetuated.

The description of the most popular form of masculinity described by research in the 1980s does not accurately describe millennial men today. Metrosexuality emerged in the 1990s as a way for men to care about clothes and style without being socially perceived as gay. This desire to look good has now moved from a transgressive notion to a valued characteristic of modern men. The British boy band One Direction best exemplify this change. These young men's gentle tactility and open displays of emotion are part of their appeal. Homophobia couldn't be further from their lips, as they thanked their army of gay fans and perform at gay venues (McCormack 2012).

This change has been explained through Anderson's (2009) inclusive masculinity theory, which connected softening masculinities with decreasing homophobia in the West across the past 30 years (Clements & Field 2014; Smith 2011). As homophobia was the policing agent of masculinity in the 1980s, the decrease of homophobia has meant that men can be more in touch with their feelings and more expressive about them publicly than they could before.

Perhaps the best example of this change is to think about men cuddling and sharing beds together. Anderson and McCormack (2015) interviewed 30 young sports men at a British university about how they related to their friends, finding that 29 of them had shared a bed with a close male friend, and 27 had spooned together – sustained cuddling in bed between two straight men. And most times, their other friends knew about this.

The relatively new sociology of masculinities, mapped out mostly by feminist scholars, has emerged as a new paradigm for examining men – one that no longer takes masculinity uncritically as a norm for male experience. Masculinities are now defined collectively in culture, and it is recognized that they are sustained by core and peripheral institutions. Masculinities today are being examined socially, historically and critically for their problems as well as their benefits.

Sexuality and homophobia

The word sexuality can have a panoply of meanings. It can refer to sexual identity, such as whether one identifies as straight, gay or bisexual; or it refers to desire – from the sex you are attracted to, to the type of bodies and specific sex acts you like. It is also used to discuss ideas of love and intimacy. We discuss many of these issues in Chapter 8. Yet sexuality is also a mode of power, and the ways these desires and practices are experienced are inherently social and influenced by cultural norms.

While sociology has a long history of research into sexuality, it has often been considered a marginal component of society – an issue of 'deviance' not particularly important to the running of society (Irvine 2003). Indeed, as gender scholarship emerged in the 1960s and 1970s, sexuality was subsumed within gender – that is, sexual desire and sexual violence were seen merely as issues within gender inequality (Rubin 1984). Thus, important ways that sexuality is understood in society – from sex work and the consumption of pornography to abortion and sexual violence – were all understood through the prism of existing gender theories.

One of the central ways sexuality has been mobilized as a source of power is through the oppression of sexual minorities. A key component of this has been the stigmatization of same-sex desire and sexual practice. Sexual minorities suffered a great deal of discrimination and oppression, including the criminalization of same-sex sexual acts across much of the 20th century (Meyer 2003). Gay people were forced to socialize within closeted subcultures for protection and safety, invisible to dominant culture.

Homophobia has been the term used by academics and activists to understand the nature and effects of prejudice and discrimination against sexual minorities. Herek (2004) argued that the term helped change the framing of anti-gay prejudice by 'locating the "problem" of homosexuality not in homosexual people, but in heterosexuals who were intolerant of gay men and lesbians' (p. 8). While terms such as biphobia are used to discuss sexual prejudice against bisexuals specifically, homophobia is still used as a term to refer to both prejudice against gay people and same-sex desire more generally, which would include bisexuals and other sexual minorities (Anderson & McCormack 2016).

Homophobia is undergoing a period of sustained decline in the West, with attitudes and laws improving across the US and most of Europe. However, homophobic laws and oppression of sexual minorities are still occurring, or even increasing, in the Middle East and parts of Russia (Smith 2011). These trends are particularly concerning, and highlight the contextual nature of homophobia and how it is a *political* mechanism used to control people within a society. Sexuality is likely to be a core way societies are divided in the future, and its study needs to be incorporated in sociology in a manner similar to class, race and gender.

CONCLUSION

This chapter has examined the ways in which societies are divided. We have focused on class, race and gender as key ways in which inequality exists in society – where one group of people gains benefits and privilege at the expense of another group. In each of these cases, the differences and distinctions are not the result of biological or inherent differences, but the ways in which society is structured. We have drawn out key theories for each of the divisions, and encourage you to look for similarities between them. The breadth and depth of social divisions means that there is much more we could have covered – both for class, race and gender but also in terms of other divisions. Societies are divided by religion, age, attractiveness, ability and many more factors. Sadly, we have to keep reminding ourselves of the black feminist poet Maya Angelou's declamatory refrain in her poem *Human Family*: 'we are more alike, my friends, than we are unalike.'

HOW WOULD...?

» How would black feminists like Patricia Hill Collins and Kimberlé Crenshaw critique second-wave feminism that focused on gender?

  » Have you noticed class, race or gender being modes of power in your own life? Have you benefitted or suffered because of them?

  » To what extent have you thought about them before?

» How would you approach studying social divisions in your own community?

  » What theoretical framework fits best?

  » How would each of the theories apply to your own context or country?

STRUCTURED FURTHER READING

McIntosh, P. (1989). White privilege: Unpacking the invisible knapsack. *Peace and Freedom Magazine,* July/August, 10–12. Philadelphia, PA: Women's International League for Peace and Freedom.

This is a piece of sociology that highlighted the powerful ways in which white people maintain privilege in society. It draws attention to a number of ways in which privilege is taken for granted, and how it requires conscious 'unpacking' of privilege to effect change.

Ghaziani, A. (2017). *Sex Cultures.* Cambridge: Polity.

An accessible introduction to understanding sex in society that views these discussions through a cultural lens. With a chapter on politics and protest, it understands the moral nature of much regulation and prejudice around sexuality and develops an argument about how to study sex and sexuality in society.

Atkinson, W. (2015). *Class*. Cambridge: Polity.
This introduction to the theories of class discusses the key theoretical traditions in research on social class, debates some of the major controversies that have shaped the field and examines contemporary class inequalities.

 Visit the companion website at **www.macmillanihe.com/mccormack** for further learning and teaching resources.

Chapter 8
PERSONAL LIFE

INTRODUCTION

This chapter focuses on issues that relate to our personal lives. Sometimes our daily routines and practices can be seen as divorced from the bigger issues of society, yet sociology helps us understand how they are connected to and impact upon each other. We examine these issues by focusing on key aspects of personal life. First, we investigate how our bodies have been understood sociologically: from how the body has been used to reproduce gender norms to the ways tattoos are used to inscribe meaning onto our bodies. We then turn to sex, and think about how this most personal of activities is connected to broader social norms – even how sex is defined. We then look at relationships, from friends to lovers, and think about diverse relationship types in contemporary society. In our Provocation, we ask whether cheating is an inherent part of monogamy, rather than proof of its failure.

THE PERSONAL

Sociology often focuses on how societies are structured and how they change. We devote Chapter 9 to this topic, including how modern societies are organized. Yet sociologists are also concerned with the most intimate parts of our individual lives – from whom we love to the rituals around death and dying. These personal aspects of life can seem disconnected from the big questions that sociology is often focused on, like globalization or social inequality, but they are deeply entwined with the social organization of society. Sociology helps us understand how and why.

We opened this book with discussions of disgust related to spit and how students attending lectures choose where to sit. These examples show the ways in which broad sociological issues, like the role of disgust in society, are reflected in everyday life. One reason that a sociology of personal life matters is that it can serve as a hook to understanding other issues. Just as listening to your favourite artist on Spotify might encourage you to see them live, or hearing one song could result in you buying their album, so connecting with sociology at a personal level can help open the vista of what sociology can offer more generally.

Yet it would be wrong to argue that the sociology of personal life is just an easy way in to, or the trailer for, macro-level sociology. We also discussed in Chapter 1 how Durkheim connected rates of suicide with the social organization of societies. This is another example of personal life interacting with broader social trends, but one which is clearly more serious. When someone contemplates suicide, they do so because of very personal feelings and experiences, yet, as Durkheim demonstrated, rates of suicide can also tell us much about the organization of a society.

In this chapter, we examine identity, society and the personal in more detail. We review how sociology has understood some of the most personal aspects of social life by thinking about the body, and the changing value and meaning attached to tattoos across time; we then explore sex, relationships and monogamy, in order to develop a sociological understanding of personal life.

From the personal to personal life

If we embrace C. Wright Mills' (1959) notion of the sociological imagination, focusing on the personal is a powerful way to develop that method of thinking that enables us to move beyond common-sense understandings of the world. In his book, Mills urged us to think about our own individual biographies in understanding how society operates. He recognized the importance of personal experiences, not least for the social justice argument that such an approach increases the likelihood that sociology will have a positive impact on people's lives.

One term sociologists use to describe the social nature of the personal is **relational**. This recognizes that behaviours and practices always occur in the context of how they relate to other people, because these behaviours and interactions occur with and between other people. Our very identities are dependent on how others see us (see our discussion of 'me' and 'I' in Chapter 2, p. 36).

Thinking about the personal enables recognition of the way institutions, culture and social policy impact on individuals. Examining, for example, how couples kiss and embrace outdoors – the infamous 'public displays of affection', or PDAs as they are known – can inform us about differences between how heterosexual and same-sex couples feel safe and able to express themselves in public venues. Even though there has been a decrease in homophobic attitudes in recent decades, you are still much more likely to see a heterosexual couple engaging in a PDA than a same-sex couple. This is not because gay couples love each other less. Rather, it is the result of historical homophobia being entrenched in culture and policy that something as simple and ordinary as a kiss on the cheek is more challenging for same-sex couples (Doan et al. 2014).

The sociology of the personal can provide information about the interrelationship between broader social norms and individuals. For example, understanding the reasons why people engage in binge drinking (the personal) can lead to nuanced interventions designed to improve public health (the macro) without relying on prohibitionist social policies, which tend to fail (Measham & Brain 2005). These policy changes can then filter down to positively impact on the personal (e.g. by reducing binge drinking or ensuring it happens in safer ways).

> **Relational:** the notion that two or more things occur in relation to each other, rather than independently

Yet the study of the personal and social interactions has not traditionally occurred under the name of 'personal life'. Rather, it will have been framed as sociology of the family or other similar terms. British sociologist Carol Smart (2007) argues that the study of personal life is an important conceptual development because it enables studies of the family and the organization of intimate life that moves beyond understandings that privilege biological relations or living together and recognizes the significant social change that has occurred in these areas. This subject has now expanded to touch upon topics as diverse as pets, public spaces and consumer culture (May 2011).

Consider how sociological understanding of families has changed over the past 50 years. In the 1950s and 1960s, the traditional, 'nuclear family' of a married, white heterosexual couple with two children (the statistical norm) dominated in many Western countries. At the time, sociology sought to connect the family with the 'normal' operation of society. Talcott Parsons' functionalist perspective (see Chapter 6, p. 134) argued that there were prescribed roles and rules that needed to be followed within the family, such as the father as breadwinner and mother as caregiver, to effectively socialize children into functional and productive citizens of this society. He suggested that deviation from this nuclear family structure and from these prescribed gender roles would be problematic both for the individual child and for society as a whole.

Over the past 50 years, sociological perspectives on the family have radically changed, with recognition of a more diverse set of relationships that include dual-heritage couples, same-sex marriages, non-married couples and many other formats. The reality of family life has been transformed, including attitudes to different family forms, and sociological perspectives have also changed greatly. We would be shocked if a contemporary sociologist shared Parsons' understanding of what comprised a 'normal' family. Much of this intellectual change was down to the increasing value being placed on understanding how the family works, not just as an institution, but also how it is experienced and lived at a personal level (see Chapter 6 for discussion of this).

Thus, a sociology of personal life examines the issues of intimacy and importance within individuals' lives, connecting these with broader social trends without losing focus of the contextual issues that influence and constrain our everyday practices.

SOCIOLOGY AND THE BODY

The body is a central component of personal life. It is, after all, the vessel through which life is experienced and lived. Our bodies are deeply personal to us and are 'with us' throughout our entire lifetime, though they inevitably change in various ways. We worry about our health. We care about how we look. Some of us spend a great deal of time and money at the gym, on cosmetic surgery, putting on make-up or choosing the right outfit. Our bodies, and how we think of them, are intimately connected with these processes.

Surprisingly, perhaps, there is a long history of *not* considering the body in sociology and intellectual thought more generally.

This is best exemplified by philosopher Rene Descartes' (1596–1650) famous phrase *cogito ergo sum* – 'I think, therefore I am'. In perhaps the best-known idea in Western philosophy, Descartes argued that the one thing we can know for certain is that we think and that, by extension, if we think we must also have to exist. He then argued that if thinking is the only way we know we exist, thinking becomes our fundamental and essential feature.

From that starting point, Descartes questioned whether we could be sure other people and the physical world existed. He felt that the most important thing that made humans special was their minds, not their senses or their sensations (or emotions). He did not value the latter two, dismissing them as things we humans share with animals. The mind, capable of knowing its own existence, is what makes humans different from animals and, for Descartes, capable of possessing souls.

This leads to what is known as Cartesian dualism – the conceptual separation of the body and the mind. Here, the body is relegated to a fleshy, finite substance that decays and dies. The body is understood as somewhat incidental, while the mind is equated with the soul that transcends human life and reaches a 'higher plane'.

The body was sometimes considered in early sociology, but it was very rarely an explicit focus of study (Shilling 1993). And when sociology touched on the subject, it was often quite abstract, using 'identity', 'the self' and other vague terms when referring to the bodily experiences of pain, emotion, injury, sickness, desire, etc. These intangible sociological terms do not exactly reflect the intensity with which the emotions are experienced.

Some research did engage more fully with the issue of the body. Erving Goffman (1963), for example, looked at how bodily practices were important in social interaction. In his book *Stigma*, he discussed how physical abnormalities could result in one being excluded from acceptable society. More generally, his interactionist approach incorporated bodily displays and interactions in this regard. Even so, the body remained a peripheral concern and not the focus of sociological thought.

In large part, sociology ignored the body because it was assumed to be purely a concern for biologists. Durkheim defined human beings as *homo duplex*, being biological bodies but also social animals. He then defined sociology as the study of the latter, not the former. This omission was particularly bad for women, whose biological differences from men were taken as a convenient catch-all to 'explain' all manner of social differences. This included employment, child-rearing, education and the right to vote (or its absence). Sociology followed society in 'taking it for granted' that the different bodies of men and women explained a range of gender inequalities and, as such, these were not studied sociologically (see Chapter 2 for discussion of sociology and women in history).

Yet sociologists have developed sophisticated theories of the body in recent years and there is a great deal of contemporary research on the body (see Waskul & Vannini 2012). A core concept is **embodiment** – which recognizes the body is both a physical object and something that is processed and understood socially. Waskul and Vannini (2012) define embodiment as 'the process by which the object-body is actively experienced, produced, sustained and/or transformed as a subject-body' (p. 3). In other words, the way we interact in society and the values we place on our bodies are understood through embodiment.

Embodiment: the process by which meaning and values are placed onto people's bodies

British sociologist Nick Crossley (2005) argues that people think about their bodies, integrating them as part of their identity. As part of this **reflexive process** – where individuals think about their actions and thus influence their behaviours – people seek to modify their bodies as a way of constructing their broader identities. In order to understand this process, Crossley discusses 'Reflexive Body Techniques' (RBTs) as a way to understand the connection between body modifications, embodiment and social identities. He defines RBTs as 'those body techniques whose primary purpose is to work back upon the body, so as to modify, maintain or thematise it in some way' (p. 9). This includes styling hair, tattoos (see p. 197 in this chapter) and permanent plastic surgery, and from what and how we eat to where and how we exercise. RBTs offer a sophisticated way of thinking about our bodies and how they interact with society, including how issues like class, ethnicity and gender can affect embodiment.

> **Reflexive process:** also known as reflexivity, it is the cyclical process whereby individuals think about their actions and thus influence their behaviours, which in turn influences their thoughts

Whose body is it?

Contrasting with Descartes' philosophy, it could be said that in many ways we *are* our bodies. After all, without a body there would be nobody left. Nonetheless, while you might arguably be your body, does your body belong to you?

Consider the fact that some societies consider suicide a crime. All societies have laws that regulate whether and how you can sell your body or particular parts of it. In the UK, men can sell their sperm but women cannot directly sell 'their' eggs because the law declares that a person cannot sell any part of their body that cannot be detached 'naturally'. Thus, you can sell your hair but not your organs. Assisted suicide, 'consenting' cannibalism and various forms of selling sex for money are all heavily regulated by law, because society claims a right over the bodies of its members. This is because societies often seek to protect their members from harm, and sometimes even claim the right and need to protect members from themselves. A significant question becomes whether these legal interventions best protect the citizens subject to them. We discuss social policy in more detail in Chapter 10.

Women and the body

Social understandings of the body have been a crucial factor in gender inequality. The fundamental difference between men's and women's bodies centred on issues of reproduction. In pre-industrial societies, home and work were not separated and so child-rearing and work went together. Yet the Industrial Revolution separated work and home (see Chapters 3 and 9), meaning that childcare and work could not occur simultaneously (Cancian 1987). Women were held responsible for raising children, to the extent that laws were passed preventing them from working outside the home so that they could raise the next generation of workers.

This socially structured division of labour was claimed to be 'natural'. Men went to work, voted and got an education. Women did not. In 1900, the average woman in England had 10 pregnancies in a lifetime, though far fewer resulted in actual births, and even fewer children survived into adulthood. Women were largely bound to a 'private' realm of reproduction which was said to be 'natural', and thus outside the realm of sociological study.

Male doctors, judges, lawmakers and even sociologists all agreed that women could not step out of their bodies. Charles Darwin pronounced that if a woman went to university, her breasts would dry up and her womb would start moving about, causing her to become hysterical (David 2005). Indeed, even the term 'hysteria' comes from the Greek for 'the wandering womb'.

While contraception did exist, it was not reliable and often in male hands (condoms). Contraception was also subject to moral and legal restriction. It was not, for example, easily available to unmarried women. Furthermore, marriage legally required that a woman make her body available to her husband to produce offspring. This was also interpreted to mean that a husband could not be accused of raping his wife because she had lawfully consented to give her body over to his use through the act of marriage. This was the prevailing common law interpretation of marriage that informed jurisprudence in England for over 250 years, until the British House of Lords explicitly ruled otherwise in 1991.

Throughout much of this time, an almost exclusively male sociology no more studied the existence of such gender roles and inequalities than they thought to study why humans cannot breathe under water. The gendered body was 'the' body, just as gills were what made fish different from humans.

To summarize a long and complex history, the contraceptive pill became available to women in the US in 1960, and later elsewhere. It was the result of much political campaigning. This oral contraceptive put relatively secure birth control into women's hands. This had a significant impact on sociological thought as well as women's lives. Research on the family had studied how the division of labour between the mother as carer and father as provider was organized socially (Parsons & Bales 1955). Yet the availability of the contraceptive pill threw the assumptions behind this study radically into question. Suddenly, the body was clearly subject to social control and could no longer be said to be 'the natural' cause of social differences. A whole social structure that assumed women's position in society was the result of their biology was suddenly, and fundamentally, discredited.

Feminist researchers in the 1960s and 1970s were the first to challenge a century of male sociology's neglect of the body, in studies of work, medicine, marriage, sexual relationships and reproduction. However, there was also later a growth in mainstream research on the body in the 1980s. There were several reasons for this trend (Shilling 1993).

First, the rise of consumer culture meant that the body was increasingly a subject of capitalist interest as people spent money on themselves as part of 'body projects'. The sexual revolution that was initiated by the contraceptive pill combined with higher wages postwar to create a consumer culture devoted to youth, lifestyle choices and adornment. The notion of the **consumer self**, where people's identities were consolidated through buying particular brands or items, meant that the body was increasingly relevant. Here, people demonstrated their consumer power on and through their bodies – in the clothes and accessories they wore or cosmetic surgery they had done.

Consumer culture became more overtly sexual and bodies – and particular parts of bodies – became more visible. Called *striptease culture* by Brian McNair (2002), bodies in sexy and sexual poses were increasingly used to sell goods and services that often had little or no romantic or sexual connotation. While women's bodies

Consumer self: the notion that people's identities are constructed and consolidated through consumerism (the purchasing of goods)

© Richard Baker/Getty Images

An(other) example of women being sexualized in advertising.

were the most sexualized in the 20th century, more recently men's bodies too have increasingly become the focus of desire – known as objectification. As the body became more visible, it came into focus for sociologists studying consumption practices.

This desire to look good is partly based on the recognition of how valued attractiveness is in society – good-looking people gain privilege because of their looks. Asch (1946) called this discrimination primary effect. He found that the first information received about a person was more important than information gained later: how a person looks is often the first information another person receives. Research has shown that good-looking people are thought to be more kind, sociable, sensitive and healthy, and are even thought to have better job prospects than unattractive people (Dion et al. 1972; Feingold 1992).

The rise and success of feminism brought the body to greater attention. Feminist research first highlighted that bodies matter through the very fact that women suffered discrimination because of their sex (i.e. the biology of their bodies) and because their bodies were deemed weaker than men's.

Feminist research also documented the ways in which women's bodies had been the property of men; that women's sexual agency was denied; and that gender research had historically tried to prove women's bodies inferior to men's. Feminists did not just discuss the role of the body; they argued that it was a central battleground in the legitimation of gender inequality.

A key site of this inequality was, and still is, the workplace. Women continue to suffer a 'motherhood penalty'. Here, women who have taken time off work to have children are disadvantaged in terms of pay, promotions, and their perceived competence and commitment (Correl et al. 2007). The reproductive function of women's bodies remains central to their inequality in the workplace. This is not a biological effect of women's bodies: being pregnant does not stop women working, nor are men physically incapable of childcare. Rather, it is how society organizes things before and after childbirth that continues to limit women's careers relative to men's.

More broadly, research also examines the presence of bodies at work through the term **body work** (Gimlin 2007; Wolkowitz 2006). We take our bodies to work every day, whether we are serving burgers in McDonald's, labouring on a building site or caring for terminally ill patients. We also use our bodies at work in very different ways. In doing so, our bodies are physically affected by the work that we do (we get tired eyes and sore feet, alongside more serious health concerns) and they are regulated by the industries that we work in (we might have to have vaccinations or wear uniforms). As such, sociology must recognize the importance of the body in our daily lives.

> **Body work:** also known as body labour, it refers to the work individuals exert on their own bodies as well as paid work that is performed on other people's bodies

Technology also had an impact on how we consider the body. Conception via *in vitro* fertilization – labelled 'test tube babies' in newspapers – brought questions about how the body and technology intersected (see Chapter 6, p. 136). Particular questions were raised about the morality of creating what were called 'designer babies' by screening embryos in order to implant those with (or without) particular characteristics. These sorts of debates are now reappearing, with recent developments in technology making the creation of synthetic cells, organs and even DNA a realistic possibility. As medical technology becomes more advanced, and an ageing population experiences their ageing bodies, there is ever more need for a sociology of the body.

Women and the body in Iran

Research on women and the body remains focused on the West. Elham Amini (2017) contributes to sociological research on women and the body internationally by exploring how Iranian menopausal women understand their gender and sexuality through pivotal bodily moments in their lives – including their first period (menarche) and the menopause. Amini showed how participants' bodies were key sites in understanding their identities, as well as sites for finding agency in negotiating patriarchal norms of Iranian culture. It was through bodily processes that participants identified themselves as entering 'womanhood' and, similarly, the onset of the menopause was seen as a significant and permanent sign of ageing. By focusing on the role of the body, Amini highlighted key issues of gender and sexuality for Iranian women. (See Chapter 4, pp. 84–85 for Dr Amini's Vox Pop.)

Tattoos

Tattoos have a long history, going back at least to the Stone Age, with evidence that the Ancient Egyptian pharaohs had them. In these ancient times, tattoos were literal signs of status or achievement. Closely related to religion and tribal affiliation, tattoos would act in a similar way to medals, denoting the achievement of the person tattooed. In non-Western contexts, tattoos were traditionally used as rites of passage. In Maori culture, *ta moko* markings on the face and body were used to document the passage from childhood to adulthood. These were done by chiselling grooves into the skin rather than inking.

However, during the 18th and 19th centuries, in the West, tattoos became stigmatized as the preserve of the lower socio-economic classes, and gained an air of disrespectability (Sanders 2008). They have also been used in slavery, as symbols of ownership.

This was partly because of criminal associations, as gang members would mark their affiliations through tattoos. Tattoos were also associated with other groups of people who were marginalized in society. Circus workers, in particular, were known for their tattoos, as well as sailors, who would decorate their bodies with tattoos from the countries (often considered 'savage' or 'primitive') they had visited. In both contexts, the tattoo was associated with wild, raucous men (and sometimes women) who did not have respectable lives or stable jobs.

Reproduced with permission from Pierrat and Guillon (2013).

From the Ancient era through to today, numerous meanings have been associated with tattoos.

Pierrat and Guillon (2013) use a collection of photos from 1890 to 1930 to show how tattoos were used by prisoners and convicts to contest their marginalized position in society (pictured). Their tattoos expressed feelings including patriotism, revenge, lust and love. During this time, tattoos were near-exclusively associated with the criminal underworld and remained very stigmatized.

Using tattoos as a form of defiance spread across Western cultures in the aftermath of World War II (Barron 2013). People were aware of the social meanings of such 'inkings', and they were interpreted by the wider populace as belonging to people who were criminals, or associated with criminality, and who used tattoos as a way to express this fact.

However, in the early 1970s the practice of tattooing began to be less associated just with criminality and deviant subcultures. Benson (2000) speaks of a tattoo renaissance in which they became a carefully chosen form of self-expression. While tattoos have always been used to communicate meaning – whether it be a medal of achievement or group membership of a gang or particular subculture – the meanings diversified, as did the people who had them. As DeMello (2000) writes, 'Tattooing began, for the first time, to be connected with emerging issues like self-actualization, social and personal transformation, ecological awareness and spiritual growth' (p. 143).

In this context, tattoos have become part of a body project in which people use tattoos to: recognize significant moments in their lives; commemorate important people; associate themselves with a particular trend; or merely to look good. Gone are fears about what the tattoo will look like when the person is old, and tattoos are widely treated in similar ways to hair, make-up and clothes — as ways to look good and stylish in contemporary culture. Even so, there is still evidence to suggest that employers may look unfavourably on people with visible tattoos (Bekhor et al. 1995; Elzweig & Peeples 2011; Miller et al. 2009).

 VOX POP Steven Hogg

Doctoral Student aged 25, from Liverpool, England

I began getting tattooed at 15. Over the past nine years since then, I've amassed a considerable collection of tattoos. My inkings are diverse, ranging from a pair of socks on my ankle to two grenade-holding squirrels on my forearm. Generally, I decide on a more surrealistic design for my tattoos and sketch the vast majority of them myself. The stranger the image, the likelier that I'll have it permanently drawn on my body. Who wants a generic tribal tattoo or a butterfly when you can imagine and create unique pieces? The recurring themes throughout my tattoos are around animals and nature, but incorporating them in an artistic and  surreal manner. My tattoos aren't to mark a specific event in my life, or have one meaning, but they symbolize different aspects of who I am and what I believe. I showcase them along with art I enjoy on Instagram, at @stehogg5.

© Steven Hogg

> » How does Steven's narrative of his tattoos correspond with the empirical research on the topic?
>
> » In what ways might Steven's tattoos be a form of body project?

This rise of the body project is part of a changing society in which meaning is located in the individual. Rather than be defined by religion, class group or profession, a person locates value in themselves and the choices they make in their lives. This is known as the **individualization thesis**; this is a significant component of personal life in the past 40 years, and will be discussed in greater detail in Chapter 9. Now, we turn to a significant issue in personal life, one in which our bodies are vital — sex.

Individualization thesis: the notion that the act of making choices about one's life is where self-worth is found

SEX

Sex is central to our lives. Even people who do not have sexual desires — asexuals — still live in a society that is infused with sexual stories and images. Sex is not just commonly held to be a vital part of romantic relationships, it can preoccupy our thoughts and is a key way to sell products and ideas. Sex is also vital to some of the big sociological issues, such as population studies and demographics — who is having sex with whom, and whether it leads to childbirth, are significant issues for countries at the macro level.

Yet there is a very basic question that is really quite difficult to answer. That is: *What counts as sex?*

If you ask your friends this question, their answer will normally presuppose that sex is a behaviour that occurs with another person. Many people will assume that person will be of a different sex, but it can of course be with someone of the same sex.

People answering this question then normally add that it includes penetration – where the penis enters the vagina. Interestingly, they will often say that penile-anal sexual activity is sex for gay men, but not for heterosexual couples.

Sociological research has investigated this issue. Sanders and Reinisch (1999) found that people had 'widely divergent opinions about what behaviours do and do not constitute having "had sex"'. The most recent study on this issue, by Peck et al. (2016), found that 97.4 per cent of participants felt that penile-vaginal intercourse qualified as sex, while 85.4 per cent thought this was true of penile-anal intercourse. Approximately 60 per cent of participants felt that oral-vaginal or oral-penile intercourse was sex.

Other forms of sexual contact – such as kissing, breast-fondling and other forms of touch or foreplay – are considered to be sex by only a small proportion of people (under 5 per cent for each).

Is there anything wrong with this?

We first need to recognize that discussing what counts as sex is actually determining a *definition* of sex. And the key component in most definitions of sex is penetration.

The focus on penetration keeps sex located in the reproductive realm. In patriarchal societies, it has always been important for the father of a child (especially an heir) to know that he was the *biological* father – that he 'has paternity'. Historically, it was difficult to ascertain this (at least before modern DNA testing advances), heightening male fear of infidelity and 'illegitimacy' of children. Moral codes were created to regulate women's sexuality, curbing their rights over their own bodies. These codes bound sex firmly to reproduction and either denied outright the concept of sex for (female) pleasure or, at best, limited it to strictly being possible within the bounds of marriage (more leeway being implicitly given to men's 'coarser natures').

Despite sex becoming more recreational rather than concerned with procreation (Giddens 1992), penetrative hetero-sex maintains that link with pregnancy and children. As such, another negative effect of believing only one kind of penetration counts as 'real' sex is a heightened risk of unwanted pregnancies and higher risks of transmitting STIs.

Changing views of sexual pleasure

What is considered sexual or erotic changes over time and depends on culture. In Victorian England, a woman displaying her ankle was considered overtly sexual – a pre-20th-century form of twerking. Similarly, when Elvis Presley shook his hips while dancing in the US in the 1950s, many in the dominant culture thought this was sexually obscene. Today in the West, however, such dancing is regularly shown on TV and in the music industry. While these physical expressions have likely always occurred, the way society views them and condemns or endorses them has significantly changed.

There is also a sizeable group of people who maintain that while oral intercourse counts as sex, it would not count as a way of losing one's virginity (Peck et al. 2016). Given that virginity is basically defined as 'not having had sex', this shows that there is a hierarchy even among those sexual acts that are widely considered to comprise sex. This speaks to the hegemonic dominance that penetration and the importance of the penis has in cultural understandings of sex – something that has been described as a *phallocentric* view of sex.

It is also instructive that people define sex through particular acts rather than experiences. While survey questions tend to structure people into answering in terms of acts, the responses are similar to our experiences of students' answers and beget the question: why focus on acts when you could focus on pleasure instead?

Indeed, the focus on penetration rather than pleasure cannot be disentangled from the problematic issues of gender in definitions of sex. However implicitly, sex defined through penetration is overwhelmingly experienced as men fucking women (or other men).

How different would sex be if we defined it through the experience of pleasure, and maybe orgasm, rather than instrumentally through particular behaviours? Would cybersex count as sex in one definition but not the other? How would the organization of personal life change if sex was focused more on mutual pleasure? We suggest it would have benefits for heterosexuals as well as sexual minorities.

Hierarchies of sex

There is an old joke that is helpful in thinking about the norms associated with sex.

> *A husband and wife are having sex. During their love-making, the husband looks down at his wife and says,*
>
> *'My dear, is everything ok?'*
>
> *She answers, 'Yes, why do you ask?'*
>
> *'Well,' he responds, 'You moved.'*

We are not interested in the joke on its comedic merits, evaluating whether it is funny, but to examine and understand why it is considered a joke at all. We suggest there are two ways of interpreting this as a joke, and the interpretation is dependent on the listener's own perspective and social context.

PAUSE FOR REFLECTION

Did you find this joke funny? Why is that the case? What do you think the joke is about? Once you have thought about this or discussed it with your peers, read on.

Originally, the joke may have been merely observational, a sexist comment on women's passive role in sex that ignored any social context for why this was so. We encountered this joke reading Margaret Atwood's renowned 1986 feminist novel *The Handmaid's Tale*. She used an austere version of it in her book, shorn of words such as 'dear'. The book is written in the style of a diary kept secretly under a totalitarian and patriarchal regime, and the words after the punchline of 'you moved' are 'Just don't move.' Here, the 'joke' is undoubtedly a commentary on the damage of misogynistic cultures where men are active in sex, and women don't move.

Yet when we use this joke in lectures, to highlight this issue, some of our students, both men and women, will laugh at it. This is not because they share those views, but rather because they are laughing at them for being archaic. The joke highlights how female sexual passivity has been a normative discourse in many societies – often known as 'the missionary position'.

The idea of the sexual passivity of women is a denial of women's sexual agency and greatly limits the ways in which women and men can experience sexual pleasure. Unfortunately, it is not the only way in which sexual activities are restricted through cultural norms that place moral values on sex.

Charmed circle: a concept developed by Rubin to visualize which sexual acts are esteemed and which are stigmatized in society

In a famous essay called *Thinking Sex*, Gayle Rubin (1984) introduced the notion of a sex hierarchy, where a **charmed circle** of behaviours deemed good, normal and natural were contrasted with those framed as bad, abnormal and unnatural (see also Douglas [1966] 2003). Her diagram (Figure 8.1) shows how people tend to think in binaries about sex, with each positive component (such as monogamous) contrasted with the stigmatized opposite (such as promiscuity).

Rubin's contribution to understanding sex in society is so valuable because she provide a method to think about how a sex hierarchy operates. She highlighted that sex was always treated with suspicion, writing that 'Sex is presumed guilty until proven innocent'. Sex is acceptable if it occurs within certain social institutions or norms – such as within marriage, for reproduction and between people who love each other.

Writing in the 1980s, Rubin powerfully underlined how society placed value on different sexual acts in a moral and political way. She offered another way of understanding the sex hierarchy, as a pyramid:

> Modern Western societies appraise sex acts according to a hierarchical system of sexual value. Marital, reproductive heterosexuals are alone at the top of the erotic pyramid. Clamoring below are unmarried monogamous heterosexuals in couples, followed by most other heterosexuals. Solitary sex floats ambiguously … Stable, long-term lesbian and gay male couples are verging on respectability, but bar dykes and promiscuous gay men are hovering just above the groups at the very bottom of the pyramid. The most despised sexual castes currently include transsexuals, transvestites, fetishists, sadomasochists, sex workers such as prostitutes and porn models, and the lowliest of all, those whose eroticism transgresses generational boundaries.

While some components of this have changed (gay men have improved their social position, and porn models perhaps face less condemnation), other acts and behaviours remain marginalized. The notion of an erotic pyramid is still distinctly relevant.

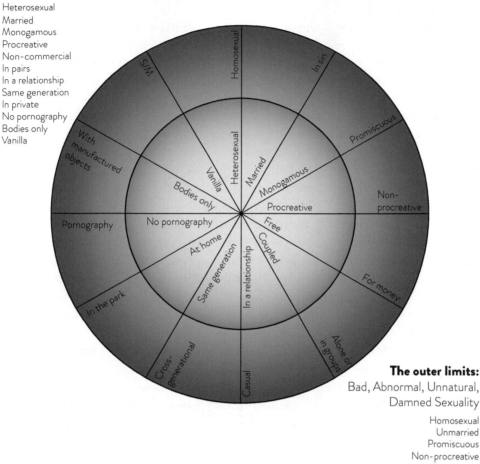

The charmed circle:
Good, Normal, Natural, Blessed Sexuality

Heterosexual
Married
Monogamous
Procreative
Non-commercial
In pairs
In a relationship
Same generation
In private
No pornography
Bodies only
Vanilla

The outer limits:
Bad, Abnormal, Unnatural,
Damned Sexuality

Homosexual
Unmarried
Promiscuous
Non-procreative
Commercial
Alone or in groups
Casual
Cross-generational
In public
Pornography
With manufactured objects
Sadomasochistic

Figure 8.1: Gayle Rubin's 'charmed circle' of sex

Source: From Gayle S. Rubin, *Deviations: A Gayle Rubin Reader.* Durham, NC: Duke University Press, pp. 137–181. Copyright, 2012, Gayle Rubin. All rights reserved. Republished by permission of the copyright holder and the publisher (www.dukeupress.edu).

Sexual attitudes are also dependent upon social norms and cultural context. One key trend in this regard is the increasing acceptance of non-marital sex (Twenge et al. 2015). The contraceptive pill meant the baby boomers began the 'sexual revolution' with far reduced risks of pregnancy. For people at the time, sexual liberation meant 'free love' outside of patriarchal controls. The 1960s and 1970s saw an increasing acceptance of casual sex and a 'free love' culture which was a rejection of earlier generations' conservative attitudes to sex in the West. What is called 'the permissive sixties' refers to the declining intervention by law and other social mechanisms of regulation into the private lives of individuals. Laws were relaxed regarding pornography, access to contraception and abortion. The grounds for divorce were also relaxed.

Sex became a matter of choice and personal freedom, not a matter for judges, politicians and priests. Sex for pleasure was no longer either shameful or wrong. This permissiveness included the rise of gay cultures in which there was a great deal and variety of sexual behaviour. There was also little condom use among gay men, because condoms were mostly seen as a guard against pregnancy – as the leading sexually transmitted diseases at the time (such as herpes and syphilis) were treatable by new generations of medication.

It was in the 1980s that gay communities were hit by the terrible HIV/AIDs epidemic, an unknown condition with no effective treatment early on. People with HIV did not have access to medical interventions to prevent the onset of AIDS and as a result died from AIDS-related illnesses. A great deal of stigma was levelled at people with HIV or AIDS, such as false rumours that HIV could be caught by a handshake or sneezing. So great was the prejudice related to HIV/AIDS that some undertakers refused to bury those who had died from illnesses related to the disease (Weinberg et al. 1994). Through media panic and homophobic political discourses, HIV/AIDS was labelled as 'the gay disease', and the prejudice and stigma applied to people with HIV/AIDS was conflated with the stigma levelled at gay and bisexual men (Hammack et al. 2018).

The combination of prejudice about HIV/AIDS and homophobia was supported by a right-wing politics that waged a culture war against homosexuality. Fears about homosexuality and HIV/AIDS were used by conservative politicians, particularly in the US and the UK, to foster social concerns about sexuality, social change and the perceived threat to so-called traditional family values. Homophobia peaked in the 1980s in part because politicians harnessed ignorance and prejudice about same-sex desire and HIV/AIDS for their own gain. This combined with the politicization of religion, with evangelical churches in the US adopting homophobic positions to increase donations during a time in which church attendance had begun to decline (Anderson & McCormack 2016).

This explains why homosexuality was placed on the outer limits of Rubin's charmed circle. Yet since then, people in the West have become generally more inclusive of same-sex sexuality, with legal and policy changes mirroring the increasing acceptance of gay people in social life. As a result, lesbian, gay and bisexual people have improved social lives, even though this is dependent on other issues, including where a person lives. Thus, the broader social organization of sexuality in society influences how sexuality is experienced in everyday life.

Moral panics about sex

A sexual component of everyday life for many people is the act of self-pleasuring – known as masturbation, but referred to by a whole host of other terms. 'Wanking', 'fapping', 'bashing the bishop' are all common terms that jokingly refer to what Christianity called 'onanism' and cast as a sin because it was deemed a waste of 'God's seed'. While terms are predominantly for male masturbation – perhaps a result of the great joy teenage boys appear to take in discussing it – there are increasing numbers of expressions to recognize that women masturbate as well.

The joking about masturbation that is a part of teenage life speaks to how it is not something that is an acceptable part of everyday conversation. Similarly, the fact that 'wanker' is used as an insult in Britain demonstrates that masturbation is not a value-neutral behaviour. The insult includes the idea that masturbation is a failure to secure sex with another person, as well as historically seen as a moral failure. Indeed, in 1980s America, a teenage boy who said they masturbated was deemed to be gay by his friends and peers (Anderson 2012).

That masturbation is treated as a joke, as slightly taboo, is not surprising. What is less well known, however, is that masturbation was once seen as extremely dangerous and even a national threat.

During the Victorian era, masturbation was understood as an epidemic sweeping Britain and America, and an emergency that needed immediate medical intervention (Hunt 1998). Interventions were devised to stop such 'self-abuse' – chastity devices including cages around a male's penis or a female's vagina, as well as machines employed by doctors that effectively masturbated women in attempt to remove their desire to masturbate (we would most likely consider this rape today).

There are several other strange aspects of the concerns about masturbation. Some foods were thought to increase the likelihood of wanking, so cereal was invented to guard against this; the use of daily baths or (cold) showers might reduce masturbatory risk; and sport became a socially valued activity in part to entertain boys who would otherwise think of playing with themselves (a completely different set of balls). It was thought that boys would become so tired from sports during the day, they would collapse on their beds and go straight into a deep 'angelic' sleep, without the time or energy to think of such vices.

This concern about sex might sound funny today – but it was deeply serious 100 years ago, and had grave consequences. Not only did it make people feel bad about a natural source of pleasure, many of the interventions were inhumane and led to a great deal of suffering. Furthermore, this Victorian puritanism casts a long shadow, and many widespread concerns about sex today can be traced back to these old social fears, at least in the UK and North America.

There was great focus on the 'solitary vice' of masturbation. But the way in which society policed and stigmatized it was not unique but rather an enduring component of sex in society – and it can be explained by the concept known as **moral panic** (see David et al. 2011).

The term moral panic was created by Stanley Cohen to understand how particular concerns in society are exaggerated and used by people in power to control others. He famously wrote that a moral panic occurs when '[a] condition, episode, person or group of persons emerges to become defined as a threat to societal values and interests' (Cohen 1972: 9).

While Cohen was using moral panic to think about the fear of gangs, and such panics are often related to crime, Gayle Rubin highlights how sex is particularly vulnerable to being subjected to moral panics.

Masturbation was an early example, and the homophobia associated with the HIV/AIDS epidemic also can be explained through the moral panic concept.

Moral panic: how particular concerns in society are defined as a threat, exaggerated and used by people in power to control others or effect particular social change

A particularly pertinent contemporary example is provided by the widespread high-profile concerns related to pornography (see Provocation 4.1, pp. 75–77).

Consider the following:

Joe and Sarah are a couple. Joe is aged 19 and Sarah is aged 16. They both live in England, where the age of consent is 16 years. It is thus completely legal for Joe and Sarah to have sex. However, if Joe were to send Sarah a sexually explicit image (if he were to 'sext' with her), Joe would be breaking the law and would face criminal conviction, including being sent to jail and put on a sex offender register.

Sexting has even seen charges of child pornography applied because the law was not able to deal with this (Best & Bogle 2014). One argument is that laws change slowly, and this is particularly true in relation to technology where there is such rapid transformation. But given our knowledge about moral panics related to sex, a better answer is that this is the result of bad laws put in place to address particular public concerns without duly considering the full policy implications (see Chapter 10).

Yet Best and Bogle (2014) argue that fears over sexting are a reaction to more general fears about 'kids becoming too sexual too soon' (p. 141). They highlight how media concern is often exaggerated and hysterical, arguing that 'contemporary legends and exaggerated fears don't help. Rather, these stories give a distorted view of youth and make it more difficult for parents or others who work with young people'.

VOX POP Alix Fox

Journalist and sex educator

Sex is a deeply human topic. It's how the vast majority of us were made in the first place, and I believe our attitudes towards it and experiences of it continue to uniquely shape us as individuals in a multitude of ways and to a profound degree throughout our existence. On both a macro, societal level, and on a micro, personal level, sex touches us all – and not just in the literal, physical sense!

© Alix Fox

I feel immensely privileged to have a career communicating about sex, sexuality and relationships. The research I do involves speaking to people in depth about their most intimate thoughts and stories; it demands huge trust.

I've chatted about everything from what it's like to be a gay man brought up in a Muslim family, to what happens if you're born with two vaginas, to how one theoretically develops a sexual fetish for the smell of fried chicken and bleach!

The fact that strangers feel confident frankly sharing such private matters with me is an enormous point of pride, and my ethics are underpinned by a dedication to be empathetic, honourable and open-minded. I grow and change with every tale I hear. I work hard to be the best listener and communicator I can be. My job very much influences who I am. My living sculpts my life.

And I have the capacity to impact upon other people's lives. I'm acutely aware that what I publish or broadcast about sex has the potential to illuminate, to educate, to make someone feel less alone or to influence them in a positive, constructive, perhaps even revelatory way. On the flipside, if I disseminate information that's medically unsound, biased or close-minded, I can do all manner of damage. My job is hilarious and fun and enthralling, but I also view myself as having a big responsibility.

Sex is about far, far more than putting something in and out of a hole. It's the ins and outs of what makes us whole. It's not merely about what goes on (or not) in our beds; it's inextricably linked to what happens in our heads. To me, it's endlessly fascinating.

» How does Alix's job as a journalist and sex educator fit with broader trends of sexuality discussed in this chapter? Does her work reflect the emergence of plastic sexuality in society (see p. 211)?

» How might Alix's job be different now compared to fifty years ago?

PERSONAL RELATIONSHIPS

Given the relational nature of being human, it is unsurprising that relationships with other people play such a vital part in all our lives. While diverse in scope, we categorize these relationships into three broad groups: friends, family and lovers.

The role of the family was discussed at length in Chapter 6 (see pp. 132–137). Traditionally viewed as a cornerstone of society, families have changed significantly. They have become smaller in size because of the availability and acceptability of contraception, while increased mobility means that members of families live further apart from each other than they used to. While family is a vital part of personal life, we focus on friends and lovers in this chapter.

Friends

Friendships hold an important part in our lives. Pahl (2000) describes friendship as a 'social glue', adding that what is important with friendship is 'the trust, security, feelings of self-esteem and feelings of being loved for one's own sake that flow from [friends]' (p. 148).

Friends also help us develop and consolidate an identity. Indeed, friends are the first step of independence from families or carers. It is through friends that we start to define ourselves – through our interests, the clothes we wear and our musical tastes. Parents who are worried about the friend who is a 'bad influence' are often just reacting to the growing independence of their child. It is worth noting that children will tend to adopt the accent of their friends rather than their parents (if there is a difference), which indicates that friendship can be just as important as family in shaping a person. Of course, your parents have a lot to do with where you grow up and which school you attend – both of which massively influence your friendship circles.

That being said, friendships are not purely the result of personal preference. While we think we select our friends, who our friendships develop with is in fact subject to several factors. As Allan (1996) writes:

> Friendships are not just freely chosen. They are developed and sustained within the wider framework of people's lives. The choices people make, in other words, are constrained by aspects of social organization over which they have relatively little control. (p. 100)

One example of this is that we tend to have friends who are like us – known as *homophily*. That is why, though this may not be desirable from a social justice perspective, friendships tend to be between people of the same ethnicity, gender, class and sexuality. They also tend to be between people of the same social status. Of course, friendships exist between different groups, but the dominant experience is *within-group* friendships.

Research has documented how friendships differ between class groups. Allan (1996) discusses how middle-class friendships develop through inviting people into different locations, until finally friendships are fully consolidated by entry into each other's houses. Yet working-class friendships are more restricted to particular settings, such as a sporting club or a particular leisure site.

Gender also significantly influences the development of friendships, with significant differences between male and female friendship groups. Pahl (2000: 112–122) highlights some of the key generalizations about gender differences in friendships:

> Men were held to be emotionally reticent – fearful perhaps of homoerotic overtones, while women were held to be more articulate and emotionally accomplished ... Men were less likely to expect to find close friends at work: the occupational communities had gone and increasing competition meant that colleagues at work became potential rivals ... Survey evidence demonstrated that [women's] regular contact with family and friends declined from the mid-1980s to the mid-1990s. This was attributed partly to the pressures consequent upon the successful juggling of family and work responsibilities. (p. 116)

Friendships also have a close correlation with mental health. Female friendship networks enabled women to talk about their problems and actively find solutions to solve them. Men, however, were prevented from discussing their concerns because this was not how male friendships were enacted.

These gender differences also emerge in childhood. When we think of boys' friendships, we tend to think of rough and tumble physical energy. But research conducted over the past three decades warns that rough and tumble play often leads to aggression and violence, and that shallow friendships have resulted in boys being emotionally stunted. Another pernicious element of boys' friendships has been virulent sexism about and towards women, and homophobia towards other men.

These damaging behaviours have tended to emerge in late adolescence. Way (2011) documents how working-class, ethnic-minority young boys have deep, meaningful friendships, where they speak about '"circles of love," "spilling your heart out to somebody," ... and "feeling lost" without their male best friends' (p. 91). Yet Way shows that as these boys get older, these friendships dissipate and older teenage boys feel socially isolated and long for the friendships of their youth.

However, friendships between boys are changing. 'Bromances' are increasingly common in British and American societies (McCormack 2012; Robinson et al. 2018). These bromances are similar to what people commonly view girls' friendships to consist of. Here, girls' friendships have been framed as oppositional to boys – intimate and tactile, whereas boys are physically and emotionally distant, lacking the fights and rough and tumble of male friendships.

While there may be truth to this, girls' friendships are more complex than this simplistic idea. In an ethnography of British schoolgirls' friendships, called *The Company She Keeps*, Val Hey (1997) explores the underlying tensions and emotions of girls' friendships in the 1990s. While less overtly homophobic than boys' friendships of that era, Hey highlights the 'compulsory heterosexuality' (see Rich 1980) of these friendships which girls would both reproduce and challenge. A different set of norms and expectations meant that girls experienced schooling and growing up very differently to boys.

We also know a great deal about how friendships develop over time. Important in any friendship is the idea of disclosure. If you tell your friend something personal, you expect them to tell you a similarly intimate detail about their own lives.

This reciprocal self-disclosure makes us feel good and is a form of sharing that bonds us together. A key component of this, though, is the idea that friends share similar amounts. If you tell your friend about your greatest fears, but they only discuss their food preferences, you would question the quality of the friendship.

Sharing too much is also considered a social faux pas. Disclosing intimate experiences or details with a casual acquaintance would be a cause of embarrassment and stigma attaches to someone who does that frequently.

Another key component of friendship is the idea that friends are supportive. A friend is someone you can rely on to offer help when required: to feed the cat while you are on holiday; or to lend you money or food in a time of need. Having a friend is, in part, being able to call on someone for a favour.

Supporting this notion, friendship is also based on interaction. We all have people who were once good friends who we no longer speak to or see. There does not have to have been a falling out for this to happen, just for the friend to no longer be part of our social lives. As social interactions decrease, so too in general does the value of the friendship. While we might hope that friendships will always exist over an extended period of time, the sociological fact is that they need maintenance through social interaction – a night out, a phone call, texts, a Facebook message – to ensure they continue. Facebook and other social networking sites has made it easier to stay close to friends who do not live nearby, but even that demands active effort to communicate.

Finally, friends are also there to offer positivity. Friends who are too negative or do not provide support in an encouraging, uplifting way tend not to remain friends for long.

Lovers

Romeo and Juliet: The most enduring example of young love, which has been echoed throughout fiction and movies ever since – from *Titanic* (1997) to almost every Disney film, the idea of 'star-crossed', heterosexual lovers is emblematic of romantic relationships.

© Maurizio Lapira/AFP/Getty Images

Tourists leave their own declarations of romantic love messages outside the entrance to the real Juliet Capulet's house in Verona, Italy.

Yet by discussing 'lovers', we have chosen a curiously vague term to describe the range of relationship types that sum up romantic relationships. After all, a lover can be a one-night stand who does not even stay the night. Or it can be a husband or wife you have lived with for 60 years.

Having made this point, given that we have discussed already the emergence of 'hook up' culture, we do not focus on casual sexual encounters. Instead, we examine longer-term romantic relationships, and investigate how they were traditionally based in marriage but have extended to other forms in the recent past.

Marriage and cohabitation

Marriage has changed significantly over the past 50 years (Cherlin 2004). Premarital sex is now considered normal, infidelity is widely acknowledged as occurring and divorce is an accepted possible end to a relationship – and almost half of marriages end in divorce.

Many of these changes can be attributed to a gradual but sustained movement away from religiosity in Western countries, an enhanced sense of self-liberty and the political victories of feminism (Twenge et al. 2015). Of course, structural changes have helped as well, with the contraceptive pill vital in enabling women the ability to have control over whether they get pregnant.

The rate of social change related to marriage and cohabitation is evidenced by the changing values attached to surnames. In the 1950s, women automatically took the surname of their husband. Indeed, cohabitating couples at the time would have the woman adopt the husband's name even though they were not married to avoid the stigma attached to living together 'out of wedlock'.

Compare this situation to today where, alongside the growing numbers of people rejecting marriage, increasing numbers of women do not adopt their husband's name but either keep their own, or both partners assume a new, double-barrelled surname. Double-barrelled names have a long history – previously the result of aristocratic marriages where both families had important ancestors. The change in the reasons for double-barrelled surnames is interesting evidence for the broader social change.

These changes have been characterized by Anthony Giddens as the move towards a *pure relationship*. The central idea here is of a shift in the meaning and experiences of marriage. Marriages were once based on issues including class and economic transaction (where women had a 'dowry'), and the woman was subservient to the man. However, Giddens argues that romantic relationships have become based on notions of equality and negotiation – and relationships only last as long as they offer fulfilment and satisfaction to both partners.

As Giddens (1992) writes, the pure relationship

> refers to a situation where a social relation is entered into for its own sake, for what can be derived by each person from a sustained association with another; and which is continued only in so far as it is thought by both parties to deliver enough satisfaction for each individual to stay within it. (p. 58)

Giddens maintains that the pure relationship is connected with a **plastic sexuality** that has emerged, where sexual behaviour has moved away from a focus on procreation to one where pleasure is privileged. True love (which Giddens calls 'confluent') is when a pure relationship exists alongside a form of sexual pleasure that sees both partners happy and fulfilled, both sexually and emotionally.

Plastic sexuality: a concept advanced by Giddens that argues sexual desires and acts are shaped by individual erotic needs rather than reproductive or economic ones

Giddens argues that this trend is the result of broader social changes in society – particularly that of individualization, which is the theoretical argument about the move from locating value in institutions to finding worth in one's self (see Chapter 9). The pure relationship has become increasingly important in a context where people locate their value in their relationships and friendships rather than institutions such as the Church or their class background.

The individualization thesis contends that it is the act of making choices about where in one's life self-worth is found. While this includes work, sense of style and other cultural choices, the primary way this is done is through one's personal relationships. The changes, Giddens argues, are big. Social and sexual life has been transformed – indeed, his book is even called *The Transformation of Intimacy*.

Giddens' argument has also been critiqued. Some scholars argue that he did not pay enough attention to differences based on class, age and gender (Jamieson 1999). They contend that while the pure relationship might exist to some extent for some people, it is not the reality for all.

What is beyond doubt is that experiences of marriages and relationships are changing – as evidenced by the decline in the number of marriages and the related rise of cohabitation. In the UK, US and most European countries, the marriage rate has been falling since the early 1970s (Smart 2011).

One clear reason for this is the age when people first get married, which has risen over the decades. Smart (2011) compared data from the US, the UK and Australia, showing that between the 1970s and the late 2000s, this age (for men and women combined) increased by approximately six years, from early 20s to late 20s or early 30s. While this is attributable in part to social changes related to work and university, it is also an effect of people increasingly feeling able to live together without marriage.

Another trend across many parts of the world is the ability for same-sex partners to get married – particularly through the campaign for 'equal marriage'. This has been seen as evidence of how marriage has changed over time – indeed, marriage between people of different ethnicities was illegal in the US until 1967. Yet despite these changes, marriage is still privileged in policy – with substantial legal and policy benefits not afforded to cohabiting couples in virtually all parts of the world.

Living apart, together

While Giddens' notion of the pure relationship captures the changes in marriage and cohabiting relationships that have occurred over the past 40 years, this form of relationship is just one of several possibilities. There are non-monogamous relationships of various forms – including open relationships, where a couple have sex with other people, and polyamorous relationships, where more than two people are in a multi-person relationship (three people together has been colloquially called a 'triogonous relationship'). In addition to that diversity, think about these situations:

Mario and Sarah became partners at high school, when they were 16. They love each other and if they had stayed in the same town they would have moved in together. However, they both wanted to pursue a university education, and while Mario's university was close to home, Sarah's was the other side of the country. Rather than break up, they decided to stay together and see each other at university holidays.

Jack, 42, and Colin, 36, have been partners for two years. While Jack has been openly gay since he was 18, Colin is bisexual and only ended a relationship with the mother of his two children three years ago. The break-up was amicable and while Jack and Colin live close to each other, everyone decided Colin should live in his family home until his two children (aged 14 and 17) left home.

Susan and Trevor met online 10 years ago, on an internet chatroom. They immediately felt a connection and communicated online for several months. They lived in different countries but after entering a relationship online, and having sex on webcam, they decided to meet in person. After several meetings, they decided to get married but remain living in different countries. They speak daily on their computers.

In each of these contexts, the couple are together, but live apart. This has been conceptualized through the phrase 'living apart together' (LAT), and it can take many forms.

An important characteristic of LAT couples is that they have two separate homes. This is different from earlier forms of cohabitation where there was one main home, and one member would live away from this for particular times, for work or other reasons.

There are several reasons why LAT relationships have emerged. There is a greater expectation that people might have to travel or relocate for their job (a trend known as the mobile workforce), and there is simultaneously *less* of an expectation that a partner will also move if this happens. This is particularly true for heterosexual couples where women increasingly have their own careers and are not able, or willing, to 'follow' their partner when they move for work. The growing acceptance of sex outside marriage also means there is less sexual need for a couple to live together.

The option of living apart has also become more palatable as the rise in technology means it is far easier to communicate over long distances – first through email and now using a range of technologies that mean couples can video call with each other over their computers or smartphones.

The increasing acceptance of diverse forms of family life means unusual forms of relationship receive far less stigma than they might once have done. Furthermore, the rise in divorce rates means that more people are single at middle and older ages and when they enter new relationships have more 'baggage' to accommodate than newlyweds in their early 20s.

Indeed, there are a number of benefits to having a LAT relationship (Levin 2004). It can avoid having to choose between a partner or caring for an elderly relative or one's own children. It also enables couples to concentrate on careers or not change jobs, and may well ameliorate tensions that can arise from 'settling down' together too quickly. Indeed, the very notion of 'settling down' has been disrupted in recent years, occurring later in life, if at all.

While technology has enabled LAT relationships to take place more easily than ever before, there are concerns about how smartphones and the internet more generally can interfere with relationships.

McCormack (2015) examined how smartphones impacted upon relationships. This research found that couples used smartphones to keep in touch – not just to organize the logistics of daily life, but also for the emotional work of caring and comforting each other. Participants spoke of the importance of texts and phone calls – short communications to check how the day was going or remind their partners that they were loved. It was also a central part of leisure time, arranging trips and dinners out or spicing up sex lives through flirtatious messages or erotic pictures and videos.

Yet the pervasive use of technology in relationships also came at a cost. For some participants in the study, smartphones undermined their trust in the fidelity of their partners. While the majority valued technology in their lives, they still expressed frustration at the tensions it caused in their relationships.

Some people were unhappy about the amount of time their partners spent on smartphone apps, as well as money spent on 'freemium' games (games which are free to play, but where there are options to purchase items within the game). There were concerns that smartphones were prioritized over face-to-face communication in the home, as well as encroaching onto sexual activity and bedroom routines. Some participants even spoke of their partners interrupting sex to answer a phone call.

Importantly, many couples had developed strategies to deal with these issues. This included organizing times when smartphones were banned from use, particularly at dinner or before sleeping. Others spoke about changing their own behaviour – deleting apps that they felt took up too much of their time. Even so, these strategies only worked in particular contexts and tensions remained with how technology intersected with their social lives.

Technology was used by couples who lived together as well as those in LAT relationships. It is possible that those in LAT relationships find fewer stresses result from technology, as its use in keeping couples together while apart is much more significant than the tensions it may cause during the (smaller) amount of time they are physically together.

Monogamy as a social construction

Although we briefly acknowledged other relationship forms at the start of the last section, a key assumption of our discussion of romantic relationships thus far has been the idea that they are monogamous.

Indeed, monogamy is an enduring component of romantic relationships in most of the Western world. Monogamy is such a well-known term that we rarely examine what it actually means – monogamy is being 'faithful' to (i.e. not cheating on) your partner.

Alas, even monogamy is not that simple – and what precisely 'cheating' consists of is far more intricate than commonly conceived.

To highlight this, think of yourself in a monogamous romantic relationship, whether it be past, present or in the future. Which of the following actions by your partner would you consider cheating?

- Penetrative sex with another person

- Received oral sex from another person

- Watched pornography

- Had cybersex with a sex worker

- Masturbated thinking of you

- Kissed another person

- Gave oral sex to another person

- Masturbated thinking of an ex-partner

We suspect that almost everyone would *not* consider their partner masturbating while thinking of them as cheating, and that penetrative sex with another person *would* be considered a violation of monogamy.

Between those two examples is where it gets interesting. Is kissing another person a form of cheating? Does it depend how long the kiss is for? What about whether your partner was drunk? Or if the person was a friend or stranger? Does it matter whether he or she enjoyed it?

In answering these questions, the first point is to recognize that different readers will have different answers regarding what counts as cheating. Ask your friends what they would consider cheating – how do they differ from you and why?

We have focused here on *sexual* monogamy. Many relationships also have *emotional* monogamy, where the other person is your primary partner and the person you love 'the most' (whatever that means). Many sexually open relationships maintain emotional monogamy.

There is still an interesting distinction here, though: In emotional monogamy, you are still allowed to have friends – to not do so would normally be considered abuse. Yet in sexual monogamy, you are not allowed, in general, a casual sexual partner. This is its own form of sexual double standard.

It is also quite likely that your friendship group might have similar perspectives on this issue – particularly if you have discussed these questions before and given that we socialize with people who share our views. There will likely be bigger differences between you and people with different experiences than you. There is greater chance of different beliefs, for example, between someone with low sexual desire and strong religious beliefs who lives in the countryside and another person who is always sexually aroused, lives in the city and likes to go clubbing at weekends.

The other key point is that answers to these questions have varied significantly historically. Masturbation was once seen as a form of infidelity by the Victorians, an attitude which was both driven by and helped inflame their moral panics against it. Watching porn has also been seen to be against monogamous norms, but now the internet has for many people made viewing porn more of a commonplace experience.

This is to say that monogamy is a social construction; that how monogamy is defined changes over time and is influenced by social norms related to attitudes about masturbation and women's rights.

And here's the thing: research into monogamy has demonstrated how it has changed. Most importantly, the central tenet of contemporary monogamy – sexual fidelity – is a relatively recent addition to the definition.

Historically, family relationships have not been monogamous. Research shows that, particularly in the non-Western world, the majority of cultures are polygamous – that is, relationships are between more than two people (Anderson 2012). Monogamy in this context refers to a coupled relationship – where just two people are in a relationship, rather than three or more.

However, monogamy came to be particularly valued in the West. Entering the modern era, as characterized by a revolution in democracy and the advancement of industry and capitalism, there was a significant move to the cities from rural areas.

It is this shift to urban living that ushered in the privileging of monogamy, in terms of coupled relationships (Cancian 1987). Whereas rural (or agrarian) living was difficult, with poor healthcare and high infant mortality rates, these improved in cities – although the very poorest still lived in squalor and in worse conditions than rural workers. Furthermore, as people living in cities moved to salaried wage (rather than living off crops grown), higher numbers of children negatively impacted on the wealth of the family, whereas previously, larger families were of benefit, offering a greater workforce for farming. Polygamous relationships moved from having positive effects to damaging life chances. Monogamy and marriage also became more formally recognized in the organization of city life as a way to keep track of issues such as tax and where one lived.

In terms of monogamy relating to sexual exclusivity, we also know this has not always been the case. In Ancient Greek and Roman times, same-sex sex was common even among married men and was not considered cheating on their wives. Monogamy as a practice of sexual restriction has a long and complex history in the West but became dominant in the late 1800s, when puritan sexual norms were to the fore.

Anderson (2012) argues that the reason why sexual fidelity became a key component of monogamy, and not polygamy, came through the widespread adoption of the French principles of liberty, equality and fraternity. These are ideas that provide the framework for Western nations; ideas that came in with Locke, Hume, Paine and Jefferson. They were adopted with the notion that every man is 'guaranteed the right to life, liberty and the pursuit of happiness'.

Thus, one reason marital monogamy is esteemed over polygamy was the egalitarian/fraternal notion that all men (but not women) were created equal, and therefore all men deserved a wife. If one man owned many wives, he would effectively be denying other men their right to own a wife. Accordingly, monogamy, as a mandated law, seems to have arisen alongside industry, democracy and political doctrines of equality. Most feminists also reject polygamy, which is largely viewed as fostering and reinforcing patriarchy when it has occurred (Willey 2006).

Since sexual fidelity became a valued part of monogamy, the definitions and experiences of it have continued to change. In the 1950s, men would date multiple women (mostly without sex, and certainly without socially approved sex), before choosing to 'go steady' with one. After 'going steady' for a while, the man would propose and, if all was successful, they would get married. After marriage, the couple were free to engage in sexual intercourse, with the expectation that this would lead to children. Sexual monogamy was then expected, both socially and religiously, for life.

Today, premarital sex is far more widely accepted (Twenge et al. 2015). Yet despite trends in sexuality in the West moving towards more liberal perspectives where people should be able to do what they want – including gay rights, divorce and kinky sexual behaviours – monogamy has retained its cultural dominance.

The cultural, hegemonic dominance of monogamy in contemporary Western societies has been called *monogamism* (Anderson 2012). As discussed in Chapter 3, hegemony is a form of power where the dominant position is maintained because people buy into the dominant belief, even at their own expense.

The basic premise of hegemony is that people will accept and even support their own subordination if the conditions are right.

Monogamism in contemporary society is evidenced by the fact that a sexually exclusive relationship is deemed the only culturally valued relationship choice available. Questioning monogamy can result in having your own morality questioned. Sexually open relationships are viewed as likely to fail, or as not constituting a 'proper' relationship.

So, the *assumption* of monogamy discussed at the beginning of this section is not a value-neutral accident, but part of the process by which monogamy is esteemed – at the heart of Rubin's charmed sexual circle, sitting atop the sexual pyramid as other relationship types are critiqued and condemned.

PROVOCATION 8: Do people cheat because they love their partners?

The prevailing cultural narrative about cheating is clear and powerful: it is a betrayal, a breaking of implicit or explicit vows, and a sign that the cheater does not love their partner. As such, a great deal of social pressure exists for the individual cheated on to end a relationship. This is one reason why cheating is the primary reason why married couples divorce.

But is cheating always a sign that one has lost love for their partner? In this Provocation, we argue that, at least for undergraduates and young adults, cheating may actually be a sign of long-term relationship commitment.

In order to make this argument, it is first necessary to think about how cheating is positioned in society in relation to monogamy, which is the personal and social expectation that two people in a relationship will only have sex with each other. The dominant view in most societies is that monogamous relationships are the only moral or even healthy form of sexual relationships, disavowing and stigmatizing those in open or polyamorous relationships.

Most people also believe that if you love your partner, you will find your sex life with them fulfilling throughout the course of your life. In other words, they believe that love makes for frequent and great sex, for ever. Some people are so heavily invested in the belief that monogamy is a sign of love, they cannot accept that a person can desire sex with someone else and still love their partner; nor can they accept that a relationship can thrive without sex.

© AntonioGuillem/iStock

The problem is, the research shows this is wrong.

Perhaps one of the longest and most consistent sexological findings we have is this: the longer a couple is together, the less frequent and erotic their sex will be. This contradicts what undergraduates normally think about sex. Young people often think that the relationship has died when the sex dies. But the opposite is true: the more love, intimacy and history a couple has together, the less sex they have together. The relationship becomes one that is based on emotional intimacy, not sex. Grandparents are not less in love than undergraduates because they have less sex with their partners.

The decrease in sex the longer a couple stay together is not the result of decreased sexual drive or horniness. People still desire sex with others even in a long-term relationship. Our argument is cheating on a partner in this context can be a sign of love, rather than betrayal.

Consider this: There are many reasons why some couples stay together, even if they no longer love each other. They might do so for the sake of their children, or because it is their only realistic option financially. They may stay with a partner out of family or cultural pressure. But for most undergraduates, these situations do not apply. Undergraduates are free to break up without causing serious financial or familial harm, and few have children to care for. In fact, there is even some peer encouragement to be single during one's youth.

So if a person cheats on their partner, must it mean that they do not love their partner? After all, they are young; they do not have kids or a mortgage together; and relative to others, their relationship is not socially expected to continue. In other words, there is no external pressure to stay together. Undergraduates have the freedom to break up simply because they no longer want to be in a relationship.

Given this, let's examine the options that an undergraduate might have after entering into a relationship, having some great sex, and then finding the sexual thrill, the passion and eroticism of spontaneous and novel sex wearing off. Eventually, the couple has to put effort into having good sex, and that very effort makes it feel as if they are trying too hard, and that makes the sex less good. Spontaneity, romance and sexual novelty can only be lived once. We are using the example of a heterosexual couple where the man is sexually unfulfilled, although the example would work equally well if either or both genders were swapped.

At this point, there are four options for the unhappy undergraduate:

1. Split up with his partner, despite loving her (and thus grow depressed in missing her and fearing that he will never be able to have a long-term partner knowing that the same cycle will repeat).

2. Ask his partner if they can be in some form of open relationship (which, given the power of norms around monogamy, he can presume would terminate or at least severely compromise the relationship, unless he has good reason to believe otherwise).

3. Only have sex with his partner, and remain sexually unsatisfied within monogamy. Men in this situation usually turn to pornography to at least partially fulfil some of their extra-dyadic desires.

   Or,

4. Cheat on his partner to meet his sexual desires, and hope that she does not find out.

Given that this undergraduate does not want to lose his partner, he rules the first option out. Given that he fears asking for an open relationship will lead his partner to break up with him, he rules the second option out. He could, of course, choose to stay with his partner, and deny his sexual desires for other people. That certainly shows that he loves his partner, because he is willing to sacrifice a real source of pleasure.

However, like many people, in this case our undergraduate finds himself giving in to sexual temptation of sex outside the relationship. He has certainly failed to signal his commitment to the relationship according to dominant norms; but can – as we propose – that cheating also signal commitment in a paradoxical way?

Here is how it can. Because this undergraduate is under no financial, familial or even social pressure to stay with his college partner, he could freely break up with that partner to pursue sex with others. The problem is he loves his partner but wants casual sex with someone else – because he is human with biological urges. Thus, he chooses to stay with the one he loves and cheat on her to satisfy his sexual urges. The cheating thus serves as an ironic proclamation of love, because he wanted the relationship with his partner to continue even as he had sex with someone else.

Knowing that research shows that up to 86 per cent of undergraduate men have cheated on their university girlfriends, the key sociological questions to consider are: 1) how much social harm is created by relationship termination because of cheating for sexual purposes? 2) What harm is caused by socially compelling people into monogamy? And 3) can open sexual relationships be a more honest and fulfilling way of doing love?

In conclusion, cheating can be a sign of love because of the cultural power of monogamy. If monogamy was freely chosen as an individual's preferred option from several equally valued alternatives (e.g. open relationship, swinging, polyamory), cheating might deserve the stigma it currently holds. But in a culture where monogamy is, for the vast majority, imposed, perhaps cheating is a rational choice and a private declaration of love.

Provoked? Read further:

Anderson, E. (2012). *The Monogamy Gap: Men, Love and the Reality of Cheating*. New York: Oxford University Press.

Barker, M. (2012). *Rewriting the Rules: An Integrative Guide to Love, Sex and Relationships*. London: Routledge.

Schippers, M. (2016). *Beyond Monogamy: Polyamory and the Future of Polyqueer Sexualities*. New York: New York University Press.

CONCLUSION

Sociology has the potential to explain and contextualize our personal lives. Experiences and behaviours that we may believe are natural or unique often fit broader social trends or societal norms. How we think about our bodies, and the nature of our sex lives, are two ways in which society has significant influence. Similarly, sociology can tell us a great deal about the relationships we have, from friends to lovers. Perhaps the great value of a sociology of personal life is that it connects broader social trends and the organization of society with the most intimate and private aspects of our lives – having great relevance to us all and illuminating the ways in which society impacts upon us.

HOW WOULD...?

» How would Gayle Rubin devise a charmed circle of sex in your own culture? What would the erotic pyramid look like?

» Draw a charmed circle and fill out what acts, behaviours and relationships are esteemed, and which are castigated. Does it still produce binary opposites as Rubin's original formulated? Which are most important? Devise an erotic pyramid that is related to this circle.

> » What similarities and differences are there between your own pyramid and Rubin's? What about your own and your classmates'?
>
> » How would Giddens' theorizing explain this difference between your own pyramid and Rubin's?

STRUCTURED FURTHER READING

Smart, C. (2007). *Personal Life*. Cambridge: Polity.
This book is a key text in arguing for a sociology of personal life that examines how families and personal relationships are experienced and connects this with broader social relations. It is written in an accessible style and focuses on core issues of family life in contemporary Western societies.

Pahl, R. (2000). *On Friendship*. Cambridge: Polity.
A key text on friendship and the importance of friends in society, recognizing friends as a form of community that can offer support and help throughout one's life. Drawing on a range of approaches, the book situates friendship within the social world.

Rubin, G. (2012). *Deviations: A Gayle Rubin Reader*. Durham, NC: Duke University Press.
This reader provides access to a range of work by cultural anthropologist Gayle Rubin. Her chapter 'Thinking sex' is a seminal text in arguing for a critical, social science analysis of sex beyond gender and feminist theories. Some other great chapters include her critique of anti-porn feminism, her discussion of gay and lesbian politics, and her ethnography of a kinky sexual community.

 Visit the companion website at **www.macmillanihe.com/mccormack** for further learning and teaching resources.

Chapter 9
SOCIAL TRANSFORMATIONS

INTRODUCTION

This chapter examines the way societies change. It is easy to think of the society in which you live as the standard form across time, yet this is not true. Societies vary far more across different eras than the most distinct cultures do from each other today. In this chapter, we focus on Western societies since the establishment of sociology as a discipline – from the mid-1800s until today. We start by examining the Industrial Revolution and explore how this has shaped our world, and the period of modernity in Western societies in the 20th century. We then investigate the mechanisms by which these societies have changed, discussing social movements and other forms of collective action. We explore globalization and environmentalism and what they mean, before discussing the contemporary era and whether we have entered a period variously known as late modern, risk society or even postmodernity. We finish by considering the future of sharing in this changing social context. In our Provocation, we ask whether we have too much rationality in our lives.

THE INDUSTRIAL REVOLUTION AND MODERNITY

Understanding how modern Western societies came to exist in the form they do today is a complex task. Ideas of politics and democracy, for example, can be traced back to the Ancient Greeks: It was during this era when institutions were created to house such debates and theories. Indeed, the current university system traces back 24 centuries to the 'Academy' founded by philosopher Plato. We do not have the scope to cover all the ways all societies have changed since then, nor can we discuss the great diversity of societies that exist across the world at any given time. Instead, we look at key moments that have influenced our contemporary world, and the creation of what have been called modern societies – and the concept of **modernity**.

Of vital significance here is the Industrial Revolution. We have already discussed this in Chapter 2, in the context of the Age of Enlightenment, where ideas of rationality and empiricism became core principles in how Western societies were organized. This was a profound change from the more mystical and diverse ways that characterized societies prior to this time.

Modernity: a term conceptualizing societies that emerged after the Industrial Revolution and when capitalism was embedded as the mode of production

221

The great transformation: the social and political changes that saw Western societies shift to capitalist modes of production

This was part of what has been called **the great transformation** (Polanyi [1957] 2002), where social and political upheavals saw a marked shift from agrarian to capitalist modes of production (Durkheim [1893] 1984; Weber [1905] 1930). Importantly, this included an acceptance of the political idea (and reality) that societies were embedded within a market economy, where a self-regulating market would be the distributor of wealth.

The Industrial Revolution was spread out across many years. Although the technological innovations that enabled it began in the 1700s, it was what historians call the second Industrial Revolution (mid-1800s to the early 1900s) that we focus on in this chapter. Here, three broad changes had a significant influence on the dynamics of these countries. First, technological advances enabled revolutionary growth in the production of material goods, transforming those economies that adopted them. Second, the emergence of efficient, affordable mass transportation, particularly the steam engine, meant that people were far less circumscribed by geography and locale. Third, improvements in agriculture and industry meant that societies could accommodate more people. Note that we do not write 'support' or 'care for' more people, as the notion of any kind of welfare state would not occur for many decades (see Chapter 10). Nonetheless, there was significant population growth across Europe during this period.

The Industrial Revolution is generally heralded as an era of great social progress – even if capitalism is appropriately critiqued for its potential to exploit people, and concerns about the dehumanizing effects of bureaucracy and rationalization are recognized (Weber [1905] 1930). Yet when one takes a more global view, it is evident that many of the harms of modernization were most acutely felt in other countries.

Colonialism: the process by which explorers and settlers take political control of another country and exploit it economically

The most obvious example of the harm to other countries caused by modernization was slavery and the global slave trade. This horrific symptom of and motive for European **colonialism** saw explorers from powerful European countries (Great Britain, Portugal, France, Belgium, the Netherlands, Germany and Spain) cross the world in ships and plunder non-Western territories, colonizing and asserting trading and social dominance over them (Smith, A.K. 1991). Williams (1972) argued that this was the result of a capitalist tendency to maximize profit and power, which trumped Enlightenment values of human rights, resulting in the degradation of human life that made the international slave trade palatable (see Chapter 7). The plundering of food and raw materials from these colonized territories was another key driver of the population growth in Europe.

Notwithstanding this deeply troubling international component, the Industrial Revolution was circumscribed by geography. China, for example, had no similar Industrial Revolution, despite having had more scientific and technological development in the prior centuries. Economic historian Joel Mokyr (2017) argues that this can be explained by the way China was governed as an empire: the singular ruling elite in China prevented technological innovation, viewing such thinking as a challenge to their authority, privileging instead the rote learning of classical knowledge.

Mokyr contrasts this with Europe, which, as a continent of independently ruled countries, was distinguished by fierce national competition, an atmosphere that drove and promoted technological innovation. While religious authoritarianism existed, the fragmentation by country meant that people who took radical intellectual positions had more chance of escaping persecution by fleeing abroad with their ideas, even though some were undoubtedly still punished (see Chapter 2). This contrasts sharply with China where, despite uprisings and rebellions, the ruling dynasty had overwhelming power to squash challenges to its bureaucratic norms. That the Industrial Revolution occurred in Europe, then, was not predetermined and could have occurred in China if its culture and politics were different.

The social valuing of sport

The development of sport may not seem central to changes in 19th-century culture, yet sport had little social value prior to the Industrial Revolution. Social historian Donald Mrozek (1983) wrote, 'at the beginning of the nineteenth century, there was no obvious merit in sport ... certainly no clear social value to it and no sense that it contributed to the improvement of the individual's character or the society's moral or even physical health' (p. xiii). However, by the second decade of the next century these sentiments had been completely reversed (Miracle & Rees 1994).

This was partly attributable to the nature of work in the city. The regularity of work meant that between blows of the factory whistle, there was time for men to play. The concept of leisure, once reserved for the wealthy, spread to the working class during this period (Rigauer 1981). And while sport was also a middle-class pursuit, this tended to be a casual mode of athletic exercise, such as tennis and golf (Hobsbawm 1987). For the middle classes, sport served as a diversion during their plenteous leisure time. This was in marked contrast to the frenetic forms of sport working-class men passionately engaged in and came to follow.

Sport also helped socialize boys and young men into the values required to be successful in the new capitalist economy (see Chapter 7, p. 178 for our Provocation on segregating sport by sex). It helped teach the qualities of discipline and obedience, and to honour the hard work that was necessary in the dangerous occupations of factory work and mining (Rigauer 1981). Workers had to sacrifice both their time and their health to earn the wage they needed to support their dependent families, and sport was a mechanism to socialize young boys early into valuing the concept of sacrificing one's body for the 'greater good' – that of the team, the family and thus ultimately the workplace. As well as producing obedient workers and students, this also served as ideal psychological preparation for soldiers going off to war, which required complete obedience to authority and acceptance of the ultimate self-sacrifice – to kill and die for others.

Most important to the bourgeois ruling class, however, was that workers needed to be obedient to authority. Sport taught boys this docility. Accordingly, organized competitive sport was funded by those who maintained control of the reproduction of material goods. For example, in UK football, the modern club system is based on teams originally associated with employers (such as particular factories) and the public school system (Magrath 2017).

 Visit the companion website at **www.macmillanihe.com/mccormack** for discussion of the ways in which the Industrial Revolution influenced gender norms and sexual identities.

UNDERSTANDING MODERNITY

Modernity and the city

The Industrial Revolution heralded the rise of the city and the arrival of a society that we would to some extent recognize today – even if we would still be shocked by significant differences, not least related to technology, poverty and the absence of social care (Pinker 2018). These modern societies across the developed world have been a key focus for sociologists, not least because they speak to our own lives and experiences.

The city can be considered emblematic of modernity. It is certainly the case that the rise of urban and city living is unique to modernity, and sociologists have documented the ways in which the city is a modern experience. Writing during the infancy of sociology, German sociologist Georg Simmel ([1903] 1976) argued that the city had a palpable influence on the mind of the individual. He contended that living in the city – which he called the metropolis – resulted in people developing 'a protective organ' to guard against the increased sensual stimuli of city dwelling. It is worth remembering here that many early cities did not have adequate sewer systems or clean water, leading to poor hygiene – the sensual stimuli of the city included this grim reality.

As a way of dealing with the increasing intensity of noise, events and interactions, the individual turns to logic and intellect – *rationality* – to process the sensory overload of the busy, bustling city. Advancing his critique of rationalization (see Chapter 2, and p. 227 in this chapter), Simmel viewed the turn to rationality as a rejection of artistic impulse and emotional response, and the potential death of culture.

French philosopher and sociologist Henri Lefebvre ([1974] 1991; [1970] 2003) developed this critique of the modern city to argue that the way space is regulated and produced in urban societies serves to reproduce capitalism itself. He maintained that the 'look' of cities – of how they are built and how space is managed and even produced – is not inconsequential but both reflects and affects the social dynamics of the period. Thus, the urban centres of Ancient Rome were markedly different from those of contemporary societies. He argued that social space is 'in addition to being a means of production [...] is also a means of control, and hence of domination, of power' (Lefebvre [1974] 1991: 26).

Sociology and the city

The city has played a key role in sociology since its initial stages. This is because early sociologists, particularly those of the Chicago School (see Chapter 2), turned to the city – and Chicago specifically – as an accessible and fertile area of study. Robert Park (1915), a leading sociologist in the Chicago School, studied how Polish immigrants to America habituated to their new culture while retaining elements of their own identity. Offering a more optimistic view of the city than Simmel and Lefebvre, he wrote:

> The attraction of the metropolis is due in part ... to the fact that in the long run every individual finds somewhere among the varied manifestations of city life the sort of

environment in which he expands and feels at ease; finds, in short, the moral climate in which his peculiar nature obtains the stimulations that bring his innate dispositions to full and free expression. (p. 608)

The research produced by the Chicago School in this early period fundamentally influenced the development of sociology as a discipline, and part of its success was how it viewed the city both as a *location* to study people and as a *topic* in itself.

While the city may be emblematic of modernity, it is also necessary to think about the key characteristics of modern societies. British sociologist Anthony Giddens has argued that there are three processes fundamental to modern societies that distinguish them from premodern ones (Giddens 1990). These are: 1) the standardization of time; 2) the disembedding of social systems; and 3) the questioning and analysis of social relations by individuals.

The standardization of time

Time is something that most of us take for granted. As you read this book, the time of day will be measured the same way for your friends, and by using the internet, you will be able to find out easily what time it is in any part of the world. Yet this has not been true across history. While people have always had an understanding of time, the nature of the concept has varied significantly.

Giddens (1990) highlights that premodern cultures' understanding of time was markedly different from our own because time was variable and imprecise and usually connected with a *place*. Prior to the Industrial Revolution, social life and work routines had generally been organized around a combination of natural markers (the seasons, sunrise and sunset – all of practical value to agrarian workers) and religious ones (daily services, feast days). As such, time was never abstract but always placed in a social or geographical context, and communities in different geographic regions would have different conceptions of time.

PAUSE FOR REFLECTION

How does time impact your everyday life?
Could you imagine your life without standardized time?
What regular occurrences in your life might you base a contextual version of time on?

Yet as work moved to factories, and the mode of production changed, time became organized not by such events but by how life ran in the city. The organization of the city meant the mechanical clock became increasingly important – the length of the working day became a battle between workers and employers rather than being determined by the sun or the weather. Workers' time needed to be synchronized, so that everyone started their shift at the same time each day and batches of goods could be shipped at the optimum time to get them to their destinations and to avoid a backlog in factories. Work did not start when the sun rose or the fruits ripened, but when the factory opened according to a time designated in that city by that owner. This also had the benefit for factory owners that they could better measure the productivity of their workers (Thompson 1967).

As capitalist life became increasingly consolidated as the organizing principle of Western societies, time became increasingly separated from the locations in which people lived, becoming instead an abstract measure independent of place.

The politics of time zones

One of the ways in which time remains organized by location is the notion of time zones. At its simplest level, when it is 2:40 p.m. in Addis Ababa, Ethiopia, it is 8:40 a.m. in Denver, Colorado, 11:40 p.m. in Seoul, South Korea, and 00:40 a.m. in Melbourne, Australia. These differences also might change depending on the time of the year, as various countries have different summer and winter times.

The rationale for this is obvious: it reflects geography and the position of a country on Earth as it rotates in position in relation to the Sun. Yet time zones are not systematically and consistently applied across the world. China, the third-largest country in the world geographically, for example, only has one time zone, yet Australia, a slightly smaller country, has six. Hassid and Watson (2014) argue that this is not a cultural quirk or an issue of geography, but reflects how State authority is conceived in each country. They understand the organization of time as a form of symbolic centralization by which a country's rulers can exert control over the daily lives of its citizens. Thus, China seeks to maintain central power through having one time zone across its vast space, while Australia has decentralized its notions of time, loosening the control it has over the everyday lives of its citizens. Time zones, it seems, are political.

The disembedding of social systems

The second key characteristic of modernity is that social systems become **disembedded** from their surroundings. In essence, Giddens argues that many of the tools we use to navigate our lives have become more abstract and no longer closely connected to the social context in which they were used.

Money is perhaps the easiest way to think of this: in premodern societies, people would directly trade something they had for something they wanted (for example, trading eggs from their hens for potatoes that another farmer had grown). They would also use forms of coinage, credit notes and other tokens, yet for all premodern societies, the metals used to make the coin had intrinsic value. Contrast this with the $50 note, for example, which is practically worthless as paper, and only has value in the form of money. This is the vital distinction that occurred as societies transitioned to the modern era.

In modern societies, money acts as a **symbolic token**. Money is not tied to a specific transaction, but has value purely because of the institutional frameworks put in place that ascribe value to it – which are invisible and disembedded from our social relations. Giddens (1990) highlights that money only works in the modern era

Disembedded: how social practices that were once grounded in the local context are no longer restricted by place and time

Symbolic token: things that can be used for exchange (such as money)

through 'the intervention of the state, which acts as a guarantor of value. Only the state (which means here the modern nation-state) is able to transform private debt transactions into a standard means of payment' (p. 24).

Giddens names symbolic tokens such as money as one of the ways society was disembedded. Another form was how expert, authoritative knowledge was perceived. In premodern societies, people were only considered experts (whether as a witch doctor, warrior, or some other figure) if others had witnessed their success. In modernity, however, people *trust* expertise, through a range of institutional systems and frameworks. Thus, we fly on airplanes because we accept that there are a huge range of safety checks and we believe engineers are well trained. Similarly, we try to eat fruit and vegetables, and not drink too much alcohol, because we trust the guidance of medical experts. Giddens refers to this as **functional specialisation**.

The trust we have in these systems is an interesting feature of modernity and can be understood as part of the move towards rationalization (see Chapter 2). In his book *The Philosophy of Money*, Simmel ([1900] 1978) argued that the impersonal nature of money – particularly when compared with interpersonal actions such as bartering – promoted rational behaviour in human affairs and supported the trend towards rationalization that yielded economic growth among the population. Giddens (1990) argues that the trust in these systems is a form of faith that is based in the reliability of the systems in producing results that were intended (see Chapter 10 for discussion of fake news and issues that occur when such trust breaks down).

> **Functional specialisation:** where trust in experts is granted through institutional frameworks rather than direct experience

The questioning and analysis of social relations by individuals

The third characteristic of modernity is the questioning and analysis of social relations by individuals. Giddens calls this the reflexivity of modernity. This is the understanding that people think of themselves *as* people and, in doing so, reflect on their actions and behaviours. As Giddens (1990) writes, 'There is a fundamental sense in which reflexivity is a defining characteristic of all human action. All human beings routinely "keep in touch" with the grounds of what they do as an integral element of doing it' (p. 36). Yet this reflexivity is part of modernity: Premodern societies placed much greater belief and importance in rituals and tradition, and did not even conceive of these *as* traditions (social constructs), but just as the natural way of things. It is a characteristic of modernity that we think about our actions, reflect on why we are reading this book, and simultaneously worry about whether our degrees will provide us with the qualifications and skills to compete in an ever-changing workforce.

This reflexivity is a vital component of modernity. Perhaps without it we would not have sociology because we would lack that desire to understand and critique the social world. Yet it was also the precursor to some more problematic shifts in society, which we will return to later in this chapter. For now, having considered how modernity was a new phase in the organization of societies, we examine the influence of the Industrial Revolution on other components of our lives.

SOCIAL CHANGE IN MODERNITY

Western societies for most of the 20th century can be understood by the concept of modernity. Yet within this overarching framework of modernity, great social change occurred. We have discussed some of these in relation to social structures in Chapter 6, social divisions in Chapter 7 and changes in personal life in Chapter 8. However, our focus was on the substantive topic (e.g. class, feminism or relationships) rather than the *way* in which change occurs. In this section, we will now focus on this sociology of social change. One of the key forms this has taken is thinking about social movements.

Social movements

Social movement: organized collective social action with political aims to challenge a problem or improve a situation

A **social movement** is a form of collective action by a group of people who seek to influence society (Blumer 1951). Social movements tend to occur when there is dissatisfaction with a current social issue, whether it be anger against an existing condition and hope for a new way of living (such as with the civil rights movement, feminism and gay rights), or against a social trend that is seen as damaging and should be stopped (such as drives the environmental movement).

As such, social movement theories place significant importance in individuals' agency (see Chapter 3). The collective agency of individuals coming together has changed cultural norms on a range of issues. This includes the understanding and treatment of sexual and gender minorities, the gradual challenging and changing of racist attitudes and institutional racism, and even the repeal of repressive laws (like the prohibition of marijuana in some parts of the world). Social movements are not always progressive and can result in reactionary and repressive behaviours or laws as well – including movements for 'white rights'.

A short description of the lifecycle of a social movement

Social movements have a number of stages, although an individual social movement may get stuck in one or take a great deal of time to progress through all of them. A complete social movement process works something like this:

» No one does something and no one talks about doing something

» No one does something, but someone talks about doing something

» No one does something, but many people talk about doing something

» Some people do something

» Many people do something

» Everyone does something, and everyone talks about doing it

» Everyone does something, but no one talks about doing it

Millenarianism: early social movements that promised transformational social change through divine intervention

Social movements existed prior to modernity. **Millenarianism** refers to the set of social movements that promised complete social change through miracles and divine intervention. Prevalent across Europe between the 11th and

16th centuries, these were particularly common among poor and marginalized groups. Vittorio Lanternari (1963) discussed a number of religious cults that emerged among many indigenous populations in Africa, Asia and other parts of the global south in response to European colonialism and the perceived failures of their leaders to repel this invasion by conventional military or political means.

© Ronniechua/iStock

Some social movements predicted the end of days.

In the early part of the 20th century, social movements tended to consolidate around religion and class. However, sociologists have identified a change, particularly after World War II, which they have termed collectively as **new social movements** (Scott 1990). While many remained based in religion and class issues (think of the transnational Occupy movement as an example of a new social movement that focused on economic inequality), they also extended further. Such movements include campaigns for animal rights, the environment, and issues related to online privacy and the internet.

> **New social movements:** refers to the growth in and change of social movements since the 1960s

The Occupy movement

The Occupy movement was an international social movement that emerged in the late 2000s to argue against social and economic inequality (Gamson & Sifry 2013). Spurred by the global financial crisis of the period, it has been described as a 'global justice movement' (Steger & James 2013: 38) because of the way it sparked protests and marches across hundreds of cities in many countries. The Occupy movement can be understood as a protest against many of the problems of a 21st-century capitalism that had rejected the job security and decent pay of what has been called Fordism (see p. 240 in this chapter). As one 2011 declaration stated:

> As one people, united, we acknowledge the reality: that the future of the human race requires the cooperation of its members; that our system must protect our rights, and upon corruption of that system, it is up to the individuals to protect their own rights, and those of their neighbors; that a democratic government derives its just power from the people, but corporations do not seek consent to extract wealth from the people and the Earth; and that no true democracy is attainable when the process is determined by economic power. (Cited in Rosow & George 2014: 153)

Perhaps the most famous protest of the Occupy movement was Occupy Wall Street in 2011. Protestors congregated, and effectively took over, Zucotti Park in New York City, staying for more than a month before being evicted on 15 November. After this, protestors occupied banks, university campuses and corporate headquarters to challenge what they saw as gross social and economic inequality perpetuated by leading social institutions (see Chapter 6).

The Occupy movement powerfully used user-generated social media, such as Twitter and YouTube, to organize and publicize their activities, making it a very contemporary social movement. Sociologists are still considering the effects of this style of protest, both in terms of the issues it was contesting and as a social movement (see Gamson & Sifry 2013).

Despite this diversity, there are some key characteristics of these new social movements (Turner et al. 1998). The first is that social movements are a *collective* endeavour. They are not the domain of individuals, but of people working together.

Secondly, social movements are related to social change. They may seek a new future or a return to a prior era, but social movements are always related to perceived changes in society, with people working together to effect such a change.

Social movements are not just crowds: they have organization and motivation. In other words, a group of people gathered together to watch a parade lacks the organization and motivation that social movements have. The people working together to effect change will normally have a sense of solidarity and an identity related to the movement.

Another key factor is that social movements are *sustained* periods of collective action. Regardless of how organized a group are, if they only exist for a matter of weeks, they are unlikely to be considered a social movement. Finally, social movements tend to occur outside of traditional institutional settings. They are normally pushing for social change, largely because their members do not have access to, or faith in, the State or institutional processes that would be able to make such change.

PAUSE FOR REFLECTION

In Chapter 7, we discussed how feminism emerged and the three stages that characterize its evolution (pp. 181–184). Reread that content in the context of our discussion of social movements and consider how many of the characteristics apply to feminism. To what extent is feminism a social movement?

Collective action as a vehicle for social change

Not all of you will consider yourselves to be an active member of a social movement. Readers who are lesbian, gay or bisexual might consider themselves part of the gay rights movement, but not all sexual minority people do (see Savin-Williams 2005). Likewise, not all women associate themselves with feminism. Membership of a social movement is for people who are particularly motivated regarding an issue – and motivated enough to commit time and resources to challenging what they see as inequality or injustice.

However, there are other more general forms of collective action that do not reach the status of social movement. One example of this is the petitions that people sign, not least on websites such as change.org. These have become so popular that some governments have incorporated them: for example, both the British and American governments recognize such petitions to the extent that, if enough people sign, there will be an official response or even a formal debate among politicians. While some petitions will be related to ongoing social movements, others will reflect more short-term or isolated incidents that capture the public's imagination.

Likewise, **crowds** are a key form of collective action that do not qualify as a social movement. Crowds often congregate spontaneously, in response to a disaster or issue that captures the imagination. Images of crowds mourning outside Buckingham Palace after the death of Princess Diana captured an outpouring of grief that was not expected or planned. These are different to crowds that occur at organized events, such as large sporting events, but in both, members of the crowd tend to have shared interests or emotions. Durkheim ([1912] 2008) described the elation that can be felt in crowds as *collective effervescence*, and he discussed how communal gatherings can intensify religious experiences.

> **Crowds:** groups of people congregated together, normally in response to a particular event

One form of group behaviour that can occur within crowds is a **riot**. Many people have negative views of riots, and they can often have deleterious effects. Perhaps the archetypal image of this kind of riot is that of the sport hooligan.

Yet just because crowds and riots are often spontaneous does not mean that there are no underlying processes related to them. In their study of football (soccer) hooliganism, Dunning et al. (1988) argue that a social and historical approach is needed to understand it. They contend that hooliganism has had a place in British football since its inception and must be understood partly as a way that young working-class men publicly express an aggressive form of macho masculinity. Furthermore, football

> **Riot:** where a group of people exhibit unruly behaviour that damages people or property

hooliganism often included fights between opposing fans that were arranged in advance. This would explain why a decrease in football hooliganism has emerged at the same time as softer masculinities flourished in competitive football (Magrath 2017).

Yet while riots are often viewed negatively and as a form of social deviance, they are also a mechanism through which significant resistance to dominant social norms are expressed (Gamson & Sifry 2013). Consider, for example, the riots that followed the death in 2014 of Michael Brown, an unarmed 18-year-old black American man who was shot by a police officer. During the disturbances (known as the Ferguson riots), residents in the area formed crowds in protest of the shooting that turned violent after clashes with police; many have argued the police exacerbated rather than calmed the process. While destructive in their initial outpouring of anger and emotion, these riots can be seen as part of the broader Black Lives Matter political protest that has drawn attention to racial prejudice in American law enforcement. As such, it is possible to view the Ferguson riots as a factor that started a new social movement about racial justice. Not least because the participants did not feel represented by, or able to effect change through, conventional channels.

© Michael B Thomas/Stringer

A scene from the Ferguson riots in 2014. Events in Ferguson have played a significant role in the broader Black Lives Matter political protest.

THINKING BEYOND MODERNITY

In this chapter, we have examined the ways in which the Industrial Revolution and the transition to capitalist forms of industrial economy saw Western societies enter a period known as modernity. We have looked at how social movements have effected social change, even if they do not change the broader structures of their society. Yet technological change has continued apace, and the form of capitalism in the late 20th and early 21st centuries is markedly different from the industrial capitalism of the early and mid-1900s. Before we discuss how best to understand society today, we first need to think about two key social trends of the past few decades: the globalization of the world and the rising importance of environmental issues.

The globalization of the world

Today, we live in a global world. The internet connects most of us to friends and family in different continents, some of whom we may have never met in person. We can order products and foods from practically any country, and have them arrive in a matter of days. And just as we can access things, opinions and information from other countries, so too our own products and influence can spread near-instantaneously across the world.

It is perhaps not surprising that such technological developments have spurred seismic social change, although few individual technological innovations have had such global influence as the internet. While the telephone was invented in the 19th century, its influence was greatest in the mid-20th century, but its impact in transforming social life does not come close to that of the internet. The internet has been the fastest-growing communication tool ever developed – whereas 140 million people used it in 1998, as of 2017, it is used by 3.7 billion people across the world (Kemp 2017).

Yet different countries were becoming increasingly interlinked even before the phenomenal growth of the internet. The term **globalization** is used to conceptualize this change, and has been defined as 'all those processes by which the people of the world are incorporated into a single, global society' (Albrow 1990: 9).

While Albrow's definition of globalization is helpful in highlighting the broad issues that globalization covers, its breadth also means it lacks specificity – it is all-encompassing. Therborn (2000) argues for a more precise definition, stating that globalization refers to 'tendencies to a world-wide reach, impact, or connectedness of social phenomena or to a world-encompassing awareness among social actors' (p. 154). In Table 9.1, we explore what each of these components means to get a better understanding of the issue.

> **globalization:** the process by which countries have become increasingly interconnected, with individual experiences and social phenomena traversing traditional economic, geographic and social boundaries

Table 9.1: Explaining the definition of globalization

Definition component	Meaning
Worldwide reach (of social phenomena)	That issues are not restricted to local phenomena but will be happening at the local level in many contexts across the world
Worldwide impact	That social phenomena (such as the environment, technology or epidemics) are not restricted to one country but experienced internationally

(Continued)

Table 9.1 (Continued)

Definition component	Meaning
Connectedness	That seemingly different issues are connected. Consider the vote for Brexit and the election of Donald Trump as parts of a right-wing populism that are connected by new forms of online media (and Russian influence)
World-encompassing awareness among social actors	That many of us do not think only about our own cultures or even societies – we also think about the world and global issues (such as climate change)

Manfred Steger (2017) argues that globalization is not a single process or a solitary concept but an umbrella term for a great many issues that are unfurling simultaneously. Steger identifies some key characteristics of globalization:

1. Globalization involves the creation of social networks and the growth of connections that traverse traditional boundaries (of geography, politics, economy and culture).

2. These social networks and relationships are expanded and stretched across the world (e.g. global financial banks operating across countries, or near-identical shopping centres in countries with distinct cultures).

3. An acceleration and intensification of social activities, primarily through the internet and online social networks.

4. The processes of globalization are experienced at a subjective level and individuals increasingly think in global terms.

Robertson (1992) famously argued that globalization represented the 'compression of the world' as technological change and new economic and cultural practices mean that once-great distances are compressed by technology. Yet, highlighting the complexities of globalization, such a term can seem distinctly jarring. For many people, their own worlds have not compressed but have opened up in ways their parents or grandparents would never have imagined possible. Cheap air flights mean that people can cross the globe and make multiple visits to countries that would have once been, at best, a once-in-a-lifetime opportunity. Globalization is simultaneously, then, a closing down and an opening up of the world.

Of particular relevance to this chapter, globalization has transformed the structures of the modern world. Perhaps most importantly, the global nature of trade and finance means that the traditional notion of the nation state that had control of its borders, economy and laws has been significantly undermined. The shift in power from nation states to these companies is exemplified by media reports of international corporations, like Amazon and Starbucks, avoiding tax in particular countries (Barfod & Holt 2013). Similarly, as the benefits of global co-operation in combatting major issues are recognized, countries have ceded power to control some of their laws – for example, to the European Union. As we discuss later and in Chapter 10, globalization is one of the key trends that has seen societies fundamentally shift from those of modernity – characterized by the dominance of industrial cities, technological innovation and the primacy of democratic principles – to a more dynamic and precarious context.

The importance of the environment

Cheap air fares are one symbol of our globalized world – showing how we are increasingly physically more connected as well as digitally. Yet air flights are also symbolic of another issue – pollution and the contribution that humans make to the degradation of the environment. Indeed, global warming (or climate change) is perhaps the most pressing threat facing us today – even potentially bringing about the extinction of human life on Earth. As we discussed in Chapter 3, the reality of climate change is not itself a sociological issue – but how we deal with the threat it poses, as well as examining who is likely to be most harmed, are important sociological endeavours. As Giddens (2013) argues, 'Human-induced climate change is without precedent in history and is one of the most formidable problems humanity has to face this century' (p. 152).

© Piyaset/iStock

Sociology has a key part to play in understanding the threat that climate change poses to human life.

When we discuss climate change, one of the key components is global warming. So-called greenhouse gases, including carbon dioxide, are trapped in the Earth's atmosphere and produce a warming effect as they block some of the Sun's heat from leaving. The problem emerged, however, when human activity, particularly related to the burning of fossil fuels, resulted in too much greenhouse gas in the atmosphere, meaning the overall temperature of the Earth is slowly increasing.

One of the key ways that sociology contributes to understanding about climate change is to theorize how globalization and the growth of capitalism has impacted upon this warming. A conference funded by the American National Science Foundation and the American Sociological Association used sociological perspectives to address the social causes of climate change, its social impacts and how societies can adapt to mitigate the effects (Nagel et al. 2010). As part of this event, York (2010) wrote:

> Contemporary global climate change (GCC) is fundamentally a social problem in two senses. First, it is primarily driven by social forces. Second, it potentially has dramatic consequences for societies. The social nature of GCC is sufficiently complex – including economic, demographic, cultural, and psychological aspects – that it requires the full sweep of social scientific analysis to gain a comprehensive understanding of it. Thus, due to the clear social aspects of both the causes and consequences of GCC and due to the traditionally broad scope of sociological inquiry, it is of the utmost importance that sociologists are active in discussions about GCC. (p. 149)

The organizers of the event argued that sociology had enabled a greater consideration of the *political economy* (see Chapter 6 for discussion of political economy approaches) of climate change – that is, the way in which political and economic power is paramount to how climate change is treated at the international level. Another component is to recognize that social policy interventions that have the effect of reducing carbon emissions are needed at an international level.

Yet global warming is not the only environmental risk to societies across the world. Dennis and Urry (2009) highlight that the global modern world is still based on a carbon economy, meaning that there is an over-reliance on polluting fossil fuels, which are both extremely damaging to the environment *and* often in short supply. They underline how the need for oil in Western countries leads to geopolitical tensions that set countries against each other in a bid for 'energy security'.

Giddens (2011) points out, however, that while there is increasing recognition of the dire threat of global warming and other environmental challenges, people are surprisingly reticent to make significant change to their behaviours to stop the threat. Calling this the Giddens paradox, he argues that the problem is that the danger of global warming is not felt by most people, so the threat is downplayed. He emphasizes the importance of national agreements to climate change, being concerned that international initiatives will struggle to gain universal agreement. Unsurprisingly, then, the 2015 Paris Agreement raised significant hope for positive change as over one hundred countries, including key countries such as America and China, signed the document that would see greenhouse gasses reduce significantly. Highlighting the challenge facing this political action, however, there remain significant concerns about America's commitment to the agreement as President Trump has announced the US is pulling out of the agreement, despite the conclusive scientific evidence on the issue.

Similarly, the way in which we understand water is liable to change as global climate change affects weather patterns. Anthropologist Veronica Strang (2004) argues that international conflicts over water are intensifying, and this trend is likely to continue in the foreseeable future. She draws on ethnographic research, cultural mapping and local archives to examine the way water is managed socially and politically in the UK, arguing that the broader political changes will be felt in local contexts across the globe. She reports that water consumption continues to increase in industrial countries at the same time as international conflicts about resources intensify. Strang draws attention to the cultural components of these issues and how cultural beliefs about the value of water inflect the debates. These debates are interlinked with the broader discussions and meanings of the climate and environment in a world that is slowly yet steadily increasing in temperature.

The sociology of the environment

Sociological investigation of the environment is an important subdiscipline of sociology (Sutton 2007). While we focus on climate change in our section on the environment, sociology has examined in detail the differences between nature and the environment. How we think about the countryside, for example, is deeply connected to the organization of the city. Consider the trend of highly paid city workers buying holiday homes in picturesque parts of their country a few hours' drive from where they work. For these rich city dwellers, the country is an idyll they can escape to, as well as a symbol of their wealth. Yet people in the countryside see this trend as an attack on their community. Fewer houses are lived in all year round, meaning that these part-timers do not easily mesh with, or spend money in and on, the wider community, while the influx of wealthy newcomers drives up property prices beyond the reach of most locals. Thus, two groups of people have very different experiences of the same environment (see McIntyre et al. 2006).

Theorizing the structure of contemporary societies

We have used the work of Anthony Giddens in this chapter to examine the structures and characteristics of societies conceptualized by the term modernity – representing Western societies for much of the 20th century. Yet since his writing about modernity and the modern era, there has been substantial debate about the nature of contemporary society, how it has changed and the key drivers of these changes.

These include arguments that people no longer find value in their lives through class and religion, but rather through social connections that occur online, crossing traditional geographic boundaries (see Chapter 8), and where people are sceptical of traditional norms and values. As German sociologist Ulrich Beck argued, 'Just as modernization dissolved the structure of feudal society in the nineteenth century and produced the industrial society, modernization today is dissolving industrial society and another modernity is coming into being' (Beck 1992: 10).

How people deal with and think about risk in society has become a central concern. Giddens (1990, 1991) argues that globalization has occurred at the same time as a growing scepticism towards institutions means that experts and expertise are becoming less trusted – having potentially serious consequences for one of the cornerstones of modernity.

A key contribution to this debate is Beck's notion of **risk society**. Beck (1992) identified risk as a new and defining feature of **late modern** societies. Whereas premodern societies had to deal with life-threatening risks – from hunger and fighting, to natural disasters attributed to local deities – modern societies have to deal with risks that are caused by humans and focused around technology. Yet these problems, while more removed than the immediacy of finding one's next meal or the impact of a tsunami, are intractable and cannot be solved easily, and certainly not by individuals.

Risk society: a framework to understand contemporary societies that have to deal with global risks that are focussed around technology

Late modern: a term that recognizes contemporary societies are markedly different from those in the modernity era of the mid-20th century

As such, we worry about global warming, what jobs will be available in the future, the state of politics and democracy in many parts of the world, all without being able to impact these in any meaningful way. These concerns are about issues at the societal level and require institutional and State intervention. And with these risks, it becomes clear that social life in late modern society is imbued with uncertainty – the 'job for life' once promised in the 20th century has been replaced by 'transferable skills' and the need for workers to have potentially many different careers in their life.

A defining feature of Beck's conceptualization of risk society is that it is distinct from earlier iterations of modernity. Beck argued that the environmental effects of industrialization were central to this shift: from global warming and more general pollution, to nuclear contamination and scares about food such as horsemeat in processed products (a scandal erupted in Europe in 2013 after foods advertised as containing pure beef were found to secretly contain horsemeat, which many countries find distasteful). All of these examples are connected to globalization processes, were not predicted and have an unknowable impact – they have all created a distinctly new kind of risk to be managed. Indeed, Beck argued that current formations of politics and the social order are not sufficient to manage them.

Other theories have emerged to engage with these new structures that are dominant in society. Writing more recently, and thus engaging with the transformative effect of the internet, spanish sociologist Manuel Castells (2005) describes the 'emergence of a new technological paradigm, based in information and communication technologies' (p. 3). He conceptualizes a **network society** – a society where key social institutions and activities are structured around digital information networks (Castells 1996). Because of this focus on the internet and electronic networks, network society as a concept is inherently tied with processes of globalization. He argues that we have moved from the industrial age to an *information age*. Castells contends that these networks have become the basic units of modern (globalized) societies, and that power now exists beyond nation states and instead in these networks. Exclusion from these networks is seen as a key form of marginalization, with power being located with those who monopolize them.

Network society: a society where social institutions are structured around digital networks of information, primarily the internet

---

VOX POP Dora Meredith

EU and Global Portfolio Manager for Innovate UK

I work for the UK's national innovation agency. Since 2007, we have invested over £1.5 billion in innovation. Innovate UK supports a wide range of technologies: from robotics for a safer world, to developing first-of-a-kind approaches for the manufacturing of medicines, to recyclable batteries to power electric vehicles. We work with industry, researchers, investors and the government to drive innovation across the whole of the UK. I work on policy within Innovate UK, with a particular focus on international strategy.

I have gained a wide variety of experience in my career so far, all with the consistent theme of working on effective, evidence-based policy interventions that improve society. I chose to work at Innovate UK, as I believe that new technologies will have a significant impact on future societies, requiring effective government policy to ensure positive ramifications.

There are many global challenges facing society: from scarcity of food, anti-microbial resistance and climate change. It is certain that new technologies will impact on these challenges. For example, we can use precision agriculture technologies to ensure more efficient farming, or further develop renewable energy technology to counter climate change. It is crucial, however, that such technology development is contextualized within wider policy, for which social science plays a key role.

It is not enough to be thinking simply about what we think can be done next in terms of technology – we need to think about the big challenges and be positive about our potential to address them. Critically, we need to ensure that challenges are addressed in a holistic manner, considering how technologies will interact with people and change our behaviour. Technologies are moving rapidly, with many businesses facing disruption within their markets, and implications upon every aspect of our daily lives: from work practices, to the way we talk to each other, to our security. Social scientists need to respond to this changing world and continue to provide crucial insight, enabling society to understand implications for the future.

(Note: Dora Meredith has made this contribution in a personal capacity. Any reference to Innovate UK should not be read as our endorsement of the views presented.)

© Dora Meredith

» How might Dora's role help combat climate change?

» What areas of research not discussed in this chapter do you think might benefit from funding?

But what about postmodernity?

An important concept in some of these debates is postmodernity. This and other similar terms, particularly postmodern and postmodernism, are used quite frequently to signify a new era, one in which Enlightenment ideals are questioned and grand narratives undermined.

We have not offered simple definitions of these terms or used them as orienting concepts for the chapter because they rely on a great deal of prior knowledge to fully understand the nuance of the debate. Thus, Giddens (1990) distinguishes postmodernism from postmodernity. He succinctly describes postmodernity: 'the trajectory of social development is taking us away from the institutions of modernity towards a new and distinct type of social order' (p. 45). Yet he contrasts this with postmodernism, saying, 'Post-modernism, if it means anything, is best kept to refer to styles or movements within literature, painting, the plastic arts, and architecture. It concerns aspects of *aesthetic reflection* upon the nature of modernity.'

PROVOCATION 9: We need less rationality in the world

A central tenet of the Enlightenment, in which contemporary Western societies have their foundation, is the notion that rational thought should be the basis for decisions and structures in society (see Chapter 2). At a time when cries of 'fake news' are part of political discourse, and leading politicians seek to deny scientific fact, we emphasize our strong commitment to this value, and its centrality to sociology.

Yet what if too great a reliance on rationality is damaging to our society? This is, after all, a concern that has a long history. English Romantic poets of the 18th century were troubled by it. John Keats, in his poem *Lamia*, worried that science would 'unweave a rainbow' and that philosophy would 'clip an angel's wings' – stripping society of magic and wonder. He probably would not have spoken highly of sociology had he known about it.

But we are not referring to Romantic literary critiques of rationality, just as we reject the mendacious claims of 'post-truth' politics where debate and even policy is framed by appeals to emotion rather than empirical reality (see Chapter 10). Rather, we want to question ways in which a narrow version of rationality is applied to benefit corporations in a globalized society, at the expense of people and the common good.

To think about this, we need to examine how technology has changed everyday life across the past century. A key concept here is rationalization – introduced by Max Weber ([1905] 1930), and discussed in Chapter 2. Rationalization refers to how traditions and rituals were replaced by more calculated, rational behaviours in the organization of societies. These processes became deeply embedded in capitalist modern societies from the 20th century.

The rationalization of work gained credibility with the theories of an American management consultant, Frederick Winslow Taylor. His argument was that the most efficient method should be used to manufacture goods, and this resulted in breaking tasks into small, manageable chunks (Taylor 1911). These principles were then adopted by Henry Ford, the quintessential American industrialist who founded the Ford motor company. The factory assembly line used by Ford made mass production of cars possible.

Ford also raised the wages of his employees, meaning that he had both a satisfied workforce *and* that there were enough people who could afford to buy the products he was manufacturing (Harvey 1989). This was part of a period of modern capitalism, from the early 20th century to the 1970s, now known as *Fordism* – characterized by relatively strong protections for workers and stable labour relations.

Relevant to our argument is the centrality of the factory assembly line and how manufacturing was rational, followed clear rules and could be transplanted from one context to another. In other words, all factories producing the same goods were practically indistinguishable and interchangeable.

Yet globalization and the continued revolution in technology development have also seen a further rationalization of the organization of work and leisure, as capitalism itself is globalized. American sociologist George Ritzer has called this process *McDonaldization*. Ritzer (2000) based his theory on Weber's critique of rationalization and bureaucracy to argue that many of the institutions where we work or spend our leisure time have undergone processes exemplified by the McDonald's fast-food restaurant chain. These processes are:

1. efficiency – minimizing any waste in the system;
2. calculability – knowing the cost and delivery time of a product, with a focus on quantitative aspects;
3. predictability – knowing precisely what the product will look like, and that it will vary only slightly, if at all;
4. control through non-human technology – machines replace workers or routinize their tasks.

In all these ways, one can see the supposed benefits of rationalization and technology. Tasks are more efficient; we know how long they will take; people (and resources) can be freed up from these tasks. These things will happen faster. There are numerous other benefits, including a greater choice of options and avoiding many of the problems of non-rational societies. Most of us at some point will have enjoyed an aspect of this process: whether it be at the eponymous McDonald's, with more upmarket brands, or in other aspects of leisure and play (see Ritzer 2010).

Yet what if, in many cases, these processes of McDonaldization do not serve to improve our services? What if they ultimately help raise profits for corporations, with little or no consideration for the experience of the user or the worker?

Ritzer argues that this is precisely what happens. He says that rather than producing positive results for people, a central pillar of McDonaldization is the *irrationality of rationality*. That is, through these processes of rationalization, there are a number of ways in which irrational effects occur. He uses the example of

© Drical/iStock

the queues at McDonald's that paradoxically make fast food very slow, particularly at times like the weekend when families are together.

Similarly, the processes of McDonaldization shifts the work from the producer to the user. That is why in most fast-food chains you clear away your own rubbish, and are not provided with proper cutlery. In the McDonaldized shopping centres, you will buy products that you put together yourself once home – such as flat-pack furniture. Arguably, the products are of lower quality, meaning that the 'cheaper' price reflects the product purchased.

The efficiency of rationalization can also lead to great waste. Have you ever wondered why, in most supermarkets, every carrot looks exactly as you would expect a carrot to look? Probably not, as it seems natural; but it is not. Supermarkets across the world – at least, supermarkets which follow the McDonaldization model – regularly throw out tonnes of perfectly edible fresh fruit and vegetables because they do not conform to their customers' expectations. Enforcing the required uniformity (the *predictability*) is fundamentally inefficient.

Ritzer goes beyond highlighting the irrationalities of McDonaldization to argue it is fundamentally *unreasonable*. Explaining this, Ritzer (1998) writes:

> Irrationality means that rational systems are unreasonable systems – they serve to deny the basic humanity, the human reason, of the people who work within them or are served by them. In other words, rational systems are dehumanizing systems. Whereas the terms rationality and reason are often used interchangeably in other contexts, here they are employed to mean antithetical phenomena. (p. 56)

These forms of dehumanization include the genuine harms of eating such foods repeatedly, and can foster negative eating habits, particularly in children. Ritzer also highlights the damage such chains have done to the environment. He is also concerned with how microwave meals can be antisocial, relegating the importance of family meals or meals with friends. Perhaps more clearly evidenced, the strict management of workers and the control of work patterns by machines has palpable effects on workers' identity and self-worth (see Chapter 7).

Ritzer (2003) sees opportunities for McDonaldization to be challenged, primarily through local cultures being able to influence and contest the way global companies develop in their areas. For example, a start-up company in California, called Imperfect (www.imperfectproduce.com), sells 'ugly' vegetables to consumers at a heavily discounted price – combatting the irrationality of strict predictability. So, while the spread of McDonaldization is pervasive, there are ways to challenge and subvert the dominant system.

In summary, while rationalization was a vital part of the Enlightenment and is a central tenet of sociology and modern societies, its expansion into many parts of work and social life can have negative effects. Counterintuitively, these effects can be *irrational* because the beneficiaries are not the consumers but those making profits. For the common good, sometimes we need less rationality.

Provoked? Read further:

Harvey, D. (1989). *The Condition of Postmodernity*. Oxford: Blackwell.

Ritzer, G. (1998). The Weberian theory of rationalization and the McDonaldization of contemporary society. In P. Kivisto (ed.), *Illuminating Social Life*. London: SAGE.

Ritzer, G. (2003). Rethinking globalization: Glocalization/grobalization and something/nothing. *Sociological Theory*, 21(3), 193–209.

Capitalism, globalization and technology

Economics is often called 'the dismal science'. This is because it often starts from the assumption that human life is a cruel competition where moral niceties cannot overcome the supposed brutal necessity of the struggle over scarce resources. Yet one of the basic insights of sociology is that supposedly **free markets**, within which people compete with one another without regulation, still require a prior level of trust: in money, credit and rights. As such, society – the structure which enables institutions (including banks, laws and systems of trust) – is a precondition of market economics (Durkheim [1893] 1984).

However, those actors who society protects with its laws and systems of property and money still use the advantages society offers them to reinforce their economic power. Marx and Weber both identified the significance of political and cultural systems in maintaining economic inequalities. Today's global network capitalism is the culmination of this long history of interplay by which economic, political and cultural spheres have been created and transformed by power and by the resistance to it (Castells 1996).

Consider the following situation: in the 1960s, people had to buy hard, physical vinyl copies of The Beatles' records to listen to their latest hit, and had to purchase physical copies of books to read the latest bestseller. Today, music can be streamed across the internet, and books can be read through electronic devices. The vital issue is that every copy of a book and song produced in the 1960s cost money, and took a finite amount of time. Yet digital technologies have made it possible to make copies of things that would have once required large amounts of 'capital' to produce.

The question is what will happen to global network capitalism if the networks that sustain it start to enable the mass production of free copies of things capitalists make a profit from selling? In other words, how is capitalism going to survive if it is no longer making money through producing all the goods?

One important argument here is that globalization has actually been a process of free markets undermining particular countries' economies. If corporations can outsource jobs to developing countries at a fraction of the wage costs, this raises unemployment in developed societies and increases the bargaining position of such transnational firms in negotiations with governments. They can also offshore activities to ensure they do not pay any tax either, further reducing the conditions of citizens. Colin Crouch (2004) has called this process *postdemocracy*.

However, this version of global network capitalism is only one aspect of the issue.

Global network capitalism is not just about deregulation and the dismantling of societies to create an unimpeded global 'free' market. At the end of the Cold War, the World Trade Organization (WTO) (1994/1995) was created to structure a new order based upon the global regulation of property rights. The first act of the WTO was TRIPS (the agreement on Trade-Related Aspects of Intellectual Property Rights), a treaty that required all WTO members to sign into domestic legislation a raft of laws harmonizing and extending the intellectual property rights of mainly transnational corporations. These regulations have continued to be increased ever since (David & Halbert 2015). Global networks are very good ways to increase markets, sales and profits, but this can only be achieved if property holders can regulate networks to retain their ownership of what is produced and circulated through them. Yet despite legal treaties, this has not been maintained.

Only a year after WTO/TRIPS, the World Intellectual Property Organisations 1996 Copyright Treaty first recognized the challenge to intellectual property

> **Free market: a system where goods and services are exchanged for money, ostensibly with no governmental control**

posed by consumers of digital recording devices, who were now able to share copies of works that were being sold in digital formats (CDs and DVDs). Only a couple of years later, the profit storm that had flowed from the CD's digitisation of recorded music in the 1980s went into reverse with the rise of the file-sharing software Napster (David 2010). While Napster was rapidly prosecuted and successfully taken down for 'contributory infringement', its closure heralded the rise of a new generation of fully peer-to-peer services that did not use a central server to mediate files, and which could not therefore be prosecuted for 'fencing stolen goods' (i.e. contributory infringement) as Napster had. The cat-and-mouse struggle between rights holders and free-sharers has continued since, with the development of torrent services, then streaming services and now cloud-based systems, each of which distributed the process of sharing in a new way that abolished whatever bottleneck rights holders sought to close down through prosecution.

One consequence of the rise of sharing networks has been the advent of illegal pirate services. Another outcome has been the rise of new legal forms of free access – such as Spotify – that fund free access through advertising. In each case, the rise of global networks has challenged traditional forms of capitalism by suspending 'scarcity', the precondition of price, and the justification of property rights within capitalist societies.

It is not just in the music industry that scarcity has been suspended by sharing networks. The ability to make digital copies whose marginal cost (the cost of making the next copy) has fallen to zero has reached ever-wider domains of what was once seen as the economy. Yet the end of scarcity will challenge some of the core tenets of accepted wisdom in economic theory and practice. Film, television, computer software and publishing have all witnessed their own versions of this struggle between sharing and scarcity-based models of production and distribution, and in each case the rationale for price and property is disproved when sharing is shown to be more efficient in production, more effective in distribution and generating higher incentives for creative innovation (David 2017).

This may sound very gloomy, but there are advantages as well. Hackers have proved more effective than corporate coders. Musicians get better paid when their music is circulated freely, generating publicity while leaving fans with more money, which has meant ticket sales and prices have increased. Sports fans frozen out by escalating subscription rates to digital sports channels can challenge hypercommercialization. Authors find wider audiences. Researchers can access more research. It is also true that the sharing revolution is spreading beyond purely informational goods. Generic pharmaceuticals mean that medicine better reaches the neediest, while research is made better and faster by free circulation from behind patent-protected barriers. 3D printers will open the post-scarcity sharing revolution even further (Rifkin 2014).

Global network capitalism requires both deregulation and new forms of regulation to profit from the global circulation of ideas and things. Capitalism has not had everything its own way. Global networks have many, diverse possible actions and outcomes from events (what Castells would call affordances), facilitating intense conflict in the world today. Just as capitalists have sought to reduce the value

© Juancho Torres/Anadolu Agency/Getty Images

This boy in Colombia receives his new prosthetic hand – created by 3D printing.

of labour by deregulating labour markets, so sharers have sought to undo the price of informational goods by deregulating property rights through global network sharing systems.

A parallel conflict is also raging among those who would use robots to replace people at work and so reduce the dependence of capitalists upon human workers (see p. 154; Cameron 2017). At the same time, workers and citizens are looking for new ways to harness the potential of machines to reduce work and help people. In an ageing society, robots may be part of the solution. Whether that solution involves helping humans or replacing them remains to be fought over. The future continues not to be what it used to be.

CONCLUSION

This chapter has developed our sociological understanding about how societies change. It has done this in two key ways: thinking about the grand social processes that see large-scale transformations, focusing at the start on the Industrial Revolution, and finishing by thinking about the radical changes in globalization and digital technologies. In both instances, sociology enables us to examine the broad trends associated with these changes. In between this macro focus, we also focused in on our understanding of how social change is developed through political action and social movements. Concluding by discussing the problems that globalization brings to the principles of capitalism, we believe that sociologists will be of vital importance in understanding these social and economic issues moving forward.

HOW WOULD...?

» Think of a social movement you or someone you know has been involved in.

  » Why would you categorize it as a social movement? Is it a new social movement? Why?

  » Are the issues it is addressing part of a modernity, or do they speak to more recent social changes? Which theorists best explain this change?

» Look in the news for a recent social event that speaks to issues of risk in society.

  » How would Giddens understand the event? What theoretical concepts of his might be useful in thinking sociologically about it?

  » How would Beck or Castells think about it differently? What are the reasons for these differences?

STRUCTURED FURTHER READING

Giddens, A. (1990). *The Consequences of Modernity*. Cambridge: Polity.
Based on a set of lectures given at Stanford University in the late 1980s, this book provides an important theoretical argument about the nature and consequences of modernity. Arguing against the notion that societies have seen a revolutionary shift, he instead develops themes of security vs danger and trust vs risk to argue that modernity has benefits and dangers; and that it is essential to develop political responses to these risks.

Dennis, K. & Urry, J. (2009). *After the Car*. Cambridge: Polity.
In this engaging book, the authors imagine what the social world will look like 'after the car'. Incorporating key themes we have discussed in this chapter – particularly around the environment and globalization – they describe how the car system may be redesigned and engineered. Yet they also offer bleak situations where the role of the digital is paramount, and policy interventions are needed to guard against scant resources and the human damage of climate change.

Kauffman, L.A. (2017). *Direct Action: Protest and the Reinvention of American Radicalism*. London: Verso.
This book provides an insider's account of recent protest movements and the potential to effect change in the US. It discusses protests on the American left since the 1960s and examines movements discussed in this chapter such as Occupy Wall Street and Black Lives Matter.

 Visit the companion website at www.macmillanihe.com/mccormack for further learning and teaching resources.

Chapter 10
SOCIOLOGY DISCOVERED

INTRODUCTION

Now you are equipped with a firm grasp of what sociology is and how it is used to understand the social world, we can turn to think about its public impact. Recognizing that people adopt sociological ideas and use them to understand diverse societies, we discuss the role of sociology in social policy before examining how recent social trends in the media affect how we engage with sociological concepts and theories. This includes the presence of fake news, and even fake sociology. In our Provocation, we ask, in sociology, whose side are you on? We finish by thinking about what a good sociology student looks like.

THE VALUE OF SOCIOLOGY

This book has introduced you to sociology. We have explained what sociology is, how it is practised and discussed some of its key empirical findings. In the later chapters, we applied sociology to a range of important topics to better understand society. Part of our job in writing this book is to ensure that you get a firm grounding in the key sociologists and their theories, to make you aware of some of sociology's central debates, and to give you an overview of the discipline that was not biased by our own preferences and perceptions.

Given that sociology is about understanding the social world, we have also sought to equip you with the intellectual tools to deal with issues that you will encounter in your lives. In short, we hope to have sparked within you a sociological imagination. The greater your sociological imagination, the more able you are to critically analyse society at both micro and macro levels. Some of these issues will be felt on a personal level, like navigating friendships and romances, and dealing with tensions that arise within them. Others will be political, like a heightened understanding of the relationship between politics, poverty, opportunity and cultural diversity. These are issues we have discussed throughout the book.

We also hope to have helped enable you to contribute to the central debates of not only our time, but of times to come. As we discussed in Chapter 9, the risks of the world related to the environment, globalization and the future of capitalism are simultaneously big, macro issues that nonetheless will be experienced by everyone in daily life. Likewise, we cannot predict what social movements around oppressed people will come next, yet understanding how past minority groups have fought for social and legal equality will help you promote other social groups in doing the same.

We believe sociology can help find the best resolution for dealing with issues you will encounter, whether at home or at work. A grounding in existing sociological research can help when the issues you face relate directly to these topics, and when it does not, we hope to have also engrained a desire and ability to locate, read, understand and critically reflect on the available evidence. While your answer is not guaranteed to be correct, sociology provides a systematic process for coming to an answer that is more than a guess and better than an opinion.

Many of you will have been undertaking a module of sociology on a different degree course – including subjects as diverse as business, psychology, medicine and criminology. If this is the case for you, we hope that you will apply the core tenets of sociology to thinking about your own discipline. Whether this is the key skills of method, theory and critical analysis, or more subject-specific ideas, a sociological imagination can and should inform your discipline (see Chapter 1).

We have drawn on Provocations throughout the book to engage with emotive issues. They are there precisely to *provoke* you into thinking differently about issues to which you may have an emotional response and perhaps have not critically thought about before. This will not have been the case for every Provocation, and the response will be different among readers, mostly based on personal experience. When you have been more familiar with the arguments, we hope these Provocations are helpful in modelling ways to engage in sociological debate rather than rely on emotional reactions.

The Vox Pops provide a different function. Sociology can sometimes be abstract or difficult to engage with. Hearing the perspectives of real people relating to sociological issues can help contextualize broader debates. We hope that hearing the voices of people with a range of backgrounds, and from several countries, has helped you engage with sociology.

We have also spoken about the importance of theory and method to sociology. Some students are captivated by theory. Just as Professor Maggie O'Neill wrote about having her worldview transformed by critical social theory (see Chapter 3), so too do many students after reading a particular theorist or how a certain issue is theorized. Yet not all immediately value the theoretical component of sociology. Many sociologists write their theories in complex ways that are not easy to understand or apply to the real world. And even when the theory is brilliantly written, it is not everyone's favourite component. If that is you, be expansive in your theory reading and find a theorist you enjoy at some level: this includes reading widely and not being put off by theory in general, even if you find some theorists boring or too difficult.

Exploring a range of theories and theorists can be a useful endeavour. It might help to think of theory as a gym for the mind: just as you get more results from the gym the more you put in, so too with theory. Sometimes, the greater your effort to understand theory and think theoretically, the more you will get back. We encourage you to put that effort in, even if in a selective manner, as theory is vital to sociology. Theory is what binds facts together, connecting them and providing an explanation for them. Without theory, there is no sociology.

The same can be said of methods: understanding the utility behind various research methods, as well as when and how to use them, can be complicated (see Chapter 4). For example, an interview may seem straightforward, yet many skills are required to interview someone successfully. These range from interpersonal and listening skills to memory and timekeeping; they require the interviewer to ask the right questions and remain in control of the conversation while also being flexible enough to be directed by the replies and interests of the interviewee.

It is helpful to think of research methods as tools in a toolbox. Just as with tools, you must know how to use each one. You can use different tools to get similar results, but the tools you use will affect the outcome. If you are trying to remove a nail, you might use a pair of pliers and have the same result as if you use the back end of a hammer. Yet if you use a saw to cut the nail off at the wall, you will be left with something different. With sociology, if you interview people privately about a sensitive topic, you will get different answers than if you use a group interview.

This tools analogy is useful in another way: to remind us that as sociologists we control our methods rather than being controlled by them. That is, the sociologist needs to reflect on the question they want answered and then use the best tool to understand it. Pick the best method for the task; do not rely on the method you like the most.

It is our hope that you develop a sociological imagination, use the tools of theory and method to interrogate the society you live in, and make choices in your life that benefit you and those around you as well as for the greater good.

SOCIOLOGY IN THE WORLD

Given that sociology is about understanding societies and social interaction, it is always, inherently, part of the world. Discussing applied sociology, or sociology in the world, can seem tautological. Yet this language can be useful to think about the influence of sociology, and the impact it can have. Thus, in the sections that follow, we discuss how sociology can influence individuals and societies, and some of the ways this can happen.

The impact of sociology on the individual

At the start of this book, we laid out what we considered to be defining characteristics of sociology. Not only is it a discipline distinct from psychology, philosophy and other social sciences, it is fundamentally different from the natural sciences. Giddens (1987) makes a useful distinction here. In the natural sciences, scientists investigate aspects of the world that are oblivious to such study. This is primarily because the objects of study do not have any possibility of 'knowing'. Rocks do not know that the geologist cares. Giddens describes this as a **single hermeneutic**, where hermeneutic means seeking understanding or interpretation.

Yet sociologists deal with people who *do* care that they are being studied. Whether it is with an international study that makes the news across the world or a student dissertation, the people in the study and the broader population who know about

Single hermeneutic: where knowledge is in one direction. The object of study does not change as a result

Double hermeneutic: the idea that people's knowledge of sociology alters how they understand the world, thus changing the world

it will be, to varying degrees, interested in the study. Giddens calls this the **double hermeneutic**.

Tucker (1998) defines the double hermeneutic as 'the interweaving of the concepts of the social scientist and everyday life, as social scientific ideas are appropriated by laypeople and become part of the new social universe that the researcher studies' (p. 3). As such, sociology can generate change through this method of changing people's perspectives of the world. Technical phrases and terms used by sociologists can become part of the wider public vocabulary, and this familiarity and (self-)awareness can alter how they are used, and indeed how they actually manifest, in society.

Tucker (1998) uses the example of role theory to illustrate this: the notion of a 'role' was developed in interactional sociology across the 20th century, and has become a popular term. Most obviously, this is about role models, but we also speak of gender roles and other similar terms. The public may not always accept these ideas or the meanings sociologists ascribe to them – but in becoming aware of the concepts, they have had to think in some way about the issues behind them.

Sociology has other ways of impacting on the individual, particularly the sociologist. Referring in Chapter 1 to C. Wright Mills' concept of the sociological imagination, we highlighted the ways in which sociology was about thinking differently. Thus, sociology changes the individual because the way they conceive the world is altered – a critical awakening that makes a person more aware of the ways in which society structures individuals' own experiences.

PROVOCATION 10: Whose side are we on?

Howard Becker's (1967) 'Whose side are we on?' is perhaps the most famous journal article in the discipline of sociology. Becker noted that while the powerful have many ways to express their interpretation of things, and to promote their interests, this is less true for the 'underdogs'. As such, Becker argued, sociology should understand and give a voice to the experience and beliefs of these underdogs. In other words, sociology should be partisan, and serve as an advocate for those in need.

Consider the examples discussed in Chapter 7 – where sociology has helped identify problems of racism, misogyny and classism among other issues. Surely, sociology is better when it is challenging oppression rather than remaining neutral or even supporting it?

The trouble is that this approach can lead to the problem of 'going native' – of becoming biased in favour of a group after spending too much time with them. Some have taken Becker to be saying that 'going native' is inevitable but not a problem; others take the view that in giving voice to a group, Becker is not suggesting the sociologist should lose their ability to provide a true account (David 2002). We therefore ask, is it the job of the sociologist to describe how things are, or to interpret the voices of those who are otherwise unheard? Can sociologists ever be neutral in who they research, the questions they choose to ask or in the results they produce?

In Chapter 5, we discussed the ethics of publishing research that might harm the group being studied, asking whether it is appropriate to suppress publication, particularly if the group is an oppressed minority. How might this discussion be advanced considering Becker's questions about whose side we are on?

Using examples of clear oppression can make it harder to think about the role of sociology more broadly: sociology should not condone racism. Hopefully, there is an internal logic to sociology that would condemn racist thinking (which tends to be based on emotive arguments that do not withstand logical scrutiny – see Chapter 7), but even if not, there are humanitarian reasons and arguments of social justice that would make that case. Given this, we turn to an example that is less clear-cut for sociologists, to consider the issue of being partisan.

In a research project looking at the local environmental movement in Kent (UK) in the early 1990s, Matthew David set out to map the network of alliances and enmities among the environmentalists and interested parties concerning a potential property development in this beautiful area. He soon found himself studying 187 different groups, all of whom claimed to be part of the local environmental

© Macmillan Mexico/Dave Cockburn

movement, but who had very different conceptions of who else was inside and outside that network. In this fractured context, what did it mean for Matthew to attend a meeting held by one particular group instead of another – was he taking a side by so doing?

This question unexpectedly became all too relevant. Having attended a meeting organized to question the development of an 'eco-tourist' holiday village in ancient woodland, Matthew's name was copied down by representatives of the developers, and passed to his then employers. Purely by attending this meeting, it was suggested that he was actively seeking to harm the local economy and to block what they promoted as an environmentally friendly development project.

Subsequently, Matthew was labelled as hostile by the company, and as a result they would not give him an interview. Yet being blacklisted by the company made it easier for Matthew to gain access to interview opponents of the scheme, because he was now seen as being sympathetic to their interpretation of events (David 2002).

In attending the meeting, had Matthew compromised his ability to carry out 'valid' research, or did being caught up in the politics of the situation give him a more 'valid' insight? What should he have done to get the best data to inform his arguments? What do you consider to be the best data in this instance, and why?

In later work, the same researcher was asked to assess the effectiveness of a scheme to provide online training in areas of rural social exclusion via local telecentres and tele-cottages (a tele-cottage is a community-based facility to assist learning). The research was funded by the agency that was organizing the programme, to evaluate its quality and effectiveness.

Matthew carried out interviews with the software developers who had written the training packages, the staff in the telecentres and cottages, and the users of the facilities. He also chose to interview a number of local employers, employees and unemployed people living in the areas covered by the scheme. This led to the identification of very different conceptions of what counted as 'effectiveness' and what helped or inhibited it.

The software developers identified the basic problem as a lack of knowledge – something that could be solved by means of their training packages, whereas centre staff and residents highlighted the residents' 'knowledge of lack' – the awareness of the material conditions of their lives which could not be resolved by any amount of training alone. The problem for Matthew was to evaluate whose position was right.

If Matthew was to evaluate the 'success' of the scheme, should he only base this evaluation on what the scheme *set out to achieve*, which was to make knowledge available? Alternatively, was it his job to evaluate the scheme according to *the definition of success offered by those whom the scheme targeted*? If the funders of the research dictate the definition of 'useful', does this require that the researcher follows their definition of 'success'? In this instance, Matthew came under considerable pressure not to publish results that highlighted the criticisms of the scheme made by centre staff and local residents. After the publication of these criticisms, the software provider was shown in a poor light, and subsequently had some of their funding withdrawn.

How should the researcher have acted in this context? Should a researcher take into consideration such a possible outcome when deciding what to publish and how? Whose experiences should be privileged in doing this?

Provoked? Read further:

Becker, H. (1967). Whose side are we on? *Social Problems*, 14(3), 239–247.

David, M. (2002). Problems of participation: The limits of action research. *International Journal of Social Research Methodology*, 5(1), 11–17.

Gouldner, A. (1968). The sociologist as partisan: Sociology and the welfare state. *American Sociologist*, 3, 103–116.

Sociology and social policy

Social policy: the way in which societies address issues of individual wellbeing, social welfare and social justice

One of the key ways in which sociology can have an impact in society is through influencing **social policy**. This is because sociology can provide an understanding of how societies operate, meaning that social problems can be addressed from an empirically informed context. Spicker (2014) highlights that social policy tends to be most concerned about people who lack wellbeing, whether it be as a result of education, health, environment or other social problems. The goal is to improve the situation through social policy – where there are clear goals and, through a process of implementation, achievable and measurable results.

Early forms of social policy tended to deal with extreme forms of absolute poverty. In the UK, for example, the 1834 Poor Law was introduced to deal with social issues at the time: one of the key ways was moving from giving money to poor people to providing institutions, such as the workhouse (Fraser 2009).

As might seem familiar with current debates around social policy in the UK, Australia and North America, key concerns were: to reduce the cost of the social provision; to encourage people to support themselves; and to take beggars off the streets. The laws were seen by many as draconian, with workhouses particularly maligned. Many of the conditions in these workhouses would not be considered acceptable today: families were separated, the food was poor quality, with silence expected at meals, and people were expected to carry out hard manual labour for ten hours a day. There was no education, people not allowed to go outside, and there was just one hour of recreation a day. They were more like prisons than provisions of support: prisons where the only crime was being poor.

The workhouses failed as social policy because they did not serve to improve the circumstances or life experiences of the people in need. A key term in understanding this failure is *welfare*. Welfare is a term used to describe the range of services which protect vulnerable or needy people – including children, the ill and the elderly (McClelland & Smyth 2014; Spicker 2014). Somewhat confusingly, in the US welfare has a much narrower definition, referring to financial aid to people in poverty.

Taking the broader definition of protecting vulnerable and needy people, there are a range of arguments for welfare. Spicker (2017) highlights some diverse, core arguments for the need for welfare within social policy (see Table 10.1).

Table 10.1: Arguments for welfare

Argument	Rationale
Humanitarian	That human beings have inherent value and societies thus have a duty to give a basic standard of living
Religious	The world's major religions have moral instructions to be charitable or offer social solidarity – much of this includes helping the poor and needy
Mutual self-interest	A recognition that supporting the poor and needy can be good for society (see discussion of *The Spirit Level* in Chapter 7)
Democratic	Welfare develops alongside democracy, because both require collective participation
Practical	Much like mutual self-interest, welfare has practical benefits for society

(Based on text of Spicker, 2017)

Social policy does not just address those in urgent need. Social policy in any country, for example, must address the education of its citizenry, the administration of tax and spend policies, and the regulation of leisure activities.

Education policy, assessment and perverse consequences

Education is a central component of social policy in most nations, not least because of its importance for the global economy (see Chapter 6). Recognizing the influence of globalization (see Chapter 9), sociologists of education Bob Lingard and Sam Sellar (2013) highlight that this has resulted in a convergence in social policy related to education across the world. While discourses of values, social solidarity and democracy persist (Hoskins 2008), the trend has been towards experienced educators having less of a role in educational policy than the increasingly influential bureaucrats and economists who seek to use educational policy to foster economic growth. Lingard and Sellar contend that various international organizations are driving this trend, not least the Organization for Economic Co-operation and Development (OECD).

They draw on an extensive case study of the OECD's Programme for International Student Assessment (PISA) to argue that schooling is now truly transnational in the way that student assessment is measured between countries. More and more countries have opted into the PISA programme, alongside education companies like Pearson. PISA has become seen as a global benchmark of how a country's education system is performing.

Yet there is a perverse consequence to this. PISA results have become increasingly important to national rankings of schools, meaning that 'PISA performance was promoted as an end in itself, collapsing distinctions between test performance and the performance of the education system it is designed to measure' (p. 34). Performing well in the measure can be more important than performing well for the students.

This problem with rankings can be seen in universities at a number of levels. In the UK, the National Student Survey asks graduating students to rate their experiences at university on several measures. Yet this survey has become so important to national rankings of universities (which themselves feed into international rankings) that there is arguably more incentive for universities to prioritize measures that keep students happy and improve their National Student Survey results, rather than focus on educational quality. Research has also demonstrated that student evaluation of teaching ratings is not related to student learning (Uttl et al. 2017).

In many countries, academics are often assessed on their teaching by student surveys – and these evaluations are frequently involved in promotion decisions as well as monitoring performance. Yet these are known to be poor measures – in sociology, optional modules tend to score more highly than mandatory ones, and methods modules often score poorly. More significantly, and across subjects, students tend to score men more highly than women (MacNell et al. 2015), and attractive people more highly than less attractive people (Felton et al. 2007).

Think about your own experiences of teaching. Are there any teachers you liked more because they were attractive? Or because of some issue that was not about teaching? When you fill out evaluations of someone's teaching, will you reflect on any potential biases you may have?

Evidence-based policy: a paradigm in which policy is based on research, supposedly free from dogma or ideology

Social policy is a fascinating area, a discipline in itself, and we do not have the scope to provide a full history of it here (see Fraser 2009). We turn instead to a contemporary trend of what is known as **evidence-based policy,** as distinct from policy that was based in ideological positions or professional or practical experience. Particularly evident in British social policy, evidence-based policy-making has become a paradigm in which research, not least sociological research, is valuable because it can provide strategies for improving social problems and influence social policy that is supposedly free from dogma or ideology (Sanderson 2011). It might seem that this is a positive trend, but it has been critiqued as well.

There are multiple ways in which evidence-based policy is practised. There is an idealistic model where academic research identifies a problem that is then addressed by policy-makers. There is a similar version where social policy-makers identify an issue and fund research to come up with a solution – that may well be positive, but it can also mean that research is quite narrowly focused through specific set government interests and lessens the chance for innovation.

A broader problem, however, is about how this evidence-based paradigm can be *misused*. Here, groups like charities or think tanks may well distort evidence to fit a particular policy agenda. This is also true of academic researchers, particularly when funding is involved. The distortion of evidence can include ignoring important information, misrepresenting or fabricating evidence, or overgeneralizing from an argument (Strassheim & Kettunen 2014). This has been called *policy-based evidence*, where such evidence is produced with the intention of supporting the desired policy. And while we have focused on the British context, there are concerns this misuse of evidence is occurring across the world (Appadurai 2001; Boden & Epstein 2006).

In an Australian context, Marston and Watts (2003) argue that evidence-based policy can be a mechanism by which the policy-makers gain power over determining what constitutes a social problem. They caution against any mechanistic process in which only narrow forms of ostensibly objective evidence are included, and seek a democratic and pluralistic form of engagement in order to make social policy. They argue that researchers and policy-makers should remain sensitive to the context of the social problem, and adapt methods and theory appropriately to understand the issue involved.

The good news is that a strong understanding of sociology equips you with the skills to differentiate the good from the bad research and to determine what is evidence-based policy and what is policy-based 'evidence'.

THE CONSUMPTION OF SOCIOLOGY

Once we step outside academic institutions, there are limited ways in which the public knowingly encounter and engage with sociology and its ideas. Unlike the highly successful lay books on psychology and economics, sociology has struggled to have a strong 'crossover' presence in selling books for, and to, the general public. Malcolm Gladwell stands out as a sociologist who has been an effective popularizer of sociology, now with a successful podcast too (see recommended further reading at the end of the chapter). Sociology is rarely taught at schools. The main way sociology is consumed by non-sociologists is through the media. As such, and building on Chapter 6, we need to think about the media and threats to how good sociology is disseminated beyond sociologists.

Thinking about the media and bias

One of the founding principles of many Western democracies is the notion of a **free press**. Also referred to as the freedom of the press, this allows people to circulate ideas in writing without being censored by government. This is part of the concept of

Free press: the idea that people are allowed to circulate ideas in writing without being censored by government

freedom of speech, where individuals have the right to speak their minds within broad limits. A free press is strongly associated with democratic countries, and countries where the press is restricted are generally deemed to be authoritarian to some extent.

China is one country where the news media is heavily regulated by the State. Freedom House, the independent watchdog organization that promotes freedom and democracy, highlights how journalists in China are regularly imprisoned and forced to air televised confessions. The internet is heavily regulated and censored, and ideas that are seen as a threat to the nation (including competing economic policies, different religions and information about sexual minorities) are blocked (see https://freedomhouse.org/report/freedom-press/2016/china).

Within Western societies, the freedom of the press is not absolute. There is some diversity across different countries, but there is general acceptance that the press should not be able to knowingly spread untruths about people or incite violence. In the US, news media can be explicitly partisan in its reporting, yet in the UK there are strict rules governing what, and how, television media can report.

The news media has evolved throughout the modern era. Cushion (2010) traces changes in how news has been generated and reported for mass consumption. It was originally communicated through oral transmission – people telling each other their news and whatever other information they had heard, upon meeting. This had many problems, not least the inaccuracies that come from recalling facts from memory, and limitations regarding how far the news could spread.

With the invention of the newspaper, news entered the written format era. Here, there was a shift from news being created during conversations to news being released and consumed periodically – when the newspapers were published. Newspapers (and other written forms of news) reduced problems of memory but entrenched new forms of bias.

© Getty Images

The news media is the main channel through which lay audiences have engaged with sociology.

This bias occurs in two forms: 1) the interpretation of news; and 2) selectivity in what news is reported. Newspapers that are more liberal or left wing will tend to espouse different theories of the world than those which are more right wing (a socialist critique of capitalism versus a free market one, for example). The second bias occurs when deciding which issues to report: Choosing to look the other way when a member of one political party is accused of sexual harassment, for example, but not when a member of another party does is a form of bias.

With the arrival of radio and then television, broadcast news emerged, but maintained the same forms of bias as print news: There were liberal news stations and conservative ones. Still, up until the 1990s, people consumed the news once or twice a day: reading the newspaper in the morning, or watching or listening to thirty minutes of nightly news in the evening. If a reported story turned out to be untrue, a retraction would be made in the press, and there would normally be consequences for the journalist.

This all changed with the invention of cable television (Cushion 2010; Cushion & Lewis 2010). In 1980, the first-ever 24-hour news channel launched in the US: Central News Network (CNN). The station gained popularity during the US invasion of Iraq in 1991, and other 24-hour news stations emerged shortly after. Also known as 'rolling news' coverage, this has become a norm for leading broadcasters. Given the limited funding for news channels, it is not possible to provide high-quality coverage all the time (Juntunen 2010). On some stations, there are a lot of repeated broadcasts played on a loop that are only updated as events evolve or new ones take precedence. But the other trend was for journalistic standards on these channels to drop and for previously un-newsworthy topics suddenly be deemed newsworthy in order to fill the non-stop demand for content.

This trend was exacerbated with the shift to online news. Mitchelstein and Boczkowski (2009) highlight that the internet has increasingly become a key source for news. It used to be that a respected newspaper, like *The New York Times*, worked on a story, paid people to fact-check that story, and ran it through an editorial board before publishing it. The general public then read the paper in the morning, and could be relatively sure that the story was fundamentally accurate. Today, however, *The New York Times* writes a story in the traditional manner, and a journalist picks up on bits of that story, that they then try and publish online. Many people read this through social networking sites and phone apps. In other words, they get their news second-hand. They may then read another internet article whose report is based not on the original news, but on the report of the news – a third-hand account. With each rewritten version, detail is lost, the initial facts hidden or neglected, and more opportunity for intentional and unintentional bias occurs.

Another bias relates to financial profit. In many countries, the news media has become guided by market principles (i.e. of profit) rather than democratic ones. If the news is guided by profit rather than serving democracy, news producers seek the cheapest version of the news that maximizes profit rather than the version that maximizes the social good (McManus 1992). This means that decisions are made not just about quality of news, but about chasing profit. While most newspapers will not remove all checks and balances – because getting sued or becoming known for poor news could affect sales and thus profit – the aim is not the best-quality news with the money available, but the cheapest (or most 'economical') reporting that satisfies a particular minimum standard.

The influence of money is more perverse and pervasive even than this. This market-driven model leads news media to report the news that meets the audience demand – in other words, audience opinions, instead of journalistic integrity or the public interest, come to dictate what is deemed to be newsworthy (Uscinski 2014). In Chapter 3, we spoke of climate change as an example of theory; it is also an example of bad news that we dislike. Perhaps it makes the headlines less than it should because the audience prefers to be uninformed about the scale and nature of the looming catastrophe.

The online consumption of news appears only to have exacerbated this problem. The way in which news spreads on Twitter as soon as events happen puts additional pressure on traditional forms of news media to report faster.

PAUSE FOR REFLECTION

Think about whether you have contributed to this cycle. Do you consume your news primarily through Facebook, Twitter or some other free social media platform? How many times have you clicked on a link because the headline supported what you already think? Yet, how many times have you investigated a link because it contradicted your values, to get an alternative view? If you follow the link more frequently – or only – when it supports your position, perhaps you are part of the news problem. What do you think might be the next step in this cycle, if we accept the premise that certain websites only report news their audience wants to hear?

Fake news

Even when a news source is biased, the media have traditionally based their stories on reporting events that actually happened, or quotes that were actually said, even if they then manipulate the context, emphasis and presentation to suit their agenda. Following the US presidential election in 2016, however, there is growing concern about the spread and effects of **fake news**. Analysing web-browsing data, the archives of fact-checking websites and an online survey, Allcott and Gentzkow (2017) found that fake news was widely spread during the election, and that it heavily favoured Donald Trump (see also Faris et al. 2017). Over half of those who recalled seeing fake news stories indicated on the survey that they believed them. Allcott and Gentzkow highlighted that fake news is of increasing importance because it is much easier to enter the media industry in the age of the internet, and then to disseminate false stories through social media.

Thus, a key difference between the 2016 presidential election and previous ones is that internet technologies transformed the circulation of news. Rather than traditional news outlets having control over what information is given – and, in general, conforming to rules related to accuracy and truth about when and when not to publish a story – internet articles were written by activists and political operatives to fabricate events and (fake) news reports that supported a political narrative

Fake news:
false stories
that are
intentionally
spread to
misinform

designed to undermine a political opponent (Allcott & Gentzkow 2017). Given the outcome of that election, it seems fake news had some success.

Collectively, the sheer volume of news we are exposed to from traditional, new and fake sources may encourage us to pay attention to less of the detail; as Allcott and Gentzkow (2017) suggest, to trust the headlines without researching the news outlet, or cross-verifying the story with other sources. With so much news populating our feeds, the opportunity is there for fake news to appear undetected and seem to be true. Indeed, given our preference for theories that are interesting (see Chapter 3) and that confirm our biases (see above), the allure of fake news is even more apparent.

The internet has perhaps been the most democratizing invention for the distribution of thought and knowledge. Yet it has also facilitated the spread of fake news.

There have since been calls for social media outlets, like Facebook, to monitor for and weed out fake news stories, as well as provide high-profile retractions and clarifications when news is discovered to be fake.

Yet to promote entirely fake news, all a person needs to do is create a rumour, or fake news story, and post it on their Facebook account. This is made possible by fake news websites, dedicated to the promulgation of fake news. This was a real issue in the 2016 US presidential election. For example, the 'pizzagate' fake news story claimed that the New York City Police Department had found evidence of the existence of a paedophile ring, operating out of a pizzeria and linked to prominent members of the Democratic Party. There was no evidence for the story because it was entirely false. Yet a man went to a pizzeria with a gun to investigate the conspiracy (Siddiqui & Svrluga 2016).

Facebook, Twitter and other social media platforms have thus rapidly moved from a place where people used to post pictures of their personal affairs to connect with new friends and maintain existing friendships to a platform for identity politics, politicking and debate. It has given power to everyone's political voice, including those who wish to be dishonest. This is a new way of creating and consuming news.

The changing nature of news and what it means for sociology

Alongside the opportunity to intentionally spread fake news, of course, the internet offers a range of possibilities for spreading real news and knowledge, including knowledge of sociologists and other academics. Supporting the notion that sociological research is interesting to a wider audience, the discipline of sociology has become an area where journalists can find news stories relatively easily. Both in traditional news sources and places like YouTube, on podcasts and e-zines, there has been an explosion in the coverage of sociology. Journalists scan journal issues and academic LISTSERVs where sociologists (and academics more broadly) discuss and disseminate their research.

This can be a fantastic opportunity, and having one's research discussed is an important part of sociology – and, by reaching the general public, a potentially important component of Giddens' double hermeneutic. Yet there is an important caveat: once research is debated beyond the scope of the published study, the sociologist loses control of the way in which it is discussed and the arguments about what claims are made. Whereas traditional forms of media had fact-checkers and rigorous systems of editing both within the institution and through legal regulation, new media have fewer if any checks in this regard, and are also more likely to post more salacious headlines to increase traffic to their websites, especially given the vast and ever-growing number of online news sources that are vying for our attention.

These issues connect with how new media is funded. Whereas old-style newspapers in general had standards and quality safeguards in place so that people would trust them and become repeat customers, new media (in most cases) does not have a purchase cost and is instead paid for by advertisers. To be successful under this business model, it is therefore more important to increase the number of visits to the website ('clicks') rather than provide good-quality news. This is conceptualized by the popular derogatory term 'click bait' – where headlines and articles are designed to motivate someone to visit the page rather than educate or inform the reader. As such, these media sites have a fundamentally different aim to sociology – one is a business model, driven to make a profit above all else; the other privileges knowledge and understanding.

© Nemoris/iStock

Clickbait websites and headlines value grabbing your attention above journalistic rigour – or even the truth.

Media sensationalism and sociological research

When Eric Anderson published research on male athletes in 2008, his findings were taken up and overgeneralized by multiple media outlets. His qualitative study examined how a group of 49 high school football players who had failed to make their university teams joined co-ed (mixed-sex) cheerleading teams (Anderson 2008). Anderson documented a resocialization processes, where the men unlearned homophobia and started to embrace tactility between male friends. As part of this, a surprisingly large number of participants engaged in threesomes with two men and one woman. While this was primarily focused on penetrative sex with the woman, several of the men had engaged in some forms of semi-sexual behaviours, such as kissing each other. A few had engaged in oral sex with the other man, when directly requested by the woman. Anderson did not argue that this change was happening everywhere, and recognized in the conclusion the limitations to generalization that come from a qualitative study.

Anderson spoke with the media about the research. A few serious reports included the headline that 40 per cent of the 49 male collegiate cheerleaders had engaged in some form of sexual interaction with another male during a threesome. Although one article in particular from the traditional media did not sensationalize the findings, blogs used more salacious headlines, including one that asked, 'How Gay are Football Players?' While they quoted the original news article that discussed some of the detail of the study seriously, they then asked: 'Wait, 40% of football players are gay?' The blog then asked a number of rhetorical questions, criticizing the research – for example, suggesting the author was biased because he was a gay man.

We have not included a link here to the blog post mentioned in this example, as our aim is not to critique that specific post, but to make a broader point: there is real danger in using online and media sources to understand a specific sociological study. Some journalists do excellent work in reporting on research, but others do not. When you find a study that is of interest to you, make sure you engage with the published research and not just the online source that has presented the most exciting aspects of the study, potentially out of context.

GOOD SOCIOLOGY Assessing Sociology in the Media

The majority of people who are not academics come to their sociological knowledge through media accounts of published (or yet to be published) sociological research. Most people will believe the results – or even just take in the headline – of that media account, regardless of how well the sociology is reported. We hope that you will, instead, be a discerning consumer of sociological. Below is a process for judging whether sociology news reports are high quality or not.

1. On first learning of an academic study of interest, identify its author. It should be in the media article. If not, you are likely not reading the original media report – search for the study, either using a search engine or following the links in the article, so that you have the name of the author and the study. Be more sceptical of reports that do not directly link to the study.

2. Open Google Scholar, or another academic search engine, and type in the name of the study. This will help you locate the study. You can now click on the abstract, where it is likely that you will already find discrepancies with what you read in the news. You will be far better informed from just reading the abstract (which is always free) than from news accounts of that research.

3. If you desire to know more about the study, you must access the article. If the article is 'open access', you can simply click on it and read it, but you should also be wary about the quality of its scholarship (as we will discuss in the next few pages).

4. If the article is closed access, you have several choices. The first is that you pay the publisher to read the article. Clearly, this is what the publisher is hoping for. The second is to access the article through a university library. If you are not a university student, or your library does not subscribe to that journal, you can often locate earlier versions of the published work by searching the internet. Sometimes there will be a university repository, or an academic's own webpage, where you can access an earlier version of the article. The final route is to email the author directly: this might take a while, but our experience is that academics are normally willing to share their research. The trick here is to keep the email short, something like, 'Hello [Name], I saw you've published some work on x and y. My institution doesn't have access to it, so I'm hoping that you might be able to send me a copy?' Most of the time this works.

The important point: whether you are reading for your own enjoyment, composing an essay, completing a dissertation or even writing your own research, it is great to use media reports of sociology to inspire your thinking, but make sure you always go to the original source as well.

But what about fake sociology?

As we have discussed, the fundamentally different aims of sociology and the media mean that reading sociology from news sources is a risky endeavour. The best way to understand a sociological argument is to read the original study in the academic journal. The next problem, however, is that you now have to be able to tell real journals from fake ones.

Traditionally, established, serious academic journals are run by a publishing house, a university or a learned society. These journals, because they have institutional credibility and a good reputation, are funded by university libraries across the world paying to have access to them: normally, this is through a print subscription (physical copies are sent to each university library) and nowadays this will usually include online access as well as (or instead of) hard copy. These journals ensure all the submitted research goes through peer review – where other academics read the research and judge whether it meets certain intellectual and academic standards – and only if approved is it then fit to be published. There is another final quality check – an editor (also a renowned academic), who makes the final decision about whether to publish. The most prestigious journals will reject many good articles because they choose to publish what they see as the best research. The author does not have to pay anything – their job is to make sure the article is good enough.

This process made it easy for people to know that research reached a certain level of acceptability – whether it genuinely contributed to knowledge in some form. It relied on the trust in institutions discussed in Chapter 9. And journalists, academics and the public at large would then know if an article had been accepted for publication in, say, *American Journal of Sociology*, it was guaranteed to be a serious piece of research.

Yet there is a new model of open access which complicates this approach. The ideal of open-access research is that it removes the paywalls around research – meaning that anyone can read it. And in a context where much academic research is publicly funded, there is a logic to the often-heard argument that the public should be able to read for free the research that their tax has helped fund. These journals are often online-only, which makes the loss of paywall income sustainable as the cost of producing each issue is therefore much reduced (see Chapter 9). The majority of these journals expect the author to pay for their article to be published.

For genuine open-access journals, this can work well. People with research grants to fund their studies can use some of that money to pay the costs of publishing in a reputable open-access journal, which can run into thousands of dollars (or equivalent) for the more prestigious titles. The general public can then read all this research. This is good, for as sociologists, we want people to know about sociology. In genuine open-access journals, the vital principles of peer review and intellectual rigour are maintained, and the cost model is completely separated from the academic decision about whether to publish.

Yet there are also problems with this new way of delivering sociological research. The key problem is that fake – or rather, *predatory* – types of open-access journals have appeared. Here, the journal publishes any research regardless of quality and solely based on whether the author can pay. There is either no peer review, or the peer review is laughably basic and positive. With many of these publications, they name an editor who either does not exist or is a real academic but has not consented to be affiliated with the journal.

To highlight this problem, scholars recently created a fictitious academic and applied on her behalf for an editor position to 360 journals (Sorokowski et al. 2017). This fictional person's qualifications were dismal for the role of an editor; in fact, on her made-up CV, it was clear that she had never even published a journal article and had no editorial experience. Yet, fully one-third of the online journals thought to be predatory accepted her as an editor without any relevant background or any invitation to interview. By comparison, she received no offers from the control group of journals that met certain standards of quality.

Worryingly, even among journals sampled from the Directory of Open Access Journals, an organization dedicated to promoting quality open-access publications while maintaining ethical standards, 8 of 120 accepted the fictional character.

Fake sociology articles

As well as fake journals and fake news, some published sociology is also fake. In Chapter 3 we discussed the hoax article by physics professor Alan Sokal (p. 66). Sokal wrote a jargon-laden piece that called for a 'postmodern science': his fake sociology was intended as a critique of poststructural scholarship that he saw as lacking intellectual rigour.

More recently, an article entitled 'The conceptual penis as a social construct' was accepted as genuine scholarship and published by an open-access journal. The paper was rather self-evidently ludicrous, and parodied gender studies as a subdiscipline of academic research. While it can be read in a similar way to the Sokal paper – as lambasting gender studies rather than poststructural theory – there were differences. Sokal's paper was published in a widely respected journal, whereas the more recent article appeared in a new open-access journal. The journal has since retracted the article, but it still published a piece of fake sociology.

Given the lack of trustworthiness of thousands of open access journals alongside the existence of respected open-access journals, it is important to be able to distinguish between them – particularly for journalists and members of the public who are not familiar with these rules of sociological publishing.

While some journals seem obviously fake or predatory, not all of them are as transparent as the fraudulent email telling you that a long-lost relative has died and bequeathed you a fortune, if you could just supply your bank details to receive the payment. Some trade on the name of prestigious academics (who are completely unaware of this). Some use titles similar to existing reputable journals. As a fictitious example, a predatory journal might try and fool people by sounding like the prestigious *British Journal of Sociology* by calling itself the *Journal of British Sociology*. In general, though, there are a number of clues that indicate if an article has been published in a non-legitimate journal:

- There is no editorial board, or the board is very small, and/or consists merely of names without any university affiliations.

- The website itself does not look as professional as those of established publishing houses like SAGE, Taylor & Francis and Springer Nature.

- Other articles in the journal look to be of very poor quality.

- Check on the Directory of Open Access Journals to see if it is listed there.

- It is also worth paying attention to national differences. Countries in the global south, for example, often have serious journals that may not have all of the above features.

 VOX POP Catherine Waite

PhD candidate, School of Social Sciences, Monash University, Melbourne, Australia

As a PhD student studying sociology and living in Melbourne, Australia, my research is coloured by the lens of my location. In particular, as a scholar of place, the cultural and geographic specificity of localities is a fertile area of research. Sociology as a discipline allows a nuanced approach in which the complexity of the social world can be made visible. This is one of the reasons why I chose to study sociology.

As a first-year student encountering the subject for the first time, I was fascinated by an approach that problematized many of the basic, taken-for-granted aspects of my own daily life. Topics like the social construction

© Catherine Waite

of gender, class and ethnicity forced me to question many of the assumptions I had made about the world.

Throughout my undergraduate studies, I have been exposed to a multitude of perspectives, and ways of looking at the world. I have explored a range of phenomena, and identified social issues across the spectrum. My knowledge and understanding of the social world has been deepened as a result. I have come to understand some of the underlying processes that underscore many of the everyday social phenomena we take for granted. While many of these processes are not necessarily specific to Australia, the specific socio-cultural milieu in which they emerge provides a unique perspective.

Most importantly, becoming a student of sociology has been a lifelong endeavour. I know that I will never stop learning, trying to identify assumptions and stereotypes or challenging societal norms and processes.

» How does Catherine's experience relate to your own experiences of sociology?

» Do you see yourself engaging with sociology in the future? In what ways?

Being a good sociology student

All of us are students of sociology. That is, we are continually learning how to do sociology, how to understand society and how to contribute to knowledge of the social world. To be a good student of sociology is to approach social issues with an open mind – not to be closed off to using different methods or theories than the ones you prefer. As we discussed in Chapter 3, human beings have agency and this vital fact means that societies can and do change. Whether it be major changes such as the creation of new technologies, or resistance to laws or norms through social movements, the sociologist's work is never done, as the building blocks of society – people – will continue to interact and thus change society in unexpected ways.

Yet while we are all students of sociology, there is also advice that we can give you, as actual sociology students, about how best to study the subject. The fundamental issue is how you *approach* sociology: with an open mind and ready to have your existing opinions challenged. This does not mean you pliantly accept what you are told or read. Instead, you should defend your views and argue your case – but still be open to the notion that you could be partially or wholly wrong. This involves giving up the notion that being wrong is bad. Being wrong is fantastic and important – it is how we learn. Realistically, if you have decided you are never wrong, you are shut off from the world and will never challenge yourself.

The famous economist John Maynard Keynes is reported to have said, 'When the facts change, I change my mind.' This is a helpful statement, but it misses a related set of issues. It is not just the facts that matter, but how you approach these facts, how you use them, and whether you are treating the facts honestly and dispassionately.

Accepting being wrong can be an odd, uncomfortable feeling, and is a hard skill to develop. This is another reason for our Provocations: as we discussed in the front matter of the book, cognitive dissonance is an important pedagogical tool (see p. xvii). When your emotions are telling you one thing but your intellect is telling you another, this is a prime opportunity to learn.

GOOD SOCIOLOGY Sociology and a Pedagogy of Uncertainty

Using cognitive dissonance in sociology, and studying difficult topics more generally, requires an element of risk: people may be upset or hurt by a topic or the way that topic is discussed. We do not advocate purposefully being shocking without carefully thinking about the consequences and how to manage them. But sitting back and disengaging, distancing yourself from the topic at hand, is the quickest, surest way to minimize the chance of learning.

Educationalist Lee Shulman (2005) emphasizes that engagement and uncertainty are vital components of learning, and that they can induce feelings of anxiety:

> That anxiety derives from the risk involved in putting forward ideas and defending them, from knowing that one must be prepared for class, from the fear of making a fool of oneself. The anxiety is either adaptive or paralyzing ... One must have something at stake. No emotional investment, no intellectual or formational yield.

Thus, learning in sociology requires active participation, accepting that you might be wrong, and revelling in that possibility.

We are not psychologists and do not have a clear set of guidelines about learning to value being wrong. We know it is not necessarily easy to do, and will depend on how you have been socialized and the values you have been taught. This learning process can include reminding yourself that being wrong can be good; it can be reflecting on prior mistakes and thinking about how to improve on them – and then developing a strategy to do so. We recommend reading Shulman's (2005) text on the pedagogy of uncertainty; trying to embrace the cognitive dissonance of learning (see Preface); and reading further around the subject – Kathryn Schulz (2010) has written an entertaining book on this.

To be able to have the discussions and challenge yourself, you also need to read. Read widely, engage with the set texts you have been given and think about their arguments. Do engage with sociological writing in the media (with the caveats mentioned earlier); listen to podcasts; talk about these readings; debate them with your friends.

Writing can also be a powerful way of thinking through your ideas. Committing words to the page is a real test of how well you know something. As such, do not save writing for exams and essays, but think about keeping a journal or blogging, whether these thoughts are kept private or eventually published for anyone to read. Writing is a cyclical process; understanding is needed to write, and the process of writing – of choosing the right words to express what you mean – hones and improves that understanding.

We also encourage you, a good sociology student, to learn to reference. It is very easy for academics to forget how confusing and arbitrary referencing seems to those new to it. Yet as people who read student work, including marking essays, being able to reference in a clear and consistent way is a vital means of showing academic rigour and demonstrating that arguments are based on academic research, and not newspaper articles or television documentaries. Your university library will have guidance on how to reference: if you do not have access to this, the American Sociological Association has a useful reference style guide (see www.asanet.org/sites/default/files/quick_tips_for_asa_style.pdf). But beware! Different institutions have different guidance: always check the required format before submitting your work.

Taking sociology into the world

Sociology is an academic discipline, but it is unusual in how it is inherently applied to social life. While sociological theories can appear abstract or inaccessible, they are all, by definition, about the world in which we live. As such, it is important that you think about how sociology will influence your life now and in the future. Sociology influences the world not just through social policy or debates in the media, but through sociology graduates – people with skilled training and an ethical ethos who use their sociological imagination and analytical skills in a myriad of careers and other undertakings. In a world of fake news and ideological debates, a sociological approach has the potential to transcend some of these problems and develop connections and mutual understanding across disparate groups. As we discussed in Chapter 3, the big picture is connected to the micro components of our own lives – by taking sociology into the world, we may help move a step closer to a more benevolent future.

CONCLUSION

Understanding sociology means that you have the intellectual tools to critically interrogate the social world. In a context where fake news is proliferating and policy can guide what evidence is collected, these skills are vital.

But finally, our main hope is that you enjoy sociology. The world is such a diverse and fascinating place, and understanding how the people in it act and interact is a fundamental component of knowing what it means to be human. We hope this introduction to sociology has enthused you and infused a sociological imagination that will stay with you throughout your life.

HOW WOULD...?

How would you improve sociology?

Over the course of this book, we have discussed the ideas of many sociologists. We have provided a history of sociology, placing it in historical and social context. We have discussed a range of theoretical positions; examined different methodological approaches; applied sociology to different topics. Now it's over to you.

» Reflecting on the chapters, what components of sociology do you like?
   » Do you have a preferred theoretical position? (see Chapter 3)
      » Do you prefer social or sociological theory? (p. 61)
      » Are you a functionalist, conflict theorist or interactionist? (pp. 59–60)

>> What parts of sociological method do you like?

>> Do you prefer a deductive or inductive approach? (pp. 56–57)

>> Do you think qualitative or quantitative methods have more value? (pp. 78–85)

>> How would you explain the importance of sociology to a friend or relative?

>> Has it changed how you think about the world? Would that help others?

>> And finally, how would you reference this book?

STRUCTURED FURTHER READING

Gladwell, M. (2016/2017). *Revisionist History*. Podcast available at: http://revisionisthistory.com/
It is vital that you read widely to be a good sociologist. But reading is not the only form of media where good sociology is present. Public sociologist Malcolm Gladwell has a great podcast that discusses moments in history whose importance has not been fully realized, and which shed light on broader social issues. Gladwell's three-part podcast on educational inequality is particularly powerful; listening to his podcasts is a great way to engage in sociology.

Crow, G. (2005). *The Art of Sociological Argument*. Basingstoke: Palgrave.
This book examines how sociological arguments are presented and constructed and, in doing so, describes several key sociologists' arguments and theories. By reflecting on the style of important sociologists' writing, Crow highlights the diverse possibilities for sociology. Strongly empirical and foundational sociologists are present, as well as more abstract writers like Michel Foucault and feminist sociologist Ann Oakley. It is an accessible and engaging book that presents sociology in a different way.

Becker, H. (1967). Whose side are we on? *Social Problems,* 14(3), 239–247.
We encourage you to read this seminal article about sociology and critically reflect on what you consider sociology to be.

Visit the companion website at **www.macmillanihe.com/mccormack** for further learning and teaching resources.

REFERENCES

Acker, J. (1990). Hierarchies, jobs, bodies: A theory of gendered organizations. *Gender & Society*, 4(2), 139–158.

Adams, J., Clemens, E.S. & Orloff, A. (eds.) (2005). *Remaking Modernity: Politics, History, and Sociology*. Durham, NC: Duke University Press.

Addams, J. ([1902] 2002). *Democracy and Social Ethics*. Chicago, IL: University of Illinois Press.

Adorno, T. (1996). *The Culture Industry: Selected Essays on Mass Culture*. London: Routledge.

Ahlum, C. & Fralley, J. (1976). *Feminist High School Studies*. New York, NY: Feminist Press.

Albrow, M. (1990). Globalization, knowledge and society: An introduction. In M. Albrow & E. King (eds.), *Globalization, Knowledge and Society*. London: SAGE, 3–16.

Allan, G. (1996). *Kinship and Friendship in Modern Britain*. Oxford: Oxford University Press.

Allan, K. (2006). *Contemporary Social and Sociological Theory: Visualizing Social Worlds*. Thousand Oaks, CA: Pine Forge Press.

Allcott, H. & Gentzkow, M. (2017). Social media and fake news in the 2016 election. *Journal of Economic Perspectives*, 31(2), 211–236.

Allport, G.W. (1954). *The Nature of Prejudice*. Cambridge, MA: Perseus Books.

Amini, E. (2017). *The Gendered and Sexual Experiences of Iranian Muslim Menopausal Women: A Biographical Narrative Approach*. Unpublished PhD thesis: Durham University, England.

Anderson, E. (2005). Orthodox and inclusive masculinity: Competing masculinities among heterosexual men in a feminized terrain. *Sociological Perspectives*, 48(3), 337–355.

Anderson, E. (2008). 'Being masculine is not about who you sleep with …': Heterosexual athletes contesting masculinity and the one-time rule of homosexuality. *Sex Roles*, 58, 104–115.

Anderson, E. (2009). *Inclusive Masculinity: The Changing Nature of Masculinities*. London: Routledge.

Anderson, E. (2012). *The Monogamy Gap: Men, Love and the Reality of Cheating*. New York, NY: Oxford University Press.

Anderson, E. & McCormack, M. (2015). Cuddling and spooning: Heteromasculinity and homosocial tactility among student-athletes. *Men and Masculinities*, 18(2), 214–230.

Anderson, E. & McCormack, M. (2016). *The Changing Dynamics of Bisexual Men's Lives*. New York, NY: Springer.

Appadurai, A. (2001). Grassroots globalization and the research imagination. In A. Appadurai (ed.), *Globalization*. Durham, NC: Duke University Press.

Appelrouth, S.A. & Edles, L.D. (2012). *Classical and Contemporary Sociological Theory: Text and Readings* (2nd edn). London: SAGE.

Asch, S. (1946). Forming impressions of personality. *Journal of Abnormal and Social Psychology*, 41, 258–290.

Ashforth, B.E. & Kreiner, G.E. (1999). How can you do it? Dirty work and the challenge of constructing a positive identity. *The Academy of Management Review*, 24(3), 413–434.

Ashforth, B.E. & Mael, F. (1989). Social identity and the organization. *The Academy of Management Review*, 14(1), 20–39.

Atkinson, W. (2010). *Class, Individualization and Late Modernity: In Search of the Reflexive Worker*. Basingstoke: Palgrave.

Atkinson, W., Roberts, S. & Savage, M. (2012). *Class Inequality in Austerity Britain*. Basingstoke: Palgrave.

Attwood, F. & Smith, C. (2010). Extreme concern: Regulating 'dangerous pictures' in the United Kingdom. *Journal of Law and Society*, 37(1), 171–188.

Bakshy, E., Messing, S. & Adamic, L.A. (2015). Exposure to ideologically diverse news and opinion on Facebook. *Science*, 348(6239), 1130–1132.

Banks, S. (2012). Ethics. In S. Becker, A. Bryman & H. Ferguson (eds.), *Understanding Research for Social Policy and Social Work: Themes, Methods and Approaches*. Bristol: Policy Press, 58–60.

Barford, V. & Holt, G. (2013). Google, Amazon, Starbucks: The rise of 'tax shaming'. *BBC News Magazine*, 21. Available online at: www.bbc.co.uk/news/magazine-20560359 (accessed 31 October 2017).

Barker, M. & Petley, J. (1997). *Ill Effects: The Media/Violence Debate*. London: Routledge.

Barron, L. (2013). *Social Theory in Popular Culture*. Basingstoke: Palgrave.

Barthes, R. (1973). *Mythologies*. London: Paladin.

Baumrind, D. (1964). Some thoughts on ethics of research: After reading Milgram's 'Behavioral Study of Obedience'. *American Psychologist*, 19(6), 421.

Baym, N. (2015). *Personal Connections in the Digital Age*. London: John Wiley & Sons.

Beck, U. (1992). *Risk Society: Towards a New Modernity*. London: Sage.

Becker, H. (1967). Whose side are we on? *Social Problems*, 14(3), 239–247.

Beer, D. & Burrows, R. (2007). Sociology and, of and in Web 2.0: Some initial considerations. *Sociological Research Online*, 12(5), 17.

Bekhor, P.S., Bekhor, L. & Gandrabur, M. (1995). Employer attitudes toward persons with visible tattoos. *Australasian Journal of Dermatology*, 36(2), 75–77.

Bell, D. (1973). *The Coming of Post-industrial Society*. New York, NY: Basic Books.

Bell, D.A. (1992). *Faces at the Bottom of the Well: The Permanence of Racism*. New York, NY: Basic Books.

Bennett, J.E., Li, G., Foreman, K., Best, N., Kontis, V., Pearson, C., Hambly, P. & Ezzati, M. (2015). The future of life expectancy and life expectancy inequalities in England and Wales. *The Lancet*, 386(9989), 163–170.

Benson, S. (2000). Inscriptions of the self: Reflections on tattooing and piercing in contemporary Euro-America. In N.J. Caplan (ed.), *Written on the Body*. London: Reaktion Books, 2334–2354.

Bertrand, M. & Mullainathan, S. (2004). Are Emily and Greg more employable than Lakisha and Jamal? A field experiment on labor market discrimination. *The American Economic Review*, 94(4), 991–1013.

Best, J. & Bogle, K.A. (2014). *Kids Gone Wild: From Rainbow Parties to Sexting, Understanding the Hype over Teen Sex*. New York, NY: New York University Press.

Bhambra, G.K. & Santos, B. de S. (2017). Introduction: Global challenges for sociology. *Sociology*, 51(1), 3–10.

Bhopal, K. (2016). Race, education and inequality. *British Journal of Sociology of Education*, 37(3), 488–497.

Bhopal, K. (2018). *White Privilege: The Myth of a Post-racial Society*. Bristol: Policy Press.

Bianchi, S.M., Sayer, L.C., Milkie, M.A. & Robinson, J.P. (2012). Housework: Who did, does or will do it, and how much does it matter? *Social Forces*, 91(1), 55–63.

Blass, T. (1999). The Milgram paradigm after 35 years: Some things we now know about obedience to authority. *Journal of Applied Social Psychology*, 29(5), 955–978.

Blumer, H. (1951). Social movements. In A.M. Lee (ed.), *New Outline of the Principles of Sociology*. New York, NY: Barnes & Noble, 199–220.

Boden, R. & Epstein, D. (2006). Managing the research imagination? Globalisation and research in higher education. *Globalisation, Societies and Education*, 4(2), 223–236.

Boden, R., Epstein, D. & Latimer, J. (2009). Accounting for ethos or programmes for conduct? The brave new world of research ethics committees. *The Sociological Review*, 57(4), 727–749.

Boliver, V. (2013). How fair is access to more prestigious UK universities? *British Journal of Sociology*, 64(2), 344–364.

Boliver, V. (2016). Exploring ethnic inequalities in admission to Russell Group universities. *Sociology*, 50(2), 247–266.

Boronski, T. & Hassan, N. (2015). *Sociology of Education*. London: SAGE.

Bourdieu, P. (1984). *Distinction: A Social Critique of the Judgement of Taste*. London: Routledge & Kegan Paul.

Bourdieu, P. (1988). *Practical Reason: On the Theory of Action*. Stanford, CA: Stanford University Press.

Bourdieu, P. & Wacquant, L. (1992). *An Invitation to Reflexive Sociology*. Chicago, IL: University of Chicago Press.

Bowles, S. & Gintis, H. (1976). *Schooling in Capitalist America: Educational Reform and Contradictions of Economic Life*. New York, NY: Basic Books.

Braverman, H. (1974). *Labor and Monopoly Capital: The Degradation of Work in the Twentieth Century*. London: Routledge.

Brooks, R. (1994). Critical Race Theory: A proposed structure and application to federal pleading. *Harvard Black Letter Law Journal*, 11, 85.

Brooks, R., McCormack, M. & Bhopal, K. (2013). Contemporary debates in the sociology of education: An introduction. In R. Brooks, M. McCormack & K. Bhopal (eds.), *Contemporary Debates in the Sociology of Education*. Basingstoke: Palgrave, 2–18.

Brown, S. (2015). The wrong type of mother: Moral panic and teenage parenting. In V.E. Cree, G. Clapton & M. Smith (eds.), *Revisiting Moral Panics*. Bristol: Policy Press, 39–49.

BSA (2002). *Statement of Ethical Practice for the British Sociological Association*. Durham: BSA. Available at: www.britsoc.co.uk/media/23902/statementofethicalpractice.pdf (accessed 31 October 2017).

Bureau of Labor Statistics (2016). *Self-employment in the United States*. Washington: Bureau of Labor Statistics.

Bulmer, M. (1986). *The Chicago School of Sociology: Institutionalization, Diversity and the Rise of Sociological Research*. Chicago, IL: University of Chicago Press.

Burawoy, M. (2005). 2004 American Sociological Association presidential address: for public sociology. *The British Journal of Sociology*, 56(2), 259–294.

Butler, J. (1990). *Gender Trouble*. London: Routledge.

Butler, J. (1997). Further reflections on conversations of our time. *Diacritics*, 27(1), 13–15.

Butler, J. (2004). *Undoing Gender*. London: Routledge.

Byerly, C.M. & Ross, K. (2006). *Women and Media: A Critical Introduction*. Oxford: John Wiley & Sons.

Cameron, D. (2017). *Will Robots Take Your Job?* Cambridge: Polity.

Cancian, F. (1987). *Love in America*. Cambridge: Cambridge University Press.

Cancian, F. (1992). Feminist stances: Methodologies that challenge inequality. *Gender & Society*, 6(4), 623–642.

Castells, M. (1996). *The Rise of the Network Society*. Oxford: Blackwell.

Castells, M. (2005). The network society: From knowledge to policy. In M. Castells & G. Cardoso (eds.), *The Network Society: From Knowledge to Policy*. Washington, DC: Johns Hopkins University, 3–22.

Cherlin, A.J. (2004). The deinstitutionalization of American marriage. *Journal of Marriage and Family*, 74, 102–127.

Chitty, C. (2007). *Eugenics, Race and Intelligence in Education*. London: Continuum.

Clements, B. & Field, C.D. (2014). Public opinion toward homosexuality and gay rights in Great Britain. *Public Opinion Quarterly*, 78(2), 523–547.

Cohen, S. (1972). *Folk Devils and Moral Panics: The Creation of the Mods and Rockers*. London: MacGibbon & Kee.

Cohen, S. (1985). *Visions of Social Control*. Cambridge: Cambridge University Press.

Collins, P.H. (2000). *Black Feminist Thought*. London: Routledge.

Comella, L. & Tarrant, S. (eds.) (2015). *New Views on Pornography*. Oxford: Praeger.

Comte, A. (1896). *Positive Philosophy*, Vol. 1. London: Bell.

Connell, R.W. (1995). *Masculinities*. Cambridge: Polity.

Connell, R.W. (1997). Why is classical theory classical? *The American Journal of Sociology*, 102(6), 1511–1557.

Connell, R.W. (2007). *Southern Theory*. Cambridge: Polity.

Cooper, D. (1971). *The Death of the Family*. Harmondsworth: Penguin.

Correll, S.J., Benard, S. & Paik, I. (2007). Getting a job: Is there a motherhood penalty? Part 1. *American Journal of Sociology*, 112(5), 1297–1338.

Craib, I. (1997). *Classical Social Theory: An Introduction to the Thought of Marx, Weber, Durkheim, and Simmel*. Oxford: Oxford University Press.

Craik, J. (2003). The cultural politics of the uniform. *Fashion Theory*, 7(2), 127–147.

Crenshaw, K. (1991). Mapping the margins: Intersectionality, identity politics, and violence against women of color. *Stanford Law Review*, 43, 1241–1299.

Cresswell, J. (2014). *A Concise Introduction to Mixed Methods Research*. London: SAGE.

Crompton, R. (2008). *Class and Stratification* (3rd edn). Cambridge: Polity.

Crossley, N. (2005). Mapping reflexive body techniques: On body modification and maintenance. *Body & Society*, 11(1), 1–35.

Crouch, C. (2004). *Postdemocracy*. Cambridge: Polity.

Cushion, S. (2010). Three phases of 24-hour news television. In S. Cushion & J. Lewis (eds.), *The Rise of 24-hour News Television: Global Perspectives*. New York, NY: Peter Lang, 15–31.

Cushion, S. & Lewis, J. (2010). Introduction: What is 24-hour news television? In S. Cushion & J. Lewis (eds.), *The Rise of 24-hour News Television: Global Perspectives*. New York, NY: Peter Lang, 1–14.

David, M. (2002). Problems of participation: The limits of action research. *International Journal of Social Research Methodology: Theory and Practice*, 5(1), 11–17.

David, M. (2005). *Science in Society*. London: SAGE.

David, M. (ed.) (2007). *Case Study Research*. London: SAGE.

David, M. (2010). *Peer to Peer and the Music Industry: The Criminalisation of Sharing*. London: SAGE.

David, M. (2017). Sharing: Post-scarcity beyond capitalism? *Cambridge Journal of Regions, Economy and Society*, 10(2), 311–325.

David, M. & Halbert, D. (2015). *Owning the World of Ideas*. London: SAGE.

David, M. & Millward, P. (eds.) (2014). *Researching Society Online*. London: SAGE.

David, M., Rohloff, A., Petley, J. & Hughes, J. (2011). The idea of moral panic – ten dimensions of dispute. *Crime, Media, Culture*, 7(3), 215–228.

David, M. & Sutton, C.D. (2011). *Social Research: An Introduction*. London: SAGE.

Davies, C. (1999). *Reflexive Ethnography: A Guide to Researching Selves and Others*. London: Psychology Press.

Davis, A. (2003). *Are Prisons Obsolete?* New York, NY: Seven Stories Press.

Davis, M.S. (1971). That's interesting! Towards a phenomenology of sociology and a sociology of phenomenology. *Philosophy of the Social Sciences*, 1(2), 309–344.

Deegan, M.J. (1990). *Jane Addams and the Men of the Chicago School, 1892–1918*. New York, NY: Transaction.

Delamont, S. (2003). *Feminist Sociology*. London: Routledge.

Deleuze, G. (1992). Postscript on the societies of control. *October*, 59, 3–7.

Delgado, R. & Stefancic, J. (2012). *Critical Race Theory: An Introduction*. New York, NY: New York University Press.

DeMello, M. (2000). *Bodies of Inscription: A Cultural History of the Modern Tattoo Community*. Durham, NC: Duke University Press.

Dennis, K. & Urry, J. (2009). *After the Car*. Cambridge: Polity.

Derrida, J. (1976). *Of Grammatology* (trans. G.C. Spivak). Baltimore, MD: Johns Hopkins University Press.

Dion, K.K., Berscheid, E. & Walster, E. (1972). What is beautiful is good. *Journal of Personality and Social Psychology*, 24, 285–290.

Doan, L., Loehr, A. & Miller, L.R. (2014). Formal rights and informal privileges for same-sex couples: Evidence from a national survey experiment. *American Sociological Review*, 79(6), 1172–1195.

Dorling, D. (2014). Thinking about class. *Sociology*, 48(3), 452–462.

Douglas, M. ([1966] 2003). *Purity and Danger: An Analysis of Concepts of Pollution and Taboo*. London: Routledge & Kegan Paul.

Drake, D. & Harvey, J. (in press). *Criminology*. London: Palgrave.

Du Bois, W.E.B. (1899). *The Philadelphia Negro*. New York, NY: Schocken Books.

Du Bois, W.E.B. ([1903] 2008). *The Souls of Black Folk*. Oxford: Oxford University Press.

Duncombe, J. & Marsden, D. (1995). 'Workaholics' and 'whingeing women': Theorising intimacy and emotion work – the last frontier of gender inequality?' *The Sociological Review*, 43(1), 150–169.

Dunning, E., Murphy, P. & Williams, J. (1988). *The Roots of Football Hooliganism: An Historical and Sociological Study*. London: Routledge.

Durkheim, E. ([1893] 1984). *The Division of Labour in Society*. London: Macmillan.

Durkheim, E. ([1895] 1982). *The Rules of Sociological Method: And Selected Texts on Sociology and Its Method*. New York, NY: Free Press.

Durkheim, E. ([1897] 2006). *On Suicide* (trans. R. Buss). London: Penguin.

Durkheim, E. ([1912] 2008). *The Elementary Forms of Religious Life*. Oxford: Oxford University Press.

Durkheim, E. ([1925] 2011). *Moral Education*. New York, NY: Dover.

Dworkin, A. (1979). *Pornography*. New York, NY: Penguin.

Dworkin, A. (1985). Against the male flood: Censorship, pornography, and equality. *Harvard Women's Law Journal*, 8, 1.

Dyer, R. (1997). *White*. London: Routledge.

Edgell, S. (2012). *The Sociology of Work* (2nd edn). London: SAGE.

Egerton, M. & Savage, M. (1997). Social mobility, individual mobility and the inheritance of class inequality. *Sociology*, 31(4), 645–672.

Ehenreich, B. (2001). *Nickel and Dimed: On (Not) Getting by in America*. New York, NY: Metropolitan Books.

Ellis, C. (1986). *Fisher Folk: Two Communities on Chesapeake Bay*. Lexington, KY: University of Kentucky Press.

Ellis, C. (1995). Emotional and ethical quagmires in returning to the field. *Journal of Contemporary Ethnography*, 24, 711–713.

Eltantawy, N. & Wiest, J.B. (2011). The Arab Spring social media in the Egyptian Revolution: Reconsidering resource mobilization theory. *International Journal of Communication*, 5, 1207–1224.

Elzweig, B. & Peeples, D.K. (2011). Tattoos and piercings: issues of body modification and the workplace. *SAM Advanced Management Journal*, 76(1), 13–23.

Engels, F. ([1883] 2004). *The Origin of the Family, Private Property and the State*. London: Penguin Classics.

Etcoff, N. (1999). *Survival of the Prettiest: The Science of Beauty*. New York, NY: Random House.

Ettorre, E. (2007). *Revisioning Women and Drug Use: Gender, Power and the Body*. Basingstoke: Palgrave Macmillan.

Faris, R., Roberts, H., Etling, B., Bourassa, N., Zuckerman, E. & Benkler, Y. (2017). *Partisanship, Propaganda, & Disinformation: Online Media & The 2016 Presidential Election*. Berkman Klein Center, Cambridge, MA: Harvard University. Available at: https://cyber.harvard.edu/sites/cyber.harvard.edu/files/2017-08_electionES_0.pdf (accessed 31 October 2017).

Feagin, J. (2006). *Systemic Racism: A Theory of Oppression*. London: Routledge.

Feagin, J. (2013). *The White Racial Frame: Centuries of Racial Framing and Counter-Framing*. London: Routledge.

Feingold, A. (1992). Good-looking people are not what we think. *Psychological Bulletin*, 111, 304–341.

Felton, J., Koper, P.T., Mitchell, J. & Stinson, M. (2007). Attractiveness, easiness and other issues: Student evaluations of professors on ratemyprofessors.com. *Assessment & Evaluation in Higher Education*, 33(1), 45–61.

Fincham, B. (2016). *The Sociology of Fun*. London: Palgrave.

Fitch, K.L. (2005). Difficult interactions between IRBs and investigators: Applications and solutions. *Journal of Applied Communication Research*, 33(3), 269–276.

Fleming, P. (2014). When 'life itself' goes to work: Reviewing shifts in organizational life through the lens of biopower. *Human Relations*, 67(7), 875–901.

Foucault, M. (1984). *The History of Sexuality: An Introduction/Translated from the French by Robert Hurley*. New York, NY: Penguin Books.

Foucault, M. (1991). *Discipline and Punish: The Birth of a Prison*. London: Penguin.

Fraser, D. (2009). *The Evolution of the British Welfare State: A History of Social Policy since the Industrial Revolution*. Basingstoke: Palgrave Macmillan.

Freese, J. (2008). Genetics and the social science explanation of individual outcomes. *American Journal of Sociology*, 114(S1), S1–S35.

Friedan, B. (1959). *The Feminine Mystique*. New York, NY: Norton.

Frith, H. & Kitzinger, C. (2001). Reformulating sexual script theory. *Theory & Psychology*, 11, 209–232.

Froyum, C.M. (2007). 'At least I'm not gay': Heterosexual identity making among poor black teens. *Sexualities*, 10(5), 603–622.

Gamson, W.A. & Sifry, M.L. (2013). The Occupy movement: An introduction. *The Sociological Quarterly*, 54(2), 159–163.

Garner, S. (2007). *Whiteness: An Introduction*. London: Routledge.

Giddens, A. (1984). *The Constitution of Society: Outline of the Theory of Structuration*. Los Angeles, CA: University of California Press.

Giddens, A. (1987). *Social Theory and Modern Sociology*. Cambridge: Polity.

Giddens, A. (1990). *The Consequences of Modernity*. Cambridge: Polity.

Giddens, A. (1991). *Modernity and Self-identity*. Cambridge: Polity.

Giddens, A. (1992). *The Transformation of Intimacy*. Cambridge: Polity.

Giddens, A. (2011). *The Politics of Climate Change*. Cambridge: Polity.

Giddens, A. (2013). *Turbulent and Mighty Continent: What Future for Europe?* Cambridge: Polity.

Gillespie, R. (2000). When no means no: Disbelief, disregard and deviance as discourses of voluntary childlessness. *Women's Studies International Forum*, 23, 223–234.

Gilman, C.P. (1892). *The Yellow Wallpaper*. New England Magazine.

Gilroy, P. (1987). *There ain't no Black in the Union Jack*. London: Routledge.

Gimlin, D. (2007). What is 'body work'? A review of the literature. *Sociology Compass*, 1(1), 353–370.

Gintis, H. (1972). Toward a political economy of education: A radical critique of Ivan Illich's *Deschooling Society*. *Harvard Education Review*, 42(1), 70–92.

Gladwell, M. (2005). *Blink: The Power of Thinking without Thinking*. New York, NY: Back Bay Books.

Glaser, B. & Strauss, A. (1967). *The Discovery of Grounded Theory*. Chicago, IL: Aldine Transactions.

Goffman, A. (2015). *On the Run: Fugitive Life in an American City*. Chicago, IL: University of Chicago Press.

Goffman, E. (1956). *The Presentation of Self in Everyday Life*. London: Penguin.

Goffman, E. (1963). *Stigma: Notes on the Management of Spoiled Identity*. Englewood Cliffs, NJ: Prentice Hall.

Golding, P. & Murdock, G. (1997). *The Political Economy of the Media*. Cheltenham: Edward Elgar.

Gouldner, A. (1968). The sociologist as partisan: Sociology and the welfare state. *American Sociologist*, 3, 103–116.

Granovetter, M. (1973). The strength of weak ties. *American Journal of Sociology*, 78(6), 1360–1380.

Green, A.I. (2007). On the horns of a dilemma: Institutional dimensions of the sexual career in a sample of middle-class, urban, black, gay men. *Journal of Black Studies*, 37, 753–774.

Green, N. (2008). Formulating and refining a research question. In N. Gilbert (ed.), *Researching Social Life* (3rd edn). London: SAGE, 43–61.

Greene, J., Caracelli, V. & Graham, W. (1989). Towards a conceptual framework for mixed-method evaluation design. *Educational Evaluation and Policy Analysis*, 11(3), 255–274.

Greer, G. (1970). *The Female Eunuch*. London: Paladin.

Guillemin, M. & Gillam L. (2004). Ethics, reflexivity, and 'ethically important moments' in research. *Qualitative Inquiry*, 10(2), 261–280.

Haggerty, K. (2004). Ethics creep: Governing social science research in the name of ethics. *Qualitative Sociology*, 27(4), 391–414.

Hall, S. (1997). *Representation: Cultural Representations and Signifying Practices*. London: SAGE.

Hamilton, V.L. & Sanders, J. (1999). The second face of evil: Wrongdoing in and by the corporation. *Personality and Social Psychology Review*, 3(2), 222–233.

Hammack, P. L., Frost, D., Meyer, I.H. & Pletta, D.R. (2018). Gay Men's Health and Identity. *Archives of Sexual Behavior*, 47(1), 59–74.

Hammersley, M. (2010). Creeping ethical regulation and the strangling of research. *Sociological Research Online*, 15(4). Available at: www.socresonline.org.uk/15/4/16.html (accessed 31 October 2017).

Hancock, A.M. (2008). Du Bois, race, and diversity. In S. Zamir (ed.), *The Cambridge Companion to W.E.B. Du Bois*. Cambridge: Cambridge University Press, 86–101.

Haney, C., Banks, C. & Zimbardo, P. (1973). A study of prisoners and guards. *Naval Research Reviews*. Washington, DC: Department of the Navy.

Harding, S. (1986). *The Science Question in Feminism*. Ithaca, NY: Cornell University Press.

Hardt, M. (1999). Affective labor. *Boundary*, 26(2), 89–100.

Harvey, D. (1989). *The Condition of Postmodernity*. Oxford: Blackwell.

Hassid, J. & Watson, B.C. (2014). State of mind: Power, time zones and symbolic state centralization. *Time & Society*, 23(2), 167–194.

Healy, K. (2017). Fuck nuance. *Sociological Theory*, 35(2), 118–127.

Herek, G.M. (2004). Beyond 'homophobia': Thinking about sexual prejudice and stigma in the twenty-first century. *Sexuality Research & Social Policy*, 1(2), 6–24.

Herman, E.S. & Chomsky, N. (2002). *Manufacturing Consent: The Political Economy of the Mass Media*. New York, NY: Random House.

Hey, V. (1997). *The Company She Keeps*. Buckingham: Open University Press.

Hiriscau, I.E., Stingelin-Giles, N., Stadler, C., Schmeck, K. & Reiter-Theil, S. (2014). A right to confidentiality or a duty to disclose? Ethical guidance for conducting prevention research with children and adolescents. *European Child & Adolescent Psychiatry*, 23(6), 409–416.

Hoberman, J. (1997). *Darwin's Athletes: How Sport has Damaged Black America and Preserved the Myth of Race*. Boston, MA: Houghton Mifflin.

Hobsbawm, E. (1987). *The Age of Empire: 1875–1914*. London: Weidenfeld & Nicolson.

Hochschild, A. (1983). *The Managed Heart: Commercialization of Human Feeling*. Los Angeles, CA: University of California Press.

Hochschild, A. (1989). *The Second Shift: Working Parents and the Revolution at Home*. London: Penguin.

Hodgson, G.M. (2006). What are institutions? *Journal of Economic Issues*, 40(1), 1–25.

Hogan, B. (2010). The presentation of self in the age of social media: Distinguishing performances and exhibitions online. *Bulletin of Science, Technology and Society*, 30(6), 377–386.

hooks, b. (1981). *Ain't I a Woman?: Black Women and Feminism*. New York, NY: Pluto Press.

Horkheimer, M. & Adorno, T. ([1947] 2002). *Dialectic of Enlightenment: Philosophical Fragments*. Stanford, CA: Stanford University Press.

Hoskins, B. (2008). The discourse of social justice within European education policy developments. *European Educational Research Journal*, 7(3), 319–330.

Humphreys, L. (1970). *Tearoom Trade: Impersonal Sex in Public Places*. New York, NY: Aldine.

Hunt, A. (1998). The great masturbation panic and the discourses of moral regulation in nineteenth- and early twentieth-century Britain. *Journal of the History of Sexuality*, 8(4), 575–615.

Illich, I. (1971). *Deschooling Society*. Harmondsworth: Penguin.

Inglis, D. (2012). *An Invitation to Social Theory*. Cambridge: Polity.

Irvine, J. (2003). 'The sociologist as voyeur': Social theory and sexuality research, 1910–1978. *Qualitative Sociology*, 26(4), 429–456.

Israel, M. & Hay, I. (2006). *Research Ethics for Social Scientists*. London: SAGE.

Jackson, B. & Marsden, D. (2012). *Education and the Working Class*. Abingdon: Routledge.

Jamie, K. (2013). Navigating the UK NHS ethics and governance approval process: The case of junior researchers. In T. Li & Q. Li (eds.), *Conducting Research in a Changing and Challenging World*. New York, NY: Nova Science, 279–290.

Jamieson, L. (1999). Intimacy transformed? A critical look at the pure relationship. *Sociology*, 33(3), 477–494.

Juntunen, L. (2010). Explaining the need for speed: Speed and competition as challenges to journalism ethics. In S. Cushion & J. Lewis (eds.), *The Rise of 24-hour News Television: Global Perspectives*. New York, NY: Peter Lang, 167–182.

Kakabadse, A. & Kakabadse, N.K. (2004). *Intimacy: An International Survey of the Sex Lives of People at Work*. New York, NY: Palgrave Macmillan.

Keating, J. (2009). *A Child for Keeps: The History of Adoption in England, 1918–45*. New York, NY: Palgrave Macmillan.

Kelvin, P. (1981). Work as a source of identity: The implications of unemployment. *British Journal of Guidance and Counselling*, 9(1), 2–11.

Kemp, S. (2017). *Digital Data & Trends for Every Country in the World*. Available at: www.linkedin.com/pulse/digital-data-trends-every-country-world-simon-kemp (accessed 5 August 2017).

Kimmel, M.S. (2004). *The Gendered Society*. New York, NY: Oxford University Press.

Kitzinger, J. (1994). The methodology of focus groups: The importance of interaction between research participants. *Sociology of Health and Illness*, 16(1), 103–121.

Kivisto, P. & Croll, P.R. (2012). *Race and Ethnicity: The Basics*. New York, NY: Routledge.

Ladd, E.C. (1999). *The Ladd Report*. New York, NY: Free Press.

Lambert, A. (2013). *Intimacy and Friendship on Facebook*. New York, NY: Palgrave Macmillan.

Lampert, K. (2012). *Meritocratic Education and Social Worthlessness*. New York, NY: Palgrave Macmillan.

Landsberger, H. (1958). *Hawthorne Revisited*. Ithaca, NY: Cornell University Press.

Lange, O. (1963). *Political Economy: Volume I General Problems*. Oxford: Pergamon Press.

Lanternari, V. (1963). *The Religions of the Oppressed: A Study of Modern Messianic Cults*. London: MacGibbon & Kee.

Latane, B. (1981). The psychology of social impact. *American Psychologist*, 36(4), 343–356.

Latane, B. & Bourgeois, M.J. (2001). Successfully simulating dynamic social impact. In J. Forgas & K. Williams (eds.), *Social Influence: Direct and Indirect Processes*. London: Taylor & Francis, 61–78.

Lawler, S. (2014). *Identity: Sociological Perspectives* (2nd edn). London: Polity.

Lefebvre, H. ([1974] 1991). *The Production of Space*. Oxford: Blackwell.

Lefebvre, H. ([1970] 2003). *The Urban Revolution*. Minneapolis, MN: University of Minnesota Press.

Lerner, G. (1986). *The Creation of Patriarchy*. New York, NY: Oxford University Press.

Levin, I. (2004). Living apart together: A new family form. *Current Sociology*, 52(2), 223–240.

Levine, M., Prosser, A., Evans, D. & Reicher, S. (2005). Identity and emergency intervention: How social group membership and inclusiveness of group boundaries shape helping behavior. *Personality and Social Psychology Bulletin*, 31(4), 443–453.

Lewis-Kraus, G. (2016). The trials of Alice Goffman. *The New York Times*, 12 January. Available at: www.nytimes.com/2016/01/17/magazine/the-trials-of-alice-goffman.html?_r=0 (accessed 31 October 2017).

Librett, M. & Perrone, D. (2010). Apples and oranges: Ethnography and the IRB. *Qualitative Research*, 10(6), 729–747.

Lincoln, Y.S. & Tierney, W.G. (2004). Qualitative research and institutional review boards. *Qualitative Inquiry*, 10(2), 219–234.

Lingard, B. & Sellar, S. (2013). Globalisation and sociology of education policy: The case of PISA. In R. Brooks, M. McCormack & K. Bhopal (eds.), *Contemporary Debates in the Sociology of Education*. Basingstoke: Palgrave Macmillan, 19–38.

Longhurst, R. (1999). Pregnant bodies, public scrutiny: Giving advice to pregnant women. In E. Kenworthy Teather (ed.), *Embodied Geographies: Spaces, Bodies and Rites of Passage*. London: Routledge, 77–90.

Lorber, J. (1994). *Paradoxes of Gender*. New Haven, CT: Yale University Press.

Lyon, D. (2001). *Surveillance Society: Monitoring Everyday Life*. Buckingham: Open University Press.

Mac an Ghaill, M. (1994). *The Making of Men: Masculinities, Sexualities and Schooling*. Buckingham: Open University Press.

MacNell, L., Driscoll, A. & Hunt, A.N. (2015). What's in a name: Exposing gender bias in student ratings of teaching. *Innovative Higher Education*, 40(4), 291–303.

Magrath, R. (2017). *Inclusive Masculinities in Contemporary Football: Men in the Beautiful Game*. London: Routledge.

Malamuth, N. (ed.) (1984). *Pornography and Sexual Aggression*. Orlando, FL: Academic Press.

Marston, G. & Watts, R. (2003). Tampering with the evidence: A critical appraisal of evidence-based policy-making. *The Drawing Board: An Australian Review of Public Affairs*, 3(3), 143–163.

Martineau, H. (1837). *Society in America*, Vols. 1–3. London: Saunders and Otley.

Marx, K. ([1867] 1965). *Capital, Volume 1*. London: Lawrence and Wishart.

Marx, K. & Engels, F. ([1848] 1967). *The Communist Manifesto* (trans. S. Moore). London: Penguin.

May, V. (ed.) (2011). *Sociology of Personal Life*. Basingstoke: Palgrave.

Mayo, E. (1949). *Hawthorne and the Western Electric Company: The Social Problems of an Industrial Civilisation*. New York, NY: Routledge.

McClelland, A. & Smyth, P. (2014). *Social Policy in Australia: Understanding for Action*. New York, NY: Oxford University Press.

McCormack, M. (2012). *The Declining Significance of Homophobia: How Teenage Boys are Redefining Masculinity and Heterosexuality*. New York, NY: Oxford University Press.

McCormack, M. (2015). *The Role of Smartphones and Technology in Sexual and Romantic Lives*. Durham: Durham University.

McCormack, M., Adams, A. & Anderson, E. (2013). Taking to the streets: The benefits of spontaneous methodological innovation in participant recruitment. *Qualitative Research*, 13(2), 228–241.

McCormack, M. & Wignall, L. (2017). Enjoyment, exploration and education: Understanding the consumption of pornography among young men with non-exclusive sexual orientations. *Sociology*, 51(5), 975–991.

McCright, A.M. & Dunlap, R.E. (2011). The politicization of climate change and polarization in the American public's views of global warming, 2001–2010. *The Sociological Quarterly*, 52(2), 155–194.

McDowell, L. (2011). *Capital Culture: Gender at Work in the City*. Oxford: Blackwell.

McGlynn, C. & Rackley, E. (2007). Striking a balance: Arguments for the criminal regulation of extreme pornography. *Criminal Law Review – London*, 677, 1–13.

McIntyre, N., Williams, D.R. & McHugh, K. (eds.) (2006). *Multiple Dwelling and Tourism: Negotiating Place, Home and Identity*. Cambridge, MA: CABI.

McKee, A. (2007). The relationship between attitudes towards women, consumption of pornography, and other demographic variables in a survey of 1,023 consumers of pornography. *International Journal of Sexual Health*, 19, 31–45.

McLanahan, S. & Sanderfur, G. (1994). *Growing up with a Single Parent: What Hurts, What Helps?* Cambridge, MA: Harvard University Press.

McManus, J.H. (1992). What kind of commodity is news? *Communication Research*, 19(6), 787–805.

McNair, B. (2002). *Striptease Culture*. London: Routledge.

Mead, G.H. ([1934] 1967). *Mind, Self, and Society*. Chicago, IL: University of Chicago Press.

Measham, F. & Brain, K. (2005). 'Binge' drinking, British alcohol policy and the new culture of intoxication. *Crime, Media, Culture*, 1(3), 262–283.

Meyer, I.H. (2003). Prejudice, social stress, and mental health in lesbian, gay, and bisexual populations: Conceptual issues and research evidence. *Psychological Bulletin*, 129(5), 674.

Milgram, S. (1973). The perils of obedience. *Harper's Magazine*, December Issue.

Milgram, S. (1974). *Obedience to Authority: An Experimental View*. New York, NY: Harper and Row.

Miller, B.K., McGlashan Nicols, K. & Eure, J. (2009). Body art in the workplace: Piercing the prejudice? *Personnel Review*, 38(6), 621–640.

Mills, C. (2014). The Great British class fiasco: A comment on Savage et al. *Sociology*, 48(3), 437–444.

Mills, C.W. (1940). Situated actions and vocabularies of motive. *American Sociological Review*, 5(6), 904–913.

Mills, C.W. (1959). *The Sociological Imagination*. New York, NY: Oxford University Press.

Mills, C.W. (1973). The meaning of work throughout history. In F. Best (ed.), *The Future of Work*. New Jersey: Prentice Hall.

Miracle, A.W. & Rees, C.R. (1994). *Lessons of the Locker Room: The Myth of School Sports*. Amherst, NY: Prometheus Books.

Mitchelstein, E. & Boczkowski, P.J. (2009). Between tradition and change: A review of recent research on online news production. *Journalism*, 10(5), 562–586.

Mokyr, J. (2017). *A Culture of Growth: The Origins of the Modern Economy*. Princeton, NJ: Princeton University Press.

Morris, A.D. (2015). *The Scholar Denied: W.E.B. Du Bois and the Birth of Modern Sociology*. Oakland, CA: University of California Press.

Morrish, I. (1970). *Education Since 1800*. London: Routledge.

Mrozek, D.J. (1983). *Sport and American Mentality, 1880–1910*. Tennessee: University of Tennessee Press.

Nagel, J., Dietz, T. & Broadbent, J. (2010). *Workshop on Sociological Perspectives on Global Climate Change*. Arlington, VA: National Science Foundation.

Ni Bhrolchain, M. (2001). 'Divorce effects' and causality in the social sciences. *European Sociological Review*, 17(1), 33–57.

North, D.C. (1990). *Institutions, Institutional Change, and Economic Performance*. Cambridge: Cambridge University Press.

Nussbaum, M. (1999). The professor of parody: The hip defeatism of Judith Butler. *The New Republic Online*. Available at: www.tnr.com/archive/0299/022299/nussbaum022299.html (accessed 31 October 2017).

Oakley, A. (1974). *The Sociology of Housework*. Oxford: Martin Robertson.

O'Neill, M. (2010). *Asylum, Migration and Community*. Bristol: Policy Press.

Oreskes, N. (2004). The scientific consensus on climate change. *Science*, 306(5702), 1686.

Pahl, R. (2000). *On Friendship*. Cambridge: Polity.

Park, J.H., Gabbadon, N.G. & Chernin, A.R. (2006). Naturalizing racial differences through comedy: Asian, black, and white views on racial stereotypes in *Rush Hour 2*. *Journal of Communication*, 56, 157–177.

Park, K. (2002). Stigma management among the voluntarily childless. *Sociological Perspectives*, 45(1), 21–45.

Park, R. E. (1915). The city: Suggestions for the investigation of human behaviour in the city environment. *American Journal of Sociology*, 20(5), 577–612.

Park, R.E. (1922). *The Immigrant Press and Its Control*. New York, NY: Harper & Brothers.

Park, R.E. (1928). Human migration and the marginal man. *American Journal of Sociology*, 33, 881–893.

Park, R.E. (1952). *Human Communities: The City and Human Ecology*. Glencoe, IL: The Free Press.

Parsons, T. & Bales, R.F. (1955). *Family Socialization and Interaction Process*. London: Routledge & Kegan Paul.

Peck, B., Manning, J., Tri, A., Skrzypczynyski, D., Summers, M. & Grubb, K. (2016). What do people mean when they say they 'had sex'? Connecting communication and behaviour. In J. Manning & C. Noland (eds.), *Contemporary Studies in Sexuality and Communication*. Dubuque, IA: Kendall Hunt, 3–13.

Pichanik, V.K. (1980). *Harriet Martineau: The Woman and Her Work, 1802–1876*. Ann Arbor, MI: University of Michigan Press.

Pickett, K. & Wilkinson, R. (2009). *The Spirit Level*. London: Penguin.

Pierrat, J. & Guillon, E. (2013). *Mauvais Garçons: Portraits de Tatoués, 1890–1930*. Paris: La manufacture de livres.

Pink, S. (2014). *Doing Visual Ethnography*. London: SAGE.

Pinker, S. (2018). *Enlightenment Now: The Case for Reason, Science, Humanism, and Progress*. New York, NY: Viking.

Plummer, D. (1999). *One of the Boys: Masculinity, Homophobia and Modern Manhood*. New York, NY: Harrington Park Press.

Plummer, K. (1997). Introduction. In K. Plummer (ed.), *The Chicago School: Critical Assessments*. London: Routledge.

Polanyi, K. ([1957] 2002). *The Great Transformation: The Political and Economic Origins of Our Time*. New York, NY: Beacon Books.

Pollack, W. (1999). *Real Boys: Rescuing Our Sons from the Myths of Boyhood*. New York, NY: Macmillan.

Putnam, R. (2000). *Bowling Alone: The Collapse and Revival of American Community*. New York, NY: Simon & Schuster.

Rawley, J.A. & Behrendt, S.D. (2005). *The Transatlantic Slave Trade: A History* (rev. edn). London: University of Nebraska Press.

Reay, D. (2002). Shaun's story: troubling discourses of white working-class masculinities. *Gender and Education*, 14(3), 221–234.

Reay, D. (2017). *Miseducation: Inequality, Education and the Working Classes*. Bristol: Policy Press.

Reed, K. (2010). The spectre of research ethics and governance and the ESRC's 2010 FRE: Nowhere left to hide? *Sociological Research Online*, 15(4). Available at: www.socresonline.org.uk/15/4/17.html (accessed 31 October 2017).

Regnerus, M. (2012). How different are the adult children of parents who have same-sex relationships? Findings from the New Family Structures Study. *Social Science Research*, 41(1), 752–770.

Rheingold, H. (2000). *The Virtual Community*. Cambridge, MA: MIT Press.

Rich, A. (1980). Compulsory heterosexuality and lesbian existence. *Signs: Journal of Women in Culture and Society*, 5(4), 631–660.

Rifkin, J. (2014). *The Zero Marginal Cost Society*. New York, NY: Palgrave.

Rigauer, B. (1981). *Sport and Work*. New York, NY: Columbia University Press.

Risman, B.J. (2004). Gender as a social structure: Theory wrestling with activism. *Gender & Society*, 18(4), 429–450.

Ritzer, G. (1998). The Weberian theory of rationalization and the McDonaldization of contemporary society. In P. Kivisto (ed.), *Illuminating Social Life*. London: SAGE, 41–59.

Ritzer, G. (2000). *The McDonaldization of Society*. Thousand Oaks, CA: Pine Forge Press.

Ritzer, G. (2003). Rethinking globalization: Glocalization/grobalization and something/nothing. *Sociological Theory*, 21(3), 193–209.

Ritzer, G. (2010). *McDonaldization: The Reader* (3rd edn). Thousand Oaks, CA: Pine Forge Press.

Ritzer, G. (2015). *Introduction to Sociology*. London: SAGE.

Ritzer, G. & Goodman, D.J. (2003). *Sociological Theory*. McGraw-Hill.

Roberts, K. (2011). *Class in Contemporary Britain*. Basingstoke: Palgrave Macmillan.

Roberts, S. (2013). Boys will be boys … won't they? Change and continuities in contemporary young working-class masculinities. *Sociology*, 47(4), 671–686.

Robertson, R. (1992). *Globalization: Social Theory and Global Culture*. London: SAGE.

Robinson, J.P. & Espelage, D.L. (2011). Inequities in educational and psychological outcomes between LGBTQ and straight students in middle and high school. *Educational Researcher*, 40(7), 315–330.

Robinson, L. (2007). The cyberself: The self-ing project goes online, symbolic interaction in the digital age. *New Media and Society*, 9(1), p. 93–110.

Robinson, S., Anderson, E. & White, A. (2018). The bromance: Undergraduate male friendships and the expansion of contemporary homosocial boundaries. *Sex Roles*, 78(1–2), 94–106.

Rose, D.B. (2000). *Dingo Makes Us Human: Life and Land in an Australian Aboriginal Culture*. Cambridge: Cambridge University Press.

Rose, H. (2000). Colonising the social sciences? In H. Rose & S. Rose (eds.), *Alas Poor Darwin*. London: Jonathan Cape.

Rosow, S.J. & George, J. (2014). *Globalization and Democracy*. Lanham, MD: Rowman & Littlefield.

Rubin, G. (1984). Thinking sex: Notes for a radical theory of the politics of sexuality. In C.S. Vane (ed.), *Pleasure and Danger: Exploring Female Sexuality*. Boston, MA: Routledge & Kegan Paul, 267–319.

Rubin, G. (1993). Misguided, dangerous, and wrong: An analysis of antipornography politics. In A. Assiter & A. Carol (eds.), *Bad Girls and Dirty Pictures: The Challenge to Reclaim Feminism*. London: Pluto, 18–40.

Rubin, G. (2011). Introduction: Sex, gender, politics. In G. Rubin (ed.), *Deviations: A Gayle Rubin Reader*. Durham, NC: Duke University Press, 1–32.

Russell, B. (1938). *Power: A Social Analysis*. London: Allen & Unwin.

Said, E. (1978). *Orientalism*. London: Pantheon Books.

Sanders, S.A. & Reinisch, J.M. (1999). Would you say you had sex if …? *Jama*, 281(3), 275–277.

Sanders, C.R. (2008). *Customizing the Body: The Art and Culture of Tattooing*. Philadelphia, PA: Temple University Press.

Sanderson, I. (2011). Evidence-based policy or policy-based evidence? Reflections on Scottish experience. *Evidence & Policy*, 7(1), 59–76.

Savage, M. (2000). *Class Analysis and Social Transformation*. Buckingham: Open University Press.

Savage, M. (2015). Introduction to elites: From the 'problematic of the proletariat' to a class analysis of 'wealth elites'. *The Sociological Review*, 63(2), 223–239.

Savage, M. & Burrows, R. (2007). The coming crisis of empirical sociology. *Sociology*, 41(5), 885–899.

Savage, M., Devine, F., Cunningham, N., Taylor, M., Li, Y., Hjellbrekke, J., Le Roux, B., Friedman, S. & Miles, A. (2013). A new model of social class? Findings from the BBC's Great British Class Survey experiment. *Sociology*, 47(2), 219–250.

Savin-Williams, R. (2005). *The New Gay Teenager*. Cambridge, MA: Harvard University Press.

Schulz, K. (2010). *Being Wrong: Adventures in the Margin of Error*. New York, NY: HarperCollins.

Scott, A. (1990). *Ideology and the New Social Movements*. London: Unwin Hyman.

Scott, B.M. & Schwartz, M.A. (2008). *Sociology: Making Sense of the Social World*. New York, NY: Allyn & Bacon.

Sennett, R. (1998). *The Corrosion of Character: The Personal Consequences of Work in the New Capitalism*. New York, NY: W.W. Norton & Company.

Sennet, R. & Cobb, J. (1972). *The Hidden Injuries of Class*. Cambridge: Cambridge University Press.

Sheppard, J. & Biddle, N. (2015). *Social Class in Australia: Beyond the 'Working' and 'Middle' Classes*. Canberra: Australian National University.

Shilling, C. (1993). *The Body and Social Theory*. London: SAGE.

Shulman, L.S. (2005). Pedagogies of uncertainty. *Liberal Education*, 91(2), 18–25.

Siddiqui, F. & Svrluga, S. (2016). N.C. man told police he went to D.C. pizzeria with gun to investigate conspiracy theory. *The Washington Post*, 5 December. Available at: www.washingtonpost.com/news/local/wp/2016/12/04/d-c-police-respond-to-report-of-a-man-with-a-gun-at-comet-ping-pong-restaurant/ (accessed: 3 July 2017).

Simmel, G. ([1903] 1976). *The Metropolis and Mental Life*. New York, NY: Free Press.

Simmel, G. ([1900] 1978). *The Philosophy of Money*. London: Routledge.

Simon, W. & Gagnon, J.H. (1986). Sexual scripts. *Archives of Sexual Behavior*, 15, 97–120.

Slater, M., Antley, A., Davison, A., Swapp, D., Guger, C., Barker, C., Pistrang, N. & Sanchez-Vives, M.V. (2006). A virtual reprise of the Stanley Milgram obedience experiments. *PlosOne*. Available at: http://dx.doi.org/10.1371/journal.pone.0000039 (accessed 31 October 2017).

Smart, C. (2007). *Personal Life*. Cambridge: Polity.

Smart, C. (2011). Close relationships and personal life. In V. May (ed.), *Sociology of Personal Life*. Basingstoke: Palgrave, 35–46.

Smith, A.K. (1991). *Creating a World Economy: Merchant Capital, Colonialism, and World Trade, 1400–1825*. Boulder, CO: Westview Press.

Smith, C., Barker, M. & Attwood, F. (2015). Why do people watch porn? In L. Comella & S. Tarrant (eds.), *New Views on Pornography*. Oxford: Praeger, 307–322.

Smith, D. (1991). *National Identity*. London: Penguin.

Smith, T.W. (2011). *Attitudes towards Same-gender, Sexual Behavior across Time and across Countries*. Chicago, IL: NORC.

Snee, H., Hine, C., Roberts, S., Morey, Y. & Watson, H. (2016). *Digital Methods for Social Sciences: An Interdisciplinary Guide to Research Innovation*. Basingstoke: Palgrave Macmillan.

Sokal, A. (2010). *Beyond the Hoax: Science, Philosophy and Culture*. Oxford: Oxford University Press.

Sorokowski, P., Kulczycki, E., Sorokowska, A. & Pisanski, K. (2017). Predatory journals recruit fake editor. *Nature*, 543(7646), 481–483.

Spicker, P. (2014). *Social Policy: Theory and Practice*. Bristol: Policy Press.

Spicker, P. (2017). *Arguments for Welfare: The Welfare State and Social Policy*. London: Rowman & Littlefield.

Spivak, G. (1988). Can the subaltern speak? In C. Nelson & L. Grossberg (eds.), *Marxism and the Interpretation of Culture*. Basingstoke: Macmillan Education, 271–313.

Stacey, J. & Thorne, B. (1985). The missing feminist revolution in sociology. *Social Problems*, 32(4), 301–316.

Standing, G. (2014). *The Precariat: The New Dangerous Class*. London: Bloomsbury.

Standing, K. (1999). Lone mothers and 'parental' involvement: A contradiction in policy? *Journal of Social Policy*, 28(3), 479–495.

Steger, M. (2017). *Globalization: A Very Short Introduction* (4th edn). Oxford: Oxford University Press.

Steger, M. & James, P. (2013). Levels of subjective globalization: Ideologies, imaginaries, ontologies. *Perspectives on Global Development and Technology*, 12(1–2), 17–40.

Strang, V. (2004). *The Meaning of Water*. London: Berg.

Strassheim, H. & Kettunen, P. (2014). When does evidence-based policy turn into policy-based evidence? Configurations, contexts and mechanisms. *Evidence & Policy*, 10(2), 259–277.

Sutton, P.W. (2007). *The Environment: A Sociological Introduction*. Cambridge: Polity.

Swingewood, A. (2000). *A Short History of Sociological Thought* (3rd edn). Basingstoke: Palgrave Macmillan.

Taylor, F.W. (1911). *Principles of Scientific Management*. New York, NY: Harper & Brothers.

Taylor, C. & Coffey, A. (2009). Editorial – special issue: Qualitative research and methodological innovation. *Qualitative Research*, 9(5), 523–526.

The Guardian (8 November 2015). Women are just better at this stuff: Is emotional labour feminism's next frontier? Available at: www.theguardian.com/world/2015/nov/08/women-gender-roles-sexism-emotional-labor-feminism (accessed 31 October 2017).

Therborn, G. (2000). Globalizations: Dimensions, historical waves, regional effects, normative governance. *International Sociology*, 15(2), 151–179.

Thomas, W.I. & Znaniecki, F. (1918–20). *The Polish Peasant in Europe and America*, 5 Vols. Boston, MA: Badger.

Thompson, E.P. (1963). *The Making of the English Working Class*. London: Victor Gollancz.

Thompson, E.P. (1967). Time, work-discipline and industrial capitalism. *Past and Present*, 38, 56–97.

Thorne, B. (1993). *Gender Play*. London: Open University Press.

Tolich, M. (2004). Internal confidentiality: When confidentiality assurances fail relational informants. *Qualitative Sociology*, 27(1), 101–106.

Tolich, M. (2014). What can Milgram and Zimbardo teach ethics committees and qualitative researchers about minimizing harm? *Research Ethics*, 10(2), 86–96.

Tucker, K.H. (1998). *Anthony Giddens and Modern Social Theory*. London: SAGE.

Turkle, S. (2011). *Alone Together: Why We Expect More from Technology and Less from Each Other*. New York, NY: Basic Books.

Turner, R.H., Killian, L.M. & Smelser, N.J. (1998). Social movement. In *Encyclopaedia Brittanica*. Available at: www.britannica.com/topic/social-movement (accessed 14 May 2017).

Twenge, J.M., Sherman, R.A. & Wells, B.E. (2015). Changes in American adults' sexual behavior and attitudes, 1972–2012. *Archives of Sexual Behavior*, 44(8), 2273–2285.

Uscinski, J.E. (2014). *The People's News: Media, Politics and the Demands of Capitalism*. New York, NY: New York University Press.

Uttl, B., White, C.A. & Gonazalez, D.W. (2017). Meta-analyis of faculty's teaching effectiveness: Student evaluation of teaching ratings and student learning are not related. *Studies in Educational Evaluation*, 54, 22–42.

Wakeling, P. & Laurison, D. (2017). Are postgraduate qualifications the 'new frontier of social mobility'? *British Journal of Sociology*, 68(3), 533–555.

Walby, S. (1990). *Theorizing Patriarchy*. London: John Wiley & Sons.

Waskul, D. & Vannini, P. (2012). Introduction: The body in symbolic interaction. In D. Waskul & P. Vannini (eds.), *Body/Embodiment: Symbolic Interaction and the Sociology of the Body*. London: Ashgate.

Way, N. (2011). *Deep Secrets*. New York, NY: New York University Press.

Weber, M. ([1904] 1949). *The Methodology of the Social Sciences*. New York, NY: Free Press.

Weber, M. ([1905] 1930). *The Protestant Ethic and the Spirit of Capitalism*. London: Unwin University Books.

Weber, M. ([1919] 1958). Science as a vocation. In H.H. Gerth & C. Wright Mills (eds.), *From Max Weber: Essays in Sociology*. New York, NY: Oxford University Press, 129–156.

Weber, M. ([1921] 1968). *Economy and Society: An Outline of Interpretative Sociology*. Totowa, NJ: Bedminster Press.

Weber, M. ([1922] 1965). *The Sociology of Religion*. London: Methuen.

Weber, M. (1947). *The Theory of Social and Economic Organization* (trans. A.M. Henderson & T. Parsons). New York, NY: Free Press.

Weeks, J. (2007). *The World We Have Won*. London: Routledge.

Weinberg, M.S., Williams, C.J. & Pryor, D.W. (1994). *Dual Attraction: Understanding Bisexuality*. Oxford: Oxford University Press.

Weis, A.H. (2010). Commercialization of the internet. *Internet Research*, 20(4), 420–435.

West, C. & Zimmerman, D. (1987). Doing gender. *Gender & Society*, 1(2), 125–151.

Whitley, R. & Kirmayer, L.J. (2008). Perceived stigmatisation of young mothers: An exploratory study of psychological and social experience. *Social Science & Medicine*, 66(2), 339–348.

Whyte, M.K., Feng, W. & Cai, Y. (2015). Challenging myths about China's one-child policy. *The China Journal*, 74, 144–149.

Wiederman, M.J. (2015). Sexual script theory. In J. DeLamater & R.F. Plante (eds.), *Handbook of the Sociology of Sexualities*. New York, NY: Springer, 7–22.

Wiggershaus, R. (1994). *The Frankfurt School: Its History, Theory and Political Significance*. Cambridge: Polity.

Wignall, L. (2017). The sexual adoption of a social networking site: The case of Pup Twitter. *Sociological Research Online*, 22(3), 21–37.

Willey, A. (2006). 'Christian nations', 'polygamic races' and women's rights: Toward a genealogy of non/monogamy and whiteness. *Sexualities*, 9(5), 530–546.

Williams, E.E. (1972). *Capitalism and Slavery*. London: Andre Deutsch.

Willis, P. (1977). *Learning to Labour: How Working-class Kids Get Working-class Jobs*. London: Saxon House.

Wolkowitz, C. (2006). *Bodies at Work*. London: SAGE.

World Bank (2015). *Internet Users*. Available at: http://data.worldbank.org/indicator/IT.NET.USER.P2 (accessed May 2017).

Worthen, M.G. (2013). An argument for separate analyses of attitudes toward lesbian, gay, bisexual men, bisexual women, MtF and FtM transgender individuals. *Sex Roles*, 68(11–12), 703–723.

Wright, P.J. (2013). U.S. males and pornography, 1973–2010: Consumption, predictors, correlates. *The Journal of Sex Research*, 50(1), 60–71.

Yardley, E. (2008). Teenage mothers' experiences of stigma. *Journal of Youth Studies*, 11(6), 671–684.

York, R. (2010). The sociology of global climate change: What we know and what we need to know. In J. Nagel, T. Dietz, J. Broadbent (eds.), *Workshop on Sociological Perspectives on Global Climate Change*. Arlington, VA: National Science Foundation, 149–150.

Zimbardo, P.G. (1972). Comment: Pathology of imprisonment. *Society*, 9(6), 4–8.

GLOSSARY

Age of Enlightenment: a period where rationality and logic became the way in which societies were organized

Agency: the ability of individuals in society to act of their own free will. This is often contrasted with *structure*, which constrains individuals to act in prescribed ways

Agrarian society: a society whose economy is based on producing and maintaining crops and farmland

Anomie: a condition felt by people in societies where there is an absence of norms or values

Anonymity: the guarantee given to research participants that they will not be identifiable in any publications about the research

Automation: the introduction of automatic equipment (robots, machines and computers) in a manufacturing or other work environment

Black feminist thought: a body of writing that argues for recognition of issues of class, gender and sexuality alongside race

Body work: also known as body labour, it refers to the work individuals exert on their own bodies as well as paid work that is performed on other people's bodies

Bourgeoisie: a term used by Marx for the class in a capitalist society who own the means of production and most of that society's wealth

Capitalism: a society whose trade and industry is owned by private citizens or corporations who seek to maximize profit through competition

Case study methods: in-depth investigation into individual cases rather than comparing variables from multiple cases

Charmed circle: a concept developed by Rubin to visualize which sexual acts are esteemed and which are stigmatized

Class: a way society is divided based on social and economic status

Coach effect: where people exaggerate a claim because of the presence of the researcher

Colonialism: the process by which explorers and settlers take political control of another country and exploit it economically

Commodification: the process of treating something as a commodity

Communism: a theory of society in which all property is owned by the community

Comparative methods: research focused on at least two locations to identify similarities and differences between them. Comparison can be made between large cross-sectional data sets or between in-depth cases

Concepts: abstract ways of defining particular issues

Confidentiality: refers to information about a participant that cannot be shared without their express consent

Conflict theories:	theories that are critical of society and seek to contest oppressive social norms
Consumer self:	the notion that people's identities are constructed and consolidated through consumerism (the purchasing of goods)
Covert research:	research where participants are not told they are part of a study
Critical race theory (CRT):	a set of critical theories that analyse society primarily through a race lens
Critical theory:	an influential set of theories that critique the social world from a philosophical perspective
Cross-sectional research:	research design that collects data at one point in time, and so is best suited to correlations, but from which causes can sometimes be tentatively suggested
Crowds:	groups of people congregated together, normally in response to a particular event
Cultural capital:	non-financial assets that can promote social mobility
Culture:	people's common goals and their ways of thinking and acting
Culture industry:	the notion that culture is the commodification of activities that reproduces power inequality by rendering the masses passive
Data:	'information' that can be analysed
Deceptive research:	research where participants are told the study is about something other than its real aims
Deductive theory:	a theory that is developed from a set of hypotheses that are then tested
Discourse:	an institutionalized or societally condoned way of speaking that controls the ways in which a topic can be discussed
Disembedded:	how social practices that were once grounded in the local context are no longer restricted by place and time
Double consciousness:	the notion of having two conflicting identities, in this case because of racism in society
Double hermeneutic:	the idea that people's knowledge of sociology alters how they understand the world, thus changing the world
Embodiment:	the process by which meaning and values are placed onto people's bodies
Emotional labour:	work that involves emotions rather than just doing activities
Empiricism:	the idea that knowledge is derived from our senses
Employability:	how attractive individuals are to employers and, by extension, how easy it will be to get a job
Ethics:	moral principles and a code of conduct that govern researcher's behaviours when doing their jobs
Ethnicity:	a socially created system of classifying people on the basis of cultural or nationality differences
Evidence:	the data required to answer a particular research question
Evidence-based policy:	a paradigm in which policy is based on research, supposedly free from dogma or ideology
Fake news:	false stories that are intentionally spread to misinform
False consciousness:	used by Marx to describe the state of mind where the proletariat are unaware of the inequality of their situation and the oppression that they suffer because class and wealth stratification is thought to be the natural order of social life

Formal institutions: rules, such as the law, that are enforced by official agencies

Free market: a system where goods and services are exchanged for money, ostensibly with no governmental control

Free press: the idea that people are allowed to circulate ideas in writing without being censored by government

Functional specialisation: where trust in experts is granted through institutional frameworks rather than direct experience

Functionalism: the theoretical perspective that all aspects of society serve a function necessary for the survival of that society

Generalizability: the extent to which the findings from a sample can be said to be true of the population that the sample is assumed to represent. Generalizability is sometimes called external validity

Globalization: the process by which countries have become increasingly interconnected, with individual experiences and social phenomena traversing traditional economic, geographic and social boundaries

Great transformation: the social and political changes that saw Western societies shift to capitalist modes of production

Going native: when a researcher adopts the views of their participants without realizing, and loses an objective perspective

Habitus: the physical embodiment of cultural capital

Historical materialism: the belief that the social world can be explained through material conditions

Human agency: the capacity of individuals to act independently and make their own choices

Hypothesis: a specific statement or prediction that can be tested empirically

Identity: the sense of self or how one gives meaning to self in a group

Individualization thesis: the notion that the act of making choices about one's life is where self-worth is found

Inductive theory: a theory that emerges from analysis of data

Industrial Revolution: the societal transition where technological change saw the economy transformed from an agricultural one to one based on manufacturing goods

Industrialization: the process by which the economy changes from a reliance on agriculture to manufacturing and the production of goods

Informal institutions: cultural customs and taboos, where rules are not written and enforced but are important to 'fitting in' in a culture

Informed consent: refers to participants agreeing to participate in a study having been informed of its aims

Interactionism: theories that focus on the ways people interact in groups

Intersectionality: the interconnected nature of social categories, particularly how they relate to oppression

Interview: a form of data collection where the participant is asked a set of questions by the researcher

Late modern: a term that recognizes contemporary societies are markedly different from those in the modernity era of the mid-20th century

Longitudinal research: research where change over time is the primary focus of attention, and which is usually interested in causal relationships between prior states and outcomes

Materialism: the belief that the social world can be explained through material conditions

Meritocracy: a social system in which people succeed and are rewarded based on talent and ability alone

Methodology:	the principles that guide methods in the attempt to generate valid results. The reason why one method might be more appropriate than another is the realm of methodology
Methods:	the techniques of data collection and analysis
Millenarianism:	early social movements that promised transformational social change through divine intervention
Miscegenation:	having children with someone from a different racial group
Mixed methods:	a research design using more than one form of data collection. How far the methods are integrated together is a source of much discussion. Sometimes called Multi-Method
Mode of production:	the way in which people's needs for shelter, food and protection are met in any given society
Modernity:	a term to understand societies that emerged after the Industrial Revolution and when capitalism was embedded as the mode of production
Modernization:	the changes that occur as a society transforms into an urban, industrial society
Moral panic:	how particular concerns in society are defined as a threat, exaggerated and used by people in power to control others or effect particular social change
Naturalistic:	a form of observation that observes people in their 'natural' settings rather than in a lab or interview conditions
Network society:	a society where social institutions are structured around digital networks of information, primarily the internet
New social movements:	refers to the growth in social movements since the 1960s
Norm:	a social expectation that guides behaviour
Nuclear family:	a heterosexual couple and their genetically related offspring
Organizations:	physical places that consolidate the norms and values and do the work of a particular institution
Orientalism:	a set of social processes by which the global north frame Arab peoples according to a range of damaging stereotypes
Paradigm:	an established theory or way of thinking that acts as a framework in sociology
Participant observation:	where the researcher participates in the activity along with participants and observes them simultaneously
Patriarchy:	a concept to understand systematic gender inequality in a society run by and for men and male interests
Plastic sexuality:	a concept advanced by Giddens that argues sexual desires and acts are shaped by individual erotic needs rather than reproductive or economic ones
Population:	all members of the category under investigation
Positionality:	the notion that the researcher has a position in the research process and that this may affect the data collected
Positivism:	the scientific search for fixed laws that govern social and natural worlds
Poststructuralism:	a set of theories that critique structuralist notions and also contest the core tenets of Enlightenment beliefs about science and empirical research
Power:	a contested term, fundamentally about the ability to produce intended effects

Preacher effect: where people underestimate a claim because of the presence of the researcher

Proletariat: a term used by Marx for the group of workers in a capitalist society who were exploited by the bourgeoisie

Public sociology: a style of sociology that seeks to inform and engage with the public

Questionnaire: a written set of questions

Racializing: the name given to the attribution of particular values or stereotypes to racial groups

Rationalization: the replacement of traditions, emotions and superstition as motivations for action by rational, calculated decision-making

Reflexive process: also known as reflexivity, it is the cyclical process whereby individuals think about their actions and thus influence their behaviours, which in turn influences their thoughts

Reflexivity: thinking critically about one's positionality and effect on data or society

Relational: the notion that two or more things occur in relation to each other, rather than independently

Riot: where a group of people exhibit unruly behaviour that damages people or property

Risk society: a framework to understand contemporary societies that have to deal with global risks that are focused around technology

Sample: a subset of a population

Sampling: the process of selecting units within a population

Sampling frame: the list of every person or thing in a population that can be sampled

Service sector: a sector of the economy focused on providing a service rather than goods

Single hermeneutic: where knowledge is in one direction. The object of study does not change as a result

Social beings: a way of understanding human beings that recognizes their actions and beliefs are dependent on their social conditions

Social capital: the cultural resources a person has based on their networks and group membership

Social Darwinism: the theory that individuals and groups are subject to the same Darwinian laws of natural selection as plants and animals (i.e. survival of the fittest)

Social facts: norms and values that do not have objective reality but exist beyond a single individual and exert influence in society

Social media: websites and apps that allow users to create and share content or connect with other people

Social mobility: the change in social status that a person achieves in a set period, between childhood and significantly later in their lives

Social movement: organized collective social action with political aims to challenge a problem or improve a situation

Social policy: the way in which societies address issues of individual wellbeing, social welfare and social justice

Social stratification: the way groups of people are divided unevenly in society

Social structures: the ways society is organized that constrain how an individual can act

Social theory: intellectual critiques of society that are connected with sociological theory but more located within philosophy

Socialization:	the process by which a person learns the accepted ways of thinking and behaving in a particular society
Society:	a collection of people who share common culture and land or territory
Sociological canon:	classical works of sociology that are seen as foundational to the discipline
Sociological imagination:	the awareness of the relationship between personal experiences and broader society
Sociological theory:	abstract propositions about society that can be tested and have empirical support
Status:	the social aspects of class, such as lifestyle and leisure activities
Stigma:	a social attribute, behaviour or reputation that is discrediting in some way
Stratification:	Weber's way of understanding social class, consisting of three elements: economic class, status and power
Structuralism:	a set of theories that contend that society runs according to a set of laws and social structures
Structuration:	structure and action are necessarily related to each other and cannot be disentangled
Structures:	the ways society is organized that constrain how an individual can act
Subculture:	a group of people who share common interests that vary from the dominant culture
Sui generis:	a term Durkheim used to say that society is unique and cannot be reduced to the sum of its parts
Survey:	the systematic collection of the same data from a specified sample
Symbolic capital:	one's prestige in a social group, such as reputation and celebrity
Symbolic interactionism:	a theoretical framework that studies how people communicate with each other to understand the meaning of actions, focusing on the symbols and signs of their communication
Symbolic token:	things that can be used for exchange (such as money)
Theory:	a proposition or a number of propositions that explain why or how something is happening
Tradition:	a belief or ritual passed down within a group, with meaning imbued to the act
Tripartite system:	the organization of state-funded British education from 1945 to the 1970s
Validity:	internal validity refers to how far data collected captures the true nature of the things being measured. This is how validity is often understood, but the term 'external validity' is used differently and refers to generalizability (see above)
Verstehen:	an approach in sociology that tries to comprehend the meanings and motivations of human action
Visual methods:	methods that enable the study of images and non-textual data
Warm bath theory:	used by Parsons and Bales (1955) to compare the nuclear family to a warm bath which men could relax into after a long day working outside the home

INDEX

Page numbers in **bold** indicate tables and in *italic* indicate figures.